Walking Point
A Vietnam Memoir

Robert "Bob" Kunkel

Thunderbrook Publishing
P.O. Box 220, Kimball MN 55353
www.thunderbrookpublishing.com
thunderbrookpub@gmail.com

Edited by Jean Doran Matua.
Cover and book design by Jean Doran Matua.

ISBN: 978-1-5136-3922-2
Library of Congress Control Number: 2018953476

Publisher's Cataloging-in-Publication Data
provided by Five Rainbows Cataloging Services

Names: Kunkel, Robert E., author.

Title: Walking point : a Vietnam memoir / Robert Kunkel.

Description: Kimball, MN : Thunderbrook Publishing, 2018.

Identifiers: ISBN 978-1-5136-3922-2 (pbk.) ǀ ISBN 978-1-5136-3923-9 (ebook)

Subjects: LCSH: Vietnam War, 1961-1975--Personal narratives, American.
ǀ United States. Army--Infantry--Biography. ǀ Veterans--United States--
Biography. ǀ Soldiers--United States--Biography. ǀ BISAC: BIOGRAPHY &
AUTOBIOGRAPHY / Military. ǀ HISTORY / Military / Vietnam War.

Classification: LCC DS559.73.U6 K86 2018 (print) ǀ LCC DS559.73.U6 (ebook) ǀ
DDC 959.704/345092273--dc23.

Dedication:

Ray Judy, Tom Gray KIA, Dennis Benedetti KIA,
Capt. John Hitti deceased

TABLE OF CONTENTS

Table of Photos and Illustrations vi

Author's Notes viii

Acknowledgments ix

Foreword x

Preamble 13

Vietnam 17

Induction 19

Basic Training (Boot Camp): 2nd Battalion, 19th Artillery . . .25

Advanced Infantry Training (AIT),4th Troop,
        12th Squadron 41

Advance Unit Training (AUT) 61

5th Battalion, 7th Cavalry, Garry Owen. 69

Battalion Goes To Vietnam, USS Hugh J. Gaffey 73

Beach Landing in Vietnam. 83

Camp Radcliff (An Khê), Building 5th Bn 7th Cav
        Compound 87

First Field Assignment: Security for Highway 19. 97

Operation Irving. 115

The Caves. 141

Operation Thayer. 149

Sore Feet Retreat 157

Retreat is Over 167

Arriving Too Early. 181

A Date with the Enemy 193

Trouble with a FNG (F---ing New Guy) 197

A Close Call 201

Communicating with the Enemy. 203

The Monsoon Rain: Heading to the Hills 209

B Company's First KIA (Killed in Action). 221

Firefight, November 1, 1966 225

Hospital (Qui Nho'n) 241

Flight to Japan 251
7th Field Hospital 257
Convalescing 269
Back to 'Nam 285
Back with the Platoon 289
A Gung-ho acting Jack 301
Move to LZ English 307
An Lão Valley 311
The Tet New Year 321
LZ Security 337
B Company to Get a New Leader 349
Easter 1967 355
Monkeys, Dogs, and Fire 357
Incoming 361
One Hell of a Firefight 365
Capture–Escape–Hero 369
Missing Funds 373
From Priesthood to General's Aide 379
LZ Security in the Mountains 385
Cam Ranh Bay 399
The Night Crew 407
Befriending the Laundress 421
Enjoying the Bay 425
DEROS 433
Back to the World 439
Going Home 447
Back to Fort Carson 451
A Civilian 455
Marriage and a Career Made for Me 461
Glossary 466
Index 469
About the Author 478

PHOTOS & ILLUSTRATIONS

Unidentified Marine walking point in Vietnam. . . . . Cover + 12

Map of Vietnam 16

Basic training at Fort Carson today 24

Basic training at Fort Carson today 24

Sgt. William Dickman, combat photographer. 40

Bob Kunkel and Eileen Wagner before Vietnam 68

The USS Hugh Gaffey in San Francisco Bay. 72

Ray Judy on ship. 78

Arrival of the 1st Cavalry in Vietnam 82

The USS Hugh Gaffey approaching a beach-head landing. . . .84

First day at Camp Radcliff 86

Defoliating the jungle by helicopter .91

Ray Olin 93

Vietnamese workers build the fence at Camp Radcliff 95

Bob Kunkel in a bunker on the green line. 96

M18 Claymore Anti-Personnel Mine. 99

Ray Kloemken. 101

Luis "Doc" Aragon, our medic. 108

Walking through a punji-staked gully 112

Operation "Irving" troops checking on a house. 114

Troops climbing a rocky mountain. .118

Captain John Hitti 123

Time magazine photo of our operation 125

Delivery of chow by helicopter 129

Infantry patrol during Operation "Hawthorne". 139

Montagnard girl watches convoy passing through 139

Checking out a cave opening 140

Ray Kloemken. 142

Entrance of a mountain cave. 147

Waving down a Huey helicopter 148

Worn out jungle combat boots 156

Smoke grenade identifies landing zone 178

Booby traps could be found anywhere 180

Luis "Doc" Aragon and Bob Kunkel. 192

Ray Judy. 192

Soldiers gather around a guitar player to sing 196
1st Infantry on search-and-destroy patrol 200
Guarding a NVA captured prisoner 204
On patrol through a heavily wooded area 208
Weary soldiers on break during Operation "Pershing" 211
Chopping down a tree to clear a landing zone 212
Vietnam-era military-issue C-Rations 217
Taking a break from the rain 219
Firing a mortar round near An Khê 219
Soldiers carry a wounded comrade through swamp 220
Helmets and equipment of U.S. casualties. 237
Bob Kunkel's sketch of firefight map 238-239
The 67th Evacuation Hospital at Qui Nho'n 240
Nurses with American soldier in hospital in Vietnam 250
Bob Kunkel in 7th Field Hospital in Japan 256
Charlie Walker Greatest Hits album. .271
Bob Kunkel, just before returning to Vietnam 284
Helicopter drop near An Khê in the An Lão Valley 306
Tom Gray on a commandeered bicycle. 319
Old and young flee Tet offensive fighting. 320
Taking cover during the Battle of Hue. 336
Quad-mount M2 .50 caliber machine guns firing 348
Catholic chaplain conducts services for troops 354
Luis "Doc" Aragon with his Bronze Star. 360
Dennis Benedetti with his medals. 360
Soldiers from the 101st Airborne duck for cover 364
M-102 105 mm Howitzer firing 384
Napalm bombs explode on Viet Cong structures 389
Some short-timers recorded time on their helmets 397
Akai tape deck advertisement 424
Personnel preparing to leave Vietnam for the U.S. 432
Bob Kunkel's Vietnam medals and ribbons. 446
Bob and Eileen 49 years married. 460
At work for the Stearns County Sheriff's Office 462
Bob Kunkel's family. 464
Tactical map of operations in Vietnam 468

AUTHOR'S NOTES:

• I have changed the names of many people with whom I served: some because I completely lost track of them and do not know how to contact them, some because I forgot the name, and still others because I want to be brutally honest in my assessment of them without damaging their reputations. My opinions are not unique; others with whom I served shared similar opinions. It is not my intention to denigrate anyone.

• During the 1960s there was a high level of racial tension in the United States. The racial tension was also prevalent in the armed services. Racism went both ways. No side was more right than the other. As I write this dialogue, I used the term black(s), white(s), as opposed to people, persons, men, soldiers, group, etc. It was a part of the social context of the time.

When we got to Vietnam, the racism issue nearly disappeared. Sometimes you depended on another person, black or white, to save your butt, and vice-versa. If you pulled your weight you were a soldier, friend, and care-keeper of one another. On the other hand, if you were a slough-off and didn't pull your weight, you were a pogue, black or white.

• The "F-word" is used occasionally in this document. It is not my intent to cheapen the material with the use of it, but rather to demonstrate the normal usage of the word. In reality, it got so you either began or ended every sentence with this descriptive word. Omitting it now would make it artificial and not true to the story being told.

ACKNOWLEDGMENTS

I thank my wife Eileen for putting up with all the pitfalls and trouble I've caused her during our 48 years of marriage. I was less than a stellar partner, especially when I was combating the effects of post-traumatic stress disorder (PTSD). A lesser woman would have left me. Eileen has stood by me through some very tough and difficult times. LOVE and THANKS!

I would like to thank Jean Doran Matua who is the owner, publisher, editor, journalist, photographer, and whatever other handle is associated with managing and publishing the *Tri-County News* weekly newspaper in our community. Along with all of these duties, she found time to edit and design this book so my words flow and look a little better for the reader. Again, a BIG THANKS!

I also would like to thank the numerous people who have read my initial version of the manuscript and have encouraged me to move forward to put it into book form. It would be impossible to name everyone, but most of you know who you are.

Finally, I need to thank the doctors, clinicians, nurses, and staff of the St. Cloud Veterans Clinic and Hospital. The doctors and staff there treat you as a valuable person as opposed to just a name and number. I've been associated with the St. Cloud VA since 1967 after completing my tenure with the U.S. Army. Just saying "thank you" does not seem nearly enough.

Bob Kunkel, 2018

FOREWORD

Bob Kunkel grew up in a large, Catholic family on a dairy farm in central Minnesota. Although he was older than some draftees, at 22, he was still young and relatively innocent. But not for long.

Kunkel recounts his experiences with so much detail that the reader can feel and smell the steamy jungle. He brings you right along with him. His story is much more than a collection of details, however. His military experience was largely mundane routine, spiced with dramatic and dangerous moments and anecdotal incidents, recounted with a dry sense of humor. Prepare for an emotional rollercoaster of a read.

Kunkel spent parts of 18 years working on this memoir. It began as general notes he wrote down in order to free the haunting details from his mind, as therapy for PTSD, It evolved into a full-fledged memoir. "Once I opened up, I could deal with it," he says. Initially, his plan was to share this painstakingly written account with family, as a sort of legacy. His story deserves to be shared much more broadly, though. It is a story of drive and tenacity, of survival, and of the power of faith and family.

We know Kunkel survived Vietnam to write this tale. Delving into these pages, however, the reader will be taken on one adventure after another, with plenty of twists along the way. It's certainly not at all like in the movies.

Draw your own conclusions on the merit, or lack thereof, of the Vietnam War. But you'll appreciate the time spent with Kunkel during his year of Vietnam duty. You will not see that war the same way after reading *Walking Point*.

Jean Doran Matua, Editor

Unidentified Marine walking point for his unit during Operation "Macon" moves slowly, cautious of enemy pitfalls, 1966. U.S. Marine Corps photo.
Photo ID 532445. Photo courtesy of the National Archives at College Park, Md.

PREAMBLE

Being drafted into the U.S. Army in 1965 turned out to be both a blessing and a curse for me, at that time then and for all time thereafter. It tested strength, fortitude, endurance, faith, and fear. It forever changed a personality and an attitude to the point where the person sometimes lost track of who he really was. His values of life and living, and even the ability to separate right and wrong based on early life's values and beliefs, would be forever altered. Passive acceptance turned to hard and critical challenge; if not outwardly, at least within one's mind.

In the span of one year, an easy-going country boy who loved baseball, hunting, and a good old beer party became a hard-nosed man, old beyond his years, who looked at the world with a new view. In his eyes, he perceived that the problems of others were actually nothing more than minor irritations. The problem, whether it went away or not, did not change the person or the standard of living.

Before Vietnam, three hours of idle chatter sometimes was not enough. After Vietnam, 10 minutes of idle chatter was almost unbearable.

During one year in Vietnam, a young man changed. But the world he lived in before, and the one he came back to after, did not change. Hardly anyone else noticed the change, but the young man, now much older by experience, was overwhelmed by it.

I can only speak for myself, but I believe the war, in a major dimension, changed everyone who fought in it. Death knocked at your door every day, at least in your own mind. On some days, the reality of death came within inches, or even fractions of an inch. It destroyed some lives physically and emotionally. It also built friendships that would last a lifetime. For many, the physical scars are souvenirs. Psychological scars are ingrained in brain cells for an eternity.

When recounting a war-related incident, the tendency is to laugh about it. Frequently the laugh is a smokescreen to keep from crying. Some stories you just don't talk about. These are the events that pry into your mind, keeping you awake at night and forever vigilant. The battles of Vietnam are over, but the battle in the mind never ends.

Over the years, I thought many times of writing this story, a history of my tenure in Vietnam. I always found ways to put it off. I always seemed to be busy with something else. In 1999 I retired from a law enforcement career. After retiring I found myself thinking about Vietnam more than I wanted. A few months without the pressure of my former position as the Jail Administrator for the Stearns County Jail, most of my waking moments were occupied by unwanted thoughts of that year I spent in Vietnam. Even old dreams came back to haunt me.

I talked many times with Terry McGee, the Stearns County Veterans Service Officer, and to a few other Vietnam vets. I was pressured into seeking counseling for what is called Post-Traumatic Stress Disorder (PTSD). After two initial visits, I was to talk with a Dr. Brown. It was advised that I jot down some notes about my time in Vietnam before I talked with him, so I would be more prepared for the interview.

As I began writing these notes, I found myself becoming very descriptive of the incidents I recalled. I brought myself back on track and began highlighting specific incidents for the notes. I decided later to go back and give the highlights more description. Thus I began writing the story of my year in Vietnam.

When telling my story, I am relaying information about me that has never been told to others before – with the exception of my wife, and a counselor at the Veterans Affairs Medical Center. Even they have not heard everything.

It has been 50 years since I was in Vietnam. I am working from old memories. The incidents as I state them may not be in the exact order they happened. But all the incidents happened, and they are told as I remember them. Many names have eluded me, but some I can never forget.

This is a view of the common soldier who saw and lived a short portion of the Vietnam War. In that war, as in most wars, the common soldier was not privileged to tactical knowledge and configurations of how operations were planned and executed. In most cases, we had only a general idea of the location where an operation was taking place. Most information we did get was on a need-to-know-only basis.

I do not believe there is ever a good war. If one has to label a war as being bad, Vietnam falls deeply within the criteria of a bad war.

Map of Vietnam showing strategic military areas during the war. Public domain.

VIETNAM

The east side of South Vietnam lies along the South China Sea between the 8th and 17th parallels. The west side of South Vietnam borders Laos on the upper one-third, and Cambodia on the lower two-thirds.

It is a long, narrow country in the north half, composed of heavy jungle, steep mountainous ridges, narrow valleys, rice paddies, flat plains, and stilted hamlets along the flooded coastline. To the south, the country widens out and is a quagmire of swamp and jungle with island hamlets beyond the populous city of Saigon (now Ho Chi Minh City), and sand dunes near the southern coast. South Vietnam has just about every type of terrain except snow-capped mountains.

Vietnam has a tropical climate with a large variety of nature's creatures. There are more than 90 different types of snakes, many of which are poisonous; a variety of lizards; and a large cross-section of birds, some with unique characteristics such as the plumes on their heads or the sounds they make. There are insects, especially the ubiquitous mosquito, and a variety of beetles and spiders, many which are unfamiliar to the average American. There are monkeys, apes, orangutans, wild cats, small deer, tigers, elephants, and water buffalo that often are domesticated and used for farming the rice crops.

I was assigned to the 3rd squad, 2nd platoon, B Company, 5th Battalion, 7th Cavalry of the First Cavalry Division, Air Mobile.

Most of my tour with the 1st Air Cav took place in the Central and North Central Highlands and along the North Central Coastline above Qui Nho'n and North to Bong Son. Military missions were labeled with operational names for specific areas, time frames, and/or the objectives of the operation.

Before any operational assignments, the battalion had to build a compound and provide security patrols until formidable security bunkers could be established. Our first operation was to provide security for Highway 19, between An Khê and Pleiku.

From Highway 19, our battalion moved into Operation Irving along the Coast of the South China Sea, then into Operation Thayer-I and Thayer-II, in Binh Dinh Province of the Central Highlands and then into Operation Pershing in the An Lão Valley and Bong Son plains.

During my year tour, B Company was involved in four major firefights with enemy soldiers. They took place November 1, 1966; December 1, 1966; February 18, 1967; and April 8, 1967. In these four firefights, more than 30 soldiers were killed, and many more were wounded. In other isolated incidents – ambushes, booby traps, mines, punji sticks, as well as self-inflicted injuries, some by accident but others on purpose – many other soldiers were killed and wounded.

INDUCTION

Sitting in a large conference room in the Andrews Hotel in Minneapolis, I was waiting for my name to be called. The Sergeant taking roll call was a tall, lean man wearing the dress green uniform of an Army soldier. He had a husky, loud and clearly discernible bass voice. As he called the first name, a young lad answered "Here," almost inaudibly. The Sergeant leaned over the podium and glared into the young man's eyes and bellowed, "When I call your name, I want to hear you answer, 'HERE!'" His voice brought everyone erect in their chairs, eyes glued intently on him. This was December 2, 1965; my first day in the United States Army.

After roll call, we took an aptitude test, and then we were officially sworn in with an oath to our country. After the swearing-in ceremony, an officer gave our group a brief historical pep talk about the world's finest fighting force: the United States Army. We were herded into a huge dining room, given lunch, and then dismissed for three hours. At 1545 hours (3:45 p.m.) we were to report to the train terminal off 4th Street and Washington Avenue.

I hooked up with two young men from Watkins, Minnesota. They were Bob Mobley and Tom Mathies. We walked around the downtown Minneapolis area until about 3:30 p.m., then went to the terminal and were directed to a train. The train was bound for Missouri, so we figured we were headed for Fort Leonard Wood. After boarding the train, we were paired up and assigned a sleeping car bunk-room. The porter giving out the assignments was a black gentleman who had a great gift of jab and jibe. He was outgoing, friendly, and had a way of joking with everyone without offending anyone. I paired up with Bob Mobley.

Around 5:30 p.m. the train began to move. The porter came through to see to it that we each knew the routine for dropping the bunks so we could use the sleeping quarters. I asked him if the train made any stops. He said it was stopping in St. Paul to pick up a couple of rail cars. I asked if there was a bar close to the St. Paul terminal, and he gave directions to one, through the terminal, a short block left, and across the street. He said that, if we were getting off the train, there would only be about 10 or 12 minutes before the train would depart. He also said that he would watch for us as best he could, but we were on our own.

Even before the train was completely stopped, Mobley and I were off the train and running through the terminal. We saw the bar down the street and ran for it. I ran into the bar and ordered four cases of Grain Belt beer. The bartender asked for IDs. I told him we just ran in from a train bound for Fort Leonard Wood, and time was important. He gave us the beer. I gave him enough money to cover it, and Mobley and I, with two cases of beer each, headed back to the train. As we ran through the terminal, the train started to rev up and began its slow takeoff. The porter was standing by the door waiting for us. Mobley pitched his beer on first, and I followed. The train was picking up a little speed as Mobley climbed on, and I had to run beside the train until he got out of the way before I could jump on. We offered the porter some beer but he declined. Mobley and I took the beer to our cabin and we each popped a can, rewarding ourselves for our fortune.

The Army issued what they called a GI bag lunch with sandwiches for our evening meal. The beer was an excellent wash for the sandwiches. At about this time, some of the soldiers were asking if we would sell them some beer. We made it clear that we intended to make a profit on our enterprise. This being understood, we sold beer for $2 a can. This was about a 400-percent markup on our investment.

There were a number of poker games taking place throughout the train. As the night wore on, and our beer supply dwindled, we raised the price another dollar. When we opened the last case, we told everyone that the beer was now $3 a can. Players at one of the poker games pooled their money and bought 18 cans. Mobley and I saved a six-pack for ourselves.

The train landed someplace in Missouri, and we were transferred to buses and taken to a restaurant to eat breakfast before going to Fort Leonard Wood.

At Fort Leonard Wood base camp we were assigned to a barracks. In the next four days, we got uniforms, our shots (about two dozen of them), and our first GI haircut. We also got our butts chewed, and often.

The second day at Fort Leonard Wood, at least 200 soldiers were bussed about one-and-a-half miles from our barracks to get uniforms. Each one of us was issued a large Army duffel bag. We stepped in line along a counter that ran the length of the building. We were told to strip down to our birthday suits and put our civilian clothes in the bottom of the duffel bags. We would not need those clothes again. One uniformed person stood behind the counter at each station. Each would size us up and issue the size and the number of that particular piece of clothing. We received six sets of boxer shorts and T-shirts. We received six pair of OD (olive drab) uniform pants and shirts. You would put the first uniform item on, and the rest you placed in the duffel bag. When you came to the end of the line, you were fully dressed in one set of Army work clothes, and the rest were stuffed in the duffel bag. The total contents weighed nearly 100 pounds.

A soldier told us how to get back to our barracks. We had to walk back. I threw my duffel bag on my back and began to walk, as did most of the others. Many of the new soldiers struggled with their loads but they were managing. About a block from the uniform dispensary, a young man was dragging his duffel bag and crying. I recognized him from the bus ride we took from St. Cloud to Minneapolis. We had been seated next to each other. I don't remember his name, but he was not going to make the trip back without wearing a hole in the bottom of the duffel bag. I felt sorry for him. I told him to carry it as far as he could and I would come back and help him. I carried my bag ahead about 200 yards, then walked back and carried his bag about 200 yards beyond where I set my bag down. I alternated carrying our bags like this until we got back to the barracks.

After we made it back to barracks and stowed our bags with the strap around our bunks, we were told to fall out and line up in front of the cadre building which was located to the west of our barracks, on higher ground. We had to line up in four columns. Then they had the last soldiers in the back of each column form a fifth column. They went through the same process to form a sixth and a seventh column. Then everyone in the first column had to fall out and line up evenly in the back of columns two through seven. They repeated this with column two and three. We were back in four columns again. By now it was time for chow, the evening meal. One column at a time was instructed to follow another cadre in an orderly fashion, without breaking the column, to the chow hall for dinner. To keep the remaining soldiers from getting bored, the cadre played the line-up shuffle again, switching columns until it was time to send another column to the chow hall. This carried on until the last of the soldiers went to chow. The same process took place before each meal.

About mid-afternoon on the fourth day, all new inductees had to be assembled in columns in front of the cadre building again. We had to bring our Army-issued duffel bags with us. There were at least a thousand soldiers in eight lines. As they called out names, you were assigned a number. You were to line up at the back of the line for your number. Once everyone was in their proper line, we loaded on buses. Once on the bus, we were told where we would be going. There were six buses just for our group. We were going to Fort Carson, Colorado, near Colorado Springs, for Basic Training (boot camp).

Fort Carson near Colorado Springs continues to be used for infantry training. These photos are from modern-day training exercises there, found online on the Facebook page for U.S. Army Fort Carson.

BASIC TRAINING (Boot Camp): 2nd Battalion, 19th Artillery

Larry Sutton from De Kalb, Illinois, sat beside me on the trip to Fort Carson. He talked about his 1957 Chevy with a 327 engine, drag racing, how he had the fastest time in the quarter-mile of all the dragsters in DeKalb, and his girlfriend. He wasn't the worst guy, but his mouth motored more than his 327 Chevy.

While riding through Kansas, I saw the name Kunkel on many small businesses: laundromats, insurance, real estate, and restaurants. It surprised me to see the name so many times.

The buses made one pit stop for chow. A Sergeant with a couple of rockers under his stripes came onto our bus to give instructions. At the time, most of us did not know the significance of the different stripes. He told us what to expect in the way of dining. We were at a large restaurant, but they could not handle the whole group at one time. We had to eat in shifts. He also said that we should get off the bus to stretch, and be ready when our turn came to eat. He asked if everyone understood. We answered in a fairly loud response, "Yes, sir." He responded, "I'm a Sergeant, I earn my wages, I'm not an officer who does not earn his wages. You call me 'Sergeant,' not 'sir.'" Then he asked again, "Does everyone understand?" We said in unison, "Yes, Sergeant." He yelled, "Louder!" We yelled back, "Yes, Sergeant!" He said, "That's better." Then he told us to fall out and stretch our legs.

We arrived at Fort Carson at around 1 a.m., or 0100 hours military time. Three of the buses pulled into an area where a number of barracks were lined up. The new recruits got off the buses and we all stood around waiting to see what happened next. There was a group of Sergeants standing off to one side. They separated and took positions probably 20 yards apart. Another Sergeant was the spokesman. He told us that we were assigned to the 2nd Battalion of the 19th Artillery. He said that he would call our names and assign each name a number between one and three. Tom Mathies and I, and a number of other people from Minnesota were assigned to the 3rd platoon. Sgt. Peyton was our Platoon Sergeant. He walked us to the back door or quadrant side of the platoon barracks. He gave us a few instructions then assigned us to either the first or second floor of the barracks. Mathies and I ended up on the second floor. We teamed up and would be partners, so to speak. I slept on the top bunk and he slept on the bottom. They allowed us to sleep until 0700 hours.

Our first training assignments were on how to make our beds the military way, and how to store our clothes the military way. We had to learn how to do the military physical training and to march in unison. In general, we did the usual training that all GIs go through when in Basic. Hour after hour of marching to commands, we eventually looked like some semblance of soldiers.

There are several incidents during basic training that are worth mention here.

Early in our training, after we ate breakfast, I had to take a dump. The latrine had eight toilets lined up in a row, with no partitions between them. While I was taking my morning dump, other GIs were cleaning the latrine. Sgt. Peyton came in, stood over me, and started to chew my butt for not taking my dump before breakfast. As he was chewing me out, I continued with the chore at hand. I wiped my butt, stood up in a crouched position, had my pants half-way up, and I looked Sgt. Peyton in the eye as I told him, "Sarge, I can bend nature a long way, but I can't change it." His eyes lit up and he stared at me for a few seconds, and then burst out laughing. From that day on, I was the person he picked on when things were dull. I also had the privilege of doing more push-ups than the average GI Joe.

One morning, after an overnight snowstorm that left about 10 inches of snow on the ground, we were in platoon formation standing on a freshly plowed road in front of an old barracks that was used for training. The door was locked and we had to wait for someone to unlock it. Sgt. Peyton yelled at me, "Kunkel, drop and give me 50." I did a right face and dropped face-first into the plowed-up snow along the road. The snow bank was about two feet deep. I would go down into the snow with my face and push out and yell out the count all the way through 50 push-ups. The rest of the platoon got a big kick out of my performance. When I completed my 50 push-ups, Sgt. Peyton had the rest of the platoon line up along the snow bank and they had to knock out 50 push-ups in the same fashion. Now that seemed funny.

One night we were laying in our bunks with the lights out. There were two low, glowing red lights on each end of the barracks. These were called fire emergency lights. Many people were talking in low voices to one another. I was talking to a black guy who was on the top bunk across the wall of lockers to my right. In our conversation, I mentioned I grew up on a farm, that our family milked cows, and the work was hard with all that was required to maintain a dairy herd. He responded that he grew up on a farm also. I thought of a quick come-back and I asked if his mother was a Black Angus. The words were barely out of my mouth and I knew that was an uncalled-for comment. The barracks became a quiet zone. Everyone else stopped talking. I jumped out of my bunk and came around the end of the lockers at the same time he did. We stared at each other before he went back to his bunk and climbed into it. I waited awhile and did the same. The barracks remained exceptionally quiet until everyone fell asleep. The next morning before we fell out for breakfast, I apologized to him. Besides the statement itself, my other regret is that I didn't apologize in front of all the people who occupied the second floor of the barracks.

One Sunday morning shortly after Tom and I returned to the barracks from the Sunday morning church services, someone came up the steps and told one of the GIs occupying his bunk with a hangover that he had a visitor outside. He crawled out of his bunk and began swearing; why would anyone bother him at such a time? He walked down the stairs in his GI-issued underwear and stumbled outside. Waiting at the bottom of the outside steps were his parents who had traveled from Wisconsin to see him. He came racing back up the stairs saying, "Oh, no. Oh, God, no." He said his parents were outside. He got himself dressed and went back outside to visit with them. They apparently wanted to take him into town to treat him to a good meal. At this point in our basic training, we were not allowed off post. They had to settle for a short visit right outside the barracks. Later on, when he returned to the barracks, he explained that he was the youngest child in his family, and his mother always treated him as her baby. It was quite a shock to her when he stumbled out the barracks and she first saw him.

On New Year's night, several GIs from our platoon went to the local Enlisted Men's Club (EM) to have a few or, more accurately, quite a few beers. We got there fairly early and lined up at least five card-sized tables together so we could sit around them in a group. About an hour later, another large group of GIs, most of them black but with a few whites with them, came in to do the same. Most of them were from the 1st platoon in our company. Besides our tables, all other tables and chairs were taken. These guys had to stand. After a short while, they began to give us crap about hoarding the tables and chairs and calling us white-ass honkies and something we would never think of doing with our mothers. Dobbins, who was with our group, went up to the bar to get a couple pitchers of beer. A good-sized black guy grabbed his chair. Lilly, who was sitting beside Dobbins, got hold of the chair and yanked it away from him. He came at Lilly showing his fists. The bartender, who resembled Hoss Cartwright from the "Bonanza" TV show, leaped over the bar, grabbed the black guy by the neck and by the seat of his pants, and ran him out the door.

As a group, we decided that if anyone had to use the latrine, we would do it with at least two or more together. Tom Mathies said he had to go to the can. I went with him. After we walked into the latrine, about eight of the other group followed us. I was about to unzip my pants when Leonard Guist slapped me on the shoulder and accused me of calling him a f-----. I told him I didn't even talk to him, so I couldn't have called him a f-----. He said, "Now you're calling me a liar?" I took a half-step back and told him that he didn't come in to talk, so let's get it on. He clenched his fist and, as he was bringing it up, I gave him a hard right jab to the face, catching him in the left eye, the first joint of my thumb hitting him on the bridge of the nose. Someone behind me hit me in the back of the head. I turned and grabbed the closest person who happened to be a small black guy named Higgins. He tried to back away but was held in place by all his buddies who had crowded in the door. I grabbed Higgins by his shirt in the neck area with my left hand, pulled him toward me, and followed through with a right fist in the face. His nose crunched and began to bleed profusely.

There was a partition between the first urinal and the door. The space between the door and partition was crowded with all these black guys. I spread my arms out and began pushing toward the door. A few took swings at my head, but my adrenaline was pumped and I didn't feel a thing. I got most of them out the door before they got some footing to push back. I put one of my feet up on the partition, let loose with a yell, and shoved forward. As I pushed, the partition broke off and pushed into the first urinal, breaking it off. The urinal was hanging down on the wall and water began spraying from it. The blacks went out the bathroom door, heading for the outside door. When the weight of the pile I was pushing gave way, I landed on my hands and knees in the hallway outside the bathroom. There was some banging and thumping still in progress inside the bathroom. I tried to get in to help Mathies. I couldn't push the door in, so I pulled it out; it swung both ways. Mathies and his victim were blocking the door from swinging inward. Mathies had a big, overweight man in a headlock with his left arm, his left hand stuffed in the man's mouth, his right fist giving him short jabs in the face. Water was spraying all over the latrine. There were three commode stools in the latrine with two partitions separating the stools. Under the partitions lay someone who was unconscious. He was face-down and soaking up water on the floor.

About this time, Hoss is standing in the door. He yelled back to his partner to shut the water off. He looked us over and said that someone's going to pay for this. There were a hell of lot of people involved, but now there were only the four of us. He said he called the MPs. I told him Tom and I came in to use the latrine and the rest followed us in to kick our butts. We only did what we had to do to protect ourselves. He kind of rocked his head up and down sighing, "Hm-m-m." After a few minutes, he said the MPs were busy and couldn't make it. He wrote our names and units down and said he would let our company Commanders handle us. The party was pretty much over so we went back to our barracks in a group. Most of the other GIs involved in the altercation were from the 1st platoon in our company. We were from the 3rd platoon. I expected that there would be an ambush party when we got back to the barracks. We had to walk past their barracks. I picked up a rock about 3 inches in diameter and said, "The first son-of-bitch who says 'boo' is going to get it between the eyes." Nothing happened on our trip back. As we went past the 1st platoon barracks we could hear a lot of "white-ass" and "mother-f------" comments.

The next morning was Sunday. Tom and I went to church. After Sunday Mass, we came back to our barracks and began playing a game of two-handed euchre while sitting on Tom's bunk. Dobbins came into the barracks and told us to stay out of the day room. He said it was full of black guys and they were talking about kicking our white asses. I looked at Tom and asked him if he wanted to play pool. He said, "Why not?" There was a loud noise coming from the day room with the usual "mother-this" and "mother-that" comments. When Tom and I walked in, they all stopped and stared at us. It got so quiet you could hear a pin drop. It appeared they were shooting four-man pool. I walked up the table, wrapped my hand around a pool ball, and asked who had the next game. No one said a word. I told those playing that Tom and I would take on the winners. They didn't finish their game. They all walked out of the day room without a word. Tom and I played pool for the next half hour.

Tom went back to the barracks and I headed for the chow hall. It was getting close to the noon hour so I thought I would eat early. Leonard Guist was standing last in line waiting his turn for lunch. I walked up behind him. He turned around and stared at me. I stared back. He had a small bruise over his eye. I figured if he wasn't over it yet, we might as well finish it sooner rather than later. Neither one of us said anything. After what seemed like at least a minute, he turned around and went into the chow hall. I followed.

Monday morning, Sgt. Peyton talked to Mathies and me. He said, "I hear you two got yourselves into some trouble over the weekend." I told him there was no trouble with us. He said the CO (Company Commander) wanted to see us A.S.A.P. He reminded us to report as we were instructed. We stepped in, walked up to the 1st Sergeant's desk, and reported in the military fashion. The 1st Sergeant looked us over, shook his head and grunted. He did this head-shake-and-grunt three times, then got up and opened the office door next to his. He announced, "The two fighters are here." We were directed into the CO's office and the door was closed. The Company Commander was a 1st Lieutenant. We reported with a salute, our rank, and last name. He returned our salute and said, "At ease." He sat there for about 30 seconds looking us up and down. Then he said, "I hear you two got yourself into a little trouble over the weekend." He waited for a response. Neither of us made a response, as he hadn't asked a question. "It sounds as if you didn't start it, but you sure as hell finished it," he said, shaking his head. Then he said, "I want you to know I don't approve of fighting, but if you have to, do it right!" He added, "It sounds like you two handled yourselves rather well. I'm proud you're in my company." Then he dismissed us. Since he didn't call the other two soldiers in, nor any of the other injured, I figured that he and the 1st Sergeant only wanted to see who we were and what we looked like.

After breakfast and roll call, we were ordered to load onto the deuce-and-a-half trucks. We were riding out to the rifle range. Cadre directed us on each truck until they were filled. I was the last person to get on the truck I rode in. As I was loading, I looked up into Leonard Guist's face. We both had a temporary startled look. He reached down and gave me a hand. We talked as we rode to the range. From that day, we became fairly good friends.

There's another incident I want to mention that happened during boot camp. We were in somewhat disassembled groups, waiting for the morning roll call. Laner, who was a good-sized boy from Baltimore, was pushing his weight around with other soldiers. He did this quite frequently. Laner stood about 6'4" and weighed about 220 lbs. He wasn't fat. A smaller guy, named Dowling, whom he had pushed, told him to knock it off. Laner braced up to Dowling and said, "What the hell you gonna do about it?" "I'm going to tear your face off," Dowling replied. Laner said, "what's stopping you?" Dowling said as he got down in a crouch with his left side out front like a boxer would do. He had his hands open. "What's this shit?" Laner asked as he mimicked him. While Laner was half-way through the gesturing, Dowling moved in with the speed of a cat and wrapped his left arm around Laner's neck. He reached up with his right hand, slid his two middle fingers in Laner's nose, pulled out with a jerk, and walked away. Laner's nose was torn from his face and hanging on only at the upper bridge. He grabbed his face and began wailing in pain. Laner disappeared for about three days. When he came back he had stitches in his nose. Laner became a much milder person after that incident. No one questioned what had happened. I'm sure the cadre was well aware of Laner's bully tactics, and they probably felt that justice had been served.

The 2nd platoon had a big American Apache Indian, nicknamed Geronimo. He was fairly tall and muscular. One morning, one of the Sergeants in his platoon got in his face over something he had done. He threatened the Sergeant with bodily harm. That afternoon, shortly after the lunch hour, the whole company was gathered in a classroom for classes in map-reading. The classroom was an old barracks, which was lined with chairs facing the far wall where there were charts and maps hanging. The latrine was off to the right side. The showers were removed from the latrine, but there were two commodes left in place. Just before the class began, the Field 1st Sergeant, Sgt. "Bull" Duggins, called Geronimo into the latrine. Duggins was a husky man, about 5'8" tall, around 200 pounds of muscle, and about 35 years old.

As soon as the door closed, Duggins yelled at Geronimo: "You threatened one of my cadre." As soon as the words came out of his mouth, there was a crunch of meat and bone, and something or someone slammed into the wall. For the next minute, the walls of the shower room were rattling, thumping and banging. Duggins came out of the bathroom and told two of his cadre to take Geronimo out and process him out of the company.

Then the Field 1st Sergeant came to the front of the class. He said, "Some of you may think you are prize fighters." He paused, then added, "I don't make such a claim. I am a *surprise* fighter." Then he said, "If any one of you threaten one of my cadre, you're gonna have to deal with me, and you ain't gonna like it."

During boot camp, after breakfast each day, we were put through the standard 12-point military exercise program.

About six weeks into boot camp, instead of that, every Wednesday we had what became known as organized grab-ass day. We would first run a mile to loosen our bodies before starting the events. The program, which was the most fun for us, was nicknamed the "dog-and-pony show." One person would act as the horse, and a second person would straddle his back as a rider. The whole company was put in a circle and we would work as a team to pull, push, butt, or do anything to knock another team down. Once you were knocked down, you went to the sideline and cheered for your favorite team still in the game. The last two men standing won the match.

Tom Mathies and I always teamed up. He was short and stocky, and he had a lot of upper body strength. I played the horse. I had strong legs and calves as well as a good strong back. Before going into the service, I was in drywall construction. I handled a trowel and mud hawk, day-in and day-out. I developed a lot of arm strength. Holding Tom sturdy was easy. At the end of the first match, Tom and I were the winners. We played a second match. Again Tom and I were the winners. A week later the event was held again. Tom and I won both matches.

By the third week, the Field 1st Sergeant worked it out with five of the teams to lay off each other so that they were all standing in the final moments of the match. Then they were to converge on Tom and me, working together to take us down. We were not informed of their game plan. When they converged on us together, I knew it was a set-up. I kept my feet fairly wide, so I would remain stable. I told Tom that I would work around and try to get them all on one side of us, and then I would rush into them and we would try to bowl them over. For about five minutes we were going at it. There were five teams of two, against Tom and me. Finally, they made a mistake and placed themselves all on the same side of us.

I think it was their intent for all five to rush us at once. We got the jump on them, and I yelled to Tom, "Now!" I started plowing and pushing forward. Tom grabbed one team in each arm and whipped them off-balance, hanging on to them. I gave out a groan and pushed, and they gave ground, stumbling over each other as they collapsed to the ground. We went down on top of them. The rest of the company, watching from the sidelines, was cheering mostly for us. When it was over, they were applauding.

Three particular guys who were black would hang together pretty much; they spent most of their time off playing poker. They were always trying to get others involved in the game with them. Not many people trusted them and most shied away from their game. Jeff Lunde, who was from Milwaukee and was in the downstairs part of our platoon, took them up on their offer to play. He played dumb like he didn't know how to play the game. He asked all kinds of questions about the game, and he seemed unclear on the order and importance of the different hands. They played a couple of practice hands and then started the game for money. Lunde continued to play dumb as the game went along. To make a long story short, he cleaned them out for more than $400. Indeed, Lunde was no virgin when it came to the game of poker.

From about week four in our barracks, people started missing items. Most of the time it was money taken from a billfold. One time a watch disappeared. Most of the time the items disappeared during the evening meal service. The thief was at it long enough that it seemed a pattern was developing. We had a buck Sergeant staying in one of the squad rooms at the end of the barracks on the second floor. He was one of the cadre and the assistant platoon Sergeant for our 3rd platoon. It was arranged that he would stay in his squad room. Another person would go to the shower room to shave and take a shower. He would leave his pants and shirt lying on his bunk, with his billfold in his pants pocket, and his watch in one of his shirt pockets with a portion of it visible. A third person would stand behind the far lockers on the end of the room, but in position to observe the clothes. He would conceal himself so as not to be seen, but could peek out to observe should someone show up. The owner of the cash recorded the serial numbers of the bills and a brief description of the watch. He kept this information with him in his personal bag with the shaving gear, toothbrush, toothpaste, and deodorant.

With the barracks seemingly empty except for the guy in the lavatory, it didn't take long for the thief to appear. He casually walked down the barracks, spotted the clothes and, after doing a scan of the area, dug in the trousers for the billfold, removed the money (which wasn't much) and took the watch. As he turned to leave, the observer stepped out and called for the Sergeant. The Sergeant stepped out of the squad room and blocked the avenue for an escape, while the observing soldier was behind him. The watch and the cash were reclaimed, and the MPs (Military Police) were called. The offending soldier, now a thief, was placed in handcuffs. The MPs took a brief statement from the person whose property was stolen, and from the assisting GIs. They also took possession of the stolen property with a receipt given to its owner. The thief was taken away and never seen again by our platoon. No one was aware of what was going down except the three people who were involved in the set-up: those three and, of course, the thief. The rest of our platoon learned of it later in the evening before bedtime.

The thief lived in the bottom level of the barracks. He was from Minneapolis and tried to be friendly with everyone.

If there is a moral to this saga, it would be, "Beware of friendly wolves."

Our company had a person who hailed from Missouri. His name was Rainer. To say the least, he was not very swift. After the lunch hour, he fell out for formation in less than a state of readiness. Everyone else had his field jacket on, but Rainer didn't. In fact, the buttons on his shirt were not in line, and it was not tucked in. His shoes were untied and the pants legs were not bloused. Each soldier was issued blousing bands, and when you put your pants on you put the blousing bands on and you tucked your pants legs under the bands just above the shoe tops. The pants legs were rolled under so there was no exposed cuff. Field 1st Sgt. Duggins took a long look at him and said, "Rainer, You're so f----- up you could f--- up a wet dream."

As part of our training, we were transported to an area that had boxed-in concrete barriers for a live grenade throw. The barrier was completely boxed-in except for the wrap-around entrance. Toward the front of the barrier, there was a hole in the concrete floor. The floor was tapered toward the hole. If someone dropped a live grenade, it would roll into the hole and come out the front of the barrier. There were six of these barriers in all. Each barrier had one drill instructor assigned. We were given instructions as a company unit. In the end, we were told that, just the year before, an instructor and a GI were killed when the live grenade was dropped and it went off before it could be recovered. When the instructions were complete, we had to count off from one to six, and then start over. I ended up with the number six as did Rainer.

There were about 16 people in each group. Per instructions, we all lined up about 10 yards behind the barrier. We were called up to the barrier, one person at a time. The instructor explained what we were to do individually. He then asked if we were right- or left-handed. He placed the grenade

38

into our hand, told us to pull the pin but retain the handle in the down position until we throw the grenade. The handle was spring-loaded and, once released, would fly off. Approximately four to five seconds later the grenade would explode. We were always told that once the pin was pulled and the handle was released, you had three seconds before it went off. I believed this was an error on the side of caution when stating this.

As it worked out, Rainer was the last person in our group to throw the live grenade. When he got in the concrete barrier, the instructor went through his instructions then asked him which was his strong hand. He did not know what the instructor meant. So the instructor asked him if he played ball, which hand he would use to throw the ball. He said he didn't play ball. Then the instructor asked him if he threw a rock at something, which hand would he use to throw the rock. He did a little try-out by waving his right hand and then left hand and pointed to his right hand. The instructor then placed the grenade in his right hand, told him to pull the pin. Once the pin was pulled the instructor told him to throw the grenade. Rainer then switched the grenade from his right hand to the left hand. In doing so, the spring lever flipped off. The instructor yelled at him to throw the grenade. He threw it halfway, underhanded, and it hit the top of the barricade. The instructor said, "You're on your own," and headed for the back opening. The grenade came back down, hit the outside edge of the barricade, and fell outside the wall. It went off before it hit the ground. Rainer was removed from the company and placed in a restructure status.

Marine photographer Sergeant William Dickman, 1967 in Vietnam. It is because of combat photographers such as Dickman that we have the photos we do today. My camera and all of the photos I took in Vietnam were destroyed by mold and mildew. The only photos I have from that time were provided by my Army buddies. There are many photos included in this book that were part of the official military record of Vietnam thanks to these combat photographers. U.S. Marine Corps photo ID 127-N-A370991. Photo courtesy of the National Archives at College Park, Md.

ADVANCED INFANTRY TRAINING (AIT), 4th Troop, 12th Squadron

After boot camp, each soldier was assigned to a unit for his particular MOS (Mode of Specialty). As I remember, two guys from our platoon were assigned to Military Police: one was assigned as a cook, some to transportation, and the balance to either artillery or infantry. There may have been one or more assigned to signal. I was assigned to the infantry.

Most of the infantrymen went to the 4th of the 12th Cavalry for Advanced Infantry Training, (AIT). The 4/12 Cav was battalion-strength, made up of four companies. Our unit was part of an armored brigade. The rest of the brigade was formed with the 1st of the 77th Armored Battalion and the 2nd of the 77th Armored Battalion.

One of the soldiers in our barracks was Roger Clark who hailed from North Carolina. He and I became fast and close friends. He was also in our squad.

Part of our training was to learn about the track vehicles we would be using. This included the trucks called the five-ton and the deuce-and-a-half, the latter being a two-and-a-half-ton truck. Among other uses, the deuce-and-a-half was the truck troops rode in for a variety of training functions.

The vehicles were kept in a fenced-in area. After our morning exercise program, we would march to the motor pool for the training. The training officer was the E-7 Sgt. First Class, motor pool Sergeant. The first thing we were told was that all vehicles, including all-track vehicles, were equipped with the 373 Chrysler engine. It was a high-performance engine that required high-test gasoline to operate. The reason this engine was chosen was because Chrysler had won a long-term bid with the Federal government to produce the engine and adapt it for all military government vehicles with the exception of the jeep and other smaller vehicles such as the smaller trucks and pick-ups. Chrysler Motors also produced the engines for those vehicles.

While we were standing in front of a PC (Personnel Carrier) that had the hood up for observation, the instructor told the soldier beside me to run to the shop and get him a "hammer for." The shop was a large building where they did maintenance work on the various vehicles. There was a parts room and a tool room on one end of the building. The young man ran off and short time later came back and asked the Sergeant, "What's a 'hammer for?'" The Sergeant replied, "It's for pounding nails." Everyone had a good laugh at the expense of this young man. It could as well have been me.

As part of our training, we had to learn how to drive the various track vehicles. An E-6, the equivalent of a Staff Sergeant, was our trip instructor. He pulled the PC out of its parked position, to allow the rear door to drop. When the rear door was down, it served as a ramp into the PC. There were 10 of us including him. This was considered squad strength. He pointed out the various parts of the vehicle, most of which was a repeat of what we heard from the motor pool Sergeant. I guess if you heard it twice it would stick to your brain cells better. He then covered the position of the driver, and the braking and turning maneuvers that were required to start, steer, and stop the vehicle. We all had a chance to sit in the driver's seat and briefly go through the maneuvers for driving the vehicle. Then he went through the command position, which would be occupied by him. He showed us how to close the hatch for the driver and command positions. You could peer through this, which would not expose you to someone shooting at you from the outside. The mirror was triple-angled so you could see forward and at an angle to the left and right. This was to protect you from bullets that would be directed at you in a combat situation. There was a place to mount an M60 machine gun just to the front of the hatch door in the roof of the vehicle. This was centered on the vehicle just to the right and behind the command position. There were two heavy metal plates on each side of the gun mount, angled back slightly from bottom to top. If someone was shooting at the vehicle, these plates would deflect incoming rounds up and over the person manning the machine gun. When our instructor was satisfied that he had covered all the aspects of driving the vehicle, it was time to put our knowledge to use. He put the vehicle back in its parked position, and we broke for an early lunch. After lunch, we were marched back to the motor pool.

He chose me to be the first driver. With a little mental hesitation, I got into driver's seat and the rest piled in. I started the vehicle, pulled out about 15 feet before making my turn so I wouldn't hit the vehicle sitting beside us, and started to drive. We exited the motor pool and went along the hillside to our left to where a well-worn trail led up into the hills overlooking the post. About 100 yards outside the motor pool I began to feel fairly comfortable driving. When directed, I turned up the trail, which angled to the top. At the top, he had me go through a few more maneuvers; I closed the hatch and drove looking through the mirrored visor. When I finished going through the required moves, he told me to stop the vehicle and secure the brakes so the next driver could get into position and learn the procedure and test his driving skills. Clark was the next driver. This went on for all nine of the trainees.

Each PC had an overhead door that opened from front to rear. It was boring to sit inside and not see what was going on. I stood up and watched. There was room for four people to stand up and have reasonable space to see what was going on to the front. As each new driver took his turn, it seemed a little rocky until they got the hang of it. The last person to take his turn driving was a big guy who, before getting drafted, was a truck driver by trade. He was older than the rest of us. I was just shy of 23, and I believe he was 25. Most everyone else was 19 or 20. He was good at talking about his truck-driving ability. He would dominate conversations to the point where it was sickening to listen to him talk. Of course, he informed the rest of us that driving the PC would be simple compared to driving an 18-wheeler.

As he started, his driving seemed more herky-jerky than when anyone else in the squad drove. At one point, he was told to turn right but instead he turned left. This took the PC over the lip of a plateau area and onto a hillside overlooking the south end of the post. There was a cliff with at least a 60-foot drop if you went too far. The farther down the hillside you went, the steeper it got. The PC commander told him to make a left turn. He did not respond. Then he told him to stop. He still did not respond. As he got closer to the cliff, the hillside became steeper. I yelled at everyone to bail out of the PC. I was the first one out and the rest followed. By now the commander was screaming for him to stop. He finally locked into the brakes, and the PC stopped about 10 to 15 feet from the cliff's edge. The Commander then told him to make sure the brake locks were set firmly. He got out of the Commander's seat and back by the open hatch. He then told him to very carefully crawl out of the driver's seat. The Commander explained that, if he bumped the brake arm and if it released the brakes, the Commander was bailing out and the driver would go over the cliff with the PC. The guy apparently used his most fancy footwork to avoid releasing the brakes. Once he cleared the driver's seat and made it to the squad area in back, the Commander slipped into the driver's seat, held the brakes secure, put the PC in reverse, brought the engine to full throttle, and started backing up the hill. He did not stop until he was on the flat surface of the plateau. He then dropped the back door and exited the PC to settle his nerves. He told the truck driver that he would never drive a PC again. When the Commander was ready, he told me to get in the driver's seat, and I would be driving the rest of the way back to the motor pool. Once at the motor pool, the back door was dropped, and the squad un-assed the PC. The back door was then closed and secured.

One of the staff at the motor pool directed me to back the PC into the appropriate place. This was done with hand signals. I caught onto this rather easily, and I parked the PC on the first try. Of course, the Commander was coaching me through the process.

After that incident, our truck driver didn't have much to say anymore. To put it mildly, that was a welcome relief. Along about the fifth or sixth day, though, he started his truck driving venture tales again. One of the guys in our squad brought up his PC driving skills. He countered that there was something wrong with the steering. I told him that I drove it all the way back to the motor pool and the steering worked perfectly. He said it was an intermittent problem, but they got it fixed now. Someone else chimed in that the only problem was when he was the driver. This made him mad and he walked away sulking. No one felt bad about his leaving.

One person in our platoon was a chronic complainer who bitched about everything we were told to do. This bitching did not go unnoticed by our Platoon Sergeant. He was an E-7 Sergeant First Class. The Platoon Sergeant stood about 4'10" tall. He was probably in his late 40s, or maybe even early 50s. He earned the label of the guy with the meanest pen in the Army. On this particular day, it was raining. The Platoon Sergeant told us to saddle up with rain gear, draw our weapons, and fall out in front of the barracks in one-half hour. We were going to march to the rifle range, which was at least a five- or six-mile distance. Our constant chronic complainer said, "This is bullshit, I'm not going." The Sergeant asked him if he was going to get ready and he said, "No." The Sergeant said, "That's okay," and he left the barracks. About 10 minutes later, he came in with two MPs and pointed out the complainer. They manhandled him into position for searching and cuffing, then they carted him away. The Platoon Sergeant told us later that he got 30 days in lock-up and then was given a general discharge from the Army. A general discharge means that the person is undesirable for the military.

About half-way through our 12-week cycle, our troop was designated the riot control unit. Stokley Carmichael, who at the time was not yet wanted for crimes, was touring the United States making speeches and stirring up the black population. He was scheduled to make a stop in Denver for one of his rabble-rousing speeches on the following Saturday.

It was the Monday before Stokley Carmichael's speech. A black man dressed in Army fatigues and bearing a Major's insignia, along with two black assistant enlisted men, drove an Army jeep up to the weapons storage armory building of the 1st of the 77th Armor. The 1st of the 77th Armor was a tank battalion with Fort Carson. The battalion was out on maneuvers. The jeep pulled up to the armory, and the man with the

Major's insignia handed a Spec-4 manning the armory orders requesting a list of automatic weapons with ammunition, which was to be used for a field demonstration for visiting dignitaries. The Spec-4, not knowing any better, turned over the weapons and ammunition. Neither the weapons nor the three black men were ever seen again.

On Tuesday we began training for riot control. Fort Carson had a made-up village that was used as a Hogan's Alley for military house-to-house war games. Another battalion was dressed in civilian clothing. They played the role of demonstrators. Our troop, dressed in fatigues, played the role of riot control. The demonstrators could do almost anything they wanted as long as it was not life-threatening or physically assaulting. They threw flour, water, eggs, and dirt at us. In a group, we tried to herd them to predetermined positions. Of course, they could resist in any way possible. We trained all day long. When one scenario was completed, another one was staged. We broke for lunch, and we ate a late supper to make sure we had a full day's training. Wednesday was a repeat of Tuesday, with variations in the demonstrations.

Thursday was another day of training. By mid-day Thursday, the training had taken its toll. We were pushed to our limits. It was no longer a game. On one occasion a demonstrator grabbed my rifle as I held it out front in the parry position. I yanked it away from him and followed through with a butt stroke, knocking him off his feet. He got up holding his jaw and said, "This is only a game." I retorted, "Not anymore." There were a number of other somewhat similar incidents throughout the unit. The powers-that-be called a halt to the training. I believe it was intended to push us far enough to see where the breaking point is for soldiers involved in riot control. Stokley Carmichael canceled his speech Saturday. I'm sure it was because of pressure from the government.

The 4th Troop 12th Cav was the Division Commander Major General Delton Maroun's favorite division unit. Because we were his favorite, we were always designated the unit that had to march in ceremonial parades in close-order drill. Close-order drill is when the whole company lines up, 12 men across, and marches elbow-to-elbow around the ceremonial parade quadrant. The tallest soldiers are placed to the front and the shortest to the back, in descending height. Many of our Saturdays were taken up practicing the close-order drills, or for the actual ceremony for which we were assembled.

4/12 Cav was part of the armored brigade made up of the 1st Bn 77th Armor and the 3rd Bn 77th Armor. The Brigade Commander Colonel Marten Stangley was going to be replaced. It was no secret that Col. Stangley liked his booze. He always had a flush face with a bulbous, enlarged red-purple nose. He always carried a large swagger stick with him. His swagger stick was about 20 inches long with a very wide handle. The top of the swagger stick had a screw-off cap. While he was out and about, which was more than usual for a full-bird Colonel, he frequently took a swig of the liquid he carried in that swagger stick.

While we were practicing for the ceremonial parade that would be the change of guard for his position, he came out to the parade grounds to watch. He climbed to the top seat of the stands along the parade grounds and he stood up on it. There was a single-back rail about 16 inches high above the seat. He opened his swagger-stick flask and, as he was tipping it, he fell over backward, off the stand and to the ground. The top seat of the stand was at least 12 feet above the ground. He had the wind knocked out of him and I'm sure he had pains, but either the booze had him numbed or he was putting on a show of toughness. He refused any medical help and crawled back up in the stand and sat down.

Night-maneuver training was part of our battalion's AIT training. We usually did this in platoon- or company-sized units. In one situation, our platoon had to do a lights-out march in the dark. We set up our positions as if we were in a combat situation. We always had to set up in a two-man position. Clark and I always worked together. We found a nice spot in some scrub brush, leveled it off, created a small bunker to our front, and pitched our tent. There were other positions on either side of us, somewhat similar to how we set up. Our squad leader at this time was a huge E-5 Sergeant. He stood at least 6'6" tall, was a little heavy on top and more slender through the hips and legs. He carried his weight well and was fairly agile. He also had a great sense of humor and reveled us in stories of his past. Everyone liked him. Once the bunkers were set up, our platoon had to muster in an open area to the front of our night positions. We had a class on night patrols, which took about an hour, and then we were dismissed until the evening meal was served. Instead of C-Rations, which often dated back to the Korean War and in some cases even back to World War II, the chow was delivered from the kitchen in insulated food containers on a truck.

The platoon had at least three hours to kill before the evening chow was served. Some people sacked out, others sat around and chatted. I was with a more venturesome group.

We had blank ammunition. We decided to make mini-missiles and competed to see who could launch them the highest. Someone had a chunk of foil wrapping that he carried around in his pocket. I still haven't a clue why he carried foil with him. We would roll the foil into a narrow cone shape, fill it with gunpowder we extracted from the blank ammunition, light it, and hopefully send the missile skyward. Most of the time the mini-missile would ignite and fall over and fizzle, sometimes spinning. After watching this, I decided that the missile needed a longer length, room for more powder, and the bottom side closed tightly. I had a government pen. I took it apart and used the writing end of it for the cone of my missile. I used a small portion of chewing gum, already chewed, to stuff the end tip of the pen shut to keep the ignition from blowing out the tip. I got a larger chunk of foil, shaped it around the pen, and sealed it to the pen with more chewing gum. I filled the pen and foil with the gunpowder and sealed the bottom shut.

Using the ink tube of the pen, I punched a hole in the side of the foil. The gunpowder was ignited with a match, and the missile lifted off. It shot up about five feet high before falling back to the ground. Two other guys borrowed my spent missile and tried to duplicate what I had done. They weren't as exact as I was and, when they ignited, they only got about a two-foot liftoff. The balance of our time before evening chow we spent BS-ing

Chow arrived, we ate, and then we got ourselves ready for the night march. We had to put small pieces of green glow-tape on each guy's back. You could see this strip from about 20 feet away in the dark of night. Beyond that, the glow strip was invisible. We mulled around for another half hour to make sure it was completely dark before heading out on the night patrol. The training officer was our patrol leader. He apparently gave us too much time to think about the march. There were four of us who decided we weren't going on the march. Roger Clark was one, and the other two shared a pup tent to our immediate right. They were part of the friendship back then, but after all these years I cannot remember their names. We lined up so we would be the last in the platoon. The patrol leader led the way. We were a long way back from him so we knew he wouldn't see us pull out. We just had to trust the few soldiers to our immediate front to keep their mouths shut.

The patrol started and we tailed along for about 30 yards and then stopped. We retreated back to an area just to the south of where we set up the pup tents. There was a high mound that had the north side weathered away and created a near cliff-like structure on that side. It was about a 12-foot drop to level ground. The rest of the rise had rounded sides that were rather steep. It was our intent to wait for the rest of the patrol to pass and slide down the embankment and fit in as the tail-enders. Even well-organized plans have glitches occasionally. When the patrol returned, and as the patrol leader was passing the mound, he thought he heard the rattle of a rattlesnake. He was deathly afraid of rattlesnakes. When he heard what he thought was a rattle, he ran right up the side of the cliff-like structure. The first thing he said was there's a rattlesnake down there. Then he asked what we were doing up there. I told him we thought we would take a shortcut back to the tent area. Then I added, "I guess it isn't much of a shortcut." I don't know if he believed us, but he didn't question us anymore.

One thing we were told back in Basic Training was to never open your sleeping bag until you were ready to crawl into it. We were told that scorpions or snakes like hideaways, and an empty sleeping bag was an ideal hideaway for either of the aforementioned critters. The training instructor slept alone. His claim was that he was too big to share a pup tent with anyone else. We all crawled into our tents and sleeping bags. Behind us someone screamed, clearly in a panicked state. The screaming didn't stop, so Roger and I with a few of the other soldiers crawled out of our sleeping bags and opened our tents to see what the uproar was all about. Sarge came running past our tent wearing his sleeping bag. A bull snake, which is not poisonous, had crawled into his sleeping bag. After Sarge had settled in, the snake began to slither around. This freaked him out and he began kicking and yelling. Through all the activity, he dismantled his pup tent, kicked holes in the bottom of his sleeping bag, and began to run. We had to calm him down and then helped him out of his sleeping bag. We shook the sleeping bag until the snake fell through one of the leg holes. This is when we discovered that it was a bull snake. It was about 40 inches long and about one and a half inches thick through mid-body. Everyone except the Sarge had a good laugh at his misfortune. All I can say is that he must have had a strong heart to live through such a traumatizing event.

The following day we got to have fun with the tanks. Sarge drove us through some very rough terrain. The ride was extremely rough, so we had to buckle ourselves into the seats that lined the outer walls of the tank. One person got to sit in the gun seat. This allowed some sightseeing. The Sarge made sure the exchange was made when the terrain was favorable for it. Sarge ran through this with four different squads. For those who did not get to sit in the gunner's seat, the ride was not a visual experience but rather a physical sensation. After the rough ride, the rest of the platoon got to drive the tank on more suitable ground for the inexperienced. There were no unusual events with the tank training.

Toward the end of our 12 weeks of AIT training, we had to make one last trip to the field.

We were told that we would be in the field for seven days and we should pack extra socks and underwear in our backpacks. When we were all set for the trip to the field we marched to the motor pool to load onto the PCs. I was designated to drive for our squad. We headed south from the camp area to higher ground. I'm not sure how far we traveled, but we averaged close to 15 to 18 miles per hour for at least four hours. We made one stop a little over halfway to our destination. The back door was dropped, and anyone who required bladder relief was allowed to take care of it. This was most of the company including myself. The PCs do not have torsion springs, or any springs for that matter. After enough time with the motion and jarring of the ride going through your body, your bladder reacts and demands relief. After a short respite, we began the last leg of the journey.

When we arrived at our final destination, we parked the PCs in a somewhat controlled order, lowered the back ramps, and the soldiers un-assed (or exited) the vehicles. In the military, the slang term "un-ass" is used rather than get out, leave, or exit. Other than the fact that it worked fine, there does not seem to be any other logic for its use. Each platoon was lined up, and instructions were given on how to set up camp. One of the most important duties was to create an outdoor lavatory. This was done with posts and canvas that was transported with us in one of the PCs. There was to be one outhouse per platoon. If the morning line for the outhouse was too long, you could disappear into the bush with your entrenching tool (a small spade or shovel that folded up and hung on the side of your backpack), dig a hole which was to be one foot deep, take your dump in the hole, then cover it up. Each lavatory had a bag of lime in it with an empty C-Ration can in the bag. When you took a dump, you had to sprinkle a little lime over it to keep it from breeding bacteria. Basically, there was a central area that was used for musters each morning after breakfast, after the noon lunch, and after the evening dinner. It was also an area where classes were held. There was a gentle slope to a hill that was clear of brush and large rocks. The soldiers would sit on this hill, and instructors would stand on the level ground to the front of it. It worked quite well as a classroom setting.

Once the minimal chores were completed, we had to put up our pup tents. Each platoon was assigned a certain area. When all the platoons were in place, a perimeter around the central staging and muster area was formed. Clark and

I selected a spot in a gully to pitch our tent. The ground was level, it had a sandy bed, and we didn't have to clear brush out of the way. It was also below normal ground level and the wind would not bother us. Once the tents were in place, we still had two hours of class time before we broke for evening chow. The cooks provided breakfast and dinner for us in the standard insulated food containers. A field kitchen was set up at a location where one of the other companies was established and meals were delivered by truck from that location. For our noon lunch, we were provided with antique C-Rations. The food was edible and that's the best I can say about it.

When the evening meal was finished, we had the rest of the day for ourselves. Some people played cards, others just sat around and BS'ed. As the evening came to an end and the sun disappeared behind the mountains, we turned in. Someone in the group would yell out, "O'Reggin." Someone else would respond with the same, "O'Reggin." This carried on for at least a half hour before it stopped and quiet came over the area. The next day we learned that the term "O'Reggin" was meant to be "nigger" backwards. This really started bad vibes with the blacks in our platoon, especially when some of them joined in on the yelling it out. Roger Clark and I missed out on the brouhaha and only learned about it later. Since we missed the first part of the training we missed out on the butt-chewing our company 1st Sergeant gave. Our squad leader asked us if we had any knowledge of the name-calling used the previous evening. We told him, no, and we had no idea what it meant. He informed us that it spelled "nigger" backward, and it was never to be used again.

Clark and I missed out on just about everything until around 0930 hours that morning. Overnight it snowed about six inches. The wind blew in the general direction toward where our platoon was staged. Since we pitched our tent in a gully, we ended up with a substantial amount of snow over the top of our tent. I was the first of us two to awake. It was very dark in our tent and I could tell that the angled sides were pushed in. I woke Clark and then opened the flap at the front of our tent. It was all snow. Since we were already dressed, we only had to put on our shoes. We also put on our field jackets. The field jackets had doubled as pillows. We rolled up our sleeping bags and stuffed them at the far end of the tent with our packs. It was a tight fit for the both of us, but we managed without clubbing each other in the process. We began to pull snow into the tent. Once we had about five bushels of snow in the tent with us, we were able to break through and escape our snow tomb.

Since neither one of us had a watch, we were hoping to catch breakfast. The breakfast truck had already come and gone. The rest of the company was in class. As we approached, our squad leader met us and wanted to know why the hell we missed out on muster and most of the first class. We told him of our snowy dilemma. He told us to catch the rest of this class and, during our break, he wanted to see our tent. There were about 10 minutes left of the class and then it was break time. Our squad leader met us and we proceeded to our tent. When he saw it, he laughed at first and then told us that we had not chosen a very good place to pitch our tent. He said that, had it rained, we would have been washed away. By this time the snow was melting at a fast rate. Clark and I selected another spot and cleared it of snow. Break time was over and we had to go back to class. During our next break time, we checked on the progress of our new tent site and then dug our tent and our backpacks out of the gully. We stretched the tent out over some brush to allow it to dry. It was soon time to go back to class. Most of our classroom training had to do with day and night patrols, perimeter defense, large- and small-patrol defense, and weapons placement, especially for machine guns and mortar squads.

During lunch break and after a quick C-Ration meal, Roger and I went back to setting up our tent in its new position. An abundance of wild stem grass-like plants was growing in the area, so we started gathering this for our tent bed and placed them in the proximity of our new tent area. By evening just about all the snow had melted and Roger and I covered the ground with the long-stem grass, pitched our tent, and made ready for sleep time. We found out that the squad leaders got to sleep in the PCs. They all had air mattresses in addition to their sleeping bags. They stayed high and dry throughout the night.

Before they allowed us to turn in for the night, the company had to assemble in the staging area to observe night flares. We first got to see how mortar flares lit up the sky. Each flare lasted for about one minute before it went out. When that was completed, someone called for artillery flares. They were much brighter and lasted about twice as long as the mortar flares. When this was finished we were allowed to crash for the night. After the butt-chewing that morning, no one yelled out any obscenities during the night.

During the next four days, we concentrated on day and night patrols with squad-sized and platoon-sized units. We set up squad-sized ambushes. Each squad took turns playing the roles of aggressor and defender. A few soldiers were sent out into the brush and told to fire blank cartridge rounds; this demonstrated how muzzle flashes gave away hidden positions. We would train long into the night, but we had more daytime to rest and relax. This training all built up to a final setting of putting our training to practical use.

On the final night of bivouac, we played war games. One platoon was designated as the aggressors. The rest of the company played the role of defenders. A group of English soldiers assigned to our company was also assigned to play aggressors. They numbered at least 20. Shortly after the games started, a few wiseasses yelled out, "F--- the Queen." This raised the ire of the English; it also increased their aggressiveness. Their role of aggressor was a lot more defined. They worked in groups of four or five, and they were much more disciplined than their American counterparts. They would identify a defender's position, catch him in a laid-back attitude, latch onto him, gag him, and tie him up. They did not tie his feet, so he could wander around looking for help. In some instances, one of the English would follow him until he led them to another victim. They would repeat this scenario. Our platoon Sergeant decided that he would rather ride the war games out hidden in some brush and lying in his sleeping bag. The English found him, possibly because he snored too loudly. They secured him more solidly in the sleeping bag and pitched him – sleeping bag and all – off the hill. The hill was rather steep, and rocks and brush intermittently covered it. He had no broken bones, but he had aches and bruises all over his body.

I was assigned to guard a tank that was near the top of a hill backed into the brush. Three aggressors, who were not English, came up behind my position and around the tank. I told them to freeze. The lead guy walked right up to me and grabbed my rifle and shoved it. The rifle went off and, since he was nearly against it, he received a burn on his chest. He asked, "What the f--- did you do that for?" I countered with, "Why the hell did you grab the rifle and push it?" I added, "If this was for real, you would be a dead man." I recognized him as one of the blow-hard wise guys in our company. Later on, I told our squad leader what had happened.

With the war games concluded, we had one last sit-down class. It basically summarized the training we concluded and critiqued our actions. While we had our ups and downs, it appeared to have been beneficial training all around. Then the PCs and tanks were lined up, each squad loaded up in their respective unit, and we headed back to main post. Roger Clark had the honors of driving the PC back.

Once back at post, besides the routine daily and exercise training, we spent time getting our gear up-to-date. There was a lot of downtime so people filled their time playing cards, shooting pool in the day room, pitching dimes against a wall, reading, or napping. Pitching dimes was a simple game. Anyone playing had to have a dime. A line was designated where you would stand. Everyone pitching had to stand in the same spot and pitch their dime to the wall. The guy with the closest dime to the wall was the winner and he collected all the dimes as his. If you hit the wall and the dime bounced back, you were disqualified. Because no one was an expert in this game, the dimes frequently shifted from player to player. Besides occupying time, the game was competitive and built camaraderie. This pace lasted for close to a week.

The last weekend of AIT training, just about everyone who did not have routine guard duty went into Colorado Springs. It was Saturday afternoon and a few guys and I also decided to head into town. Clark, Kultzer, another guy (whose name I don't remember) and I and got ready to go. There was a black guy who lived in the same barracks as Clark and me but on the first floor. He was sitting on his footlocker by himself when we came down the stairs to leave. He struck up a conversation with us and asked where we were headed. We told him into town. He asked if he could tag along with us. We told him that would be great. We went next door to meet with Kultzer and his friend and then out to the main drag to catch the bus. This black gentleman always hung by himself. He was quiet and pretty much kept to himself. While waiting for the bus, Kultzer asked him why he didn't go downtown with the other blacks. He mulled the question over for a while then said, "I shouldn't say this, but they're mostly niggers and I just don't like the way they act." Then he added, "They'll go down to the Cotton Club and meet more of the same and shuck and jive each other." (The Cotton Club was a bar that catered to blacks only. If a white guy showed up, there would likely be problems.) He added, "That's not me. I'd like to think I'm a little more refined than that." Through additional conversation, we learned that he had graduated from college with a teaching degree in math and got drafted as soon as he graduated.

When I say he was a quiet guy, that rang true only until he had a few bottles of beer in him. Then he opened up and he was quite a card. We hit a few bars and somewhere around 5:30 in the afternoon, decided to get something to eat. We went to a pizza place to have a large pizza. A waitress came to our table and told us she couldn't serve us unless the black guy left. I told her he's been with us all afternoon, he's a friend, and he's good enough to be served the same as anybody. She said she would talk to the manager. A short while later she came out and took our order. When she brought the pizza and set it on the table it didn't look right. Another guy and I tried it. It had the regular pizza crust, but the ingredients were nothing more than rendered lard chunks. I spit it out into a napkin. Kultzer said, "This is bullshit," and we got up to leave. We were almost to the door and Kultzer said, "Wait a minute, I forgot something." He walked back to the table, picked up the pizza, and dropped it topside-down on the floor.

We figured they would call the cops, so we walked down to the corner of the block, turned left, walked another half block and were about ready to go into a Mexican bar. A police car with red lights flashing and siren blaring pulled up to the pizza joint. We went into the Mexican bar and asked if they served blacks. They did. They served finger-type Mexican food on platters. We ordered three platters and, with some beer, we satisfied our hunger.

ADVANCE UNIT TRAINING (AUT)

After 12 weeks of AIT, we went into Advanced Unit Training (AUT). The troop was realigned, and I was assigned to a barracks with 48 soldiers. There were no American Indians and no Hispanics in our barracks. Of the 48 people assigned, there were six male Caucasians; it should be easy to figure out who the rest were. Consider that this was the mid-1960s and there were racial demonstrations and rioting going on all over the country. This proved to be an interesting period.

As it turned out, Roger Clark moved into the same barracks as I did. All the whites moved to the second floor. Two guys, both squad leaders, grabbed the two squad rooms on either side of the stairwell. I took the first bunk on the left at the top of the stairs, and Clark took the second. Blake, who hailed from a suburb near Los Angeles, took the third and Fitzpatrick took the fourth bunk. Along with the two squad leaders, we did our thing and the blacks did theirs. When we made the transfer, our Platoon Sergeant transferred also. The little pencil-pusher must have liked us.

It was the Memorial Day weekend. Roger Clark and I went to Denver for the weekend. We rode the bus from Colorado Springs. As we were walking around Denver, some guy stopped us and said we looked like two guys who were about to go out and get into trouble. He said he wanted to talk to us, and if we didn't like what he said we could just leave. We told him to go ahead, interested in where this might go. With that, he started preaching fire and brimstone, hell and damnation. Roger and I busted out laughing and walked away.

We walked for another three blocks and found we were in the rougher part of town. There were transients sitting in doorways, empty wine and liquor bottles lying around, garbage strewn all over the place, and the buildings were in run-down shape. We walked by a second-hand store that had a big beefy man standing in a double-wide, open doorway. About 15 feet beyond was a duplicate of the double doorway with another big beefy guy standing in the doorway. They looked as though they could be identical twins. As we passed the first guy, he said to the other one, "What do you think?" The other guy said, "Why not!" He stepped out in front of us and the other came up behind us. I yelled at Roger to hit it. We both ran at the man who stepped out in front of us and hit him on each side of his body, toppling him over. We ran for about two blocks before we looked back. No one was following.

We found a cheap motel that was very simple but clean so we checked in for an overnight stay. We paid for one night in advance and asked the person who checked us in how to get to Colfax Avenue. This is where all the night action is located. In a span of three blocks, there are probably 20 or more entertainment clubs, some with live music.

According to hearsay, among the younger population, Denver had about four females to every male. We found Colfax Avenue and began walking west in the direction of the clubs. The so-called female jet-setters catered to the Air Force cadets from the Air Force Academy which is located about 20 miles north of Colorado Springs along I-25. Denver is 60 miles north of Colorado Springs. For some reason, they generally disapproved of Army personnel. Once we found Colfax Avenue, within the first block a car pulled to a stop with two young females in it. They asked if we were Army or Air Force. I quickly told them we were Air Force. They told us to get in, so Clark and I crawled in. They went up the street another block, made a left turn and drove around another block to come back to Colfax Avenue and headed for the club area. We were almost to the section of the street where all the clubs were located when Clark said something related to Fort Carson. One of the girls said, "You're Army, aren't you?" I told them, "Yes, but we're not animals. We are still decent people." The driver pulled to the curb and told us to get out. At that point, there was nothing we could say that would change their minds. We gained two beneficial things in that short ride: (1) what we heard about Air Force versus Army in Denver was true; (2) instead of walking we got a ride, getting us at least eight blocks closer to our destination. We spent a couple of hours checking out a few of the clubs and found out again that Air Force was much preferred over Army. We walked back to the motel, discussed our night in Denver, and eventually fell asleep.

The next day, Sunday, I woke up and looked in the phone book for churches; I did not find any close by. I went to the office and checked with the girl in charge as to where the nearest Catholic church was and they had no idea. Denver did not appear to us to be a very religious town.

Roger and I checked out of the motel and headed for a park that was within 10 blocks of the bus station. We spent at least three hours there before we headed back to the bus station to catch a ride back to Colorado Springs. We then hitched a ride back to Fort Carson, arriving at around 1700 hours (5 p.m.). We went to the barracks and the second floor had at least 15 black guys standing around a little portable record player, with the volume turned up to the max, playing soul rock. It seemed they were all trying to talk over the sound of the music. We went to the dining room for chow and came back to the barracks. We showered, got into clean uniforms and, since the noise was still intolerable, went to the day room, shot pool, and watched television until 2200 hours (10 p.m.).

The next day, Memorial Day, both Roger and I would have KP duty. We crawled into bed, thinking they might turn the music down and quiet down themselves. It didn't happen. I got out of bed and went to talk with them. I told them we had KP the next morning and we needed sleep. All I got for my efforts was a, "F--- you, white ass," and other slurs. I went back to my locker, pulled out my portable radio with four brand-new D-cell batteries, tuned in the local Country Western/pop station and turned the volume as loud as it would go. My radio was louder than their record player.

For a few minutes they stood there glaring our way, "mother-f---ing" us and throwing us other insults they knew. The noise was too loud to hear anything, but it wasn't hard to read lips. After a short while, the whole group came over. Their lead man said that, if I didn't turn that radio off, he was going to kick it out the window. I got down in a crouch, opening my hands as if ready to charge him. I told him, "Before it hits the ground, you will be a dead man." He backed away, now unsure of himself. About this time, Nowacs, who was a squad leader and who slept in one of the cadre rooms, came out of the room. He told them it's time to shut the noise down so people could sleep. Now there were three of us. Because we took a stand, you could sense the group was losing their confidence. About 30 seconds later, the Sergeant of the day came storming up the steps, taking about four steps at a time. This Sergeant was a big, lanky guy who was from the south. He grabbed the soldier who was going to kick the radio out the window and threw him toward the stairs saying, "You don't even belong in this barracks. Get out!" The man's feet never caught up with the rest of his body. He pile-dived into the hallway below. The day Sergeant grabbed for another guy and shoved him toward the stairs. By now the rest were getting out of the area any way they could find. A few went out the fire escape. After it was over, Clark looked at me and said, "You're f---ing nuts!" I told him, "Sleep tight." There was peace and quiet for the rest of the night.

A few days later, we were standing in the lunch line for the noon meal. There was a big black guy in front of me. His name was J.T. Jones. He had a close friend whose name was J. Jones. J.T. Jones was about 6'2" and was a little on the fat or heavy side. J. Jones was about 6'6" and built like Carl Eller, a Minnesota Vikings defensive tackle. J. Jones walked up to the back of the line; the line was stretched out with at least 30 soldiers behind me. J.T. Jones looked around and told J. Jones to come up to him. J. Jones walked up and stepped in front of me. Without thinking about it, I grabbed J. Jones by the belt, which was slightly lower than my shoulders, and swung him around and out of the line. I got down in a low crouch and told him, "I started at the back of the line and that's where you can start unless you can go over or through me." He assessed me for a few seconds then walked to the end of the line. It was a quick reaction on my part, and most likely I would never have done such a thing if I had a little time to think about it. I'm sure if J. Jones had wanted to, he could have wiped up the ground with me.

A few days later, after the lunch hour was complete, most of us fell out for the afternoon formation. The Platoon Sergeant could see that a few troops were missing. He told me to go to the barracks and tell anyone in there to fall out. As I went in about three guys came out. J.T. Jones was sitting on his footlocker not doing anything. I told him the Sarge wants everybody out. He told me, "One of these days, you're going to get your ass kicked." I told him, "You're not going to do it, and the Sarge says to fall out. You can take it up with him. Right now I'm going out to tell him I told everybody to fall out." He begrudgingly got up, grabbed his hat, and came out behind me.

Orders came down for most of the soldiers in our AUT to be transferred to the 25th Armored Cav unit based near Indian Gap, in Pennsylvania. Once everybody with orders left, there were now only about 30 enlisted men remaining in the unit. I happened to be one of them. Rumor had it that we would be training cadre for new recruits.

We were all moved to one barracks kitty-corner across the compound from where I was located. I found a bunk on the ground floor. There was a guy in our barracks who was a comedian. He must have come from S-1 Intelligence. His name was Stawicky. He thought it would be a good idea to form our group into its own identity.

He said that, wherever we went as a group, we would display this identity. We went outside to do a short practice session. He lined us up into two separate groups, and the two groups would march side-by-side. The first group formed an "F" and the other group formed the "I." The F group always marched to the left of the I group. Since Stawicky dreamed up this idea, as a group we thought it best that he should command it. When we fell out for any type of training, we formed outside the barracks into the "FI" pattern and marched to the start of the military formation. When we fell out for chow, we would form the "FI" formation and walk to the chow hall, which was directly across the compound from our barracks. One day we were marching to the chow hall and the Captain stopped us. Stawicky called us to a halt, told us to stand at ease, faced the Captain and saluted per instructional training. The Captain asked why we walked around in the unique "FI" formation. Stawicky told him, "This represents our identity and attitude." The Captain asked, "And what is your identity and attitude?" Stawicky responded, "F--- it." The Captain laughed and told him to carry on, then walked away. He didn't even wait for a salute as is the norm.

Prior to this, I had tested for a position as a helicopter pilot. While I didn't think I wanted to be a helicopter pilot, at least not during this period, I still wanted to find out more. I went to the Orderly Room and requested permission from the 1st Sergeant to go to main post, Division Headquarters, to talk to someone about being a pilot. I forget what the office was called, but at the time I had the information with me. We unkindly referred to our 1st Sergeant, whose last name was Franchez, as 1st Sergeant Pig. He was a short stocky guy with a Spanish background. His jaw jutted out so his face looked like the face of a pig. Of course, no one called him that to his face.

Sgt. Franchez told me I didn't want to be a helicopter pilot and that I should forget about going to Division. I bypassed his recommendation, as I was allowed to do, and went anyway. Once there, I was given a pass to cover me in the event I got stopped. Soldiers were not allowed to wander around Division Headquarters without a specific purpose. The next day, right after lunch, Sgt. Franchez called me into his office. He said, "So you want to go to Vietnam? Well, you're going, but not as a helicopter pilot. Here's your orders for the 5th Battalion 7th Cav. Report there immediately."

Bob Kunkel, home on leave before going to Vietnam, with girlfriend Eileen Wagner.
Eileen lived and worked in Minneapolis at the time.

5th BATTALION, 7th CAVALRY
Garry Owen

The 5/7 Cav was located about one mile south of the 4/12 Cav. Between them, military buses traveled the strip about once every hour. I put my gear together, said some goodbyes, and went out to the road to catch the first bus.

This was in late May, and the 5/7 Cav had been training hard for the past five weeks, getting in shape for Vietnam. There were stories about how tough their training was and how many miles they ran, every day. For at least the last 16 weeks, we had it pretty easy with the 4/12 Cav. I was expecting a tough time of it before I got into good enough shape to stay with these guys.

The 7th Cavalry is nicknamed the Garry Owen Brigade. There's an old Scottish marching song called Garry Owen. The history of the Garry Owen and the 7th Cavalry dates back to the Civil War and to the Indian battles of the 1860s.

When you are with the 7th Cavalry, you always saluted an officer with the greeting, "Garry Owen, sir." If he was an officer from the 7th Cav, he returned your salute with, "Garry Owen, trooper."

I was assigned to the 2nd platoon. I made it just in time to fall out for the afternoon exercise session. The last time I went through a training session like that was in Basic. The next morning we were awakened at 0500 hours to fall out for the morning run. The Battalion Commander, Colonel Sweat, led the run and set the pace. Everyone in the battalion ran, except for the cooks, and the Day Sergeant who had to man the Orderly Room office.

We took off from the barracks compound and headed to the end of post property. We went out past the south gate and continued down the highway toward I-25, which runs from Colorado Springs to Pueblo. Five miles off post there is an overpass which allows access to the freeway. This is where the formation turned around to head back to post. About three miles out, I noticed a few guys fell out of the run. My guts seemed as if they were about to burst open, but I hung in there. Even though Colonel Sweat was more than 40 years old, he set a pretty fast pace. He had a lean, runner-type body. About four miles out, I just couldn't take the pain in my gut and sides. I fell out and walked. By the time they turned around and back to where I was walking, I had recovered enough and fell in line and ran with them back to post.

After training for the day, and before evening supper, the battalion fell out for the afternoon exercise drill. At the completion of the drill, and before heading back to the barracks, one of the cadre called out names. I was among the names called. We were told to stay in place while the rest were assembled and marched off. Another cadre, who appeared to be a fitness guru, told us, "You fell out of the run this morning. You will not fall out tomorrow morning." For the next two hours, we drilled and were pushed to what seemed the extreme end of pain endurance. When we were done, and thoroughly convinced this would never happen again, we were marched back to the barracks. I forgot about supper. I collapsed on my bunk and awoke the next morning, in the same clothes I was in when I landed there the previous evening. We fell out for the run. I told myself, I would die falling before I quit this run this morning. It's funny how a little incentive can bring more out of you.

I trained with these guys for the better part of seven weeks before we were given passes to go home before we departed for Vietnam. I got to know the guys in my platoon very well and became friends with many of them. Little did I know how deep that friendship would run in the next 12 months.

Toward the end of our training, we had to make a long march with backpacks and a full web belt. The march was nearly 30 miles. It was more of an endurance march than anything else. On the plus side, we did not have the morning run or the one hour of the 12-point military exercise program that day. When the march was complete, we walked to a road and sat down to wait for some deuce-and-a-half trucks to take us back to the compound.

Once we were loaded onto the trucks we learned that there was a grass fire going and we were the closest unit to the fire. We were trucked about five miles in the direction toward the fire. The trucks left the road and got us as close as they could to where the fire was located. The terrain became impassable for vehicles so we had to hike the final leg, which was somewhere between one and two miles. We left all our gear behind except our entrenching tools and jogged the rest of the way. We were spread out on the down-wind side of the fire and began beating the fire out. By now it was fairly widespread. With about 180 people beating on the fire, we finally got it out. It took at least two hours. Once we were sure it was completely out, we headed back to the trucks. We were all parched dry, but there was no water to quench our thirst. We had to wait until we got back to camp.

We were at the end of our training and were allowed a 10-day pass. A few people took a couple of extra days, and when they came back they got a good ass-chewing. One more day and they would have been listed as AWOL (Absent Without Leave).

The USS Hugh Gaffey going under the Golden Gate Bridge, departing from Oakland, California, for Vietnam. Commissioned in 1942 by the U.S. Navy, the ship was used by the U.S. Army to transport men and material to American installations throughout the Far Est and Pacific Ocean until late 1968.

BATTALION GOES TO VIETNAM
USS Hugh J. Gaffey

When we got back from leave, we had three days to take stock of all gear, pack, and prepare to move out.

1st Sgt. Dayton Hare was the 1st Sergeant for B Company. He had four roosters he kept as pets, or maybe they were fighting cocks. With him anything was possible. He kept the roosters in his office. He had to get rid of the roosters before departing post, and he did not want to give them to anyone else. Two nights before we were to leave Fort Carson, he drank at least a half bottle of Jack Daniels whiskey and, using his service .45-cal. pistol, he shot the roosters while still in his office. There was an immediate call for the MPs. They found him drunk and with the gun and the dead chickens, and they arrested him. Capt. Hitti was called and he arrived before they could haul him away. Hitti tried to convince the MPs to turn Sgt. Hare over to him. They were reluctant to do this, so Capt. Hitti called the Battalion Commander, Colonel Sweat, who convinced the MPs to place Sgt. Hare under the control of Capt. Hitti.

On August 2, we were bused to the Colorado Springs airport, loaded onto commercial jets, and we flew out to Oakland, California. From the Oakland airport, we were bused to a pier where we loaded onto a troop ship called the USNS

General Hugh J. Gaffey. I don't think many people knew about Hugh J. Gaffey, or what he did to get a ship with his name on it. At the time I really didn't care.

As we loaded onto the ship, we were directed to a troop passenger hold located close to the ship's waterline, in the middle of the ship. Later in the voyage, we would learn how lucky we were to have this location on the ship for sleeping and living quarters. After we were assigned a bunk and had our duffel bags secured to the post, we could go up topside to watch the preparations for departure. We had about a four-hour wait before the ship would be towed by tugboat away from the harbor.

We pulled out of the Oakland harbor at about 1630 hours (4:30 p.m.). Nearly all troops and hands were on deck to watch as we passed under the Golden Gate Bridge. For many, this would be their last view of America. I couldn't help having this thought as the ship passed from the San Francisco Bay into the open ocean.

Before the California land mass disappeared, everyone was told to report to their quarters for a short review, and then topside for instructions on procedure to abandon ship should the need arise. We were also told to bring with us the life vest that was on our bunk. In our troop hold, there were only a few life jackets. Our platoon Sergeant, Sgt. Inez, gave us a briefing of expectations while on the ship. We then had to report topside with the life jackets, at least those who were lucky enough to have them. In explanation, we were told that more life jackets would be issued and everyone on board eventually would have one. We were shown how to use and inflate the life jackets. One of the lifeboats was uncovered, and we were told how to board the lifeboat once it was in the water, and instructed on how many to fit into each lifeboat. The ship was designed to carry approximately 4,800 troops. There were

5,800 soldiers on board. This did not include the ship's crew. There were 12 lifeboats. Each lifeboat would hold 72 persons. If this ship went down, almost 5,000 soldiers would have to tread water until they could be rescued. The life-saving pep talk was completed, and that was the end of the life jacket shortage. There simply were no extra life jackets to be had.

The days on board ship seemed to drag by forever. The bunks were stacked five-high, with no room to move around. If you wanted to turn over in your cot, you had to get out of the bunk. You either lay on your back or stomach. The air circulation was not adequate for the volume of people. During the day, the troops would sit around on the deck and find corners to play cards, shake dice, or pitch pennies, dimes or quarters. The ship had a commissary that would open around 2 p.m. nearly every day. It was suggested that people with turbulent stomachs purchase saltine crackers to stabilize them.

About the third day, word was sent down that the 5/7 Cav troops would have to go through PT exercises each day. In company-sized units, we were taken to the front deck area of the ship to go through the majority of the standard military exercises. Being stationed in the center of the ship, we did not notice the up-and-down motion that others experienced on the front or back of the ship. When we did our exercises on the front deck of the ship, the bow would rise and fall as much as 15 to 20 feet, even when the weather did not seem all that windy. Running in place or doing push-ups as the ship would rise and fall put extra strain on the body. As the ship went down, you had to try to catch up to the floor. When the ship's bow came up, your body weight seemed to triple and you had to push the extra weight away from the floor. If you got caught going down as the ship started to come up, your arms would literally collapse, driving you into the deck.

On the third night of the trip, for entertainment, there were boxing matches on board. Anyone interested in boxing could sign up for the matches. The matches were similar to a Golden Glove tournament. Boxers were put in weight classes, and each fight was a three-round match of 90 seconds each. If you lost, you were out. If you won, the following night you fought again. This went on until there was a final winner for each weight class. If anyone had boxed professionally before their service time, they were paired with other professional fighters. There were three professional fighters who signed up. One was considered lightweight and two were considered heavyweight. The lightweight ended up fighting the light-weight winner of the non-professionals. He was short in height but had arms that were extremely long proportionately. He would throw a series of right jabs to set up his opponent, and then come across with a left hook that would catch his opponent nearly in the back of his head. Every time he threw the left hook, his opponent went down. He had two knockdowns; the first round and one early in the second round and the fight was called: TKO in his favor.

The two heavyweights were both 5/7 Cav troops. Their last names were Hawkins and Sandoval. Hawkins was the more aggressive fighter in the beginning. He won the first round easily. Sandoval started to come on in the second round and it was scored even. Sandoval took the third round with some punishing jabs and hooks. The fight ended up a draw and got a rousing standing ovation from the troops who were watching.

Sgt. Silsby (a.k.a. "Slick") of the 1st platoon had a little Derringer .38-cal. pistol. The barrel flipped from the bottom up over the grip for loading. A few too many people knew he had the gun. Word came down from Battalion Headquarters that no soldier was allowed to carry an unauthorized/

non-military-issue weapon. If anyone had such a weapon, they were to turn it over to Battalion immediately. There was also a warning that all bags would be searched for non-issued weapons and, if any weapons were found, there would likely be a court-martial of the guilty party. Slick decided to get rid of the gun. He sold chances on the gun for $1 each, and there would only be 100 chances sold. The 100 chances were sold within an hour. A drawing was held and a guy from New York, named Murgatroyd, won. He was in our platoon. I offered him $20 for the weapon. He initially turned down my offer. A couple of days later, though, he decided to sell me the gun.

There never was a search of our duffel bags, but to be on the safe side I carried the gun in my pocket for about three days before securing it in the bottom of my duffel bag. We never heard about non-issue weapons again.

I eventually sold the gun to another GI; he, in turn, sold it to someone else. The weapon eventually ended up in the hands of a CID (Civil Intelligence Division) officer in Taipei, Taiwan. As it turned out, the guy who tried to sell it to the CID officer ended up getting arrested; the poor guy was on R & R and just needed a little extra money. The authorities held him overnight, then released him and sent him back to his 5/7 Cav unit.

Feldkamp, Kampa, Heronema and I were in line at the commissary on ship. The commissary was in a lower deck with a narrow hallway leading past it. While we were waiting in line, a call went out that B Company 5/7 Cav was to report to the front deck for PT. The intercom system did not reach this portion of the ship, so obviously we missed the call. The next day, Sgt. Inez called all four of us aside on a lower deck of the ship. We were located in the walkway along the right (or starboard) side of the ship on the outer rail. Sgt. Inez accused the four of us of intentionally skipping PT. I am not sure of the exact words exchanged, but Feldkamp said something that irritated Sgt. Inez. Inez struck Feldkamp in the face with his fist. Sgt. Inez stands about 5'7" tall and weighed about 135 lbs. Feldkamp stands about 6 feet tall and weighed about 190 lbs. Feldkamp grabbed Sgt. Inez and lifted him up, pushing him over the ship's railing. I grabbed Feldkamp's arm, and Sgt. Inez by the shirt, and pulled Inez back inside the rail. Inez threatened to have the four of us court-martialed. Later in the day, Capt. Hitti had a talk with the four of us to hear our side of the story. It was the last we heard of the incident. There would be times in the upcoming months that I wished I had never stopped Feldkamp from throwing Sgt. Inez overboard.

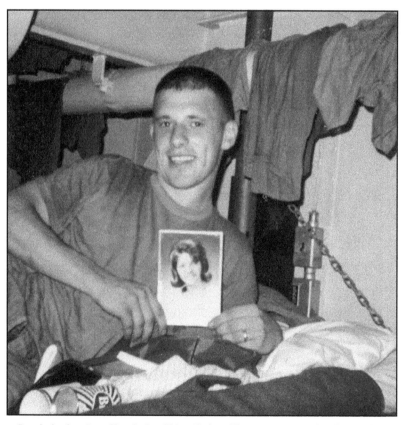

Ray Judy showing off a photo of his wife Ann. They were married on leave after boot camp, before shipping out for Vietnam.

The further into the Pacific Ocean we traveled, the warmer it got. With mostly clear skies and the sun reflecting off the water, it was nearly intolerable to be out of a shaded area. Soldiers would find nooks and crannies on the ship to stay out of the sun and play whatever game they preferred to pass the time. Fay Mathews was from our platoon. He had the foresight to bring a cribbage board and a couple decks of cards along. Not many people played cribbage or knew the game well enough to play it. He and I spent a lot of time playing the game. If I remember correctly, Tom Gray and Ray Judy also played cribbage.

The nights were a little better, but it was still extremely warm. Sleeping in our compartment was like taking an overnight sauna. A few from our Company decided to sleep on the upper deck, commonly referred to as the sun deck. There were about 10 lounge chairs on it. There was a larger patio deck just below the sun deck. There were another 24 lounge chairs on the patio deck. The line troops made good use of the two decks for two nights. Then word came down that only officers were allowed on the two upper decks. This meant during daytime hours also. It seemed like a big kick in the shorts for those of us who first saw the benefit of using the upper decks.

Rather than sleeping below in the sauna-like heat, a number of troops decided to sleep in the walkways on the outer perimeter of the ship. You had to leave enough room for ship personnel to walk around the decks. There were a number of setbacks along the outer corridor and this is where you had to fit yourself in. The rails were not enclosed. There was at least a space of 10 inches under the bottom rail. If you moved in your sleep, you easily could slip under the rail and into the ocean. Keep in mind that most of us were quite slender from the hard training and running we had gone through during the previous few months.

The troopship bypassed the Hawaiian Islands about 60 miles to the south. Beyond Hawaii and before Okinawa and the South China Sea, one of the ship's officers noticed a lighted buoy floating on the ocean, in the wake behind the ship. The buoy was not seen as the ship approached that area of the ocean. Maritime rules of the ocean are that a lighted buoy means a man overboard. The ship had to circle around to look for someone in the ocean. The ship made two complete circles, with a three-hour delay before it could continue on with the journey. It was determined that the buoy came from the USS Hugh J. Gaffey. An officer from the ship used a shotgun to knock out the light of the buoy. This apparently was less costly than trying to retrieve it. The buoy was destroyed to prevent other ships from suffering the same fate as the Gaffey. The usual inquiries were made, but no one admitted to throwing the buoy overboard. Talk among the troops was that someone from C Company of the 5/7 Cav was responsible for the juvenile act.

We made a day stop in Okinawa and had a chance to get off the ship and get our land legs back. After standing around in the hot sun for about two hours, some trucks came and transported us to an American Legion Club on the base in Okinawa. Once at the club, we asked to fill out a short form making us honorary members of this Legion Club. After a few hours of drinking, we were trucked back to the ship. The ship set sail right after dark.

Tom Jettis got on the wrong side of 1st Sgt. Hare. Sgt. Hare told Jettis he was not allowed to leave the ship when the rest of us went ashore. Jettis ignored Sgt. Hare's orders and went ashore, to the NCO Club with the troops. When he came back, Sgt. Hare was on the deck waiting for him. Sgt. Hare had done a little imbibing himself on this stop. He appeared to be drunk. As Jettis stepped on board, Hare grabbed him and shoved him into the ship's wall. Hare told Jettis that he was going to pay with his life for disobeying his order. He held Jettis by the front of his shirt and dragged him along toward a cabin. Terry Olexy was a pretty good-sized boy. Hare told Olexy to follow him. When they got away from the crowd and inside the cabin, Hare told Olexy to watch and make sure to stop him before he actually killed Jettis. Hare then pounded on Jettis. He tried to get Jettis to fight back, but Jettis wouldn't do it. After giving Jettis a good working over, he stopped himself, calling Jettis a wimp and a chicken-shit.

A day or two out of Okinawa, the ship ran into a typhoon. Only the ship's crew were allowed on deck. This was out in the South China Sea. The storm lasted for nearly three days.

Our cabin was just above the natural water line when fully loaded. We had a few small round port windows we could see out. Looking out the windows between the waves, there was a wall of water that seemed to reach 50 feet high. When the storm had ended, we were told that the ship had sailed through 60-foot waves that brought water washing over the deck. All troops were kept below deck and seasickness was prevalent, with vomit and body stench throughout the storm. Being located in the middle of the ship turned out to be a blessing. People who were in cabins in the front and the back of the ship had the ride of a lifetime.

Our bathrooms, better known as "heads" when at sea, were located at the tail end of the ship. During the storm, if anyone had to use the head, he had to grab a rope that ran along the far wall and hang onto it to walk toward the back of the ship. Without the rope, it was possible to get washed over the back of the ship. It was very difficult to stand and urinate into a urinal. As the tail went up, the pee flow stopped. As it went down, you almost had to catch up with the flow. At any rate, it was a messy chore, to say the least.

Once we passed through the storm, life on ship became more bearable, although most of the balance of the ride seemed a little rougher than when we were in the Pacific Ocean. One morning we woke up to a strange quietness. The ship was anchored in Qui Nho'n Bay. Most everyone came topside to look toward shore at Vietnam. We stood around for close to an hour. We were then instructed to go back to our cabins, retrieve our duffel bags, and bring them topside. This was August 22.

Arrival of U.S. 1st Cavalry Division (Airmobile) in Vietnam Sept. 14, 1965. The 15,800 men and 424 helicopters and planes disembarked from troopships and carriers at Qui Noh'n and then immediately moved inland by air and convoy to their assigned tactical operations area at An Khê. Men of the 1st Battalion 77th Artillery watch from the lou as their comrades in arms disembark from the troop transport USNS General Simon Buckner. Photo courtesy of the National Archives at College Park, Md. Original photo from the Records of the Office of the Chief Signal Officer. Photo ID 530609.

BEACH LANDING IN VIETNAM

Of the 5,800 troops on board, the 5/7 Cav was the first to load into LSTs for what they called a beachhead landing. An LST is a landing craft that is used to transport soldiers and equipment from a ship to the shore. 1st and 2nd platoons of B Company were the first troops to load on the LSTs. We left our duffel bags behind. They would catch up to us later. We were dressed in full combat uniform to include loaded weapons, and web belts equipped with canteens, ammunition, pouches, grenades, and bayonet. I was compacted to the front of the LST and would be one of the first ones to hit the beach. The LST stopped too far from shore and we were ordered to un-ass the LST. One other soldier and I went into the water with full gear and sank. I am not sure how deep the water was when we went in, but I never touched bottom. I estimated I went down 15 feet or more before I began fighting my way back to the surface. I managed to come up with all my gear, including my helmet. The other soldier took off all his gear before he came up. (Throughout my youth I swam a lot and was a strong swimmer.)

We were pulled back on board and I had more than a few choice words for the LST driver. The craft then pushed up to shore and again we were ordered off. This time the water was only about three feet deep. As we came up on the beach, a military band played "Stars and Stripes Forever" as a greeting.

The USS Hugh Gaffey approaching a beach-head landing.

There were news reporters and photographers waiting for us also. This so-called beachhead landing was featured in *Stars and Stripes*, the overseas military paper. From what I heard, it also made some headlines back in the States. No mention was made of the near-drowning of two soldiers.

The sun was bright and the heat was nearly suffocating. We stood around in platoon groups waiting for the rest of the company to make it to shore. Our duffel bags were brought onto shore later with a follow-up LST and more battalion troops. Once we all assembled, we loaded onto buses for a short ride to the airport and then loaded into C-130 airplanes. The C-130s had no air pressure equity. We were tucked into the back of the plane, with no seats. Our duffel bags became our seats. We were flown to Camp Radcliff near An Khê and trucked from the airport at Camp Radcliff to a place on the north end of the base camp.

End of day one at Camp Radcliff.

CAMP RADCLIFF (AN KHÊ)
Building 5th Bn 7th Cav Compound

The An Khê River made a quarter-moon bend partially around our battalion area before it straightened out and flowed east, away from our location. Six hundred meters east of our battalion area was a bridge that crossed the An Khê River. Just west of the bridge the river was wider; it was cordoned off there as a protected swimming area. The An Khê River averaged about 40 to 50 feet wide and it was fairly deep, much of it 20 feet or deeper.

There had been previous crude excavating of the terrain which was to become our base camp, but most of the work was yet to be done by troops, with shovels and a variety of hand tools. Areas were staked out where each platoon-sized tent was to be erected, and the troops were assigned to begin digging ditches around each of these sites. The digging was mostly in clay ground and it was very difficult. Additional ditches were to be dug between each tent. We did not finish these ditches, but at least we made a recess into which we could crawl in the event of a mortar attack. Near dark on that first day, we set up the tents and unfolded Army bunks for sleeping. We also had to put mosquito netting around each bunk.

lieve that I was the first casualty of the 5/7 Cav. I

I believe that I was the first casualty of the 5/7 Cav. I had a short-handled shovel. While I was digging, I was bending over the shovel and pushing it into the dirt. Another person, whose name I do not remember, was throwing a shovel-full of dirt out of the trench. I bent into the line of his shovel toss and got hit in the left temple area of my head. It put a gash there and I was bleeding from the wound. One of the Sergeants looked at it and said I had to go to the Aid Station which was a 20-foot by 20-foot tent located across the trail northeast of our platoon tent areas. The tent sides were rolled up with a screen at the sides. Two medics were in the tent. They got the bleeding stopped, dressed the wound, gave me a tetanus shot, and sent me on my way.

As soon as the sun set, the mosquitoes came out. There were hoards of them. The night air was a mass of black buzzing insects looking for bare skin to drill into for their evening meal of warm animal blood. The human animal is their preferred menu choice because the skin is not as coarse as other creatures. We were all given a small plastic bottle, OD green in color, of mosquito repellent. It had an Army issue number. In civilian terms, it was actually 100% DEET. The DEET kept the mosquitoes at bay, for a short while, but they were constantly circling, buzzing and bouncing off your head looking for an opening into which they could sink their blood-sucking proboscises.

Someone had a portable radio. It was tuned to the station out of Hanoi. This station played American pop and rock music. It came in very clearly. They boosted their power for the sake of American soldiers. Between songs, Hanoi Hannah would come on the air and mess with American soldiers' minds. Hanoi Hannah welcomed the 5th Battalion 7th Cav to Vietnam. She even mentioned some soldiers by name. She welcomed Robert Phillson by name, said that his girlfriend was now dating someone else, and she even gave the name of the new guy she was dating. Phillson went a little spastic. He knew the guy Hanoi Hannah said his girlfriend was dating. It turned out to be true. Two weeks after getting to Vietnam, we had one of our first mail calls. Phillson got a "Dear John" letter from his ex-girlfriend and she confirmed what Hanoi Hannah had said.

Hanoi Hannah kept us updated on how the war was going. Of course, we were losing every battle fought. She encouraged desertion rather than getting killed.

The second day we continued digging ditches, making them wider and deeper. The ditch-digging and grooming of the base camp continued for a week or more. We then started to fill sandbags and placed them around all tent structures as walls for more protection. This included the mess tent, supply tent, command headquarters, all the platoon tents, and any other structure that was made of canvas.

Just before midnight of the third day, we got our first mortar attack. It was raining at the time, and we all had to get into the ditches. The bottoms of the ditches had water in them, and the wet clay/mud made them greasy. We hunkered in the wet ditches until the mortars stopped. The only casualty was a near direct hit on the Battalion Commander's personal tent. His tent was across the trail and north of the company tents. When the mortaring began, he immediately joined the troops in the ditches. No injuries were reported, but we had our first combat experience.

The next day we had to put extra effort into building higher sand-bagged walls around the tents. It was hot and muggy. We had been working from daylight to near dark. We were not accustomed to this intense heat and humidity as yet, and everyone was tired. Sgt. Moore, who was an overweight

Field First Sergeant and who had just come to the battalion before we left the States, came by riding on the back of a jeep. He was sitting above the rear seat cushion on a box. He had the driver stop and he commenced to raise hell with soldiers who were taking a break, or who were not in the actual act of shoveling dirt or piling sandbags. He then motioned his driver to go. The driver took off with a jerk and Moore toppled backward out of the jeep, landing on his neck. A few soldiers had a laugh but quickly sobered as the Sergeant quivered and shook intensely for a few seconds and then was still. There was an ambulance at the medical tent, and it was summoned. Moore was loaded on a stretcher and hauled away. We heard later he had a broken neck and fractured spinal cord, and probably was permanently paralyzed.

Following the mortar attack, we began conducting patrols to the north of the base camp. A typical patrol would be anywhere from an eight- to 10-man squad and sometimes even as large as a 30-man platoon. We would start late in the afternoon and continue all night long with some sit-down time to catch some rest and minor Z-time (sleep). This was also good training in preparing us for the next year. As long as we continued the patrolling, we did not get mortared again. During the time we were building up the battalion base camp, the Vietnamese were clearing about a 200-meter wide opening in all trees and brush just to the north of the An Khê River. Eventually, towers and ground bunkers were built to the north of the river, with floodlights scanning the open area toward the jungle. This was tied in with the rest of the 1st Cav Division's Camp Radcliff.

2nd platoon was out humping (walking) beyond the river. It was extremely hot. We still weren't used to the heat, but it was getting more bearable. Small bubble helicopters with tanks and spray attachments were flying overhead and spraying defoliant on us. The moist spray actually gave us some relief from the heat. Only the Lord knows what damage it did to us in the years that followed. Agent Orange was still being used in the defoliant at this time.

We stopped to take a break in a partially wooded area with high grass. Some soldiers were able to lie down, and others found a spot to sit. Zachery, a Spec-4, was lying down. Sgt. Silsby (Slick) was sitting near him. He told Zachery there was a snake crawling up to him. Zachery sat up, took a look but didn't see the snake. He thought Slick was pulling a scam on him so he lay back down. Slick took his rifle and pinned the snake to the ground. The snake was about 16 inches from Zachery's head. He told Zachery to take a better look and then tell him there was no snake. The snake was a bright green color with very narrow, darker green stripes on each side of its body. It was about 18 to 20 inches long and had a head

Defoliation mission in Vietnam, July 26, 1969. A UH-1D helicopter from the 336th Aviation Company sprays a defoliation agent on a dense jungle area in the Mekong delta. Photo courtesy of the National Archives at College Park, Md. Original photo from the Records of the Office of the Chief Signal Officer. Photo ID 111-C-CC59950.

larger than the body of the snake. Slick seemed well versed in snakes. He said the snake was a green bamboo viper, and very poisonous. It responds to heat, and when Zachery lay back, most likely the snake targeted him because of the heat coming off his body. Slick also said the snake will attack as easily as it would flee when threatened. If bitten by the snake, you would have to immediately amputate the infected area before the infected blood reached the heart. Once the blood got into the body, you would need an immediate antidote or you would die. This snake was nicknamed the "ten-stepper." In theory, if the snake bit you, you would take ten steps and die. In reality, if the snake bit you, it would take at least an hour to die, the last half hour of which you would be convulsing in pain before you finally die.

When we came back to camp later that afternoon, there was a crumpled-up bubble helicopter lying on the ground beside the trail which ran to the south and downhill side of our tents. The helicopter had landed, dropped off a ranking officer, and then took off. As the chopper swerved, the chopper blades struck the top of a tree, snapping one blade off. The chopper crashed back to the ground and the pilot was killed.

Once our company was settled in, Capt. Hitti allowed soldiers to go into An Khê on a pass, similar to the routine in the States. There was old An Khê and new An Khê. Old An Khê was made up mostly of straw huts with dirt floors. New An Khê capitalized on the soldier trade and had hard-walled construction, much of it metal hammered out from tin crating, beer cans, or other light metals that could be flattened. Much of the building materials were thrown-away junk and crating from the military. The buildings were tightly bunched together so a single wall separated one building from the next. The noise from one building would flow over into the next. There were bars, open-front shops, barber shops, souvenir shops, and anything else where a buck could be made. The town had a carnival atmosphere. There must have been eight bars, and each bar had rooms in the back for the prostitutes. Vietnamese children were running around either trying to sell some trinket or looking for handouts. If you gave a child anything, there were 30 more grabbing at you looking for something. If you were in the crowd, someone would try to dig your billfold out of your pocket. Before we left the ship, we had to turn in all greenback money for military scrip (Military Pay Certificates). The Vietnamese barterers, traders, and businesses preferred our scrip instead of their piasters (Vietnamese money). If you didn't cup your money or hang onto it securely when bartering with the merchants, the kids would try to wrench it out of your hand and run.

Ray Olin pulled his own weight but didn't take military life seriously.

Ray Olin and Allen Ascher were close friends, and both PFCs (Privates First Class, or E-3). Neither one took military life seriously. Even at this point, in Vietnam, they did not get serious. I wouldn't call them screw-offs, because they weren't afraid to pull their load when it came to work. They went down to An Khê with a few other soldiers from our company. After a few drinks, Ascher became enamored by one of the prostitutes. For 400 P she took him to one of the back rooms for a quick fling with the skin. When he disappeared, Olin and another soldier, I'm not sure which one, paid another girl 400 P to use the room next to where he went. Ascher had all his clothes off and was mounted on top of the prostitute. Each room had a pan of water sitting on the floor to wash with after intercourse. Olin and the other soldier moved the cot against the wall and stood on it to see over the wall into the next room. Olin took the pan of water and, just as Ascher was about to get his rocks off, he dumped the water over his ass. That took the life out of his jiggle stick, and the prostitute was more than a little upset. Ascher wanted his money back, but she wouldn't give it to him. He took her underpants; they were a light lavender color.

When they came back to base camp and walked into the company area, Ascher had the underpants pulled over his head. Some of us were working on building up the wall of sandbags around the tents. Everyone stopped to check out Ascher. Sgt. Milbur, who was an NCO with Headquarters Company, started to give Olin and Ascher hell for being drunk and carrying on in a non-military fashion. Ascher took the underpants off his head. Olin was giving crap back to Milbur. Ascher slipped around behind Milbur and pulled the underpants over his head. Olin gave Milbur a hard right jab and drove Milbur into a trench. Milbur pulled the underpants off his head and went into the typical court-martial threat. Ascher grabbed the underpants. Milbur tried to get them back. Ascher told him, "I paid for it, so I'm keeping it." The next day the two

94

were demoted from E-3 to E-1. An E-1 is the lowest rank for enlisted men.

The day before we went out on our first mission, we got a visit from General William Westmoreland, who was a Four-Star General and the Commanding Officer of all armed forces in Vietnam. Col. Trevor Sweat, the Battalion Commander, gave a short speech of introduction, and then Westmoreland gave us a rabble-rousing speech about kicking the Cong's ass and driving them back above the 18th parallel. His talk lasted about 30 minutes. He got thunderous applause, a standing ovation, and he walked through the crowd of soldiers as he left us. He presented a very impressive image.

Local workers wearing the familiar Vietnamese straw hats and pajama-like clothing construct a barbed-wire barrier around Camp Radcliff in 1966. The rolls on the ground are concertina wire, which has razor-sharp hooks and stretches out like a Slinky. Concertina wire can stop infantry by snagging on their clothing, and can entangle and stop vehicles as well. Soldiers caught in concertina wire typically require assistance to get out. Photo courtesy of Army Heritage Center Foundation in Carlisle, Pa.; *www.armyheritage.org.*

Bob Kunkel in a bunker tower on the green line at Camp Radcliff.

FIRST FIELD ASSIGNMENT:
Security for Highway 19

For three weeks we had built up and fortified the base camp and patrolled the adjacent jungle to our north. Then we were given our first field assignment. The whole battalion of the 5th Bn 7th Cav was assigned to pull security and handle patrols along Highway 19, which runs from Qui Nho'n west through An Khê and onto Pleiku, which was near the Cambodian border. The area of concern for B Company was west of An Khê, covering three bridges and the Mang Yang Pass. 2nd platoon spent the first day and night securing Highway 19, in the hills on either side of Mang Yang Pass. As night fell, the wind coming through the pass seemed to amplify and it created an eerie and almost evil sound. Everyone seemed to be tensed up waiting for the shit to hit the proverbial fan. Stories were being passed around about how the French had an entire battalion or brigade wiped out in the pass back in 1954.

The platoon set up in two-man positions and each position was spaced about 15 meters from the next. I was teamed up with Spec-4 Tom Manning. Manning was a small guy who stood about 5'2" tall. Manning and I dug a foxhole in the side of the hill facing the jungle away from the road. We used some of the dirt we dug out to level off a spot above the foxhole where we could take turns sleeping. As dark came, I agreed to take the first two-hour watch. When staring at nothing in the dark, two hours drag on forever. Once my two hours were complete,

I woke Manning to cover for me while I slept. It began to rain, so I pulled my poncho over my head and body in an attempt to stay dry. I had just fallen asleep when a trip wire ignited in front of a position next to ours. The position next to ours opened fire and immediately other positions began firing. This woke me up. I threw the poncho back and was just sitting up, grabbing for my rifle when a black silhouette shot up over the bank from our foxhole position. My reaction was that we were being over-run. I immediately swung a well aimed, haymaker punch at the silhouette. The punch landed square in its face. The figure toppled back, falling head-first into the foxhole, moaning and swearing. By the voice, I could tell it was Manning. Manning was not wearing his helmet when he came over the bank. He was pretty sore at me for the rest of the next day. He had a black right eye and a large bruise under it. As it turned out, either the wind or an animal had set off the trip wire. Our Platoon Sergeant, Sgt. Inez, raised some hell with us in the morning over the unnecessary shooting. Most everyone else got a kick out of it.

The next day we were transferred west beyond the third bridge and were given an area to make camp and set up a perimeter. The squad leaders came around and told us where to set up positions and we began digging in for what was supposed to be a three-week stay. After digging in two-man foxholes, we set up a string of concertina wire around the outer perimeter. We tied empty C-Ration cans to the concertina wire and placed a few rocks in each can. If someone would try to crawl over or through the wire, the rocks in the cans would rattle, giving us advanced warning. Just inside the concertina wire, we set up Claymore mines.

We were told how Charlie (nickname for Viet Cong) liked to come into camp during the night, turn the Claymore mines around, and then snipe at the perimeter positions so we would set the Claymores off at ourselves. We decided to booby trap the Claymores with hand grenades. We would set up the Claymore as usual and tie a trip wire to one of the posts. We would cut a trench in the ground and bury the trip wire to the grenade. We pulled the pin on the grenade and slipped the grenade into a C-ration can. If anyone attempted to turn the Claymore, they would pull the grenade out of the can and within five seconds it would go off. We never had any problems with anyone trying to mess with our Claymores.

A rule was made among the troops. The only person who disarmed a booby trap was the one who set it up. To be on the safe side, it was always two people who set up any booby traps so that, if one got wounded or killed, the other one would know where the booby trap was located and how it was set up.

After a full day-and-a-half of grooming the area, we had some fairly elaborate positions. Since it rained daily, we

The M18 Claymore Anti-Personnel Mine, U.S. Army Center of Military History. Public domain photo, from Wikimedia Commons.

put tops on our bunkers to keep the rain out. As soon as there was a dry spot from the rain, rats and other jungle creatures would move in. Rats were the biggest problem, some of them were the size of muskrats. After a while, you got used to them. As long as they had a little food, you were left alone; it was common, however, to have them run over you as you slept or relaxed. There were always war stories going around about how rats chewed chunks of meat out of soldiers as they slept. To my knowledge, our platoon never had that problem.

Every night the mosquitoes plagued you. If you tried swatting them they would drive you crazy. You used the DEET and did your best to ignore them. If you had enough dirt and grime on your body, and your clothes looked as if you grew in them, the mosquitoes were not so bad. They loved clean fresh meat, but if you started to smell like the earth itself, you were somewhat exempt from their vicious swarming attacks. Also, if you had been bitten enough, you developed a resistance to their bites and the itching that came with them. We learned to deal with mosquitoes. If you feel the bite, brush the mosquito off, don't slap it. When you slap the mosquito, you usually break off the blood-sucking stem and it embeds in your skin causing the itch.

One morning, just as daybreak was opening a new day, there was a blood-curdling scream that came from the position to our right. Danny Bentz woke up looking into the eyes of a large-horned rhinoceros bug. The creature was about three inches long, nearly two inches wide, and two inches high. It was black in color and had a rhinoceros-like horn extending out on its head; that is why we labeled it the rhinoceros bug. Bentz's partner, Ray Kloemken, picked the bug up by the horn and the bug began to thrash its wings and feet; it let out a grinding-like buzz that could be heard beyond the bunkers on either side of their position. Over the year we saw many of these bugs, but not another one that big.

On the third night in this camp, we got a visitor. He came into the perimeter and went to Ray Judy and Tom Gray's bunker. He went into their bunker and took the chocolate candy Gray had saved from his C-Rations.

A portion of the next day was spent building a bamboo trap for a monkey. Bamboo was cut and driven into the ground on four sides leaving a small area on one end for a door. Additional bamboo was tied across the top to form a bamboo cage about three feet long and two feet wide. At the door entrance, the bamboo was split apart creating a channel on each side of the door. The door was also made of bamboo, wired together with Como wire (two-strand, rubber-coated wire used for land communications). The door would slide up and down inside the bamboo channel. A wedge was slipped under the bottom piece of Como wire to hold the door up. The wire was then tied to an empty C-Ration can and candy was put into the can. The

Ray Kloemken.

wedge was set so that very light pressure would release and drop the door.

Early in the morning, at least three hours before daylight, the door dropped and trapped a monkey in the bamboo cage. The monkey began screaming, and everyone in the camp and for about a mile in any direction could hear the scream. After a few minutes of wild screaming, the monkey became quiet. The cage was right beside the bunker for Judy and Gray. Tom Gray could see the monkey trying to squeeze through each opening in the bamboo. After about 40 minutes, the monkey found an opening in the top of the cage through which, with great effort, he managed to squeeze out. He was not done yet. He reached through the bamboos, pulled the can over and took the candy from inside before leaving. As he ran off, he gave laugh-like screeches, as if taunting us.

The following night, we received another visitor. This one was not as genteel as the monkey. Along about midnight, the cans in the concertina wire started rattling. I was sleeping at the time. Manning was scared and woke me. The wire squeaked, and there were a series of grunts. Someone shot up a hand-held flare. When the flare ignited, the intruder became startled and took off on a run away from our bunkers. The thing was hooked pretty solidly in the concertina wire. But with his size, he managed to drag and stretch out the concertina wire for about a hundred feet before he pulled loose. It turned out to be a huge orangutan.

Sgt. Inez was not the most liked person in our platoon. If you asked any of the troops, Sgt. Inez was probably the most disliked person in the Army. He was of the assumption that someone, anyone, was doing something wrong, but he just had not caught him yet. He would sneak around the bunkers at night trying to catch someone sleeping while pulling guard duty. One night, he thought he had caught Matera sleeping, but by morning his word did not hold up against Matera's word.

He was not to be undaunted in his efforts. The following night, he again started to sneak around the bunkers trying to find someone sleeping. The night was warm and I was pulling guard. I decided to sit up outside the bunker rather than inside. I saw Inez crawl up alongside the bunker to my left. I got down behind my bunker and waited for him. As he came around to the front of the bunker to take a peek inside, I came up behind him. Just as he shined his small flashlight into the bunker, I put my rifle barrel behind his ear and told him if he moves he was dead. He didn't move until I had him fully identify himself. I told him he was within a hair's breadth of buying the farm. I also told him that, in the future, anyone sneaking around the bunkers at night would be considered an enemy and would be treated as such. This apparently scared him, and he never tried his sneak attacks again.

Along about the fourth day at this location, a group of six soldiers including me were led by Sgt. Patino on assignment to go on an overnight ambush patrol. We left camp, headed west, and then cut back north, heading for higher elevation. We had traveled about a mile and came across some fairly recent spider holes, also known as gook foxholes. We moved to a slightly higher elevation, a short distance from these spider holes, and set up an ambush site that allowed us to cover the spider holes should the gooks return. Just as we were settling in, we heard a gook patrol passing below the hill to our east, heading in the general direction of our platoon camp. They were very noisy and talking in steady Vietnamese. They must have been telling jokes because they were laughing constantly. My thoughts were that these were very undisciplined soldiers. I suggested we sneak down and catch them by surprise. We estimated there were only four or five of them, and with the racket they were making they would've been easy pickings. Sgt. Patino did not want to take any chances, and a few other troops agreed. Sgt. Patino logged the activity. After they got out of hearing distance, Sgt. Patino tried to call our platoon on the PRC 25 radio. Because of the heavy jungle terrain, we were unable to make contact. We spent the rest of the night without further incident, other than a series of rain showers. At daybreak, we had a quick meal of Cs (C-Rations) and headed back to camp.

Later that same afternoon, Sgt. Miles was assigned to lead out a patrol that was to cross the road to the south of our camp and set up an overnight ambush site along the river. There was a trail that showed fairly heavy foot traffic that ran along the river. The patrol set a wire-triggered trip flare along the trail and put out two Claymore mines to cover the trail just inside the flare. The patrol then took up positions along the trail. As luck would have it, a gook patrol set the trip flare off and exposed at least seven or eight gooks before they ran off. Sgt. Miles would not let the patrol shoot or set off the Claymores. When the squad came in, the talk was about the gooks they had a chance to kill. Lt. Frank, our platoon leader, made inquiries of the troops and then had a talk with Miles. After conferring with Capt. Hitti, B Company Commander, Miles was demoted to a Spec-4.

As a rule, I always pulled guard duty first when we set up at night. I would let Manning get about two to three hours of sleep, depending on how tired I felt. Manning had a Seiko watch, which did not have a band; he kept it in his shirt pocket. We would swap the watch back and forth when we pulled guard duty at night so we knew when our two-hour watch was completed. It had rained late in the afternoon and it was one of those heavy low-pressure nights. I pulled guard for about two-and-a-half hours and then woke Manning to cover for a couple of hours. I was very tired by now and fell asleep immediately.

After what seemed a short time, Manning woke me and told me it was my turn. I told him I didn't think I had slept two hours. He said I did. I sat up but my eyes didn't want to stay open. I pulled my poncho over my head, lit a cigarette, and checked the watch. It showed a little more than two hours past the time I went to sleep. When I smoked, I would cup the cigarette and bend my head down behind the bunker wall so as not to display any light. After the cigarette was finished, I crawled out of the bunker to get the blood circulating. On a hunch, I walked to the next position and got their attention before walking up. I asked them what time it was. Their watch was one hour earlier than Manning's watch. I set the clock one more hour ahead and woke Manning to cover guard again. I told him to pull the full two hours this time. He argued that he did. Of course when morning came, his clock showed it was around 0900 hours, everyone else's was 0700 hours. I never told him I had set the watch ahead by an hour. I gave Manning my form of a lecture about pulling his weight and, if he didn't want to do that, he would have to find a different partner.

During one of the days, we had another jungle visitor come into camp. It was a 30-inch lizard, and it took up a post on a rock close to the platoon CP (Command Post). After a few hours, the lizard wandered off. One of the troopers had a camera and flashed a few photos for a keepsake.

The three-week stay at this camp was cut short by two weeks. We were told to leave everything as it was, pack up all our gear, and load on trucks waiting on the road to our south. As we were moving out, another squad from another Cav battalion began moving into our camp.

On Highway 19, between An Khê and the Mang Yang Pass, there were three bridges crossing a rather turbulent river. Highway 19 was used to run supplies from the dockyards at Qui Nho'n Bay to Camp Radcliff near An Khê and to Camp Holloway near Pleiku. The gooks liked to blow up the bridges to slow down the supply route. For that reason, it was necessary to have security on all bridges.

Our platoon was divided into three squads, and each squad was assigned to one of the three bridges located on Highway 19 between Mang Yang Pass and An Khê. The 4th squad was our heavy weapons and machine gun squad. As a rule, the heavy weapons squad was comprised of two three-man machine gun crews and one three-man mortar team. After a short while in country, and since the artillery was very accurate and readily available, we canned the mortar team and made a third machine gun team. Each squad had one machine gun team assigned to it. Our 3rd squad was assigned to cover the third bridge. When we arrived, the old positions were not up to snuff. They were poorly built, and not in the best positions. We began dismantling the old positions and building new ones more suited to our preferences. When assigned to maintain a temporary-permanent position, the days were boring. With not much else to do, rebuilding bunker positions gave us something productive to do, and it allowed us to use our creative skills.

Again, we were told that we would probably spend close to a month guarding this bridge. Tom Manning and I decided to make a very elaborate bunker. There was no shortage of sandbags and dirt. Also available were sections of portable landing strips. Each section was about eight to ten feet long and about 20 inches wide. They were corrugated to allow for carrying extra weight. With a center support, we could stack sandbags three or four deep on top. The outer walls were about two feet thick. We used most of the sandbags from an old bunker close to where we were constructing the new bunker.

During dismantling, I found a large spider burrowed into a crease between the old sandbags. The spider appeared to be dormant. I found an old flat board and, with a stick, I slid the spider onto the board. The spider was about five inches in diameter with the legs, and the body was about an inch-and-a-half across. I took a piece of brittle elephant grass and pierced the spider, killing it. Initially, I had the thought of weather-drying it and then mailing it home as a souvenir. The following day that thought no longer appealed, so the spider was tossed.

Manning and I built the bunker on a slight knob so that the ground all around the bunker was lower than the bunker. This allowed rainwater to run away from our location, and the slight elevation gave us a better field of vision. We had to clear brush away from the bunker to allow for visibility and shooting alleys. We did not have any concertina wire, but we did put out Claymore mines and booby-trapped them as before. We also set up booby-trap hand grenades with tripwire.

On the second night, I was on guard duty and I heard a noise out in front of our position. I crawled out of the bunker and went to a mound where an old bunker was located. I wanted to draw fire so I could locate the position of the intruder. I struck my cigarette lighter and held it up thinking it would draw fire. I was crouched down behind a hump of dirt. No fire came, but there was an explosion. I crawled back to the bunker. By this time Manning, who had been sleeping, was awake. He was pissed that I didn't wake him up before leaving the bunker. Neither one of us was interested in checking out what had caused the explosion in the dark. The next morning we went out and found a dead wild cat about the size of the

American bobcat. It was a dark, almost black, striped feline that had tripped one of the hand grenade booby-traps.

During this time, it seems everyone got the squirting Hersheys. We had been getting drinking water from the river and putting iodine tablets in it for purification. Apparently, we did not use enough tablets to prevent dysentery. Our butts became our biggest enemy for a while. We had no toilet facilities, and we had to dig a hole and bury our excrement as we went. With everyone's butt inflamed, Doc (the medic, Luis Aragon) dug out some type of powder in little OD green cans and gave a can to each one who wanted it. He told us to

Luis "Doc" Aragon, our medic.

use it after crapping. The first time I used the stuff, I wanted to scream at Doc, but my mouth was too puckered to get any words out. After about 10 minutes, the inflamed tissues got a cooling effect that lasted for about two hours.

The third bridge, where we were located, was about one klick (1000 meters) from the Mang Yang Pass. Highway 19 followed the path of the river, and the river basin followed the ridge. The ridge was to our south, heavily foliated and considered jungle. The base of the ridge was about 300 meters from Highway 19. At the base of the ridge, just east of the third bridge was a Montagnard hamlet. The hamlet started about 200 meters off the highway and pushed to the base of the ridge. There was a narrow trail running from the highway up to the first group of hooches (single-family dwellings).

The engineers had cleared back the trees and bushes that were close to Highway 19. This was done so the Viet Cong could not get close to the road for ambush. They pushed the trees and brush onto piles next to the standing jungle. The Montagnard women would go to these piles of wood and brush and cut off pieces small enough for them to carry back to their hamlet. One morning, there was a Montagnard woman trudging down the road bent under a very large tree branch. The branch was about eight inches in diameter on the large end and about four inches on the narrow end. It was about 15 to 16 feet long and twisted. I would estimate it weighed at least 200 pounds. The big end was over her shoulder and small end dragged on the ground behind her. As she approached the bridge from the west, she was stooped over so her shoulders were horizontal to the ground. She was wearing a black pajama-type gown that had openings below the armpits. The upper portion of the gown was hanging down, exposing the upper part of her body. When she was about 50 feet from our location, she stopped, straightened up her body, pulled her clothing tight so it covered her breasts, and continued trudging down the road to the hamlet. In total, she had to travel at least 500 meters with her load and stopped only long enough, that one time, to adjust her clothing.

One morning at least eight Montagnard women came down to the river near the bridge to wash themselves and an assortment of clothes. They would tie the clothes to a crude rope and throw them in the river, and let the current wash as the clothes rippled in the water. While they were waiting, the women sat, one behind the other, with their legs straddling the one in front of them. They picked bugs, ticks, and probably lice out of each other's hair. They would go through the hair of the person to their front, taking a few strands at a time and pull their finger through the hair. Whenever they found a tick or lice, they would put it in their mouth and eat it. After a while, the last person would rotate to the front of the line.

As a rule, we would crush our C-Ration cans so they could not be used against us. But for the Montagnards, we would leave the opened cans whole. The cans were used as cups, for digging, and for a number of other uses. The Montagnards were considered friendly, although they kept to themselves. The word was spread, "Don't do anything to piss them off." They had crude ways to even the score. There was a rumor that some ARVNs (ARVN stands for the Army of the Republic of South Vietnam, or South Vietnamese Army) who guarded the bridge previously, had raped a young Montagnard girl. The next night some Montagnard men stole into their camp, killed four of the ARVN, and cut off and stuffed their genitals down their throats.

There was an old trail that followed the river into the jungle. This trail had been used frequently in the past. To make sure the Viet Cong could not get close to our position and snipe at us, during daytime hours we had to post a guard along this trail. We dug a foxhole in a bank above the river. This foxhole was about 200 yards upstream from the bridge. We would take turns, in four-hour increments, one person at a time, sitting in this foxhole watching the trail. Red ants moved into the hole, so we would sit up above the hole and jump in only when necessary. While we were at the bridge, it was never necessary to use the hole. To kill time, I would pretend the ants were Viet Cong, and I was in a plane overhead. I would take rocks and drop them on the ants. It seemed like child's play, but it helped to pass the time.

On one particularly hot day, Spec-4 Miles was assigned to take out a patrol along the trail that ran along the river. He selected me, along with six other troops, to go on the patrol.

Miles openly stated he did not like to be in charge and did not trust himself with other peoples' lives. We did not follow the trail for fear of booby traps, but we walked along the river away from the trail, breaking a new trail as we went. About a mile from the bridge, we found a series of punji pits. There were about five or six pits sporadically spread out to cover about an acre of land. Each pit had about 40 or 50 punji stakes driven into the ground. The punji stakes are slices of bamboo stems, sharpened, dipped in excrement, and then driven into the ground at angles, usually in high grassy areas. The tip of the punji stick is about 12 to14 inches high. The idea is to have the punji stick poke you in the leg about calf-high. The excrement will infect the wound causing an injured person to be medevaced out of the field, reducing the number of troops. It is more of a harassment tactic, but some injuries from punji sticks became quite severe for the damage caused.

As we were patrolling, we found a small tributary river running into the main river. We followed it into some very thick jungle. As we walked, we heard a faint noise coming from upstream. The further we went, the louder the noise became,

111

A Marine of Company H, 2nd Battalion, 4th Regiment, walks through a punji-staked gully; January 28, 1966. U.S. Marine Corps photo. NARA 532439. Courtesy of the National Archives at College Park, College Park, Md.

and finally we could make out the sound of bubbling water. The river water had a more swift current here and the water was more active. It became obvious that we were approaching a waterfall. The water was pouring over the rocks about 70 feet above us. We had walked into a box canyon but, because of the heavy jungle growth, we did not realize it until we came to the waterfall. We were surrounded on three sides by cliff walls. The waterfall was a beautiful spectacle of nature. The air had a nearly suffocating effect. But nearer the waterfall there was a cool, tropical-plant fragrance, similar to what you find in a botanical garden. We now knew we were in a box-type canyon and, if the gooks knew we were there, we could easily have been trapped. We said to hell with it, took off our clothes, and took a cool shower under the waterfall. We did leave two people on guard to watch our back trail and, when the first group was finished, they took their turn. This time near the waterfall is one of my fondest memories of Vietnam. Vietnam was a pretty country, but so much of its beauty was destroyed by years of war with France and later the United States.

While stationed at the bridge, we had a couple of days of extremely heavy rain. The river ran over its banks and flooded some positions that were in the lower ground. The bunker Manning and I had built stayed high and it was relatively dry in spite of so much sogginess everywhere. PFC Kampa and another trooper had put out a booby-trap grenade that became submerged in water. When the river went down, they could not find the grenade or the wire. They figured the raging water washed it away. About a day later, Kampa found the grenade. It went off as he walked down to the river to get some water for bathing. He received what was known as a million-dollar wound. He got a piece of shrapnel in the ass.

Our highway assignment, which was relatively easy compared to what was to follow, lasted for 13 or 14 days instead of the 30 we were expecting. One morning we were told to pack everything up; we were being replaced. A group of deuce-and-a-half trucks dropped off our replacements and we loaded up for a trip back to Camp Radcliff. We were stacked in the trucks so tightly that everyone had to stand up. Just before we got to the southeast entrance, PFC John Wren's rifle discharged. He had it aimed up, so the slug went straight up, but it scared the hell out of everyone. The driver slammed on the brakes, stopping the truck, and he bailed out and dove into the ditch. The front-seat passenger did likewise. The one who seemed the most scared was Wren. He crapped in his pants. Of course, everyone gave him the raspberries for the rest of the day.

Troops of A Company, 1st Air Cav. Div. (Airmobile) check a house during patrol to clear the area of North Vietnamese soldiers. Part of "Operation Irving," the 1st Air Cavalry was tasked with clearing a mountain range about 25 miles north of Qui Nho'n which lies 400 miles NNE of Saigon. Credit Laurence J. Sullivan SPC5. October 6, 1966.

OPERATION IRVING

As soon as we got back to our battalion area, we had to get our gear in order. We were told that the next morning we were headed out on some operation with other troops from the 1st Cav. Once we had our gear together, and an inspection was complete, we were told we had the rest of the day pretty much to ourselves. Some of us made a tour of Division Headquarters to see how the pogues (rear-echelon paper-shufflers) worked. We visited the PX, purchased some beer, crackers, and canned foods. This became our food staple for the rest of the day. Only E-5s and above could buy liquor.

A supply Sergeant on main post asked if any of us could type. He was looking for a typist. He said that he could get a good typist transferred to supply. Since I had typing in high school, I gave it a try. I wasn't good enough. Oblad tried it and impressed the Sergeant. The supply Sergeant put him to work for about two hours typing up some forms. Before he left, the Sergeant took his name and told him he was going to have him transferred to his supply unit. That was the last Oblad ever heard of the transfer.

Before dark, we headed back to battalion headquarters. Some other guys from the company were going down to the 8th Engineers' EM Club, about 500 meters south of our unit. There was a wooded hill separating us from them. The Engineers had access to materials and equipment, more so than any other unit. As a result, they built themselves quite a nice EM Club, with slot machines, a bandstand, indoor toilets, and even a small dance floor. Not long after we arrived, a fight broke out involving some of the 5/7 troops so we were asked to leave. With some reluctance, we left.

Bull-shit talk floated around in the tents until after midnight. We eventually got to sleep and had an early morning awakening. We were rushed through breakfast, packed up our gear, and waited along the road that went past our tents. A group of trucks came by, picked us up, and transported us to the helipad airfield. We loaded onto choppers, 10 troops to each chopper, and we were airlifted to a hilltop overlooking a large valley and a series of villages, hamlets, and a river that flowed to the ocean. We were told that we were about 35 klicks north of Qui Nho'n. Our battalion and three companies from the 1st Bn 7th Cav were to spread out in the valley and drive the gooks out to the South China Sea. We were clearing the valley of all Viet Cong influence. This was called Operation Irving. The ocean was about 15 miles away, but we could make it out through a mist that seemed to rise along the shore. There was a large ship sitting offshore; we later learned it was a gunship, used for ground support.

We were assigned positions and told to dig in. The hill was composed of mostly rock, so digging in was not an option for most of us. Instead, we dragged anything bulky into a position that would create a sight barrier and possibly stop or deflect bullets. The position Manning and I were assigned to, as well as those on either side of ours, was on an extremely steep hill that was wooded with a gnarl of brush and prickly-like ash, like what we are accustomed to around the northern plains of the United States. I checked the front of our position and was satisfied that no one (i.e., the enemy) would attempt to come up the hill in our defense sector. Once through the first brush, it was a shear cliff-like structure out in front of us. I expected to sleep at ease that night. I was wrong.

Shortly after the noon hour, Sgt. Nehr told me I was going on a night ambush with him and a few others. Sgt. Jeffery Nehr was the squad leader for the 3rd squad of the 2nd platoon. He was from Florida and lived close to the ocean. He told me that since I was from Minnesota, and was used to hunting, I might be the best one to lead point to the position where we were to set up the ambush. He and I sat down with the map and looked it over. From the hilltop, we could see the area where we wanted the ambush. It was about 1500 meters to our south and east. The only problem was, to get there we had to travel north off the hill, then northeast to get to the basin, and then south to get to the ambush location. This had to be done after dark.

The map had grid lines marking out the ridges and basins, and the steepness of the drop in the terrain. We ate an early evening meal, prepared our gear, and waited for dark. When dark rolled in, I noticed the ship on the ocean had two low lights that were visible. As I started out down the hill, I kept track of the lights to maintain a sense of direction. We had to zig and zag back and forth to descend the hill to the basin. Most of the time, I could see the lights on the ship. Once we got to the basin, the ship's lights were no longer visible. It was extremely dark, but by now my night vision allowed me to see the outline of the hill we just came down. I began walking south along and slightly away from the hill. We came to some fields that had been recently tilled. Hedgerows surrounded the fields. We were still on the declining ground at the base of the hill, and the hedgerows kept the ground from washing away with all the rain.

Once at the basin, our patrol walked southeast for almost two klicks and stopped. I looked back to the hilltop to

Troops climb up a rocky mountain during "Operation Thayer II," a search-and-destroy mission against the Viet Cong in the An Lao Valley about 400 miles northeast of Saigon. This photo is Company A, 1st Bn 5th Cav, 1st Cav. Div. (Airmobile), February 7, 1967. Credit Robert C. Lafoon. U.S. Army photo. NARA 111-CC-38401. Photo courtesy of the National Archives at College Park, Md.

get my bearings. Sgt. Nehr asked me if I had an idea where we were at. I told him our ambush site should be about 100 meters to my front and left. We walked about half that far and found the exact spot we were looking for. There was a cut-away in the ground. Here in the States, we would call this structure a gully. This gully is usually used to channel rainwater from the hills to the rice paddies below where it is stored in dug-out pools in the dry season. Once the rice paddies are planted, the pools of water are drained or siphoned into the newly planted rice beds. It was still considered the dry season, even though we got an inch or more of rain nearly every day. This gully was also used by the gooks as a means to travel in and out of the hamlets at night undetected. There was about a 45-degree bend in the gully and we wanted to set up to cover this bend. In studying the map and terrain during the daytime, and with the help of the ship's lights, the outline of the hill, and a little/lot of luck, I put our ambush squad on the exact spot we wanted. We had to travel about two miles in the dark, starting in the opposite direction to get to our spot. I did it as if I knew exactly what I was doing, never second-guessing my decisions. Sgt.Nehr and everyone else in the squad marveled but had no idea how I did it.

We all sat awake throughout the night but had no contact with the gooks. As soon as daylight came, we headed back toward the top of the hill. It was now during daylight hours that I could see the real distance we had traveled, and the type of terrain we came down. It was a bear getting back up. As soon as we got back to Company Headquarters, Sgt. Nehr told the Captain and all other B Company officers and Sergeants about how I took them in the dark to the exact location we wanted. This one excursion marked me as the number-one point man for the company from then on.

When we got back to the hilltop, the morning breakfast choppers (sorties) arrived. We had breakfast and were told to saddle up: we were going down into the hamlets. Our mission, along with two other companies from the 5/7 Cav and three companies from the 1/7 Cav, was to line up and sweep the hamlets all the way to the ocean. The hamlets were located along and away from both sides of a large river and were between two long ridges that extended nearly to the ocean. It was our job to clear this valley of all people. The civilians were loaded onto helicopters and flown to civilian camps. All Viet Cong were either killed or, if they surrendered, they were hauled back by helicopter to Re-Ed (Re-Educational) camps for interrogation and restructuring.

D Company was assigned to provide backup support with mortars and troops if necessary. They would also secure and control the civilians and Viet Cong soldiers who were captured. These people would be flown out by Chinook helicopters (twin-bladed helicopters capable of hauling 50 to 60 people) to one of the aforementioned camps.

The ROKs (South Korean soldiers), some Aussies (Australian soldiers), and the mortar platoon from D Company were covering the ridges to prevent Viet Cong soldiers from escaping. Before this mission was completed, more than 2,500 Viet Cong would surrender and 780 were killed. From what I understand, four American soldiers died, and around 10 were wounded.

The first day off the hill, we searched a series of island hamlets. Rice paddies surrounded the hamlets. We would wade through the rice paddies, go through the hamlets, get all the locals out of their huts and bunkers in the ground, and search for weapons and ammunition. The locals and any Viet Cong were escorted back to the staging area for eventual extraction from the valley. We then would burn their huts and destroy their rice. The goal was to remove all civilians, destroy all the food, and burn the hooches so there would be no sanctuary or food for the Viet Cong when we left the area.

When we stepped into the rice paddies, you could see the leeches. They seemed to sense flesh and swam to you. We bloused our leg bottoms over the top of our boots. To get to your skin, a leech had to crawl up your clothes and find an opening under your shirt, or the neck area. When you're out in the open of a rice paddy, you have little or no cover. Our concentration was on watching the hamlets for activity and not looking for leeches. Frequently throughout the day and night, we had to do a search of our bodies for leeches. If a leech burrows into your skin deep enough, they can do damage. We found out that there were two types of leeches: water leeches, and sand leeches that thrived out of the water. Sand leeches would hang in trees and drop on you as you walked under-neath them. They would crawl up on you as you slept.

In every hamlet, there was at least one bunker. Someone had to crawl into the bunkers to check them out. Since I was skinny and not overly tall, I was one of the tunnel rats. The bunkers were made for people smaller than the average American GI. There was usually one entrance which went down at an angle and then in. The inside was constructed of split bamboo, stacked upright and leaning toward the peak, with the rounded side facing in. Dirt was thrown against the reeds and bamboo. The floor of the bunker was about 2 feet wide, and the peak was tight; the height was about 30 inches. I could not sit upright in a bunker. Getting in was not very difficult; I had to turn sideways to get through the opening though. To get out, you had to turn around, as it was too tight to back out.

In every hamlet, we would find from five to ten women, about 20 children under 10 years of age, and maybe two or three old men. Not every hamlet, but many, also had one person, usually a young male adult, who appeared to be mentally retarded, many times from old head wounds. When we first come across these people, we thought they might be Viet Cong. But the rest of the locals would yell, they were Dinky Dau, their term for mentally retarded.

As we worked our way from hamlet to hamlet, we were getting closer to the ocean and finding fewer rice paddies and more of what was called mangrove swamps. Fishing the swamps and eating and trading fish seemed to be how the locals lived. Many hamlets also had one hut with chickens.

Our first night in the valley, B Company took over a village that we had cleared earlier in the day. We had left all the buildings intact so we could use this village as Command Post (CP) headquarters overnight. Part of the 3rd platoon got to set up in the village with the CP. They had the high ground. The rest of us set up on the dikes in the rice paddies. Shortly after dark, it began to rain. It rained a deluge throughout the night. When I set up in my position, I was sitting on the dike and would have stayed dry had it not rained. Before daylight came I was sitting in water that was at least a foot higher than the dike I was sitting on. We were close to the main river and it over-ran its banks. No one in the rice paddies slept that night. This was back-to-back nights I did not get any sleep. Going without sleep for two and three nights at a time would become common practice for the time I spent in the field.

After daylight, we all went into the higher ground of the village. A sortie brought in our breakfast and extra C-Rations. After breakfast, we began sweeping hamlets again. We came into a larger-than-normal hamlet; it could be construed as a village, along the river's edge. It had about 70 inhabitants. There also were a few solid-constructed buildings. Almost all other hamlets were constructed of straw-and-stick huts. This village was the last sizable one of its kind that we encountered before we entered the numerous mangrove swamps that lay along the ocean.

As we went through the village, the locals seemed much more ill at ease than what we had previously experienced. We did a cursory search for weapons, ammunition, and Viet Cong, and then called in the choppers for evacuation. This village was used as a staging area for the evacuation.

On the far side of the village, the water was about three feet deep off the bank. About 50 feet out from the edge of the village, there was a large tangle of mangrove bushes. Just above the water, but under the mangrove, was a platform-like base. It looked as if a coconut was floating under the platform.

Capt. John Hitti.

Ray Judy and I went into the water to check out this mangrove. When we were about 20 feet from the mangrove, the coconut changed and now looked like the head of a drowned person. Capt. Hitti and a number of other soldiers were watching us. Hitti said to be sure the person was dead and not playing possum. I raised my rifle and shot the head. The jaw started opening and closing, and it made a moaning sound. We moved in on the mangrove. Judy stood back and covered me with his rifle. I reached under the platform and grabbed the hair and pulled it out. As I pulled the body out, another male about 20 years old rushed out from under the mangrove with his hand leading the way. Ray shot him, hitting the hand, tearing the index and middle finger completely off, and then the bullet grazed the right temple of the gook. He apparently was giving himself up. As soon as we cleared him out of the way, another person came out from under the mangrove. We held our fire. Capt. Hitti told us to get away from the mangrove.

We sent the two Viet Cong to shore, and I dragged the dead one up to the bank. When we pulled the gook up on the bank, we saw it was a female, probably in her mid-20s. The top of her head was blown off and part of her fore-skull was missing. Her face was grossly distorted. The M16 round hit the water just before striking her head, creating much more damage than a direct hit would have. This was the first confirmed kill our company had made, and it turned out to be a female. Through our interpreter Sgt. Nguyen, we learned that there was at least one more person under the mangrove. We lobbed three hand grenades at the base of the mangrove and then ran a 50-shell belt from the M60 machine gun under the platform base strafing the water top. No one came out. We went back out to the mangrove and began tearing it apart. In a rush, a gook came out of the water and grabbed Benedetti by the neck. Ray Kloemken shot and killed him. We then had the uninjured gook search the area for weapons or any other device that may have been left behind. We did not want to take a chance on finding something that may blow up in our face. We did not find anything. Through the interpreter, we learned the gooks under the mangrove were Viet Cong. I do not recall the military group they were with. The female was a Viet Cong nurse.

While Sgt. Nguyen and the Captain were interrogating the gooks, we decided to break out the C-Rations for lunch. I was sitting on the bank of an underground bunker with the dead woman right by my feet. A man dressed in clean jungle

AIR CAVALRYMEN RETRIEVING VIET CONG BODY
The price of an irresistible potshot.

42

One of the members of B Company removing a dead Viet Cong nurse from the water, from *Time* magazine, October 14, 1966. This was the U.S. version of the magazine. The Asian edition used a photo of Bob Kunkel eating his lunch near the dead body.

Here is the paragraph in *Time* related to this photo:

South Viet Nam: Down to the Sea
"Finding the enemy is often half the battle in the Viet Nam war. To keep from being found, every Communist soldier is under orders not to give away his unit's position by firing needlessly at an Allied reconnaissance plane. Last week more than 1,000 Viet Cong and North Vietnamese lay dead in the rice fields rimming Sweet Water Bay north of Qui Nhon, and another 950 captured – all because a Communist took an irresistible potshot at a helicopter of the U.S. 1st Cavalry (Airmobile)."

fatigues came up, snapped a photo of me and the gook, and asked me how I could eat with the ghastly sight of the dead body right next to me. I told him, "I guess after a while you get used to this, and it doesn't bother." This photo and an article with my comment appeared in *Time Magazine*. Later, when I returned to my company from the hospital, Ray Judy showed me the article. He was keeping the magazine for me. But, like everything else, things got wet and rotted due to the extreme heat and high humidity in Vietnam.

I visited various libraries looking for that article in old *Time Magazines*. I called Ray Judy and he confirmed that it was *Time Magazine*; he had purchased it in Taiwan when he was on R & R. From a recent issue of the magazine I located a phone number for the magazine and I was informed there was an Asian version of the magazine, and the person I talked with gave me a phone number and an E-mail address for the magazine which is published in Singapore. I made contact by E-mail and was informed they keep back issues for only 12 months. This ended my search with negative results.

Capt. Hitti told Doc (Luis Aragon) to patch up the wounded gook. Doc was a Hispanic American from California. He told the Captain he would not waste his supplies on the enemy, as they were more valuable for our own men. Hitti reinforced his directive, telling Doc we'll get re-supplied when we need more. Doc began the routine of getting the wounds cleaned. He picked up scissors as if to cut some bandage, and with a single thrust drove the tip of the scissors into the gook's temple area where the wound was. The gook let out a scream, convulsed for a short while, and died.

We went back through this village and gave it a more thorough search. We found a shallow underground bunker, built tight to a stucco house. There was a wood barrel sitting on top of a small wood slab. The slab was covered with dirt.

126

We removed the barrel and scraped the dirt away to expose the bunker. There were two rifles, ammunition, and a fancy wooden box in the bunker. The box was wrapped in plastic and on a shelf built into the bunker. I handed the box out. It was locked and 1st Sgt. Hare pried it open with a knife. The box was about 24 inches long, 16 inches wide, and six inches deep. Inside was a removable insert with additional room below the insert. The insert and the bottom layer of the box were divided into 2-by-2-inch squares. The entire inside of the box was lined with a soft felt-like material. In each of the squares were six small plastic packs of a white powdery substance. The powder in each pack would not quite fill a shot glass. Sgt. Hare said the substance was heroin. He also said that, if it was pure which he believed it was, the contents would be worth about 5 million dollars back in the world (the United States). We took the box and, under supervision, opened each pack and dumped it into the river.

This stucco house belonged to the village chief. It is believed that he was the chief of the entire valley we were sweeping. When the search of the village was completed we recovered five or six guns, some ammunition, and some old-fashioned booby-trap mines.

Once this village was cleared, there were only hamlets between it and the sea. The company was divided into platoons and each platoon began searching the remaining hamlets, dividing them into sectors to cover the remaining ground more rapidly. The 2nd platoon headed away from the river toward a hamlet that was surrounded by water. The water was about three-and-a-half feet deep. The hamlet was much smaller and had five or six huts and an underground bunker.

There was a large berm (a large dike-like dirt bank used as trails and to control water) that ran from the village to this hamlet. Of course, we didn't use the berm. We had to get in the water to get there. The berm extended from this hamlet to another island hamlet further out toward the ocean.

John Petters, a career Spec-4, had a brown-gas grenade. This was something he apparently brought over from the States; it was not Vietnam-issue. For some reason, he thought it would be a good idea to pull the pin and toss it into the underground bunker. When he did this, the gas poured out of the bunker and hung in the air. The gas seemed to bother us more than the locals. The locals got teary-eyed, and they laughed at our discomfort. Petters caught hell from just about everyone. On the positive side, two women and three or four children exited the bunker. I still had to check out the bunker. Instead of crawling in, I slid down the hole headfirst, shined my flashlight to look around, and had a couple of other soldiers pull me back.

While we were in this hamlet a two-man bubble helicopter flew over, heading toward the sea. This chopper flew around quite regularly, scouting for us as we moved along. It was about 300 yards from our position and it banked to make a turn. Rifle fire erupted from the ground along the berm, and the chopper lost steering control and had to make an emergency landing. Our platoon was closest to their position. We headed in their direction, about belly button-deep in water. With all of our gear, and the depth of the water, we could not make fast tracks. We wanted to provide protection for the pilot and his scout until they were rescued. We hadn't moved more than a 200 feet when we heard a barrage of small arms fire. As we closed in on the helicopter, rifle fire was directed at us. We fired back and the snipers withdrew into the mangroves. When we got to the helicopter, we found both the pilot and scout had been shot and killed. It appeared they landed, in very close range of the snipers. Lt. Frank called in a chopper to evacuate the pilot and scout. Some items were removed from the chopper and also loaded on the evac helicopter. We destroyed the rest of the helicopter with the use of grenades that were designed to melt metal. The chopper was left where it went down.

We then moved to another island hamlet, where we continued the search and removal of civilians. It was getting late in the day so we set up a security perimeter for the night.

Supplies of hot food and fresh water are unloaded at a mountain camp 60km northwest of Qui Nho'n for C Company, 7th Cav., 1st Cav. Div., during "Operation Thayer II." Oct. 29, 1966. U.S. Army Photo. NARA 635080. Photo courtesy of the National Archives at College Park, Md.

As we were waiting for choppers to bring out the evening meal and supplies, the 3rd platoon took on some sniper fire. They exchanged fire. The skirmish lasted only a minute or so, but a young NCO was hit in the groin area. Word had it that he was begging someone to kill him. Apparently, he got married while he was on leave before coming to Vietnam and he felt this injury left him totally useless as a man.

Choppers eventually came and delivered the evening meal to the village where 3rd platoon and headquarters were set up. The injured Sergeant was put on the chopper to be medevaced to the field hospital.

Half of our platoon went to chow, and the other half pulled security until they returned. I went to eat with the second group. By the time the first group got back, it was pitch black. We followed a large berm back to the chow point and walked about three meters apart so we did not present a single large target.

By now, we had driven the Viet Cong as far to the ocean as they could go. Apparently, some of them tried to escape over the ridge to our north. At about 2030 hours (10:30 p.m.) a firefight broke out on the ridge. The next morning we were told that the ROKs, who were in a blocking position on this ridge, had killed about 180 gooks.

The next day, as we moved through the mangrove swamps, hundreds of enemy decided to surrender. As we lined up to move to the next hamlet, they came out with their hands in the air. None had rifles or ammunition; through the interpreter, we learned that they had left them lying in the water before surrendering.

We came to a large mangrove that was about 60 to 80 acres, with a large berm surrounding it. To our north was the river and just beyond the river was a platoon from the 1/7 Cav.

We moved over the berm from a smaller mangrove swamp and were about 40 meters into the larger one. Small arms fire broke out from the mangroves about midway through the swamp. Bullets were splattering the water all around us. We got down so only the upper half of our face and helmets were out of water and backed up toward the berm. We then slipped over the berm and began firing back into the mangroves. Benedetti was the machine gunner and he opened fire, raking the mangroves just above the water. Two gooks broke out of a cluster of mangrove about 200 yards out and headed away from us. Murgatroyd carried an M79 grenade launcher; he raised the barrel high and fired a round that landed between the two gooks who disappeared under the water.

When the gooks fired at us, they also fired at the platoon from the 1/7 Cav. We were shooting back across the water toward the 1/7 Cav, and the 1/7 Cav was shooting in our direction. The gooks had drawn us into a long-range firefight with our own troops. The shooting lasted for at least five minutes before someone realized what happened. A cease-fire was called. Lt. Frank called in gunships, which are helicopters with M40 rockets and two machine gunners, one out each side door. They flew over the mangroves firing their machine guns and the M40 rockets.

From radio communication with the 1/7 Cav, we learned that the only American casualty in the skirmish was a radio antenna. When the firing started, their RTO ducked down, but his antenna was sticking up and a bullet knocked it off.

We waited about an hour and then began our push through this mangrove swamp. Everyone was more alert than usual. As we moved toward the middle of the swamp, the water was getting deeper. My partner Manning was hanging onto my shoulder pack and bounced along behind me. When the water got deep enough for me to have to bounce along, I could no longer help Manning. Bentz was about 6'4" tall, so Manning hung onto him. As we passed through the center of the swamp, the water gradually got shallower. Eventually, Manning could walk without our aid.

As we were passing between the mangroves, Manning caught sight of a gook who had slid under the water behind a mangrove and was swimming between him and me. I was looking into the water but could not see anything. The gook almost swam into Manning. He put his rifle into the water and fired. The water near Manning began to turn red. Manning bumped into the gook with his feet, screamed, and got the hell away from him. Bentz and I stomped around until I hit him with my feet. I reached in and pulled him up. Bentz reached down and pulled up a rifle. I got a hold of the gook's shirt by the neck, dragged him across the rest of the swamp to the next berm, and pulled him out of the water. He was holding an American hand grenade with the ring hooked in his thumb. The pin was hanging in the clip by only a quarter of an inch.

Two days later, we went back to this same mangrove with three rubber rafts that were flown in. We searched the mangrove from the rafts and found 13 dead bodies floating in the water. We also found a lot of dead fish. Throughout our stay in the mangroves, we would find a few dead fish, but in the mangrove swamp where we had the skirmish, there were hundreds of them floating around. Many of them looked like eels.

After searching the gook, we crossed the berm and moved into another mangrove. At the far side of this mangrove were two small hamlets about 200 yards apart. Since we had been making more resistive enemy contact, we were extra-cautious as we approached the first hamlet. There was a hut with stilts holding the side nearest to us up off the water. This hut extended out on a point and it concerned us. Heronema carried an M79. The Lieutenant asked if he could put a round through the window of the hut. He said with a little practice that he might be able to do it. We were about 180 yards from the hut. He aimed a little high on his target and the first round went through the window exploding inside. There was a lot of squawking of chickens with some flying out the door into the water and onto the berm. In all, there were about two dozen chickens, most were dead or dying. We killed the wounded chickens and left the live ones to make it on their own. We snipped the heads from five chickens and cleaned them for cooking. We searched the hamlet and found no other animals or people.

We moved to the next hamlet, which was larger and had one solid-frame building without a roof; it may have been a church at one time. We decided to set up for the night in this hamlet. Again, there were no locals in this hamlet. The chow chopper landed on the hamlet island where the company head-quarters was stationed. We were about 400 meters from their position, but we had to walk the berms to get to them. The berms did not go in a straight line, so we ended up traveling almost twice as far. Again, half the platoon went for chow while the other half pulled security.

Since we had the five chickens, some of us, mostly 3rd squad, decided against walking the dikes to the next platoon area where Company headquarters was set up. We cleaned the chickens, removing internal organs and skin, and put them on a bamboo spit. We made a fireplace of old brick and slabs we found around the church. We cooked the chickens, two at a time, taking turns turning them on the spit. We even heated our C-Ration biscuits, which made them taste much better than normal. The taste of the chicken was tolerable, but it was so tough that we could not chew it down to swallow. We chewed the flavor out of it, and then spit most of the meat on the ground.

Everyone was told to be extra-careful because we had pushed the gooks about as far as we could before the water would get too deep. It was felt that they would try to break through the ranks during the night to get behind us. Therefore we had to set two-man security positions along all the dikes about 40 to 50 yards apart to stop them. We were told to make sure one of us stayed awake all the time. We were also told that a couple of nights before, someone fell asleep while pulling his guard and he and his buddy were captured. They were found the next day, by another platoon, in one of the hamlets tied to a tree naked; they had been skinned alive, their testicles and penises had been cut off and shoved down their throats. I am not sure this was the truth, but the story was effective in making sure someone was always awake and alert.

The next day would be our last day in this valley. We had to clear a few more hamlets, one of which we knew was inhabited. The whole company moved into this hamlet and found about 20 civilians. One woman was lying on a floor mat in a hut, giving birth. Capt. Hitti told Doc to help her and told me to assist Doc. My job was pretty simple. All I did was watch and only once, after the birth, handed Doc some heavy padded gauze from his pack. Soon after the birth, choppers arrived and we loaded the civilians on the choppers, including the new mother and her son, and we sent them on their way. We spent the rest of the morning searching the rest of the hamlets in the valley and then we were flown by chopper to the ridges overlooking the valley and sea.

All along I was thinking that, once this operation was over, we would be flying back to Camp Radcliff for a break. I think many of the other soldiers thought the same thing. We all were wrong. I didn't see base camp again until the end of January.

By now we had been in water for about five days straight. Our feet were shriveled and colorless. We were told to set up in four-man positions and rest, taking off our shoes and airing our feet. The 2nd platoon was assigned an area where the ROKs had the firefight two nights before. They dumped the dead bodies into a deep crevice in the ridge. After two days with temps well over 100 degrees, and the sultry air, the decaying bodies were very ripe. The wind was coming off the sea and blowing the smell toward us. The view overlooking the sea and valley was great, but the smell was horrendous.

Headquarters learned that there was a small hamlet over the ridge that was used by gooks as a source of food and shelter. It was in a remote, rocky area north of the ridge we were on. Battalion Headquarters wanted a squad to find the hamlet and ambush it in the night. Sgt. Nehr was assigned to lead the squad. He chose me for point and recruited other volunteers. The sky was clouded over and, as usual, there was a threat of rain. We waited until nearly dark and headed west away from the sea. I did not have a topographical map of the area to study before heading out. For me, it is important to know the lay of the land. Based on that knowledge, I have a general idea of where we are located especially when it comes to sharp drops or rises of the terrain. We were walking to the left of the highest part of the ridge. Because of the blackness of the night, I could not use the outline of the ridge to stay on course, as was my custom. The hillside kept getting steeper to our left as we moved forward. This gave me the only indication that we were traveling in the right direction.

We were walking in a tight column, about one long step apart to keep from losing each other without making noise. One step I was on the side incline, and the next step the ground

135

fell away from me and I dropped down a hill that was barely shy of a cliff. I bounced end-over-end, somersaulting down the hill; I probably was touching the ground half the time. I ended up buried in a thicket of prickly ash-like brush. I do not remember yelling, but the rest of the squad said I yelled all the way down. Sgt. Nehr yelled to me to see if I was okay. I yelled back that I needed a flare so I could see what the terrain was like. I also yelled that I lost my rifle and most of my gear.

When we left on this patrol, I was carrying an M16 rifle, a Claymore bag that had 22 clips of M16 ammunition, four hand grenades, my web belt with two canteens of water, and my poncho rolled in a tight roll, tied to the back of my web belt. After freeing myself from the thicket of prickly brush, I took inventory and found that I still had my web belt, and three of the four hand grenades. Everything else was strewn somewhere on the descent of the hill. Nehr called Company Headquarters and gave them the Sit/Rep (Situation Report); he asked for an artillery flare at my request. It took about 10 minutes to finally get the flare. Apparently, this was supposed to be a priority-type mission, and Headquarters was reluctant to authorize a flare which would give away our position. With more explanation, the flare eventually was sent up. An artillery flare ignites about 1000 feet above the ground and lights up the sky for a good half-mile around.

When the flare ignited, I damn near shit in my pants. All I could think of was that God was watching out for me. If I had been 50 feet to the right or left of where I was at, I would have dropped off a cliff into rocks that were from 60 to 100 feet below the hilltop. My fall came in the only area where there was an angle to the drop. Slowly I made my way up the hill, literally bracing myself against rocks and brush as I went up. While I crawled up the ridge, I found most of my lost gear. I found the ammo bag, but over half the clips were missing from it. I found most of the ammo clips, both water canteens, and my poncho which had come unraveled, as I crawled back up the hill. I did not find the missing grenade and three ammo clips. After three flares and 20 minutes of searching and climbing, I finally reached the top of the hill.

I told Sgt. Nehr that, without daylight, to go any further would be suicide. He sent this information by radio back to Company Headquarters. Company Headquarters contacted Battalion Headquarters with the information. Battalion, through Company, told us to move on, regardless. I told Sgt. Nehr that I would not go another step, as it would be suicide. I also said that, if anyone else wanted to lead, I intended to be walking at the rear of the group. Sgt. Nehr told Capt. Hitti that I would not go any further, regardless of orders. Capt. Hitti apparently trusted my judgment and told us to pull back and set up for the night. We pulled back about 200 yards and found an area where we could prop our feet against some rocks and lay back on the ground. There were eight of us, so we broke into two groups of four each. We covered ourselves with two ponchos, one for each four-man group, lay back and went to sleep. During the night we got a heavy downpour that lasted about an hour, but we remained fairly dry.

At daybreak, we made our way back to our platoon area. The stench of the rotting gooks seemed even more vile than the night before. A chopper brought out our breakfast and a few supplies. The platoon Sgt. Inez told us to pack our gear; we were going to find that hamlet we didn't find the night before. I think he was trying to insult us. We took the same route we walked the night before, retracing our steps for a third time. We got to the point where I did my quick descent the night before. The platoon leader, Lt. Frank, decided this was taking us away from our target. The high point of the ridge was only 30 yards to our right. Everything from our location as far as we could see around the ridge was cliff. We crossed over the top of the ridge and still found the terrain was cliff. At the highest point, the cliff dropped at least 100 feet. We worked our way down the ridge to where the drop was about 50 feet. The ground below was a jagged rock bed. This is what I was looking at the night before when the flares went off.

It was decided that we would repel over the cliff. We tied a rope around a rock, and I believe Sgt. Nehr was the first one to go down. His descent was slow, likewise for the next soldier to go over. It was apparent that this move would take all morning. Lt. Frank decided that he would send a six-man squad down the ropes; they would check out the hamlet and wait for the rest of us. Since I had already been down the hill the hard way, I was to lead the rest of the platoon down that same hill and take the long way to the hamlet.

We went down the hill, bracing ourselves against rocks and brush until the bottom of the hill leveled off. Once off the sharp incline, we veered to the right, the direction of the hamlet. We crossed through the lowest area of a valley where there were some old, unused rice paddies. Just beyond a heavy wooded hillside, we found the remains of the hamlet. It took us about 90 minutes from the time we left the six-man squad to get to the hamlet. The six-man squad had not yet arrived. There were four burned-down huts and a rock wall on the high hill-facing side of what had been the huts. I think the wall was used to divert the water as it came down the hill during the rains. About 20 minutes after our arrival, Sgt. Nehr and his advanced squad showed up. Their route had been hampered by rugged terrain with more cliff-like drop-offs. They had to work their way slowly down the hillside.

An infantry patrol moves up to assault the last Viet Cong position after an
attempted overrun of the artillery position by the Viet Cong during Operation
"Hawthorne" at Dak To, Vietnam, June 7, 1966. U.S. Army photo, ID 111-C-CC35682.
Photo courtesy of the National Archives at College Park, Md.

A Montagnard child watches a convoy moving toward Plei Djerang and carrying
men and equipment to the armed assault, May 14, 1970. Photo courtesy of the
National Archives at College Park, Md. Original photo from the Records of the
Office of the Chief Signal Officer. Photo ID 111-CC-65723.

Sgt. Ronald A. Payne, squad leader of Company A, 1st Bn, 5th Mech Inf, 25th Inf. Div., checks a tunnel entrance before entering it to search for Viet Cong and their equipment during "Operation Cedar Falls." Credit Robert C. Lafoon, January 24, 1967. NARA 111-CC-38112. Photo courtesy of the National Archives at College Park, Md.

THE CAVES

The platoon took another 15-minute break to give the squad a chance to catch their wind. We then began working our way around the north base of the ridge back in the direction of the ocean. We went about 800 meters and had just rounded an outcrop of rock. Our point man and the soldier following him saw two gooks lying spread-out on a flat rock above them on the side of the ridge. The gooks were about 500 feet above the base of the hill and apparently had been sleeping. They woke when they heard us below. It was extremely hot and there was a punishing midday sun. We were packing all our gear, which was about 50 to 60 pounds for each person, and we were a cranky bunch. We were anything but quiet.

The gooks jumped up and disappeared into the rocks. We spread out and took up positions that gave us some cover and got ready for the fireworks. It did not come. The platoon leader asked for volunteers to go up and check out the area. Four soldiers – Sgt. Nehr, Sgt. Crockett, Kloemken and, I believe, Benedetti – went up the hill and found a cave in the side of the mountain. They found a rifle, a bag of ammunition, and some bloody bandages right at the mouth of the cave. They stood guard over the cave, and at least 10 more soldiers went up the hill to their location; I was one of the 10. The rest of the troops stayed below and were expected to provide what backup they could, if needed. Lt. Frank came up the hill with us. Sgt. Inez stayed below with the backup troops. While we were making our way up the hill, Sgt. Crockett checked out a trail that led east along the ridge. About 50 meters east and about 60 feet lower on the hillside, he found another cave with a smaller opening.

Sgt. Nehr, Kloemken, Gray and I went into the upper cave. The cave had about a three-foot-wide by four-foot-high opening. It was hidden behind the rock the gooks were laying on when we first spotted them. To get through the opening, you had to crawl up and over a rock. The cave then dropped about four feet down inside. The formation seemed to be naturally made and not excavated. The opening allowed some light into the cave. We needed a flashlight to go deeper into the cave. The inside of the cave was about 12 feet in a rough circumference. It was about 10 feet high in the middle of the inside dome, and the ceiling part gradually rounded down to about four feet high at the outer walls. The outer walls were a jagged mass of rock. The whole cave was a hollow in a rock formation and it had a damp smell about it.

Ray Kloemken.

At the back wall, away from the opening, there was a head-high opening that descended downward like a tunnel structure to the left. When quiet, we could make out the sound of running water somewhere below. Sgt. Nehr held the flashlight, and I walked beside him with my rifle ready. We began a slow descent down the tunnel. It made a wide sweeping bend to the left, similar to a half-spiral staircase. The tunnel dropped at nearly a 45-degree angle. Water was seeping out of the side walls in a few places making the rock base of the cave wet and slippery in spots. As we continued our descent, the sound of the running water grew louder. The tunnel stopped about 60 feet from where it began in the domed area at the entrance. There was an underground river at the lowest part of the tunnel. The river was about six feet wide and about two feet deep. The water was extremely cold. It came out of the rock wall on our right, bubbled and rippled for about 12 feet, and disappeared into the rock on our left. Where the water went into the rock, it had eroded a side cave that disappeared below the water level.

We went back up to the dome and outside to daylight. At the bottom of the cave, the temperature must have been about 50 degrees. Inside the opening, the temperature was probably 80 degrees. Outside, the temperature was at least 110 degrees.

We talked briefly about someone going under the water, upstream, to see where it led and what was beyond. If the gooks were in another area of the cave, even if they did not have weapons, going in one at a time would be suicide for us. We dismissed the idea as too dangerous.

The cave that Sgt. Crockett found had a smaller opening, and it opened up inside similar to the one we were in, but with smaller quarters. This one had a small opening that veered off to the left. Instead of going down, it had a slight angle upward. Sgt. Crockett crawled through the tunnel, which was about 20 inches in diameter. About 40 feet in, it opened into a larger, rock-walled room. There were bamboo slats woven together for cots, and medical supplies in this cave. We searched up and along the hillside for more caves but found none.

Two gooks had gone into a cave, and none came out. We made a thorough search of the entire hillside and found only the two caves. Logic told us these two gooks were still under the hill, and most likely holed up beyond an opening in the underground river.

Lt. Frank had radio conversation with Capt. Hitti. It was decided to have some troops wait inside the caves to see if the gooks would come out later in the day. Lt. Frank asked for volunteers. Sgt. Nehr, Kloemken, Tom Gray, and I volunteered to stay in the upper cave. Sgt. Crockett, Benedetti, and two others volunteered to stay in the lower cave. At around 5 p.m. the rest of the platoon made a departure from the ridge, walking across some rice paddies toward a small ridge across the valley. In daylight, they set up for the night. The ploy was to make any gooks, if they were watching, believe we had abandoned the cave mission.

Each group had one flashlight, one radio, our weapons, ammunition, C-Rations, and our personal supplies to include cigarettes. It was decided, among the four of us, that we would each pull one shift during the night, staying awake and listening for the gooks. Kloemken would pull first watch for three hours. He would wake me, and I would pull second watch for two-and-a-half hours. I would then wake Gray and he would pull third watch for two-and-a-half hours. Sgt. Nehr would pull watch until morning.

Sgt. Nehr rigged his poncho into a hammock. There were rock outcrops along the walls of the cave. He tied the foot end around one of these outcrops and ran a rope outside the cave and tied it to some rocks outside the entrance. His hammock was tight against the wall of the cave to the right of the entrance as you came inside. Gray found a level spot at the foot end of Sgt. Nehr's hammock. Kloemken found a level spot to the left of the opening, and I found an acceptable spot almost directly under the opening. While Kloemken was awake, I tried to sleep. The rock bed was not very comfortable, the temps dropped after dark, and I was tense and edgy.

I had just dropped off to sleep, and Kloemken woke me for my turn. I stood up to get the blood circulating and, when fully awake, I sat down. About 20 minutes into my watch, I heard the rippling water below change sounds. There was a sound like a large bubble bursting in water, and then the dripping of water. Then I heard a sound as if someone were walking in water and then stepped out of it. There was a dripping of water on the rocks. My immediate response was to take out a hand grenade and throw it down the tunnel. I pulled the pin on the hand grenade and then realized, because of the dark, I was not sure where the descent tunnel began. If I did not get the grenade down the tunnel, or if I hit the backside of the cave and the grenade bounced back, I would kill all four of us. I held the hand grenade in my right hand and searched in the dark for the flashlight. I could not find it. By now, I had a death grip on the hand grenade. I still had the pin, so I tried to put it back in the grenade. The tip of the pin had a small spread in it, and I could not get it back in the hole. I was getting worried. The grenade seemed to get heavier, and my right hand began to tingle and shake. The dripping water was slowly coming up the tunnel. Kloemken whispered to me asking whether I was awake and heard the noise. I whispered back that I had a live grenade in my hand and I couldn't find the flashlight to see where to throw it. He said that he had it. I told him to turn it on. As soon as there was light, I threw the grenade down the tunnel.

The grenade went off, and from that moment, everything turned into a Keystone Cops production. Sgt. Nehr bolted upright, striking his head on the rock ceiling, and he collapsed back into his hammock. He was in la-la land for about 10 minutes. Gray jumped up and hit his head. He remained conscious but had a severe headache. We all had temporary deafness.

The four troops in the cave below us did not know what to think. They tried to call us by radio and got no response. I don't think the signal would carry through the rocks but, even if it did, none of us could hear anyhow. The Lieutenant tried to call us. After numerous tries, they went to calling once every half hour. The four troops in the other cave requested to check on us, but the Lieutenant said to stay put and wait until daylight. If we were dead, they did not want other unnecessary casualties.

As soon as daylight arrived, Kloemken and I went down the tunnel with rifles and the flashlight. We did not find a body, but we found bits of meat and clothing. From my understanding, this was reported as two enemies KIA (Killed in Action). We assumed we got one, and the other had dragged the dead or wounded one back into the cavern where they were hiding the day before.

When we came out of the cave to daylight, the other four-man squad was just coming up to our position. By now we could hear again, and we told them what happened. They said they had to put the radio antenna out of the entrance hole to make contact with Platoon Headquarters below. We radioed down that we were okay, and we would explain when we got back. The eight of us made our way down the ridge joking about the previous night's activity. We went to Platoon Headquarters and relayed the event to Lt. Frank. Through the night, everyone had thought we were dead. They were rather excited and happy to see us.

I did not know it at the time, but this was the conclusion of Operation Irving.

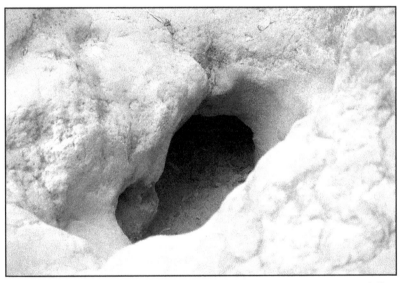

One of many cave entrances in the mountains. Whether natural or excavated, the Viet Cong made effective use of caves and spider holes throughout Vietnam.

A U.S. Army soldier directs a UH-1 helicopter approaching to pick up injured after a paradrop in South Vietnam, October 1966. U.S. Air Force photo, ID 342-AF-100513USAF. Photo courtesy of the National Archives at College Park, Md.

OPERATION THAYER

The morning chopper came and dropped off our breakfast. We ate and waited for it to return to pick up the food canisters. Because we had been constantly in water for such a long time during Operation Irving, many troops developed a type of foot rot. The feet turned white and shriveled, and the constant walking caused them to develop sores. The best cure was to take your shoes off, prop your feet up, and allow the sun to work its healing magic. It usually took about three or four days to get the feet back to normal. The trooper with the worst foot problem was Sgt. Nehr. Nehr stood about 6'4" tall, and he wore a size 16 shoe. Even for his size, his feet were large. They could not find jungle boots large enough for him, so he had to wear his regular combat boots from the world. Combat jungle boots would allow the water to run out through screened holes in the side, just above the sole. His regular boots held the water in, and he constantly had to remove them to pour the water out. Sgt. Nehr and at least three others got onto the breakfast chopper and returned to camp for foot repair.

The rest of us waited and, after an hour or so, a sortie of choppers came in, picked us up, and flew us inland and further north. We were dropped on a small LZ (landing zone) that was no more than a half-acre hump in a valley. We crossed some lowland and came to the base of a very steep ridge. It was almost too steep to climb straight up, so we went up at an angle following an old trail. The hill was empty of trees but had some small brush clumps and many rocks. We began our climb with 1st squad in the lead, followed by 3rd squad, and then 2nd squad.

I believe this was the start of Operation Thayer. I'm not sure how the military came up with the names for operations, but many operations are named after people.

The sun was high, and temps were well above 100 degrees. There was no wind, and it took effort just to breathe. Lt. Frank was near the front of the formation, and Sgt. Inez followed near the rear of the formation. About a hundred feet from the top of the ridge, Lt. Frank stopped and called Sgt. Inez up to him. By now everyone was tired, hot and cranky. The trail was narrow and, when we stopped, we braced our feet against something so there was not so much pressure on the ankles. Inez came trudging up the hill, cussing as he walked. Rich Aby, who stood about 6'2" tall, had red hair and was from North Dakota, was standing on the trail but off to the lower side. As Inez came up to Aby, Inez pushed him aside and down the ridge. As Aby fell, he reached out and grabbed Inez by the shirt, pulling him up and over him. As Inez went over him,Aby gave Inez an extra shove and threw him. This effort stabilized Aby and allowed him to catch his balance, going only a few feet down the ridge. Inez landed about 15 feet below Aby and, with momentum, toppled most of the way down before coming to a stop. He came walking back up the ridge, cussing Aby all the way. As he approached Aby, he told him he was going to have him court-martialed. When he was within arm's reach, Aby let fly a sharp right jab and drove Inez about 40 feet back down the ridge. The next time Inez came up the ridge, he made a wide berth around Aby.

Lt. Frank saw what happened but didn't say a word. I believe he told Capt. Hitti about the incident. Word came back later that, when Sgt. Inez reported the incident to Hitti, Hitti told him to go back to his platoon and behave himself.

150

Before we went over the top of the ridge, we were spread out along a line. As we topped the ridge, all we found was the slant going down the other side of the ridge. The jungle began about halfway down the ridge. I felt a little too much exposed being on an open hill walking down the ridge toward the heavy tree line. We made the tree line without any problems. We again formed a column and began picking our way through the jungle again. About 300 yards into the jungle, we could see an open valley with rice paddies. There were a number of straw huts lined up along the edge of the rice paddies. There were some huts to our right, but most of them were to our left. At the end of the valley, there was a large hamlet. We worked our way through the trees and came down into the first huts. Again, we were checking for Viet Cong and weapons. The locals did not give us their usual cheerful smiles as they had in the past. I had a strong sense they did not trust us, that they did not want us around. This made us more cautious and on-edge.

If one of our goals was to win over their confidence, it was not working in this valley. Of course, we had just come from an operation in which we removed all the locals from their land, burned out their homes, and destroyed all their food. Who would think that would bother these people? (Of course, I am being cynical now.)

We began working our way northward, along the rice paddies, checking every hut and bunker. We did not burn any huts, we did not destroy their rice, nor did we evacuate the people. The hamlet at the head of the valley was even larger than it looked when we first saw it. There were many more huts stacked behind the ones that were visible from the rice paddies. They extended back to the base of the ridge. We made our searches and got the same cold-shoulder treatment. After searching this hamlet, we moved around the head of the valley

151

and down the far side of the valley. There were a few scattered huts there, but they eventually ran out and we found an area at the far end of the valley in which to set up defensively for the night. We were not getting an evening supper chopper this night. We had to settle for C-Rations.

After dark, Lt. Frank sent out a squad to recon the hamlet we just searched. We wanted to know if any VC would come down out of the hills during the night. I was selected to walk point. Ray Judy was put in charge. The two of us, along with four other troops, made our way into the outskirts of the first few huts, moved toward the base of the ridge, and found a cemetery that was surrounded by a hedgerow. We set up behind the hedgerow to watch the hamlet for enemy activity. Since we were inside the hamlet, everyone stayed awake and alert. Nothing happened, so at around 4 a.m. we left the cemetery and worked our way back toward Platoon Headquarters. We found a spot in a heavily brushed-in area, and set up for the rest of the night; we managed to get an hour of sleep. To avoid getting shot by our own men, we waited until after daylight before going back to the platoon.

For breakfast, we had C's again. When we set up the night before, we were located at the far end of the valley away from the hamlet. We were out on the point of a ridge that separated one valley from the next. There was a large jungle-cover ridge that separated the two valleys. We walked around the ridge and into the other valley. Like the others, the basin was covered with rice paddies. There were more huts along the edge of the rice paddies and below the ridge. As in the previous valley, there were more huts concentrated in one area to form the nucleus of the hamlet.

This area of Vietnam was made up of ridges and valleys, with hamlets and hooches at the base of the ridges, and rice paddies in the valley bottoms. These were simple people, farming simple crops to sustain life for themselves. Five hundred years ago they lived like this, and I'll wager 500 years from now they will still be living like this. Who's going to prove me wrong?

We headed out of the valley, up through jungle terrain, over the top and down again. Toward the base of the ridge, the jungle opened up with high grass and fewer trees. We walked through the high grass along the ridge and came to a trail. We were spread out in a skirmish line. The trail led up into the jungle. Just before the edge of the jungle, and in the trail, lay a dead gook. He had been there from the night before last. A Company had sent out an ambush patrol. They set up in the jungle covering that trail. They put a Claymore mine out along the trail, with a trip flare in front of it. The gook was ditty-bopping up the trail and tripped the flare off. He dropped down about six feet in front of the Claymore. He was severely shredded, and most of his head was gone. I believe that Lt. Frank had guided us to this on purpose.

We moved along the ridge to the next valley and started the same routine: search hooches and bunkers, and disrupt simple lives. We stepped up the searches, finishing the entire valley before day's end. We then headed up the next ridge, through the jungle, and came to a clearing just over the peak of the ridge. We set up a perimeter and prepared for the evening meal chopper. Since we had depleted our C's, we got a shit load of C-Rations with our supper. As soon as the chopper took off, we moved down the ridge to the base of the hill along the next valley. We found a good site to set up for the night. There was a hamlet at one end of the valley. As before, we sent out a night squad to recon the hamlet and watch for activity. Nothing changed: I walked point, and Ray Judy was put in charge. We came in the next morning with an empty report. Everybody seemed satisfied with the report, but we could tell the others were getting lackadaisical and letting their guard down. There was more complaining and petty bickering. A little action would have broken this attitude, but no one wanted to see it.

After breakfast C's, we broke camp and began the search again. We made good time going through this valley and one more valley before the end of the day. By 0900 hours, the sun was high enough to make the temperature extremely sultry, always exceeding the 100-degree mark, and sometimes going over 110 degrees. Every day, and sometimes two or three times a day, we would get a heavy rain. As long as we were already wet with sweat, the rain felt good and cooled us off. As soon as the rain ended, the sun would come out and make the humid air hot.

We moved over the next ridge, found an area for platoon perimeter, and sent out another night patrol. You guessed it: again I walked point and Ray Judy led the squad. We set up at the outskirts of the hamlet in a brushed-in area where we watched and listened. Shortly after we set up, we saw some people walking outside one of the huts and then disappear inside. There was some chanting and wailing (that is, crying) coming from inside the hut. From what we could gather, someone had died and this was a burial ritual, similar to a wake back in the world. A little more than an hour later, the ritual broke up, and about 20 people left this hut and returned to other huts. We could not see them clearly, but it did not appear that there were any young men in the gathering.

We made it back to Platoon Headquarters shortly after daylight and made our report. Again, after a breakfast of C's, we searched the huts and hamlet. Just outside the main hamlet, in a cemetery plot, we found a freshly dug, empty grave. The grave was a round circular hole in the ground about 3 feet deep. This confirmed what we had surmised the night before. In the hut where the gathering took place, there was a corpse wrapped and bound in a fetal position. The Vietnamese always buried there dead in a fetal position to use less room for the grave. Someone suggested that we check out the corpse to see if it was a Viet Cong, but this was vetoed. The locals indulged us, for now, but they certainly were not welcoming us. Desecrating their dead would not win us any peace medals. We completed our search of the valley and moved to the next valley. This valley was much smaller and had only about 20 huts located along the one side.

We walked around to the far side of the valley and headed up through the jungle ridge. We found a spot that we could clear in order to get the chopper in and began the work of clearing. After working for awhile, we were told we were not getting a chopper. We would have to eat C's again.

By now my feet were getting very sore and walking was becoming painful. We moved down into the next valley and set up for the night. This valley did not have any rice paddies and there were no hooch structures. We were getting a hot meal again. Along with the meal, we got mail. Powell, a tall black guy, got a package from home. In it were at least 10 cigars. After supper, he lit one up. Sgt. Inez saw the cigar and asked him where it came from. Powell told him, but he said it was no concern of his. Inez took one of Powell's cigars and lit it. He was standing in front of Powell, cigar in his mouth and a shit-eating grin on his face. Powell hit Sgt. Inez in the face with a hard right, driving the cigar halfway down his throat.

Lt. Frank assigned Fernandez to take the night patrol. Even though there were no huts or hamlets, he wanted some assurance that we were alone in the valley. Fernandez came to me and asked me to walk point. I told him I had not had any decent sleep for four days, my feet were killing me, and I would

155

not go. He got a little pissed but didn't push it. I don't know who walk point, but they came back the next morning.

The next morning my feet were so sore I had a hard time walking. I took off my shoes and carried them. Doc looked at my feet and talked to Lt. Frank. Frank took a look at my feet and told me I would be going back with the chow chopper to see the doctor.

The breakfast chopper arrived. Sgt. Nehr and the three soldiers who had left with him four days earlier were also on the chopper. Nehr still had his old combat boots. He took a bunch of shit about having water skis for feet. I asked Nehr how things were going back at Camp Radcliff. He said he hadn't been there. He said they were at a forward base camp called LZ Hammond, about 15 minutes flying time from our present location. He said it was a drag because there was nothing to do but play cards.

Combat boots worn out in service in Vietnam, taken May 23, 1970. U.S. Marine Corps photo, ID 532489. Photo courtesy of the National Archives at College Park, Md.

SORE FEET RETREAT

The chopper flew over a ridge that had artillery guns entrenched near the top, and about 300 meters beyond and below this ridge there was an assortment of about 30 tents. The helipad was a flat area about 150 meters from the first tent and just below the ridge where the artillery was sitting. As soon as the chopper landed and I got off, I could see the medical tent as it was clearly marked with a red cross. I went in and found a medic sitting at a small table, typing. He finished the report he was working on, pulled it out of the typewriter, and then looked at me. He had the look of someone extremely bored. He asked what I needed. I told him about my feet. I still was carrying my shoes. He looked at my feet and said, "You got the rot, too." He took out a small OD-colored jar of salve. He said the Doc ain't back from breakfast yet so I should wait. The walls of the tent were rolled up so the air could flow through. By now, the sun was higher in the sky and giving off its penetrating heat. There were sandbags all around the tent, about three feet high. I crawled up on the sandbags and lay down on top of them. About 10 minutes later, the doctor came in, looked at my feet where I lay, and told the medic to give me the salve. He told me to keep my shoes off and my feet clean, to rub the salve on them once every two hours, and expose them to as much sun as I could take. I don't know if the salve kept them from burning from the sun, or if it had some healing power. I didn't ask either. He told me there was a tent at the far end of the camp that had other soldiers with foot problems. He told me to join them and enjoy a few days out of the field.

The tent was the last one in the group and was on lower ground than the rest of the tents. There were four or five soldiers on the south side of the tent, sitting on sandbags with bare feet. They were all 5/7 Cav soldiers. I knew the faces but not the names, except for Mitzner. He was short, about 5'6" tall, but a rather well-built guy. He said, "Take a seat, there ain't shit to do." There was a large insulated water jug hanging just inside the tent. I took a canteen cup, drew some water, sat down on some sandbags, and poured the water over my feet. I let the feet air-dry and then rubbed some salve on them.

I sat beside Mitzner for about an hour and we talked. He said, "I know you're with 2nd platoon, but I don't know your name." When I told him, he said, "So you're Kunkel?" I asked him why that surprised him. He said, "Man, you've got a reputation among the troops." I told him I wouldn't know why. He said, "You're labeled a killer, and you got balls." He also said, "You're like a cat, you can see in the night." I told him I had only shot one gook, and it happened to be a woman. He asked, "What about the gooks in the cave?" I said, "Oh, I guess I never thought about them." I told him I think I only got one. He said, "That ain't what I heard. You killed the first Cong and blew up two others." I told him I never thought much of it, but secretly I liked his assessment of me.

After sitting there for about an hour, I decided to make my seat more comfortable. I took some of the sandbags around the tent and made a makeshift easy chair that I could lay back in. It took at least 15 sandbags. I set the chair up in front of the hole I made in the wall, but this still left a hole. Within a few minutes, a Sergeant came by and gave me hell for taking the sandbags off the wall. I told him to get me some more sandbags and I would replace the wall. I also told him that, as long as

I had to sit here, I was going to make myself comfortable. He said he would send someone down with some bags and a shovel. He pointed to a pile of gravel and told me to use that. He said he didn't want any holes in the ground.

An hour later, a mule driven by a PFC arrived with 100 bags and a shovel. A mule is a motorized cart about four feet wide and eight feet long. The motor is underneath the carriage, and the only seat is in the left front for the driver. It has a low- and high-speed transmission, a gas pedal, a brake, and a steering wheel with a shift lever on the column. There is a six-inch high metal bar running all around the bed to hold or keep the freight from sliding off. They are used in base camps to haul supplies around, and to and from the helipad. Before setting up this LZ, the engineers had leveled off the ground for the tents and built trails running through the camp and to the helipad. They also pushed up piles of gravel in various locations for filling sandbags. I filled about 20 sandbags and carried them over to the tent. I filled in the hole I had made and then used a few more bags to make my chair even more comfortable. Mitzner told me I did too much work for the short while I would be there.

Right after I finished with the sandbags, there was a call for lunch. A large tent made up the kitchen and mess hall. We walked barefoot to the mess hall and got a tray of food. I'm not sure what we ate but, when back in camp, lunch frequently was bologna or other cold cuts with bread. Iced tea, or most times not-so-iced tea, was a favorite drink. We could sit inside to eat or find a place outside. We ate outside that day. When lunch was finished, we went back to our tent. Mitzner tried out my chair, and told me I did such a good job I should build him one. I pointed to the sandbags and the shovel and told him he saw how it was done. He filled about four sandbags and threw them in place for his own chair and sat down. He sat for a few minutes then readjusted the sandbags. He squirmed around a little more then went back to the sand pile to fill some more sandbags. By now, one of the other guys was filling sandbags to make himself a chair. As soon as he laid the shovel down, Mitzner took it and filled a few more sandbags.

I washed my feet and rubbed some more salve on them. About mid-afternoon, someone brought out a deck of cards. Mitzner and I and two guys from C Company played a couple of games of 500 Rummy. We had to keep score on the ground since we didn't have any paper. Nobody really gave a shit whether they won or lost; we were content just having something to do. After a while, this got boring also so I went back to sitting and watching the sky.

At about 1630 (4:30 p.m.) some mules went up to the mess tent to pick up the evening meal for the field troops. It took about 40 minutes to transfer the food and other supplies to the choppers and send them out. Most of the chopper pilots were Warrant Officers. As a rule, they didn't act as high-handed as the regular officers. They had no problem bullshitting with the enlisted men, and often times preferred them to the regular officers.

Once the choppers were loaded and gone, the evening meal – supper or dinner, however you want to have it – was ready for those in camp. When in Vietnam, field soldiers always had preference over rear-echelon soldiers. The mess hall closed at around 1830 hours, so we had about an hour and 20 minutes to eat. The food was not extravagant, but the cooks did a good job preparing it and giving us as much variety as possible.

At about 1900 hours the sun began its disappearance over the western horizon. By 2000 hours, it was dark. I took my poncho and covered my easy chair to make sure it didn't

160

get wet if it rained during the night. We didn't have any rain during the day, so I figured it surely would rain during the night. Mitzner was told he would be flying out with the morning choppers, so he had to have all his gear and be ready on the helipad by 0700 hours.

I had not had one good night's sleep since we got to 'Nam. I figured my body was ready to sleep all night. I crawled under my mosquito netting at about 2000 hours and was just dozing off when the artillery guns opened up just above us. They fired six rounds and then it was quiet. A short while later, they fired six more rounds. This went on all night. This is called H&R fire (Harassment and Repel). When the field troops set up for the night, the Company Commander selects predestined areas about 400 meters outside their perimeter for the artillery to shell throughout the night. They will usually select two or three areas for the H&R around each company field headquarters. If night patrols go out, they had to move beyond the area of the H&R fire. The artillery alternates which sector to fire at, so the enemy cannot gauge where it will come next. The goal is to dissuade the gooks from congregating to plan an attack on the company. Since the guns support more than one company, they are firing ammunition frequently. About an hour after hitting the sack, my mind adjusted to the firing and I fell asleep.

Soon I was walking through the jungle, with jungle vines getting thicker until I had them wrapped all around me. I was caught in them and was fighting to get free. I woke up with my head caught in the mosquito netting. I pulled the netting away and sat there, all tensed up. Everyone else seemed to be sleeping. I sat there for about five minutes and the artillery sounded off again. I lay back on the bunk but could not sleep. When the guns were not firing, I could hear the sound of the generator running. There was the sound of mosquitoes and other bugs. The night seemed alive with sounds, yet it was relatively quiet until the guns sounded again. I thought about home and tried to picture what was going on. This was October. They were probably picking corn. These thoughts were making me homesick, so I put them out of my mind.

I decided to say some prayers, so I started a Rosary. I don't remember getting to the first Mystery before my mind was full of other thoughts. I started the Rosary again. And again my mind was diverted to other things. I gave up on the Rosary and said an Act of Contrition. I don't remember finishing it. I finally said a short prayer that was not in the books; it came from within me. This one I finished. I asked God to accept it.

I lay there wondering if I would ever see home again. I didn't like these thoughts, so I tried to put them out of my mind. I wondered who was out on night patrol from our platoon, and who was walking point. I thought about the wake we witnessed a few nights earlier. Getting out of the field took away that intense caution. I had too much time to think about things that I wouldn't think about if I were still in the field. I must have lay there close to four hours before I fell asleep again.

I didn't sleep very soundly and, as soon as the sounds of morning came, I was awake. I got up, walked to the piss tubes and took a leak. When I came back, Mitzner was getting his shit together to go out to the field. I thought of the Derringer pistol I had in my pack and thought I might do some target shooting later in the day. I only had about six cartridges for it. The chopper pilots carry .357-cal. Model 29 Smith & Wesson revolvers. They fire .38-cal. ammunition. I walked up to the helipad to wait for the pilots to show up. The crew chief and a door gunner were already at the chopper. I told them about my pistol and asked if the pilots had any extra ammo they did not need. He told me they usually do, but I would have to ask them. Two pilots came up and the crew chief told them of my problem, if we can call it a problem. One of the pilots

162

reached into the chopper, took out two boxes, 50 rounds each, of ammunition and gave them to me. He said he gets all the ammunition he wants, so I could have these. I thanked him and stood around watching the routine. Ten minutes later, the first mule came up carrying breakfast chow. He loaded the chow onto the choppers, and they took off. I hooked a ride on the mule back to the kitchen. Mitzner was waiting to ride up to the pad with the next mule. I said my goodbye and told him not to stop any bullets.

By now it was obvious, I was not going to sit around all day in the sun. I did not put the salve on as often as I should have, but I did walk around barefooted. I went back to the tent and washed my feet. I rubbed in some salve and waited for it to dry. After breakfast, I asked one of the cooks for some tin cans for target practice. He gave me as many as I could carry.

I walked out behind the tent we used as our sleeping quarters and set two tin cans up on a bank. I paced off 15 steps, about 45 feet, loaded the revolver, and fired at one of the cans. I missed it. I fired the second shot and missed again. I walked about 20 feet closer and fired again. This time I hit the top of the can. A couple of guys from C Company came back from breakfast and came to watch. I let them fire some rounds. The Sergeant I talked to about the sandbags the day before came down to see what the shooting was about. He apparently was responsible for overseeing that the camp was kept in order and that chores were tended to. I told him it was too boring to sit around so I was doing some shooting. This didn't seem to bother him, but he told me that, if I wanted something to do, he needed some sandbags filled. I told him that, if he got me the bags, I would fill them. One of the guys from C Company told him to get us another shovel. After Sarge left, we continued to fire the pistol, shooting up one whole box of shells.

About 20 minutes later, a black PFC came down with a mule. He had 200 bags and an extra shovel. No one worked really fast, but we worked fairly steady.

About mid-morning two soldiers from B Company and one from C Company came down with their bare, sore feet. They weren't bored enough yet, so they were content to sit in the sun and watch us fill sandbags.

By noon, we had most of the sandbags filled and stacked in two piles. It was lunch time so we went up to the mess tent for lunch. We took our tray of food outside, and Sarge came by on his way to lunch. He asked how we were doing on the sandbags. I told him they were almost all filled, and the pile of gravel was almost gone. He said he had more bags and more gravel. One of the guys from C Company told him that, as long as he didn't push us, we can fill sandbags. When I first met Sarge, he had that "I'm in charge, asshole" attitude. Now he was just one of the guys, and he actually had a sense of humor.

After lunch, we sat around and bull-shitted. We passed jibes back and forth and played Monday morning quarterback with how the Army was running the war. I always thought that, if we had to fight the North Vietnamese, why didn't we take the war to them. There was always talk about the 17th parallel dividing North Vietnam from South Vietnam. If we attacked North Vietnam and even Hanoi, Ho Chi Minh would have to pull his soldiers back home to defend their country and that would leave just the Viet Cong Rebels in the south. From our experience in Operation Irving, which we had just completed, the Cong were not a formidable force. Without the North to back their play, they would probably quit.

The PFC came down on the mule with 200 more bags. He dumped them off at the gravel pile and started to load the filled sandbags onto the mule. Two other guys and I went over to help him. As we were loading and bull-shitting, he told us, "Man, you know, the more you guys work, the more I have to work."

That afternoon we took our time filling sandbags. We decided to work a half hour then sit for half an hour. One of the new guys had a bellyful of sitting around, so he decided to help. Three more times the PFC came back and got a load of filled sandbags. We could get about 40 sandbags on the mule. We told him to take a break and we loaded the mule for him. I asked him if he had any help unloading the sandbags. He said, "Yeah. I get them the sandbags, and there are two other guys who have to stack them."

When night came, the artillery started again. We sat around and bull-shitted until dark, and then crawled under our mosquito nets. I slept a little better but woke up almost every two hours. I was more relaxed than I was the night before. Morning came. I was the first one up. I went to the piss tube, came back, poured some water in my helmet, washed my face and got out my razor to shave. We did not have a regular bathroom structure, so we used our steel pot for a sink. I could go about three or four days between shaves. I didn't have the rough facial hair that a lot of guys had. I washed my feet and rubbed the salve on, and waited for breakfast. Shortly after the choppers took off, we could go up for breakfast.

My feet seemed to be healing fairly well. I was getting anxious to get back in the field. I would wash and rub the salve on them five or six times a day. As long as they were bare, walking around on them didn't seem to harm them. Since I came out of the field, I believe it only rained a couple of times. We still had the heat, but it didn't bother us as much as it did at first.

The rest of the day went about like the day before, except we slowed down our sandbag filling even more. We had just about depleted another pile of gravel. About mid-afternoon I went up to the medic tent to let the doctor look at my feet. He said I could go back out to the field if I wanted to the next day. He also said that, if I wanted another day in camp, he would authorize it. I decided to go back to the field. I had gotten pretty close to some of the guys, and I wanted to get back to them. Besides, even filling sandbags had become boring.

Vietnam-era military-issue jungle boots.

RETREAT IS OVER

The next morning I was waiting at the helipad and jumped on the chopper going to B Company. We dropped chow off at 3rd platoon which also had Company Headquarters, then 2nd platoon where I got off before the chopper moved on to 1st platoon. I was happy to see the guys. Nothing much had happened while I was gone. They were still searching hamlets, huts, and bunkers. The locals were still apprehensive if not unfriendly.

After breakfast, the chopper came back to pick up the food canisters, and we saddled up and took off. The area did not have the big rice-paddy valleys now. There was more high ground, and the rice paddies were smaller. There was a series of hamlets surrounded by rice paddies. Usually, around each hamlet, there was a deep ditch that carried water for irrigation. There were more trees in and around the hamlets. This meant more cover for the enemy, if they were present. We had to spread out and walk through the rice paddies from hamlet to hamlet. Usually, there was one large dike that connected the hamlets; this was used for transportation, mainly walking. As we were walking through a rice paddy, the sole of one of Sgt. Nehr's boots came off. The rest of the shoe rode up his leg a few inches. He said he was waiting for that to happen. The sole on the other shoe was ready to come off, too; he tore it off. When we came out of the rice paddy, he took off his shoes and walked around barefoot the rest of the day.

We didn't come across any gooks that day but, according to our interpreter, they were around; they just didn't choose to come out and fight yet. When evening came, Lt. Frank chose to set up camp in a hamlet. It was an island-type hamlet, surrounded by rice paddies. We did not dig in but arranged positions behind trees and banks. The interpreter instructed the locals to stay in their huts and told them that, if anyone came outside during the night, they risked being shot. When the choppers dropped off our chow that evening, they had to hover over the rice paddies until we got the canisters unloaded. Sgt. Nehr got on board and went back to camp.

After chow, Lt. Frank directed Ray Judy to take out a night ambush patrol. I was asked to take point. We were to go out about one klick (1000 meters) from camp, along the dike trail connecting the hamlets, and set up an ambush site. We walked into and through the next hamlet. No one was moving around, and it seemed that all locals had bedded down for the night. We did not want to set up on the dike in the middle of the paddies without good cover. So, on the far side of the hamlet, we picked a spot that would cover the trail. We set up two Claymores, one out about 60 meters and the other about 90 meters out, and wired a trip flare between them. The flares were set one on each side of the trail and covered with some grass. If gooks came up the trail, the first ones should trip the flare about four meters from the Claymore. The last ones, if it were only a squad, would be within killing distance of the second Claymore. If there was more than a squad, we would set off the Claymores, give them everything we had for a minute, and then get the hell out of there. We figured we could be half-way back to camp before they could pull it together. Our luck held out and no one came through that night.

In the morning, we ate breakfast and loaded onto choppers to fly to another area. We flew over some dense jungle and landed on a small hill that had a heavy tree line on one side that was about 100 meters from the landing zone. We were told that we were going into a hot landing. A hot landing is one that most likely will have gooks shooting at us when we come in. We were going to be the first sortie flying in. (A sortie is a group of helicopters transporting soldiers into the landing zone.) Once down, we would set up security for the remaining sorties. I never liked the idea of getting shot at while in the chopper. You're too big and an easy target, and there is damn little you can do about it until you're out of the chopper and on the ground. As the choppers came down, we could see muzzle blasts coming out of a tree line. The doors were open so the door gunners could fire. I was sitting on the right side of the chopper closest to the door, facing the chopper tail. I tried to shrink back into the seat, to make myself a smaller target. I probably gained only an inch of safety, but mentally it made me feel I was doing something to keep from getting shot. Just before our arrival, artillery softened the LZ with a barrage of artillery rounds. The LZ had smoke rising off the ground from the artillery rounds. The choppers were not going to land. They were going to strafe along the ground and we were to jump out of them on the move. When the chopper was still six feet off the ground, someone yelled, "Hit it!" I jumped out, did a half-roll, scrambled away from the landing area about 5 meters, dropped to the ground, and began firing at the tree line.

There were six choppers that came in at the same time and, within a few seconds, they were all on their way out. The door gunners continued to fire at the tree line until they were well out of range. Lt. Frank told us to move out about 25 meters, take up position, and be ready to return fire when the next sortie arrived. To move a whole company, it usually took two or three sorties, depending on how many choppers were in each sortie and how many soldiers were in the company. We could usually get 10 soldiers onto one chopper.

When we arrived in Vietnam, there were 182 soldiers in B Company. This is considered strack because every position was filled. With the scammers figuring a way to get out of the field, and with injuries and other problems, we were now a company of about 140 soldiers.

The next sortie came in and the door gunners opened up on the tree line again. We also fired rounds into the tree line. No one fired back. They were either gone, or they were keeping their heads down.

Once the whole company was on the ground, we spread out and made our way toward the tree line where the firing had come from. We searched the tree line looking for dead or wounded gooks, or possible weapons or ammunition. We found empty cartridges and nothing else. Knowing how things went, I am sure the enemy body count was 10 or more.

We broke into platoons and were assigned areas of operation. We worked our way down the sloping terrain along the tree line and into a valley. It was a small valley surrounded by jungle. It had the usual small rice paddies, and small, heavily wooded hamlets. The area was labeled unfriendly. The people were either Viet Cong or those sympathetic to them. Our mission was to search and destroy. We were to go into the hamlets, clear them, search them, burn them, and destroy the rice or any other food.

We spread out and approached the first hamlet through some rice paddies. Everyone was waiting for the shit to hit the fan. Nothing happened. The hamlet was empty. No one was around. There were still dishes on the tables in the huts, and there was a fire in an old open, rock-made stove. It looked as if someone was making a slatted bamboo mat, which was partially completed. It appeared that, just before our arrival, everyone in the hamlet took off, leaving everything as-is. This was the first time this had ever happened to us, and it was mystifying. After all, we were supposed to be the good guys.

The hamlet was divided into two portions with a canal between them. 2nd platoon was clearing hamlets on one side of the irrigation ditch, and 1st platoon was doing the same on the other side of this ditch. As we watched the huts burn, a loud explosion came from the next hamlet. Everyone dropped down and found something to get behind. No one fired, and nothing else exploded. Lt. Frank called on the radio to see what happened. 1st platoon had an injured soldier and needed a medevac. He also said there must have been a mine in one of the huts that went off when it was burned. I believe the injured soldier was Reiser. He was assigned to carry a LAW (Light Anti-tank Weapon). He didn't have the LAW on him. Reiser was hit in the groin area, and he was still conscious and talking. Some of our platoon crossed the canal to 1st platoon's location. He said he laid the LAW on a table and he was going back to see if he could retrieve it when the explosion came. As near as could be figured, it was the LAW that exploded and sent a round into his groin. Doc, the medic, gave him a double-dose morphine shot. Reiser was laid out on his poncho, and we waited for the medevac. By now the morphine was doing its work and Reiser started laughing. He gave us some shit about us being stuck in 'Nam while he was going home. He was still in good spirits when he was loaded on the chopper.

1st and 2nd platoons parted ways again, with each platoon taking a different valley to search. The valley we were searching had a trail that separated rice paddies on each side of it. The valley was only about 120 meters wide with heavy jungle cover going up into the hills on each side. We stayed off the trail for fear it may have been mined. The platoon was divided in half, and each half walked along each side of the valley in the jungle, making sure that we did not walk into an ambush. When we came to the next village, there were two old ladies and an old man in it. Since one side of it lay along and below the jungle ridge, half the squad spread out searching the jungle so we did not get a surprise attack. Again, we searched and destroyed the huts except for one, which we left for the old locals. The trail led off on a near 90-degree angle, toward another part of the hamlet. There was an old metal gate with a fence on both sides, it led to a trail out and along the rice paddies. Before opening the gate, Gray looked it over to check for booby traps. There was an old cylinder-type Chinese grenade tied up to the fence with a pressure switch. As soon as someone opened the gate, the pressure switch would flip open and set it off. Since we had never seen one like this before, we left it alone and cut a wide berth around it.

We again spread out into the rice paddies and walked toward the rest of the hamlet about 150 meters away. The trail split as we came to the hooches. Right at the "T" in the trail, there was an old wood-framed signpost, with an old slate board, similar to the old chalkboards we had in school. The slate board was about two feet wide and four feet high. Someone had written on the board, "Yankee Number 10," and "Yankee go home." As we were looking at the board, Gray said, "I'm not a Yankee; I'm still an old Dodger fan." (Tom Gray was from a suburb close to New York City.) This village was completely empty. We did our search-and-destroy and moved on. This was a narrow valley that S-curved between some heavily wooded ridges. When we moved past this end of the hamlet, the ground gradually dropped into a larger and wider river-bottom valley.

We moved out of this valley and into the next. There was a large hamlet off to the right. We were to meet up with

172

the rest of the company in this hamlet. There was a series of these narrow valleys with ridges on both sides, leading to the bigger river bottom. 1st and 3rd platoons each had a similar route to cover. We had the shorter route and arrived first.

We came to a hamlet ahead of the rest of the company. As we came up to the hamlet, we could see people moving around in a manner unlike what we were accustomed to. This tipped us off that things were not right. We did a quick search. Murgatroyd was walking along the edge of the hamlet. A channel ran around the hamlet, separating the hamlet from the rice paddies. There was a bank on the far side of the channel.

He saw someone swimming underwater in the channel. He followed the figure along until it surfaced about 15 feet from him. He shot and hit a gook in the middle of the back, in the spine. The gook clawed up at the grass along the bank and just lay there, his head and shoulders out of the water. He was frozen in position. The gook was bare-back. He had a large hole in his back where the slug had struck him. Murgatroyd carried an M79 grenade launcher. When a round is fired, it has

Tom Gray.

to travel at least 60 feet before the grenade is armed to explode. The round spirals as it leaves the gun; the spiraling arms it. When the slug tore into the gook, it had not made enough spirals. This was bad for the gook but good for Murgatroyd. If the round had exploded, Murgatroyd was close enough to have been injured or even killed by the explosion.

Capt. Hitti and the rest of the company met us. He had planned to set up the CP in this hamlet but changed his mind. He did not want to take a chance on a dead gook exploding on us during the night. We moved out of this hamlet to the next one. We searched it and set up security positions. It would be more than an hour before the chow chopper would arrive. Capt. Hitti said to relax, but he wanted the positions

Capt. John Hitti during a search-and-destroy mission.

174

maintained, and one person in every-other position alert and watching. This was a chance to get some rays (a catnap).

At about 1700 hours the chow chopper came in. We ate in the order Capt. Hitti established. Half the soldiers from 3rd platoon lined up for chow. There are two people in each position. One from each position lined up for chow. When a person returned to his position, his partner would line up, repeating until the whole platoon was done. The line-up was called in reverse order, with 3rd, then 2nd, and 1st platoon eating last. Usually, three or four soldiers are selected to serve the chow. The servers were the last to get their food, but the officers always ate last, after the servers served themselves. Capt. Hitti always was the last person to eat. When in combat, that's the military code of ethics.

The next day we swept through the valley, 2nd platoon covering all the villages and huts on one side of the river and 1st and 3rd platoons covering the villages and huts on the other side. When we got to the far end, 1st platoon had to cross the river. The river widened out a little, and there was an old wood-rail fence coming down into the river from the far side. There was a sandbar extending from our side toward the fence. I was walking point. I walked out onto the sandbar and off the sandbar into the river. The water was about calf-high on my legs, and murky. I took another step and disappeared under the water. I thrashed and fought like hell to come back up. I was in a current that pulled me down river. I finally came to the surface, made my way up on the far bank, and crawled out. I kept my gear. The rest of the platoon had to walk up the river about 100 meters before they found a safer place to cross.

From this valley, we headed up the ridge into the jungle. We spread out about 3 meters apart and began sweeping the ridge and jungle terrain back along the valley. We walked about a mile through some heavily tangled jungle growth, and gradually the heavy trees gave way to high grass and fewer trees. The ridge came down to a point, and close to the point we flushed up about a thousand parrots. They seemed as thick as blackbirds in a cattail swamp in Minnesota in the fall. They were a very bright green, and many had plumes on their head. The parrots were near the point of the ridge and, when they flushed, they circled around behind us and back to their trees. Apparently, this was a nesting area for the parrots.

When Manning came to Vietnam he had fewer than 90 days left in the service. He was now a short-timer, with only a week or so left before he went back to the world. He was scared and always serious. He was afraid something would happen before his DEROS (Date Eligible Return from Overseas). This did not stop him from giving everybody shit about his being a short-timer. After about five weeks in Vietnam, he was promoted to an E-5, or Buck Sergeant. When he got the promo-tion, he tried to throw his weight around a little more. Since he was my partner, he tried to order me around. I would have none of it. I told him he was the same person who came over on the ship and, if he's lucky, he'll be the same person going home. Since Manning was such a small person, he naturally developed that small-person or Napoleon syndrome. While he took himself seriously, no one else did.

From the point where we saw the parrots, 1st platoon was sent up the valley beyond the ridge. This valley was higher ground that was not usable for rice paddies, so there were no villages or huts in it. There were no clouds in the sky and, to my recollection, it was the hottest day we had for the year I was stationed there. We were told it hit over 130 degrees. It felt all of that. We walked about a mile and sat down to take a breather. I tried to lay down in the grass, but the sun seemed as if it was baking me. We had no shade. After about 10 minutes, we decided it would be better to walk than to sit. At least we had a little air movement around us while walking. About two miles up the valley, we crossed over to a higher ridge. The ridge was sparsely covered with trees and more high grass. We walked this back and located a depression about 200 meters across. The depression was about 10 feet deep. We were standing on the edge of the depression and spotted a company of ARVNs (South Vietnamese soldiers) another 100 meters beyond the depression. For some reason, they began shooting at us. The bullets were popping over our heads. A few guys fired back, but most of us dropped down the ridge into the depression. Lt. Frank got on the radio and, through Company Headquarters, got word to them that we were friendlies. The shooting stopped and they departed.

We had to crawl out of the depression. The bank was steep. I was going up and Manning told me to give him a hand. I had to go back down and hoist him up so he could crawl over the bank. We walked about another two miles through some old, dried-up rice paddies. There were places where the ground was lower and muddy. The mud built up on our feet. We made it across the old rice paddies and had to crawl up a bank at the edge of the paddies. As I was crawling up, Manning grabbed hold on my rucksack to help himself. (A rucksack is a shoulder pack to hold your personal supplies.) He pulled me back down and he went with me. I spun around on him and gave him a shot with the butt of my rifle. I hit him in the chest and it knocked the air out of him. I asked him what the hell he was doing? When he caught his breath, he said, "I'm just a little guy and I need help." I told him, "I've been pulling your weight since we were stuck together, and for the few days we have left you're going to have to pull your own weight." Once we got up the bank and into position, Lt. Frank came over and talked with us. He said he didn't want us hurting or killing each other, and he would separate us if it were necessary. I

told Frank that I could live with Manning for a few more days.
I also told him that with heat and the long walk, fuses get a
little short. Manning was okay with this.

Lt. Frank told us that the Brigade Commander was
coming out to visit the company. He wanted us to make our
positions invisible from the ground and air. We built our
positions in brush and broke off more brush and added it to
each position. When the Brigade Commander came out, he
first dropped into Company Headquarters. After talking with
headquarters and 1st and 3rd platoons, he had the chopper
come to our position. They flew over us about three times
and then radioed to throw smoke so they could identify our

A "Purple Haze" smoke grenade identifies the landing zone for a UH-1D helicopter
carrying the brigade commander of the 101st Airborne Brigade during "Operation
Cook" in the mountains of Quang Ngai Province. The brigade commander was
making a visit to receive a briefing from the commander of the 2nd Battalion,
502nd Infantry, September 6, 1967. U.S. Army photo. NARA 111-CCV-349-
CC43096. Photo courtesy of the National Archives at College Park, Md.

position. Greek (nickname) threw a yellow smoke grenade out into the rice paddy. When they identified yellow smoke, Lt. Frank called them in.

Whenever a chopper is coming in, the pilot requests the ground force to throw smoke. Once they identify the color, it is safe to call them in. Prior to our time, some choppers were blown out of the air when the ground forces threw smoke and called the color for identification. As soon as the gooks heard the color they threw the same color and the chopper would come into the gook position. The Brigade Commander walked around our positions admiring the camouflage job we did. He gave a pep talk and then went on his way. We were already set up for the night, so we stayed where we were. Lt. Frank sent out one listening post, about 200 meters up the ridge from the platoon's position. This was to give us advanced warning if the enemy attacked from the heavily wooded ridge, the most obvious location for such an attack. Other than the normal night sounds and the sounds of distant artillery, the night was quiet and uneventful.

The next morning, Sgt. Nehr arrived, with his brand-new jungle boots, along with the breakfast chopper. Apparently with Capt. Hitti's call to battalion, and battalion's call up the line, got some action on locating size-16 jungle boots. A pair was located at Cam Ranh Bay, and it was flown in with the first supply mission north. I believe they got at least two pairs of size-16 boots. Under the conditions, boots did not last forever.

Besides Sgt. Nehr, a priest came out with the breakfast chopper. I don't remember what the occasion was, but we had a priest to say Mass. He was on a tight schedule since he had to catch the ride back with empty breakfast containers. He held a quick Examination of Conscience prayer, gave General Absolution, and went right into the Mass. We ate breakfast as he prepared and began the Mass. He was distributing communion when the first sortie came in. 2nd platoon was going out on the first sortie. I took communion and grabbed my gear then headed for the pickup zone. There were a number of us in the same situation. I guess the war would not wait for a full Mass.

Much of the terrain in Vietnam is hazardous on its own, but the Viet Cong built booby traps using whatever materials were at hand. Punji sticks, trip wires, and repurposed Chinese or American mines and other weapons.

ARRIVING TOO EARLY

We were told to expect another hot LZ. We landed on an open ridge next to a higher jungle ridge. The door gunners opened fire on the tree line as we came in for the drop. Again we were out of the choppers on the move and they were quickly airborne, circling away from the jungle. We moved out and set up a defense line between the jungle and the drop zone and waited for the next sortie of choppers to bring in the rest of the company. When the whole company was on the ground, we lined up in a skirmish line and moved into the jungle. The jungle was heavily foliated. You could hardly see through the brush and vines, much less walk through it. You could easily lose sight of the man next to you. It was impossible to hold the skirmish line. Capt. Hitti directed everyone to form a column. 1st platoon took the lead. There was a trail that we followed. Someone else was walking point, and this suited me just fine. The trail ran out so we had to break one. The lead person had to use a machete to hack and cut the undergrowth vegetation. Three or four men would alternate on point when cutting a path through the jungle. When one would get tired, another would take his place. Movement was slow. It would take three hours to move a klick (1000 meters). It took the company about three hours to move to the very top of the ridge. Capt. Hitti had everybody spread out, and we took a long break.

Going down the hill went a little faster. About mid-afternoon, the ridge began to level off and we could make out more light penetrating the tree line ahead. We were coming into a valley. I was on point and we no longer had to cut a path. We came down to the rise above some rice paddies. There was a small hamlet about 80 yards out into the paddies. Two gooks carrying rifles and their ammo bag broke out of the hamlet and went running across the rice paddies away from us toward another hamlet about 200 meters on the far side of the valley. I opened fire, and three or four guys behind me opened up. The rear gook went down. The other one was about halfway between the two hamlets when he stumbled, nearly going down, but he recovered and made it the rest of the way. It was obvious that he was hit. We were cussing our luck or, more likely, our stupidity for shooting too fast and not taking a better aim.

Capt. Hitti called the machine guns up and had them set up on the edge of the tree line. He spread out the rest of the company in flank coverage and then sent a squad from 1st platoon out to check the hamlet. Once they gave a clear sign, Hitti had the squads he put out on flank watch the back trail while the rest of the company moved into the rice paddies and converged on the hamlet. The gook who fell was dead. We dragged him back to the hamlet and put him in a sitting position up against a tree. We burned the huts and moved to the next hamlet.

We came down in the upper part of a large valley. We were in a dogleg off to the south side. There was a fairly large river meandering through the valley. It came out of a deep ravine between two steep-pitched mountains to the west. 2nd platoon took the far side of the valley. We had to cross the river. When crossing a river this wide, we set up at least one machine gun and two posts about 30 meters out from the machine gun. As each man crossed the river, they spread out in defensive positions on the far side. This was a search-and-destroy mission. As we checked out the huts and hamlets, we burned them as we went. There were only a few civilians, and we would leave one hut in each hamlet for them.

Lt. Frank selected a hamlet to set up camp. It was on slightly higher ground and had clear land on the backside and rice paddies on the front side. Instead of two-man positions, we set up in three-man positions. This meant a little more sleep than normal. I teamed up with Ray Judy and Tom Gray. Manning would be leaving the next day; Lt. Frank told him he would spend the night at Platoon Headquarters. Manning gave me his watch and told me to keep it. He said I would need it more than he would from now on. He and I had not talked much to each other since I gave him the butt of my M16. I took this as a sign that everything was cool. We didn't get a chow chopper, so we had C-Rations for supper. Judy, Gray and I had strung together two ponchos tied down on the sides, with a three-foot peak in the middle, which we tied front and back. We were on a bank facing the rice paddies. We found a chunk of log and some rocks. We built a wall with the log and rocks, and we dug some dirt to mix in with them. We were in Vietnam for two months and still had not been attacked during the night. Other than some sniping, we had not been attacked at all. It wasn't that there weren't any gooks; they just chose not to mess with us up to this point.

As soon as dark came, so did the rain. It poured all night long. Those who built a good position stayed dry. Those who didn't put effort into it got wet. Judy, Gray and I were dry. The rain stopped just before daylight.

The next morning, Capt. Hitti summoned Lt. Frank to come across the valley to his position. We broke camp early and headed out. The river was at least twice as wide as the day before and the current was fast. We found a spot that normally should have been safe to cross, but as soon as the point man got waist deep, he lost his footing with the force of the current.

He was swept downstream about 30 meters before he got back to water shallow enough to let him get back out.

Lt. Frank decided to form a human chain to cross the river. We slung our rifles and locked wrists, feeding the human chain out into the current. As soon as the first man got waist deep he would lose footing. The second person would hold him until he lost footing. By the time the third person was floating, the fourth person had the weight of three men loaded with their gear and a heavy current pulling on him. This was not going to work, but Lt. Frank insisted we keep feeding it out. Manning was just in the water by a few feet. I was out beyond him. Manning was very small and probably didn't weigh more than a hundred pounds. He released his grip and the line beyond him collapsed, sending the last three soldiers downstream. They all went under water. The first man came up about 30 meters down and got control. The other two were out in the current further and they got swept further downstream. It seemed like an eternity before the first head popped up without his helmet and gear. He managed to make it back to shallow water. We were all thinking the other guy didn't make until we saw him pop up further downstream. This was Heronema. He was well over 100 meters from us, and he chose to float downstream at least another 100 meters before he started swimming toward the bank. He was from California, spent a lot of time on the beaches, and was a good swimmer.

Sgt. Nehr said he would tie a rope around his waist and swim across using the current to get him to the far side. There was a bend in the river and the current was strongest on the far side. He went above the bend about 100 meters and tied a 200-foot rope around his waist. Benedetti and Kloemken went with him. As Nehr swam out, the current started sweeping him downstream. Benedetti and Kloemken followed him down the river's edge, feeding him rope as he swam. When he got to the bend in the river, the current swept him to the far side. He stayed there next to the bank until the river straightened out, and the current shifted back to the middle of the river. He crawled out and tied the rope around a tree. The rope was tied off on the near side to another tree. One by one we crossed the river. The last person untied the rope from the tree, tied it around his chest, and he was pulled across.

Breakfast was waiting when we arrived at Company Headquarters. We ate in a hurry and were told that we were moving to another area. The chopper came back to pick up the chow canisters, and Manning was leaving with it. We were saying our goodbyes, and he broke down and cried.

An hour later, eight choppers came in to pick up at least half the Company. Another 30 minutes later they came back to pick up the rest of us. 2nd platoon went out with the second flight. We were dropped on an open hill about 400 meters from a heavily walled jungle. We had to go down a ravine and then up a steep incline to get to the jungle. We were walking in a column with flank squads out 100 meters on each side. When we reached the edge of the jungle, Capt. Hitti directed a perimeter be set up. He called the platoon leaders (Lieutenants) and platoon Sergeants together. He said he wanted 2nd platoon in the lead and wanted me to walk point. He told the platoon leaders that we were looking for a company of NVA (North Vietnamese Army) in the area, and we should expect to make contact.

Capt. Hitti set the direction and I took off. He wanted the second person to keep contact, but he wanted me as far out front as I could be to still maintain contact. In some spots, three meters seemed too far, and in other spots, 25 meters didn't seem far enough. I didn't like being separated by too far a distance so, when we could see, I stayed about 20 meters out front. As a rule, Capt. Hitti walked in the middle of the 1st platoon formation. For this mission, he was about fifth in line. He placed Lt. Frank in the back of 2nd platoon. Shortly after we got into the jungle, we got one of those 20-minute downpours. It dumped about an inch of water and then stopped. The sun came out as fast as it disappeared. The temperature was well over 100 degrees. Since we were in the jungle, the rain didn't penetrate too much. However, after the rain stopped the dripping continued for another hour. We were always wet, either from sweat or rain. We adapted to the conditions.

The jungle terrain went up for about 1000 meters (one klick) and then started a gradual decline. About 200 meters from the peak, the terrain almost fell away. As I went down, I would slide into trees to stop myself from going too fast. The rest of the company followed suit. The slide-and-stop routine worked fairly well as long as you did not take too big a chunk of the hill at any one time. As we were coming down, there were times I could see open terrain through the trees. The trees were not as thick on the hillside as they were up on top of the hill. Once we reached the bottom, we were about 200 meters from the open valley. Capt. Hitti said we came down the wrong finger. We should have veered to the left before coming down. He said he wanted to reach a certain village that had a church in it. I told him that as soon as we hit the valley we could move up the valley toward the village. He told me that he thought this was a different valley and we had to go back. Better than half the company was waiting on the hillside braced into trees to stay put. Hitti told everyone else to take a breather, and we – Hitti, Sgt. Nehr, Benedetti, Walters and I – walked close to the edge of the jungle. Across the valley stood a single, large hooch with a tree line beyond it. Hitti insisted that we were in the wrong valley. I told him to remember that hooch.

186

We started back up the hill. This time each man had to grab the tree in front of him and pull himself up. As I started to climb, my mind went into a pain-free, euphoric state. I passed one person after another until only Lt. Frank was in front of me. Lt. Frank was a Ranger, was well built and he had an athlete's look. I could have passed him, but instead gave him the distinction of getting to the top first. Twice he looked back at me. When we made the top, he said, "Damn, you push hard!"

It took an hour for everyone to get back to the top of the hill. Capt. Hitti decided to take a break. He asked me how I was doing on point and if I wanted a breather from it. I told him I could handle it. We moved out heading west for 300 meters before the ridge dropped away. The heavy trees opened up into a few trees and some high grass. I was sliding down the ridge on my butt and my feet got caught in a tangle of vines and brush. My feet stayed but the rest of my body kept going. I vaulted forward and landed hands-and-face-first in a dry creek bed. I was just picking myself up when Kloemken landed on top of me.

Along the creek bed was a stand of elephant grass. Elephant grass looks somewhat similar to cattail reeds but stands about eight to ten feet high. The blades of grass are sharp and will give superficial cuts when it strikes you. It grows so thick that it is nearly impossible to walk through. The elephant grass extended south along the rise of the creek bed for quite a distance. The ground to the right dropped straight down. The grass bed was about 100 feet wide. I handed my rifle and gear back to Kloemken, rolled down my shirt sleeves, buttoned my shirt to the neck, turned my collar up, and pulled my right hand into the sleeve of my shirt. I put my right arm in front of my face and neck and rolled into the elephant grass.

I broke the grass over and stomped it down. I repeated this until I crossed through to the other side of the elephant grass.

My clothes were cut to shreds, I had numerous superficial cuts up and down my body, and blood was mixing with my sweat, which made it look more severe than it was. Doc sponged off the blood and put antiseptic on the cuts. The antiseptic stung at first and then numbed the cuts. Capt. Hitti asked if I still wanted to walk point. I told him I came this far, I might as well finish it. We walked another 300 meters and came to a trail. The trail looked as if it had been used recently. Capt. Hitti had everyone spread out at least 5 meters apart. He put Sgt. Nehr second, and told him to stay at least 20 meters or more behind me. He designated groups of four to hit the flank on either side of the trail when he ordered it. Capt. Hitti was exceptionally well versed and well prepared in these types of situations.

The trail meandered but headed pretty much northwest along the top of the jungle ridge. Gradually it went downhill. I rounded a bend and in front of me about 40 meters was a fresh pile of dirt. I stopped the column and went back to Sgt. Nehr and told him what I had. Capt. Hitti put his flanks out on both sides of the trail and he and Sgt. Nehr came forward with me to where we could see the pile of dirt. They took up positions on each side of the trail and I went forward. When I got about 10 meters from the dirt pile, I could see over it enough to see there was a hole dug into the high side of the trail. I got down on my hands and knees and crawled up behind the dirt pile. I took a rock, about the size of my fist, and tossed it in the hole. I heard it hit the ground inside. I took another rock and threw it to the left side of the hole. It hit the ground. I peeked over the lip of the hole and found it empty. I stood up, turned around to wave the Captain and Nehr forward and saw at least a hundred more piles of fresh dirt and spider holes scattered in the jungle on the upper hillside of the trail. I jumped into the spider hole in the trail. Just as I jumped I thought, what if the hole has a mine in it? I was already committed, mid-jump, and I landed in the hole. It didn't blow up. I poked my head up, but could not see any movement in the other holes. I looked downhill and saw at least 10 more fresh piles of dirt. Capt. Hitti and Nehr could not see the holes from their position. Without yelling, and talking just loud enough for him to hear, I explained the situation to Hitti. He put the whole 1st platoon on a flank to the high side of the trail, and most of the 2nd platoon on a flank to the low side of the trail.

The flanks slowly walked forward on a line and checked out each spider hole. They could not see the holes until they were almost on top of them because of the way they were camouflaged. The holes were all empty. I don't remember the count, but there were about 150 freshly dug spider holes. We found an American-made entrenching tool (small fold-up shovel used to dig foxholes) and a web belt that had a canteen and ammo pouch strapped to it. The ammo pouch was full of .30-cal. ammunition, used in an AK-47. It appeared that whoever was digging the spider holes had left in a hurry.

We continued to move slowly through the jungle with flanks out on each side of the trail. The trail continued on a downward incline for at least a klick and then leveled off. We were coming to an open valley. Somewhere during the trip through the jungle, a sand leech must have dropped down my neck and worked its way under my left armpit. I could feel it but, with all the gear strapped to me, I couldn't get at it. We eventually came out of the jungle into a dogleg of the upper part of a large valley. The trail coming out of the jungle tied in with a large dike trail through some rice paddies and across the valley to a village that had a church. We could see a large hole in the roof of the church. We spread out in the rice paddies and walked toward the village. No one trusted walking the trail.

We came into the village and did our search. The church sat on the highest ground and had a semi-circle of hooches around it. In one of the hooches, we found three gooks, all with fairly recent injuries. Capt. Hitti set up Company Headquarters in the church. The three gooks were split up, and one at a time taken to the church so Hitti and Sgt. Nguyen could talk to them. Through the interpreter, they said they were NVA soldiers and part of the company we were looking for in the jungle. We had come onto them before they had a chance to complete and camouflage their spider holes. It was their intent to ambush us as we passed them on the trail. We came onto them too soon, so they left in a hurry. The three of them were holding up the rest of the company, so they stayed behind and hid out in the hooch until we found them. The rest of the company had headed west into the jungle beyond the village where we found the three NVA soldiers.

Once we stopped, I took off my gear and shirt. The leech had wormed its way into my skin under my armpit. Doc Aragon told me not to pull the leech out. He lit a cigarette, and he touched the leech with the hot ash of it. The leech pulled back a little. He continued this until the leech backed out of the hole it had bored into my flesh. There was a strong blood flow coming from the entry hole. Doc said to let it bleed out so the infected blood would come out. It was bleeding much worse then he thought it should. He was concerned it may have gotten close to my lungs. After an appropriate amount of blood flowed out, he put a compress bandage on the entry hole and told me to put pressure on it.

Doc started a fire in the back of the church where there was a hole from artillery in the roof. The church was completely empty and had a slate floor. He piled brush and chunks of wood on it until the flames were about three feet high. He let it burn down. Meanwhile, he cut off a green branch and whittled a point on it. He snipped off the tip so it wasn't sharp and put the tip in the fire. I was holding the compress bandage tightly against the wound. He kept turning the stick until the tip was a red glow. When it was ready, he had Sgt. Nehr and Lt. Frank hold me steady. I pulled the compress away and he stuck the hot tip of the stick into the wound, searing it to stop the bleeding. I gritted my teeth and let out a low groan. Doc then boiled some water in the fire and washed out all the cuts I got from the elephant grass and applied more antiseptic. Again, there was the sharp sting followed by a numbing sensation. He taped rolled cotton strips above and below the wound, so my arm would not make contact with it. Doc said he wanted to watch the wound to make sure I didn't have internal bleeding, and he wanted to keep me dry so the wound would not get infected. I would be staying with the CP overnight in the church.

The next morning, the company split into platoons and swept through the valley. This was considered a hostile area, so we burned all hooches and destroyed all the rice. We moved down the valley three klicks and came around a wooded ridge point stuck out into the valley. As we rounded the point, I could see that the valley beyond looked familiar. Capt. Hitti was behind us, so I dropped back until he came along. I asked him if anything looked familiar. He saw right away that we were close to where we had been the previous day after descending the steep hill. I think Hitti knew all along where we were the previous day, but he was more interested in finding the company of NVA we flushed; it was our primary mission. This valley had a river meandering through the middle of it. It seemed the norm for all large valleys. This valley got wider as we moved from west to east. I believe we were getting closer to the ocean again.

Luis "Doc" Aragon and Bob Kunkel.

Ray Judy.

A DATE WITH THE ENEMY

After searching part of this valley, we moved to a low hill with a flat plateau on top. We had a new mission and were waiting for the choppers.

As we sat around, Sgt. Crockett started talking about how good it felt to be with the guys in our platoon. He said his life in the Army was better than anything he ever had growing up. He never knew his father, his mother was an alcoholic, he said he never had enough to eat; his clothes were so badly worn that he never wanted to be seen by other kids. For the same reason, he didn't want to go to school, so he skipped often. He got into trouble with the law, and the judge told him to join the Army or go to jail. He said that, once he got in the Army, things went better for him. He said he had no reason to go home, so he intended to stay in Vietnam until the gooks got him. He insisted that he would die in Vietnam.

About mid-afternoon, choppers came in and lifted the company west to an open LZ between two narrow ridges. Capt. Hitti sent out squads to secure the wooded ridges. He called the officers and platoon Sergeants together and gave them our new mission. He called Sgt. Nehr, Ray Judy and I to his location and gave us what information he thought we needed to know. He said we were making a night move and had to be camouflaged in a blocking position by daylight. Our target area was close to 15 miles from our present site. He told me that I would be walking point, and Ray Judy would take over if I got tired. Sgt.

Nehr would walk second in line, and Hitti would follow fifth in line. I asked to see the map so I could get a lay of the land. Hitti, Capt. Grady (the Company XO), Lt. Frank, Sgt. Nehr, Ray Judy and I, went over the route we would be taking. The first five miles would be easy. We were between two ridges and I figured to use the skyline of the ridges as a guide. The ridge on the left extended at least a mile beyond the north ridge. Beyond the ridges was a valley with rice paddies and hooches. We would walk right through the middle of this valley. The valley hooked to the right, but we would go up and over the ridge guarding this valley. Once beyond this ridge, if the weather cooperated, I should be able to guide us onto another low ridge to our left. This ridge would blend into where we would set up our blocking positions.

The night started out with an overcast sky. We began the walk right after complete darkness. We did not want any VC scouts to know we were on the move. Even in the darkness, I could make out the ridges. Shortly after we started, we had a good downpour hampering vision of the ridge skyline. As long as I didn't go uphill either way, I figured I was still going in the right direction. Nehr had a compass and could steer me as needed.

About four miles into the walk, Capt. Hitti wanted to take a compass bearing. Hitti, Grady, and Frank pulled a poncho over themselves and checked out their maps and compass readings. We were right on course. The light they used had ruined their night vision, though. We had to wait at least 10 more minutes before we could move on. Since time was important, Hitti trusted my judgment to get us into position before daylight.

We came out on target as expected and set up on a skirmish line below the skyline of a ridge overlooking a series of hamlets in the valley below us. C Company and two platoons from A Company were going to sweep the valley. D Company was set up to our left at the end of the valley, and the 1st of the 7th Cav had A Company across the valley from our position. We were after the NVA company we had rousted the day before. Intelligence figured they would be in this valley overnight and, at daylight, A and C Companies would drive them out and into the blocking forces. This is the only time during my stay in the field that B Company set up a blocking force. Until now, we always were the company doing the driving, with other Companies doing the blocking.

Light was just starting to appear over the far horizon where the 1st of the 7th was set up. We could hear the choppers long before we saw them. At the south end of the valley, what appeared to be at least 20 choppers descended into the valley and immediately lifted out again. We could only see them after they got above the ground line. Everyone was pumped up, waiting for the gooks to show themselves and for the fireworks to start. About 15 minutes into the sweep, we heard some shooting coming from the valley. It was a small volley of gunshots that lasted only about a minute and it was over. About 15 minutes after the first shots, the 1st of the 7th Cav opened fire. Again there was a fairly small volley, lasting no more than a couple of minutes and it was over. By now, we could see the soldiers from A and C Companies. It took at least another hour for them to sweep the entire valley. There was no other enemy activity.

When they started the sweep, they apparently surprised an eight-man squad of gooks. The gooks ran. This was the first volley of shots. When the gooks headed out of the valley, they ran into the 1st of the 7th Cav. That was the second volley of shots. For those gooks, the war was over.

Capt. Hitti sent out squads in two directions to check the area surrounding our position. He told the rest of us to relax. We had about a four-hour wait for choppers to take us out of there. Most of us heated C-Rations and ate, then lay back to get some sleep, which we missed during the night march.

The 1st squad had Juan Velasques as their squad leader. He was from West Texas, near El Paso. He wrote three songs for the 7th Cav. One song played to the tune of the "Ballad of the Green Berets," and the other played to the tune of the Beatles' "Yellow Submarine." I don't recall what tune was used for the third song. I don't remember the words either, but they sounded and sang well to the tunes mentioned. After a couple of hours of rest, to idle the time away, he sang the songs for the rest of us. Pretty soon, most of us were singing along with him.

Following a hard day during Operation "Yellowstone," a few members of Company A 3rd Battalion 22nd Infantry (Mechanized) 25th Infantry Division gather around a guitar player and sing a few songs. U.S. Army photo, January 18, 1968. Photo courtesy of National Archives at College Park, Md. Photo ID 530617.

TROUBLE WITH A FNG
(F---ing New Guy)

The choppers came early afternoon and we flew out in platoons. 2nd platoon was taken to an open ridge next to a higher jungle ridge. We made a sweep up the jungle ridge and worked our way down the other side. As we came down to the edge of a tree line, a gook broke out of the tree line ahead of us and began running away from us to our left. The point man and a couple of others started shooting at him. He went down. When the first rounds were fired, the rest of the platoon dropped to the ground and began firing out to the left and right. Lt. Frank called a cease-fire. It appeared that he was the only gook in the area, and we had surprised him. We checked the body, but could not find any bullet holes. We took off his clothes to get a better look at him and still did not find any bullet holes. It was assumed he had died of a heart attack.

Lt. Frank selected an area to set up for the night. We prepared positions in the wooded area along an open grass valley. We didn't set up the poncho tents as normal. We left this area and headed about one klick further along the base of the ridge. This time we set up positions, making it obvious that this is where we would be spending the night. We built our poncho tents, dug in, and piled dirt around the positions, and then we waited for the chow choppers. For all intents and purposes, we had set up for the night. Once the chow was dropped off and we had eaten, we made final adjustments to our positions. As soon as it was too dark to see, we tore down our positions and moved back to our previous location, to the positions we had worked on earlier. We always assumed that we were being watched, and often times we were. The idea was to fool the gooks into looking for us at the wrong location. With any kind of luck, we might be able to spring our own surprises.

The next morning we got three FNGs (F---ing New Guys), arriving with the morning chow. Since Manning left, I did not have a partner. Lt. Frank had one of them team up with me. Even though he was the same age as most of the guys in the platoon, for some reason he seemed much younger. The daily grind and routine for the past two months made us seem much older. This kid, I don't remember his name, since he was with us for such a short time, had an attitude problem. He acted cocky and sure of himself. It was only a false front covering his fear. We crossed a small river and headed in the direction of some hooches on the far end of the valley. We hadn't gone very far, and I noticed this new kid had his gun off safe. I told him to put the safe on. He clicked it on. About 20 minutes later I saw the safe was off again. I told him to put his damn safe on. Again he clicked it on. I watched him more closely now. We walked about 20 feet and he clicked the safe off again. I took his gun away and told him that, if he wasn't going to keep his gun on safe, he was not going to have one at all. He told me that he wanted to be ready in case the gooks came. I told him that, if the shooting started, his first move would be to hit the ground, and then he could put his gun off safe. I gave him the gun back and we started walking again.

For the next 20 minutes, I checked on him often to make sure the gun was on safe. It was. I figured he had learned his lesson, so I ignored him for a while. About 30 minutes later, he tripped over some clods in the high grass and he fell forward. His gun went off. Kloemken was walking about 4 meters in front of him. When the gun went off I swore it was aimed right at Kloemken's back. The bullet just missed him. Before the new kid could get up, I jumped on his back and began beating him in the back of his head with my fists. Ray Judy and someone else pulled me off him. Kloemken wanted a piece of him too. Lt. Frank saw what happened and asked why I was so upset. I told Frank how often I had warned the kid about carrying his gun off safe, and that the f---ing punk wouldn't listen. I also told Frank that, if I had to be his partner, I would kill him before he had a chance to kill me or someone else. I had his M16, and I told Frank that I wouldn't give it back to him if he had ammunition in it. Frank told me to give him back his gun and told the kid that he would be walking point and that everyone else would be behind him. He also told him that the gun had better not go off unless it's pointed at a gook. The kid walked point for the balance of the day. I walked second and made him walk at least 20 meters in front of me. He tried to slow down, but I kept pushing him. When the chow chopper came that night, Lt. Frank called the kid over, had a talk with him, told him to get on the chopper and sent him out. I never heard what happened to him, but I believe he went to another company.

One of the other FNGs was a fairly tall one. He was assigned with Sommers, I believe. This guy did nothing but bitch. He complained about the humping, the heat, the weight we had to carry, the rain, the food or lack thereof, and anything else that was not comfortable or perfect. The third FNG was a pure red-headed kid from Georgia. He had a slow drawl and easygoing talk and manner about him. He was the exact opposite of the complainer. He was teamed up with Rohl who was also an easygoing farm kid from Wisconsin.

Troops of C Company 2nd Brigade 1st Infantry (Airmobile) move through an area that had been previously cleared by supporting artillery, near Xa Cam My during "Operation Abilene," a search-and-destroy mission. Photo courtesy of the National Archives at College Park, Md. Original photo from the Records of the Office of the Chief Signal Officer. Photo ID 111-CCV-CC34049.

A CLOSE CALL

The following morning we were again air-lifted by chopper to another ridge overlooking a long valley. The valley ran mostly east and west with a river running down the middle toward the sea. 1st and 3rd platoons went west, and 2nd platoon went east. Since the valley was considered an unfriendly zone, our mission was to search and destroy. There were no hamlets. However, there were a number of hooches scattered along the rice paddies and below a heavy jungle ridge. This ridge was high enough to refer to it as a mountain. Down the middle of the valley, close to the river, were a series of wooded islands, uninhabited by humans. We would search the hooches along the lip of the rice paddies, and then swing out and sweep through the islands.

We swept through the first island and then headed back to the line of hooches. As we came off the rice paddies, the bank above it was steep, and in one place a trail led up the bank. This was the only place nearby to get out of the rice paddies. I took point and began walking up the trail. John Ward was about four meters behind me. I was looking for signs of disturbance on the trail but saw nothing that raised suspicion. As I was nearing the top of the trail, Ward yelled, "FREEZE!" I froze in my tracks. He told me to look down at the back of my right leg. There was a thin wire stretched across the trail. I had stepped over the wire and nicked it very slightly with my heel. The wire fluttered or bounced slightly and the sun reflecting off it caught Ward's attention. I followed the wire to my left and saw where it was tied off on some brush. I followed the wire to my right and saw an old Chinese-style cylinder grenade. It had a cork-like cap and, when the cap came out, the grenade would explode. It was five feet to my right and tied to a bush about 8 inches off the ground. Had it exploded, most likely Ward and I would have been killed, and at least one man behind Ward would have received injuries.

Walters was the assistant machine-gunner. He carried a 100-foot rope with a weight attached to one end. Everyone except Walters backed off well over 100 feet. Walters ducked down behind some built-up turf to our left and threw the weight attached to the rope up on the bank above the trail. He lay flat on the ground and gave the rope a tug. The weight came off the bank, down the trail and wrapped the rope over the top of the wire. He tugged the rope again and the grenade went off. I raised my eyes to the sky and gave God a big "THANK YOU!" I gave another "thank you" to Ward.

On the plain, above the rice paddies, stood five hooches. There was a pregnant woman in one of them. Also in this hooch was a young man, who was obviously a Dinky Dau (mentally retarded). Dinky Dau had a permanent grin etched on his face. We burned all but the hooch she was in and destroyed all but a small amount of rice, which we placed in a large clay jar we found. She started bawling, but orders were orders. There were a few hooches further down the valley, so we moved on to them, and burned them down as well.

COMMUNICATING WITH THE ENEMY

We worked our way back to the hooch with the pregnant woman and went back out to sweep what was left of the wooded islands. As we came to the first island, I was walking point. A gook came out of the brush with his hands folded across the top of his head. This is the sign of surrender. The interpreter was with Headquarters. Headquarters was with 1st and 3rd platoons, so we could not interrogate him. We discussed shooting him, but no one wanted to be the one to do it. Lt. Frank said he surrendered to me, so I was responsible for him. The platoon swept through two more islands, and Lt. Frank, Sgt. Inez, Aragon the medic, the gook and I walked around it on the rice paddy dike. The gook was walking behind Lt. Frank, and I was walking behind the gook. Frank turned around and said he was getting too close. I grabbed the gook, and pointed to Lt. Frank's feet and then to his feet. I was talking to him as I did this, but I don't believe he understood what I said. I hung onto him and let Frank get about 5 meters in front of him, and then I pointed to his feet and made a stepping motion with my hands for him to go. We had walked a short distance and Frank stopped. The gook was in mid-stride with his leg in the air, and he froze in that position until Frank started walking again. I think we had communication.

We came up along the river and Frank said to look for a place to cross. I walked along the bank and indicated to the

Corporal M.R. Carter guards an NVA soldier he captured during a ground movement 10 miles northeast of An Hoa, November 20, 1968. U.S. Marine Corps photo, ID 532503. Photo courtesy of the National Archives at College Park, Md.

gook that we would cross here. He shook his head vigorously back and forth indicating "no." I grabbed him by the arm and we both jumped in. Immediately I understood why he did not want to cross here. We went under. This time we did not have good communication. We both fought to get back above water and, as soon as I came up, someone was stretched out on the bank and reached out his hand. I grabbed it and, between us, I pulled myself out. Someone else helped the gook out. When I had jumped in, two C-Ration cans came out of the leg pockets where I carried them and floated downstream. We walked about another 200 meters downstream, and the gook looked at me and indicated we should cross at this location. He and I jumped in and the water was about waist deep. It stayed the same depth across the river.

We walked down river and came to a hamlet site that had been previously burned out. We were not getting a chow chopper that night, so we had to eat C-Rations. I shared what C-Rations I had left with the gook. Even though we did not understand each other's language, we managed to communicate. As night fell, a few guys again talked about killing him. They did not want a gook on the loose near them in the dark. I said that I would tie his hands and legs and stay awake all night with him, and we would put him on a morning chopper back to battalion or wherever they would take him.

On the back side of the burned-out village, there was a large dirt bank with a wall of rocks on the uphill side of the wall. The hamlet had been built below two ridges that came together to form a ravine. With heavy rains, the bank steered the water around the village into the rice paddies.

At about 0400 hours it began to rain. By daylight, it was a heavy downpour. Capt. Hitti had called by radio and told Lt. Frank to get us across the river before the river rose too high to cross. We were supposed to meet the rest of the company at the site of the hooch we left standing for the pregnant woman. We packed up to go. Lt. Frank came to me and said we were not taking the gook with us, and we were not leaving him behind to pass information to other gooks. I told Frank that I had sat up with him all night. Even though we didn't talk, we sure as hell had communication. Sgt. Nehr said, "I know what it's like. I'll take care of it." I walked away with Frank and, as soon as I disappeared below the bank, there were two shots. Sgt. Nehr caught up to us. When we crossed the river, it was armpit high to me. A few shorter soldiers needed help crossing. The rain was still pouring when we came to the trail leading up to the lone standing hooch we left the day before.

About a third of our platoon was above the bank when 10 gooks broke out of the hooch running for the trees. I was just coming up the trail when the shooting started. I ran ahead and hit the ground behind a clump of brush. Then I could see the gooks were running away and our troops were the only ones shooting. The lead squad was in our way, so we could not shoot. A few other soldiers and I ran around the far side of the standing hooch. The pregnant woman was standing in the doorway bawling. Dinky Dau was standing behind her with his permanent grin. I looked into the hooch; no one else was there. I took off and ran through some high grass in the direction the gooks ran. About 60 feet from the hooch, I stepped in a small ditch covered with a grass entanglement. Something moved underneath me. I shot into the movement and the movement stopped. Something else moved under the grass to my right. I shot into that movement. There was no more movement. I could make out the outline of the ditch, so I put my M16 on full automatic and sprayed bullets up and down the ditch. I pulled the grass away from what I shot at below me when I stepped in the ditch. The face of a young girl, maybe in her mid-teens, stared up at me. As I was staring back a glaze seemed to come over her eyes. She died as I was looking at her. I looked over at the spot where I saw the other movement. I stood there for the better part of a minute and then walked away. I did not want to find another young child. To this day, I wonder if I left a child laying in that ditch to suffer a long agonizing death from wounds I had inflicted. The death stare of that young girl as she died is forever etched in my mind.

The first squad up the bank gave chase to the gooks who ran. The rest of us followed to back them up. Sgt. Inez told the medic Doc Aragon to guard Dinky Dau. He was left behind as we went ahead. We were about 50 meters ahead of Doc, and he started shooting. We all looked back and Doc was running to catch us. He said, "The guy ran, so I shot him." All Doc carried was a .45-cal. automatic. We traveled about another 200 meters and the lead group came back and met us. Lt. Frank spread some of the squad out to sweep the wooded jungle foliage at the base of the ridge. Two gooks had been killed when they ran from the hooch, and a few had been wounded. He was looking for the wounded. He told Sgt. Inez to take some of us back to the hooch and take a better look around. When we got back, Dinky Dau was still alive, but he was thrashing around on the ground, raising up and flopping back down from side to side. It was still raining, and Dinky Dau had created a mud wallow where he was thrashing around. His whole body was covered with mud. I said someone has to put him out of his misery. No one else offered, so I shot him behind the ear. I stayed away from the ditch.

Men of C Company 1st Bn, 7th Cav. 1st Cav. Div., move on patrol through a heavily wooded area surrounding their mountain-top camp during Operation "Thayer II" 50 km NW of Qui Nho'n, October 29, 1966.

THE MONSOON RAIN:
Heading to the Hills

Capt. Hitti and the other two platoons were just arriving at the hooch. Lt. Frank updated him, by radio, after the shooting as to what had happened. Lt. Frank and the search squad came back. When everyone had gathered around, Sgt. Inez said there were four dead gooks. I'm assuming they counted the girl and Dinky Dau.

Capt. Hitti said the forecast was for rain for the next four or five days. He told us that the choppers could not fly in this weather, so we were stuck in the boonies. He said we were going to the top of the mountain to clear out a drop zone for supplies when the weather let up. He wanted 2nd platoon in the lead, and he wanted Ray Judy and me to alternate on point. Shortly after starting the uphill climb, the foliage became so thick that we again had to cut through it with a machete. I slung my rifle and began hacking the vines, cutting them away to make a trail. The mountain was extremely steep, and I had to brace myself against trees and rocks to keep from sliding back. I would hack for about 20 minutes, then Judy would hack for 20 minutes. We were not moving very fast, but we were moving. We came to a trail and started walking it. When Capt. Hitti came out on the trail, he told us to get off the trail unless we wanted our asses blown up. We got off the trail. The mountain was at least 1500 feet high and the distance to the top, since we couldn't walk in a straight line, was almost twice that far.

We were about half-way up the mountain, and I had just taken the machete from Judy. I started hacking at the foliage. I looked over to my left and saw two gooks, wrapped tightly in their ponchos, walking on the trail, up the hill beside us. They were only about 12 feet from us. I had not realized that I got so close to the trail again. With their ponchos over their heads, all they must have heard was the rain beating on the plastic. I sure made enough noise while I was swinging the machete.

Sgt. Nehr was the first person behind me. I pointed to the two gooks. I whispered, asking him if they were the national police that traveled with us occasionally. He replied that, if they were, they're dead. He took the one behind, and I took the lead gook. We both opened up. Immediately, the rest of the company dropped to the ground and laid cover fire out right and left. Nehr shot his man in the head and he died instantly. I shot my man in the side. He slumped forward. I walked toward him. He raised his hand as if trying to give up. It was understood that we were not taking prisoners. My mind was fighting with my conscience. One part said to finish him, the other part said not to shoot. Then I thought, if our positions were reversed and he had caught me off-guard, I would be dead. As I made up my mind to finish him off, the gook must have seen the look in my eye. He turned his head down, and I swear he said, "Oh, God, no!" He began to cry. I put the barrel about one foot from his head and pulled the trigger. His face contorted, the left side of his upper jaw below the ear blew out, and he collapsed face-first into the ground.

Both gooks were wearing rucksacks. Capt. Hitti and Grady came forward with Sgt. Nguyen, the interpreter. The lead gook turned out to be a Colonel in an NVA unit. This is equivalent to a U.S. Army Battalion Commander. He had maps, documents, and data for their military activity. He also had some letters from his wife and three photographs of her and three children. Sgt. Nguyen read one of the letters from the wife. He also said it was signed "Love," and he gave the wife's name. Ray Judy looked at me and said that they're no different than us.

The Colonel was carrying an M1 Garand rifle. This is a World War II, American-made Army rifle. The other gook was carrying an old French .43-cal. rifle with a swing-out triangle bayonet attached. Sgt. Nehr and I took the rifles for souvenirs. We carried the souvenirs with us for the next four days. They were sent back to our company supply. Once these souvenirs were out of our sight we never saw them again.

The Captain and interpreter spent at least an hour going through the dead gooks' belongings before we started

Members of the 1st Cavalry (Airmobile) take a break while patrolling the Lao Valley during "Operation Pershing," 1967. U.S. Army Photo. NARA 639913.
Photo courtesy of the National Archives at College Park, Md.

our trek back up the mountain. We got to the top about three hours later. Capt. Hitti immediately sent out three scouting squads to make sure we did not get any unexpected company. The rest of us started clearing an area to make a drop zone. At the very top, the trees were not as thick as on the hillsides, but there was still a lot of cover. A helicopter from above would not be able to see into the jungle. We worked until dark before calling it a day. Almost everyone was out of C-Rations, so we did not eat. The rain had not let up all day. We put up positions, each platoon in their own group. Capt. Hitti didn't think we would get any company, but he wanted one position on our back trail and one position out in each direction on the mountaintop. I teamed up with Tom Gray and Ray Judy. We put up the two ponchos and tied them tightly to the ground on two sides. We put about a 24-inch peak in the middle front that sloped down to our backside. We built a trench that carried water around the poncho tent to the downhill side. When we

Sgt. James E. Knauls, C Company 1/327th Infantry, 101st Airborne, chops down a tree to clear a helicopter landing zone. Photo courtesy of Army Heritage Center Foundation in Carlisle, Pa.; *www.armyheritage.org.*

crawled under the ponchos, we were completely protected from the rain.

The three of us lay in the dark, bull-shitting until late in the night. We were all due to get out of the service within a few days of each other. When I got out, deer hunting would be over in Minnesota so I would have to miss it again. Ray Judy said it would just be starting in Pennsylvania. We would be getting out of Vietnam on August 1st. After a 30-day leave, which we were entitled to, we all had about three more months to serve in the Army. We decided that we would all put in for finishing our military tours at Fort Dix in New Jersey. Gray was due to get out of the service on November 27, Judy would get out on November 30, and I would get out on December 1, 1967. The three of us would meet at Ray Judy's home in Lucinda, Pennsylvania, and go deer hunting with him.

It must have been after midnight before we fell asleep. I woke up at about 0400 hours shaking. I noticed that Judy and Gray were also shaking. I asked if they were awake. They were. Judy said it was cold enough to be snowing. It was cold, but I think the absence of food made it seem colder. Our body heat had dried the ground under us, so at least we had a dry bed now. I fell asleep a little before daylight but was awake as soon as people started to mill around.

It rained all the next day and we cleared more brush and trees. We had one axe so we took turns swinging it to drop trees. The rest of us worked with our bayonets and the machetes. We had three machetes for the company. By late afternoon, we had a fair-sized opening. It was still raining too hard for the choppers to fly. We were going without food for another day. Some of us talked about going hunting, but the Captain wouldn't allow it. We started making jokes about whom we would eat first. Someone suggested that we go back down the hill and get a chunk of gook meat. This was all said in jest, or at least I hope this was the case.

Sgt. Nehr was interested in the M1 Garand that I got from the dead gook Colonel. He finally asked if I would be interested in trading souvenirs. I told him I would. I pictured the French-made blunderbuss of a rifle hanging over a fireplace in my home on some future day.

Gray, Judy and I were under the poncho tent long before dark. Judy talked about his wife, Gray talked about living in New York, and I talked about Minnesota lakes and growing up on one. We talked about President Johnson, about the chicken-shit ARVNs, and almost anything else that came to mind. At one point, Judy said, "I'm serious about the three of us hunting deer after we get out of the service." We all agreed that it would happen.

Again, the night was bitterly cold compared to the normal temperature. The rain continued. The next morning it let up to a drizzle, but there was a heavy haze in the air. The choppers headed out to our position but had to turn back. Word came that the choppers were on standby and that, as soon as they could fly, they would come to drop in C-Rations. The heavy rain started again. By mid-afternoon, it was apparent that we would not be eating again today. By now, our stomachs were tied in tight knots from lack of food. I went past the point of hunger. We heated water to put something warm in our stomachs. Any body reserves that we had were getting used up. The rain kept pounding. It was getting monotonous. As long as we had others around us, we kept our sanity. A person alone would have lost it.

The next morning, the rain diminished to a slight drizzle. The air was still sultry, and a fog was settled in the top of the trees. We crawled out of our tents and anxiously waited for the choppers. Capt. Hitti said they were airborne. Minutes dragged on. The choppers had to fly above the fog, and visibility was still severely hampered. Apparently, they flew off-course far enough that we could not hear them. Capt. Hitti had radio contact and told them to make wide circles to see if we could pick up their sound. We finally heard chopper sounds. Hitti used his compass and got them to turn in our direction. When they got close enough, we threw smoke. The heavy air pressure kept the smoke close to the ground, so they didn't see it. Hitti talked them over our position. We finally could make out the bottom of a helicopter. Hitti told them to kick the C-Rations out. Case after case of C-Rations tumbled out of the helicopter. Some of the tents got smashed, but no one really cared. We had food again.

The C-Rations were gathered into a pile. The Captain insisted on an orderly distribution. He told everyone to make sure that they heated their C-Rations before eating them. He also said to eat a small amount and wait; eat another small amount and wait. Capt. Hitti was one officer who had his shit together. Most people listened to him. Gray, Judy and I had set up a little open-rock stove. We stuck a chunk of C-4 in between the rocks, started it burning, and held an open can of C-Ration over it. C-4 is an explosive putty used in Claymore mines. It also came in one-pound bricks shaped like a pound of butter. It will burn very hot, but needs a cap charge to set it off as an explosive. We took turns heating our food a little at a time. If you held the can over the fire too long, it would burn the food on the bottom of the can. I saw the bottom burn out of a can that was left over the C-4 too long. My first meal was a can of ham and lima beans. By soldiers' standards, this ranks near the bottom of the 12 varieties of Army-issued C-Rations. Given the circumstances, once the canned ham and Lima beans were heated, a rib-eye steak could not have tasted any better. I ate slowly and savored the food. Some soldiers rushed it and ate their food cold and in a hurry; within a minute or two they were puking it out. Those who followed Capt. Hitti's instructions were able to keep it down. One can of food and I seemed full. I could not eat any more just then.

The C's had a plastic pack in each box with sugar, salt, pepper, cocoa packs, Chiclets gum, and a box with four or six cigarettes in it. My box had a pack of six Camels. We had been getting Kent cigarettes in the S.O.S. packs. Their taste was bad by my standards. The Camels did not have filters. I lit one up. It gave me a high. After about an hour, I heated a can of beans and wieners and ate that. By now my hunger was satisfied. Everyone was in a better mood. Capt. Hitti sent out a squad to walk the top of the ridge one klick each way.

It never quite quit raining, but it slowed considerably. A couple of times during the day we got a heavy cloudburst, but it would let up after about 30 minutes. During the night, it stopped raining completely. The morning had some brightness to it. After breakfast C-Rations, we packed our gear together and moved in file off the mountain. We made a new trail down, but it was much easier than the climb up. 1st platoon led the way down.

During the past four days, the spoiled FNG bitched and complained to anyone who would listen. I finally told him that, unless he got injured or killed, he had a whole year of this same shit coming his way. It wouldn't be getting any better, and it might get worse. I told him that I was speaking for the whole company. He could quit his pissing and moaning; no one was interested.

We came down into the same valley we left four days previously. The whole valley was flooded with water making it look like a lake or a wide river. Mama-San, the pregnant woman, was gone. The dead gooks were all gone. We moved up the valley and up the ridge to the LZ where we had unloaded five days earlier. Choppers came in and picked us up and flew us to an artillery base. We set up perimeter around the base to reinforce security.

2nd platoon had to send out a forward post. We were to go out 400 meters, no more, and set up the post. The artillery would be firing H & I (Harassment and Interdiction) fire. They wanted to make sure that we didn't get out too far and get caught in the fire. Six of us went out. I stepped it off to the 400 meters. Ray Judy did the same. We set up in two positions about 100 meters apart.

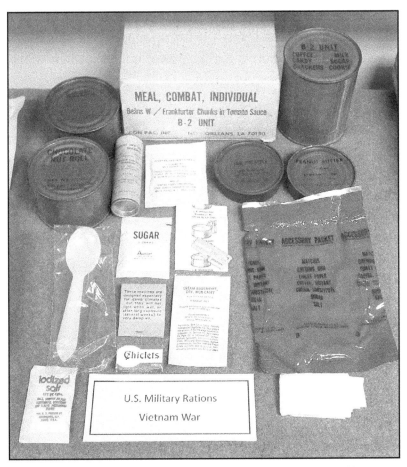

Vietnam-era, military-issue C-Rations. Photo courtesy of Fort Devens Museum.

We were in position for a couple of hours before the first H & I rounds came in. The first one landed about 150 meters beyond us. The second round landed about 100 meters from us. Judy had the radio. I told him those rounds were getting too close for comfort. The third round came whistling in. Everybody pulled their heads down and flattened to the ground. The round landed between our two positions. Large chunks of shrapnel came whistling over our heads, skimming through the brush, and tearing off branches in its path. Judy got on the radio and yelled for "Comanche Brave 6," Capt. Hitti's call sign. He came on the air immediately. Judy told him that the H & I was landing almost on top of us and to tell the artillery to stop the firing. One more round landed within 100 meters of our location before the firing stopped. The rounds were coming from another artillery location. Somewhere along the line, the grids got screwed up.

The next morning when the chow choppers came in, Sgt. Nehr got on the return ship. The Army had decided to send out Long Range Reconnaissance Patrols (LRRPs). Sgt. Nehr was selected to be one of the squad leaders for a patrol. This was only supposed to be a temporary assignment, but there were still some sad farewells. Sgt. Frank Cooper from 3rd platoon requested to take Sgt. Nehr's place as squad leader for 2nd platoon.

A break in the rain: two battle-weary leathernecks of the 26th Marine Regiment take a break, rain and all, during Operation "Bold Mariner." The cordon operation on the Batangan Peninsula in Quang Ngai Province was aimed at uncovering and destroying the Viet Cong and their political infrastructure. U.S. Marine Corps photo, ID 532462. Photo courtesy of the National Archives at College Park, Md.

Members of E Company 14th Infantry fire a mortar round at a platoon-size element of Viet Cong during the night at Fire Base "Abby," located about 30 km northeast of An Khê. Photo courtesy of the National Archives at College Park, Md. Original photo fromt he Records of the Office of the Chief Signal Officer. Photo ID 111-CC-66727.

Soldiers carry a wounded camrade through a swampy area. Credit Paul Halverson SSG, 1969. U.S. Army photo. NARA 111-CC-651408. Photo courtesy of the National Archives at College Park, Md.

B COMPANY'S FIRST KIA

Late that morning, choppers came to fly us out to our new mission. 3rd platoon was headed for Happy Valley. Happy Valley was anything but happy. Happy Valley was inhabited by Montagnards and considered Viet Cong by the military. In truth, they were neither Viet Cong nor were they pro-South Vietnamese. They had their own old-established culture and they wanted to be left alone. Anyone who came into their valley was an enemy. 3rd platoon was to make a sweep through part of the valley. Frank Glowiak was walking point. He tripped a homemade mine, and it killed him and wounded three other soldiers including their platoon leader. The home-made mine was made of a can, shreds of metal, and rock chips. Glowiak was the first person killed in B Company.

2nd platoon went to a jungle ridge just north of Happy Valley. We had seen enough sign of enemy activity, but we did not make any contact. When we stopped for evening chow, we heard about Glowiak. He was kind of a quiet guy and every-body liked him. Most of the guys called him "Pollack." Charles Love was a black guy with 3rd platoon. He studied theology for the ministry, and he was an ordained minister. He led 3rd platoon in prayer for Glowiak, i.e. on the tiger's back.

I walked point for a night patrol that night. We went out about one klick from platoon CP and set up an outpost, staying put until we returned to the CP the next morning. Just about daylight, there was a lone shot from our platoon. We waited a few minutes, and then called that we were coming in. Nothing was mentioned of the shot over the radio. When we got back to the platoon, we learned that the bitching FNG had shot himself in the foot. He was claiming it was an accident, but his partner now, the other FNG, the red-head, said that he was awake when he shot. He was laying back in the position, and he saw the guy aiming at his foot. He didn't believe the guy would fire, so he tried to get back to sleep. After a few seconds, the FNG shot himself in the foot. He reported this to Lt. Frank. The new guy who shot himself was not too bright. The front and back sights of an M16 sit about 3 inches above the barrel. He was aiming down the sight at where he wanted to hit his foot. Instead of the bullet going in through the top of his foot, it went through where the barrel was pointed, at the top of the ankle. His foot was almost amputated, hanging on by a few muscles and tendons. When an M16 round hits a bone or other hard surface, it rips and tears, sometimes at weird angles. He had to wait for the chow chopper before going back for treatment beyond what treatment he received in the field.

When the chow chopper arrived, word had come down that Ray Judy should go back with it for R & R (Rest and Relaxation). Each soldier was entitled to six days of R & R during his calendar year in Vietnam. Lt. Frank or someone above him had canceled the R & R, indicating that we were too short on manpower. When Judy didn't arrive on the chopper the Battalion Commander, Trevor Swett, apparently became a little upset. He put out orders, "No one would be denied R & R." The next chopper out would bring Ray Judy back to camp so he could go on R & R. That evening, Judy got on the chopper. He said he was headed for Taipei, Taiwan. Our platoon patrolled jungle and open grass ridges most of that day. By late afternoon we were settled in on a heavily brushed knoll overlooking a narrow rice paddy area.

When the chow chopper came in, two Hispanic-looking soldiers got off the chopper. Pabone (I don't remember his first name) was one, and Jesse Samaripa was the other. Lt. Frank told Samaripa to team up with me. He told him, "Kunkel's a good soldier. Listen to him and he'll keep you alive." He looked at me and told me to teach him the tricks that would keep him alive. Sam (his nickname) and I set up our position and talked. I should say that most of the time I talked; he was pretty quiet. I suspected that he was scared. Anyone who wasn't scared when they first came to the field was a fool and was not to be trusted. Bravery was usually a smokescreen for fear. Apart from the distant and not-too-distant artillery shelling, the night was quiet.

Morning came, and Lt. Frank told us to saddle up: we would fly out shortly. We were flown to a knoll outside the perimeter of an artillery base. Breakfast chow arrived right after we did. The platoons were mixed together while we ate. Bob Schuck from 3rd platoon was one of the company clowns. He was very sober this morning, and not up to his usual antics. Someone asked him why he was so serious. He said, "I'm going to die today!" Someone else told him to knock off that bullshit talk. He said it wasn't bullshit. "I'm going to die today. I know it. I can feel it in my body. I won't be here tomorrow." Most people tried to brush it off, but for others the day took on a more serious tone. After breakfast and some milling around among the different platoons, the platoon leaders called everyone in their platoon into a group. They told us to have our gear ready and that we would be flying out in platoon order within about an hour. An hour came and went, no choppers. Another hour rolled by, still no choppers.

A couple of days earlier, Sgt. Inez had left the field. In his absence, Sgt. Carter became the Platoon Sergeant. Around noon, Sgt. Carter told us that the 1st Bn 9th Cav had a recon platoon searching for an NVA company. It was almost certain when they found the force, that we would be flying in to take over on an assault. After listening to what Schuck had said I got a really bad feeling about what was coming. As long as I was in 'Nam, I never had a feeling like this. I believe everyone else had the same feeling. There was damn little talk and even less bullshit. I said an Act of Contrition and thought about the events of the last week or so. I asked God to forgive me if I was wrong in killing the gook on the hill, and the girl. I asked God to forgive me for not checking the ditch after spraying it with gunfire. I prayed, if it was a child, that I didn't hit it, but if I did, that it was a clean kill without suffering.

I tried to pray a Rosary. I could not keep my mind on the praying. I finally said a prayer that I pulled out of my heart. I think this is a better way to pray than saying "Our Fathers" and "Hail Marys" from memory. When you say prayers from memory, your mind tends to wander. When you make up the prayers as they come to you, you think about what you're saying. I guess I did a lot of reflecting on what had happened in the past three months. Until now, I hadn't given it much thought. We left Oakland three months ago. I asked Lt. Frank what day of the month we were on. He said November 1. This was All Saints' Day. Tomorrow is All Souls' Day. All around me, everyone was somber and quiet. There was always some bull-shitting going on when we weren't walking, but not now. This did not seem like the same group of men. That bad feeling stuck with me. I think we all had it. I started thinking that, if we were going into something heavy, it would be better to get it on. This waiting was really working on our nerves. At the same time, though, I wasn't anxious for anything to start.

❦ FIREFIGHT, NOVEMBER 1, 1966

At noon, Lt. Frank told us that the platoon from the 9th Cav was pinned down by a small NVA company. We were going in to bail them out. He said that the choppers would be here in less than 10 minutes. The choppers came and we loaded onto them in platoons. I made sure that Sam was with me. 2nd platoon was the first sortie out. Sitting on that chopper, no one said a word. I said a few prayers. Around 15 minutes later, we could see smoke rising out of a series of wooded knolls and cultivated fields. There were hedgerows around the fields. The knolls had trees and heavy brush covering them. The chopper banked away from this area. When it turned, I could see a number of soldiers lying on the ground, hidden behind a hedgerow and trees. They had their backs to the open rice paddies. To their front was an open field, about 100 meters wide, with hedgerows at the base of a wooded knoll. The chopper dropped us on an open knoll on the far side of the rice paddies, about 600 meters from where the platoon was pinned down. We were the first platoon down and, as soon as we got out of the way, another group came in. B Company supplied the 2nd and 3rd platoons, and A Company supplied one platoon for this mission. A Company landed west of the 9th Cav and we landed south of the 9th Cav.

We took off running across the rice paddies. Our feet sank in the mud, which slowed our speed. It also tired us out much faster. B Company came out of the rice paddies to the right of the 9th Cav. A Company came out of the rice paddies to the left of the 9th Cav. The 9th said there was a small group of gooks that had cover beyond the field in the brush and hedgerows. They said they had two of their own dead and three wounded. We could see two dead gooks. One was in the hedgerow across the small field, and one was at the end of the hedgerow to the right of the 9th Cav. He apparently tried to flank them, but they saw him and killed him.

3rd platoon was to the right of the 2nd platoon. 2nd platoon was now linked up with a platoon from A Company. I was the far left man on the skirmish line for B Company.

I was to keep linked with the far right man with A Company. Together both companies laid down a field of fire and we advanced forward. We laid out enough firepower to kill some of the gooks and drive others back. A Company advanced through the open field. I fired a few rounds, but the return shots were being fired at the mass of A Company. When A Company got to the hedgerow, heavy fire came off the wooded and brushed-in ridge. They were stopped. Advancing was impossible without having numerous casualties. I still had not seen a live enemy soldier. The fear I had known was no longer there. Now it was a matter of reacting to the circumstances.

By now Lt. Frank was into it. Until now he always seemed to be in control of himself. He had a good head on his shoulders. But with this firefight, he came unglued. He yelled, "CHARGE! ATTACK! Kill them f---ers!" I couldn't see the gooks so I didn't know whom to kill. They were well camouflaged. I yelled at Lt. Frank that A Company could not advance. I suggested we sit tight and call artillery in on the hill. He continued to yell, "Charge!" Days later, I reflected on his actions. He must have been waiting for this opportunity to show his leadership under fire. He probably had visions of his chest lined with ribbons of valor. As I watched, I knew that, at this point, he was a dangerous man. Not one person reacted to his yells. I figured we were on our own until this fight was over.

Within a very short time, the skirmish line was in disarray. There was confusion. Frank ran out front, and then came back. He continued to yell his war cries. No one charged. We were advancing on a hedgerow to our front. We were now out to the right front of A Company. The far right line of 2nd platoon was over a rise and out of sight. 3rd platoon was beyond them. As we advanced on a hedgerow about 200 feet to our front, we began to get flanking fire from our left. I hit the dirt. I looked back and Sam was standing, watching me. I yelled at him to get down. He got down right behind me. I yelled to Frank that we should sit tight and drop artillery on the hill. He yelled, "3rd platoon needs help, follow me!" and he ran to the right. No one followed him. The rounds were constantly popping over our heads. I told Sam, "When you hear a snap or pop over your head, you are getting shot at, so don't stand around, get on the ground." I would run a few steps and when the rounds popped over my head I would hit the ground. Twice more I had to yell at Sam to hit the ground. Sam seemed like a decent enough guy, but I was beginning to think that maybe he was not too swift. The 3rd squad advanced to the hedgerow to our front and took up positions. There was a dead gook lying just beyond the hedgerow. Someone must have got a lucky shot. I still had not seen a live gook, and we were taking all kinds of light arms fire.

I placed Sam to my right and told him when I go, he should go; when I hit the dirt, he should hit the dirt. Sgt. Cooper was to his right. I asked Cooper, "What the hell happened to Frank?" He said, "The f---er's gone nuts on us."

I yelled back that we were on our own. Frank came running back and yelled for us to move out. We crossed the hedgerow, into an open field with a sorghum-type plant about 6 inches high. The edible part of the plant was underground. It looked like a giant white radish but tasted similar to a rutabaga. We often would slice flakes of this sorghum into our C-Rations to flavor them.

The ground to our front was on an upward angle forming a hill at the far end of the field.

There was another hedgerow beyond the field. We were out in the field about 50 feet when we started to take shots from the hedgerow at the far end of the field. We hit the dirt and returned fire. We would shoot, jump up and run, hit the ground, and shoot again. We repeated this as we moved across the field. As we closed in on the hedgerow, Lt. Frank gradually worked his way toward our flank. He seemed to have settled down. He asked me where A Company's right flank man was. I told him they were behind us about 300 meters. He told me to go back and link up with them. I asked him, once I link up with them, then what? "Come back here and tell me where they are." I told him they were about 300 meters to our rear left, taking heavy fire, and that they couldn't move forward. He insisted I take Sam with me and go back to find out where they were.

Sam and I ran back to where the shooting started. As soon as we crossed the hedgerow, the gooks began firing at us from our right. I hit the ground and Sam just stood there beside me. I grabbed him by the belt and pulled him down. I told him that you don't hear the shots when they are right at you. You only hear a snap over your head. Since we were the only two people in the field, there was more shooting directed at us than when we came through it the first time. I started crawling. The gooks apparently couldn't see us, because the shooting stopped. I got up and ran, and the shooting started up again. I hit the ground, and this time Sam dropped right behind me. I crawled some more, then jumped up and ran. There were more snaps over my head. I dropped back to the ground.

I finally came to the first man from A Company. I verified that he was the right flank person. The man next to him told me that we were nuts for charging across the open field like we did. I told him that someone should tell our officers that. For a brief moment I had the thought to stay with A Company, but decided against it. I asked Sam if he was ready to go back through the fireworks again. All he said was, "I guess so." I told him the closer we stayed to the hedgerow on our left, the more cover we had. I started to run. Again we got shot at. I hit the ground and Sam followed. We went through this run-and-drop cycle about six times before we got back to the hedgerow. Once we got past the hedgerow, the firing stopped. The rest of the platoon was right where we had left them. They were tight up against the hedgerow at the end of the field. They were getting shot at in short volleys from high grass and brush to their front. They fired back. Off to our right and over an incline, all hell broke loose. 3rd platoon was really catching hell and they were giving it right back.

I located Lt. Frank and told him A Company was right where we had left them earlier. I told him they had enemy to their front and couldn't move forward. Frank spread Sam and me to the left flank again. Immediately to our right was Sgt. Cooper. Frank decided that we were going to charge the hill. He yelled, "Fix bayonets!" and "Charge!"

A well-trained American GI is a very formidable battle combatant. A well-trained American GI is not necessarily a highly disciplined GI. At least four or five well-trained

American GIs yelled back, "F--- you!" No one fixed a bayonet. It's rather stupid to use a bayonet when you still have ammunition.

We moved through the hedgerow. Sgt. Cooper, Sam and I all came out into an open field that I believe was freshly planted with sorghum. No plants were out of the ground as yet. To our right was another hedgerow, separating the high grass hill from the open field. Until now all we heard was light arms fire. Now, what sounded like a .50-caliber machine gun opened fire. The sound of it sent a shudder through me. Brush, dirt, and debris might deflect a light-caliber round if shot at you, but the .50-caliber round will penetrate and pass through more than one foot of dirt, a large tree, and even an inch or more of metal. Frank yelled at Ward to help the guy on the hill with the machine gun. Ward yelled back, "F--- you! He's a f---ing gook, and he's shooting at us." The gook he was referring to had the .50-caliber machine gun.

When I passed through the hedgerow, I could see a hamlet to my left front and at the base of the incline I was on. To my left, the incline descended 40 feet and then made a fairly sharp rise to a narrow ridge with a heavy brush line. The brush line was at the top of the ridge. I looked at the brush line and hoped it didn't have any gooks in it. At this point, I was so damned tired from all the running and eating dirt, I had the thought that dying had to be easier than what we were doing. We had been in this firefight for a little more than two hours. I had no idea how many casualties we had but I suspected, with all the shooting, that we had some. With all the shots that whistled and snapped over my head, I was thinking that the gooks couldn't hit shit. I threw caution to the wind and walked out in the open field, not giving a damn whether I got shot or not. My mind got to that point where it didn't matter. I had no fear. Off to my right, the rest of 2nd platoon was engaged in heavy shooting. I couldn't see what was happening beyond the hedgerow near the top of the hill to my right.

As I was walking along the hillside angling toward the hamlet below the hill, I saw a gook, carrying a rifle, run from a hooch toward a bunker. He was about 100 meters to my left front. I took aim at him and something smashed into my back. I went down, face first, and let out a loud yell, dragging the yell out for about 10 seconds. My helmet fell off my head and rolled down the hill about 20 feet. My first impression was that someone took a white-hot broad axe and smashed me across the back with it. There was a severe burning sensation across the back of my shoulders. Then I realized that I had been shot. The second thought I had was, why did I tell Mom I might not come home alive? When I was home on leave before coming to Vietnam, I was talking with Mom as she was washing clothes. I told her that people were dying in Vietnam and there was a chance it could happen to me. She told me not to talk that way. She also told me to pray it didn't happen. Now as I lay there I felt bad about telling her that I might die.

I opened my shirt to see if I had a wound in the chest. I had never been shot before, and I didn't know what to expect. I was thinking the bullet may have hit me in the chest and, when it came out the back, it tore the meat and skin out, and that was what I felt. There was no hole in my chest. I said a prayer, asking God to take me to Heaven if I died. I asked forgiveness for my sins. I don't believe the prayer lasted more than 10 seconds, but I felt I was ready to die. I was lying in an open field with no cover. I never expected to make it back to safety alive. I expected to die. Other than what I had told Mom, I wasn't worried about dying. I was expecting it and I felt at peace with the thought. Then the thought struck me that I had no children of my own. I would have no descendants of myself. This thought bothered me for a moment.

I could feel blood seeping under my armpit. I started to rationalize and figure out from which direction the shooting came. Based on how I was standing when I got hit, I figured the shooting was coming from the brushed-over ridge on my left. I felt naked and exposed without my helmet; I crawled down the hill and got it. Once I had my helmet on, I swung around and put my back to the brushed-over ridge. For some reason, if I was going to get shot again, I didn't want it in the face or front. I looked back at the ridge to see if I could make out any movement. I could only see the brush. I put my rifle on full automatic and sprayed a burst of rounds into the brush. I always taped two ammo clips together for a quick reload. I would slip the empty clip out, turn it over, slip it back in, and be ready to fire. Just before crossing the last hedgerow, I had put a full set of clips in the rifle. I emptied both clips into the brush and was reaching for another clip. As I was reaching with my right hand across and under my prone body, I raised my head up to get my arm under the body. I heard a clink and instantly felt a heavy smash to my head, and then nothing. I was unconscious.

I don't know how long I lay there. When I regained consciousness, my head was partially in my helmet and the helmet was soaked with blood. It took a minute or more for me to come to my full senses. It wasn't raining before I went unconscious, but it was raining when I woke up. The rain was mixing with my blood and it made the bleeding look much worse. I always carried my billfold and a couple of packs of cigarettes in my helmet liner. This was the only way to keep them dry, and even that didn't work all the time. I could see my billfold had a tear in it from the bullet. The whole right side of my head was numb and throbbing. It felt like a part of my skull was gone. I reached up and could feel my head was intact, but I could also feel that my scalp was split open. I tried to put my helmet back on, but it was painful. I left it lay. I looked up the hill to where the rest of the platoon was supposed to be. I could see Sam lying in the dirt. I could see movement of other GIs beyond the hedgerow.

The shooting coming from the hill had stopped. It appeared that 2nd platoon took the hill. I started to crawl up the hill. It was difficult crawling with my rifle, so I left it lay by my helmet. As soon as I would crawl, I would hear shots snapping over my head. I would lay still. I was closer to the gook or gooks who were shooting at me than I was to my platoon. There were stories about people who were wounded and executed by the gooks after dark. My desire to live was much stronger now than what it was when I walked out in the open field. So I crawled again. And the shooting started again. As long as the rounds were snapping over my head, I thought staying close to the ground offered at least some protection. I kept my head down and pulled myself with my elbows and pushed with my toes. I crawled and, when the shooting started again, I stopped. I would lay there faking dead and then crawl again. Each time I moved, shots would snap over my head. I didn't trust staying in the field. I felt I had to get closer to our platoon before dark. After numerous sequences of crawl — get shot at — play dead, I made it up the hill to where Sam was lying. I grabbed him by the shirt and yelled at him to come with me. He moaned. He moaned about five or six times. I pulled on him and turned him. I could see he was shot through the head right below and behind his ears. There was a bullet hole in and out. I knew his wound was serious and I was sure he would die soon. I thought to myself, "You poor bastard, you didn't last one day in the field."

I tried pulling Sam with me as I crawled. I could not move him. He was stocky and had not lost any fat cells from the daily humping. While I was trying to pull him, I felt a thump on my right foot. It felt as if someone had kicked me in the heel. Sam was the only person close to me and he didn't kick me. I gave up on trying to pull Sam with me. The gooks were shooting at me. I felt if I stayed close to Sam, I was increasing his chances of getting shot again. I decided to move away from him. I headed for the hedgerow. I crawled ahead and my shoe almost slipped off my foot. I looked back and could see the canvas part of the shoe was torn right above the heel, right behind the ankle knuckle. I realized that I was shot in the foot, but the bullet went through the right edge of the boot heel and ripped the canvas up along my leg. No part of my body was hit with that shot.

My shoulders were aching and they were getting stiff. When I got about 6 feet from the hedgerow, I looked for a hole I could crawl through without exposing more of my body. There was an occasional snap over my head every so often as I crawled. Where the hedges were growing, the ground was higher than the field. I figured that if I tried to crawl through the hedges I would expose myself and give the gook a better shot at me. The best way to get to the other side of the hedges would be to jump up and dive through them. I wasn't even sure I could rise. My upper back and shoulders were extremely stiff and painful. I let out a yell – more to absorb the pain than anything else – jumped up and dove through the hedgerow. Just as I was diving through the bushes, I felt a sting in my right rump cheek. The son-of-bitch gook had shot me in the ass. It stung like hell, and it made me furious.

When I dove through the hedges, I landed on Alan Ascher's feet. He was lying face down on the ground. At first, I thought he had been shot. Then he said something, I can't remember what. Allen carried a grenade launcher. I took it from him and told him to give me rounds for it. I started firing it across the open field into the brush where the shots were coming from that hit Sam and me. I fired the fourth or fifth round and, without realizing it, I was rising up into a near standing position. Doc Aragon ran into me, gave me a shoulder block and knocked me back down. He yelled at me asking, how many times did I want to get shot? He then started to bandage my wounds. I told him that Samaripa was still out there. He said he knew where Sam was and that they would get him after it was dark. He asked if I was hit any place other than the back and head. I told him that I had a new hole in my ass. He cut my pants open and bandaged that wound also. He gave me a shot of morphine to ease the pain. He got Ascher and someone else to help him. They took my poncho from my web belt, laid me on it, and dragged me back through another hedgerow. There was another body lying on the ground and they laid me beside it. I asked who he was, and someone said it was Sgt. Cooper. They took me off the poncho and covered me with it.

Somewhere I had lost my shoe. I didn't remember when it came off. While I was lying there, I began a steady digging with my right foot into the ground. I didn't even know I was doing it. Capt. Hitti came and looked at Cooper and me and asked how I felt. He set up CP headquarters close to the wounded. Capt. Hitti was on the radio with, I believe, the Brigade Command helicopter. I overheard him say we had seven dead, and 14 wounded. He said three of the wounded had to be medevaced out tonight. Hitti must have called for Puff the Magic Dragon (AC-47 gunship with the Gatling gun). Puff can cover an area the size of a football field with a round landing every square foot in three seconds. The rounds come out so fast you do not hear a shot. The shots are a steady drone that sounds like a loud hum.

After a short while, it was fairly dark and they brought Samaripa to where Cooper and I were located. I heard Capt. Hitti calling for the medevac chopper. Apparently he was told that, as long as we were still in a hot zone, they would not risk coming out. I'm not sure what else they told him, but I believe they wanted to wait until morning. I overheard Hitti say that we would lose two more soldiers if they didn't get here tonight. He also told the listener on the other end that, if they waited until morning and the soldiers died, he would shoot them out of the air himself when they came in the morning.

The Brigade Commander cut in and said they were in the air in the vicinity and they would come in and take out the severely wounded. Before the Brigade Commander landed, Doc gave me another morphine shot. The ground under me had dried out from the draining heat of my body. Doc thought I was going into shock. Samaripa was still moaning and unconscious, and Cooper was unconscious and quiet.

When the chopper came in they loaded Sam and Cooper on the chopper first; they took up all the floor room. I was placed on the bench seat. The door gunner jumped off the chopper to help load the wounded. He got back on the chopper and sat down in his seat. It was now completely dark. My head was laying on his seat so he sat on my head. The chopper was already in the air. I yelled. He leaned forward and ahead. The door of the chopper was open and all he had between himself and the air was the machine gun pedestal. I shimmied back and repositioned myself so he could sit down.

The two morphine shots were doing their trick. I wasn't feeling any pain, and I was ecstatic that I was getting out of the field. I thought I might even get to go home, but I put that out of my mind. It was just a damn good feeling to be on this chopper. As high as I was on the morphine, I still took a few seconds to thank God that I was still alive and getting the hell away from the gooks and the fighting.

The flight to an aid station lasted at least 20 minutes. We were all unloaded and taken into a large tent used as the field hospital. If you ever watched "M.A.S.H." on TV, that's where we were at. They took a look at Cooper and Samaripa and called for a medevac chopper to take them to Qui Nho'n. They changed the dressing on my head wound, gave me another morphine shot, and put me on the same chopper to go to Qui Nho'n.

Photo depicts helmets and field equipment taken from 1st Cavalry Division (Airmobile) casualties during "Operation Long Reach" near the Cambodian border in Republic of Vietnam, November 20, 1965. Photo courtesy of the National Archives at College Park, Md. Original photo from the Records of the Office of the Chief Signal Officer. Photo ID 111-CC-32731.

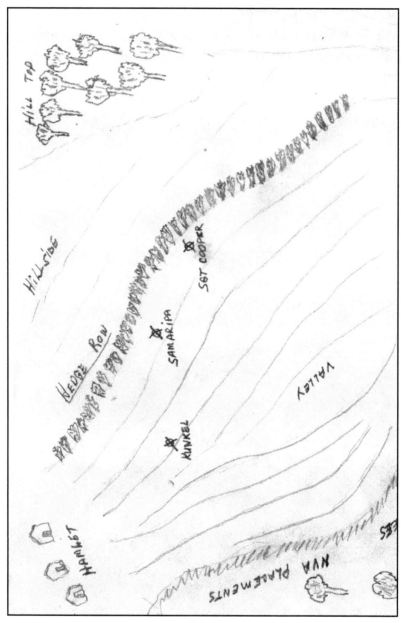

Layout of Nov. 1 firefight, as I remember it. (top half)

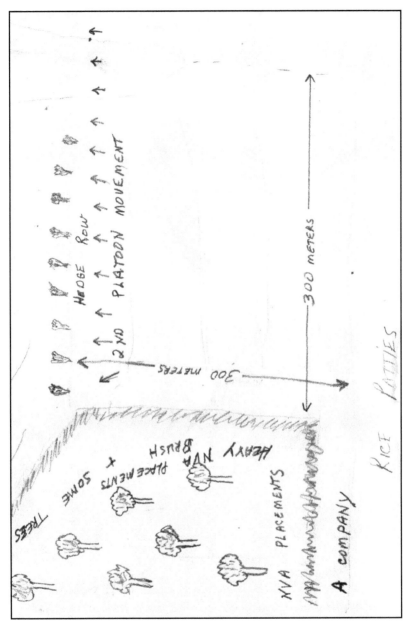

Layout of Nov. 1 firefight, as I remember it. (bottom half)

The 67th Evacuation Hospital at Qui Nho'n, Vietnam, as pictured in the USARV Medical Bulletin, USARV PAM 40-3 May/June 1967, p. 18. Photo courtesy of U.S. Army Academy of Health Sciences, Stimson Library. Photographer unknown.

HOSPITAL (QUI NHO'N)

The medevac arrived at the hospital in Qui Nho'n about 30 minutes later. With the morphine in my body, I had no pain. Actually, I felt very much relaxed and at peace. I had to feel myself to see if this was real. I could not believe I made it out of that battle without dying.

Hospital staff moved me from a field stretcher to a hospital gurney. Someone checked my wounds and then put me off to one side while the staff worked on Cooper and Samaripa. Twenty minutes later I was rolled into an operating room. A nurse, a Captain by rank, gave me another morphine shot. I didn't need another shot, but I wouldn't tell the nurse as much. This was the first time I had morphine, and it was a trip unlike any other I ever took before. (I never used recreational drugs other than alcohol.) I didn't have a care in the world.

The same nurse began cleaning my wounds. After she scrubbed the wounds, she tried to insert an IV in a vein in my forearm. She made three attempts on my right arm and then switched to my left arm. As soon as she opened the flow valve, the vein would bulge up. I was thin as a rail and very much muscle-bound. The muscles pressed against the blood veins and would not allow the IV fluid to flow. I was giving her static about it. She talked to her supervisor, a fairly plump Major. The Major attempted to place the IV. She had the same problem and I continued with the static. As loose as I was at the time, I was enjoying the attention. A doctor came to the gurney and requested some special insertion needle. It was at least 8 inches long and quite large in diameter. My right arm was taped to a straight board, and he began inserting the needle below the inside of my right elbow and slowly fed it through the vein and past the muscle. I told him this is a dry well, you might as well give up. He told me it was okay to have my fun now, but come morning you'll think this is a log sticking in you. He wasn't lying. Once the flow valve was opened. I was out.

I'm not sure how long I was out, but I believe it was near daylight when I came around. I woke up screaming for Samaripa to get down. Immediately a nurse came to my side. I asked her if Samaripa made it. She said he's okay. I told her no, he isn't. I saw where he got shot and he would not be okay. She began to rub her hands up and down my body talking softly, slowly and deliberately, trying to settle me down. Off to the left of my feet, I could see a gurney and someone on it was making moaning sounds. It sounded like the same moaning sounds I heard from Samaripa after he got shot. I wanted to get up and go over to him but the nurse said I couldn't.

I was now lying on my back and tied securely on the gurney with what I believe were sheets. The board was still taped to my arm, and the arm and board were taped securely to the side of the gurney. Like the doctor said, it felt as if there was log inside my arm. My whole body ached, unlike anything I had ever experienced before. The needle inside my arm gave me the most pain. My head was wrapped in a heavy bandage. I could tell my back across the shoulders and my butt were heavily bandaged. The nurse continued to rub and softly touch me. I was in an extremely agitated state. What parts of my body could move were in constant motion.

During this whole time, the nurse did not leave my side. Other than the night before, it had been a long time since I had talked to an American female. Even with the pain and agitation, it was a great experience. I still had pain, but my body movements began to slow down. By now my bladder seemed about ready to bust. I told the nurse I had to piss. I guess I still had my field manners. She held the bed urinal for me and I let it flow. The urinal filled up and a little spilled over me. I managed to hold the rest back while she got another urinal so I could finish the job. Since I was fully undressed under the sheet, it was easy to clean me up.

When I was finally settled down, the nurse left my side and went about her other duties. Eventually, the moaning from the other gurney stopped. Samaripa is listed as a KIA on November 2, the day after the battle. He most likely died in my presence.

The longer I lay there, the stronger the pain became. My back across the shoulders was throbbing. The needle caused a sharp stinging in my upper arm. My whole body ached from being secured flat on the gurney. I could see the bottle that was supplying the juice in my arm was slowly getting empty. When it finally drained down, I expected the nurse would remove the needle. Instead, when it was almost empty, the nurse put a full one up again. I tried to convince her I didn't need any more, but she wouldn't hear of it. I made up my mind to shut off the pain. I began thinking about going home. I wasn't sure what would happen, but I wanted to believe that, once I was stable enough, I would be sent home. I said some prayers thanking God that I was still alive, and I prayed for Samaripa. I tried to look around the room I was in but, because I was secured flat on my back, I was limited to what I could see. I eventually fell asleep but it didn't last long. I woke up yelling at Samaripa. The nurse was by my side again rubbing me and talking me down. I had to pee again, so we went through the routine as before. This time I didn't fill the urinal.

By mid-afternoon, the IV bottle was nearing empty. The nurse came by, pinched the flow off, and said that she would remove the needle. She pulled the needle out slowly but steadily. It felt as if someone was sticking little pins in my arm as the needle came out. Once it was out, the relief was overwhelming.

The bonds holding my arm were released, and the sheets holding me to the gurney were untied. A short time elapsed and I was carted from the recovery room to a small room where I was weighed. My weight was 112 pounds. I knew I was thin, but I didn't think I was quite that light. Considering I had had nothing to eat since breakfast the day before, and after the doctors were finished carving on me, it was more understandable. Although we had no scales to weigh ourselves, I believe my usual body weight was roughly about 130 pounds. (Unknown to me at the time, I had a wide trough cut across my back, and another one cut through my right buttock.)

I was transferred to a regular room. Even with the wrapped-up head, two soldiers from the 3rd platoon recognized me and came over. They had been injured at the time Coviak was killed by the booby-trap mine. One was Lt. Merten and the other was James Underwood. I filled them in on what I knew about the firefight. We talked until a nurse came to give me a double penicillin shot. With my muscles bound as tightly as they were, the shots were painful. I received these shots every four hours.

Shortly after the shots, the evening meals came in. I had forgotten about food, something I got used to in the past three months. There was nothing spectacular about the food, but it sure tasted good. I would eat a little bit and feel full. I waited a short while and ate more. When the stomach shrinks, it does not take much to satisfy it. Lt. Merten and Underwood were bunked at the opposite end of the ward. After supper, I decided to get out of bed and visit them. Every move I made getting up felt like it was driving pains through me. A nurse saw me struggling, came to my side, and wanted to know what I was doing. I told her and she instructed me to wait until she could find a wheelchair.

I talked with Merten and Underwood for at least two hours. The nurse told me it was time to get back in my bunk. I was located at the opposite end of the room across the center aisle and up against the wall. The bed next to me was empty. It felt good getting back in the bunk. I was tired and I fell asleep quickly. Because of the damage to my back, I slept face-down.

The night nurse woke me for my double shot of pain (the penicillin). As soon as she touched me I jumped and twisted, ready for the attack. It sent a searing pain across my upper shoulders. After the shots, I could not get back to sleep. A million things ran through my mind. As always I found time to say a few prayers. I sat up for a while on the edge of the bed and watched over the room. About once every 30 minutes a nurse would walk through, take vital signs on some, check IVs on others. This was my first time in a hospital so watching the routine, while not exciting, was interesting. This was before the "M.A.S.H." series on television, so what I was seeing was new to me.

About the time I finally fell asleep, I was awakened again for the next double shot of pain. As before, I awoke with a jump, and again there was the pain across my upper back.

It took about three weeks to get over these jump-starts when waking up.

I slept for a short while and then breakfast came in. I was extremely hungry and displayed as much with the way I gulped the food down.

Off in another room, I heard someone screaming in what must've been severe pain. The screaming continued for a few minutes. Another 20 minutes later two medics brought another patient into the ward. He was pale in color and in obvious pain. They placed him into the bed beside me. Both of his legs were bandaged from toe to the hip. For about 15 minutes he received all the attention in the ward. They kept the IV bottle with tubes attached to him. Once the staff left, he fell off to sleep. For the next two hours, he slept but talked and even yelled, mostly incoherently, while he slept.

A couple of hours later he woke up with a jump. He slowly looked around the room, apparently trying to orient himself. I sat up and welcomed him back to the world. I asked him how he was doing. You could see the pain etched on his face as he told me his legs were all torn up from hand grenades. He appeared talkative, so I asked him how he got wounded. He was with the 4th Division. Their position was overrun by a human wave of gooks. He was on a machine gun. He said a gook came running at him with a grenade in each hand. He fired into the gook's body but he kept coming until he fell right in front of him. He said the grenades rolled out, one on each side of him, and went off. When the gook was running at him he had the barrel pointed right on his chest. So many bullets went through the gook, he could see right through him, yet he kept coming at him. He said that other gooks ran right past him, thinking he was dead. When the medics finally got to him, they said the attacking gook had syringe needles taped to both arms. The Viet Cong or NVA soldiers would shoot themselves up with heroin when going into the fight. The reason they taped the needles to their arms, was to give them a quick fix if they started to come down before they died or the fight was over.

He asked me what outfit I was with and how I got wounded. I gave him a short version of my experience. A nurse came by, took his vitals and asked how he was doing. He said he had a lot of pain. She told him that he would have to wait another hour before she could give him another shot. She also said that he still had shrapnel in his legs and that is why the pain was so sharp.

By now I was tired enough to try sleep again. It didn't last long. A nurse came by to administer my double shot of pain again. My muscles were still tight, and the injections were painful. Considering what the guy next to me was going through, I gritted my teeth and kept my mouth shut.

Lunch came and I ate everything. The guy next to me had his first meal and, like me, could only eat a small amount at a time. He did not finish his tray before they came to pick up the empties. He slept some more, and Underwood came over and talked to me. He said he had heard they were going to ship a bunch of the wounded to Japan the next day. I guess we hoped we would be making the trip.

About midway through the afternoon, a nurse and medic came to get the guy next to me. The nurse said they had to remove some more shrapnel from his legs. He asked why they couldn't put him under for it. She said something about needing to know what was the extent of nerve damage on his legs. He was in tears as they rolled him away. A few minutes later the screaming started again. It seemed to last forever but probably went on for about 20 minutes. About 20 minutes after the screaming ended the nurse and medic wheeled him back into the unit. Again he was as white as a sheet and heavily sedated. Even with the pain, he dropped off to sleep. He slept nearly two hours. When he awoke, the nurse brought in about a pint-sized jar, three-fourths full of chunks of shrapnel. She said it was cleaned up and he could keep it for a souvenir. He asked whether they got it all. She said there were some chunks still in his body, but that they were too deep; if they had to come out, they would take them out in the next hospital he went to from Qui Nho'n. I looked at the jar and told him if that came from two grenades, at least half of all the metal went into his body.

The rest of the day progressed in most likely what was routine for the hospital staff. The penicillin shots came on schedule, vitals were taken as needed, and the evening meal showed up on time. By now the rumor was out that many of the patients would be leaving the next day for Japan. The guy next to me still had enough pain, but his spirits seemed to be better. By 10 o'clock most everyone was sleeping. It seemed I slept more in the last two days than I had since arriving in Vietnam. The only way I could lie was face-down, so if I couldn't get to sleep I would sit up. I got pretty adept at rolling myself up into a sitting position without straining my back too much. After the lights went down, I sat up in bed and watched little or nothing going on. There were 24 beds in the ward, and only a few of them were empty. I seemed to be the only one awake. Every so often someone would talk in his sleep. I'm sure most of the dreaming was none too pleasant. I managed to say a few prayers, but the mumbling and sleep-talking broke my concentration.

Close to midnight, my eyes were drooping. I knew I was due for the penicillin, so I decided to stay awake until I had that behind me. The new nurse for the midnight shift came in with a single syringe. She was slightly older than the other nurses and was a little on the plump side. She said I would only get the one shot and the Doc said to give it every six hours instead of the usual four hours. I put myself in the face-down prone position. She pulled my pajamas down a few inches, rubbed the alcohol over the target area, and then gave my butt a hard slap. By the time the sting went out of my butt from the slap, she had given me the shot. I hardly felt the pain. I told her to teach the other nurses how to do it that way. She told me to get some sleep and she would see me at 6 in the morning. I slept straight through and, true to her word, she was there at 6:00 a.m. She gave me the shot and told me to get more sleep. It seemed only like a few minutes and at 8:00 breakfast was served.

After breakfast, a doctor came through checking on the patients. He removed the bandage from my head and said I didn't need it any longer. The right half of my head was shaved. There were 22 stitches in my scalp to pull it back together. The gash in my scalp was about 4 inches long. The Doc told me I was very lucky with the wounds. He said if the bullet had been an eighth-inch lower, it would have gone into the skull, and another fraction of an inch, the bullet that went through my back would have hit the spine causing paralysis.

As soon as the Doc went on his way, someone called me Comanche. The nickname stuck until the hair grew out and I got the whole head cut to the same length.

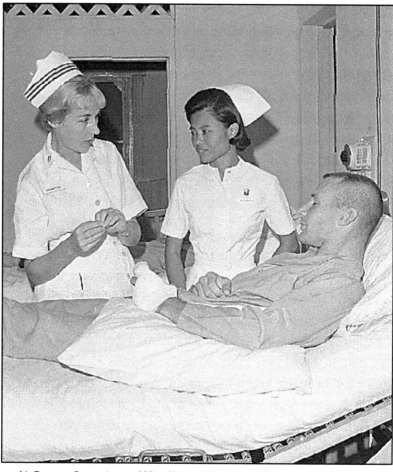

Lt. Frances Crumpton and Miss Nangnoi Tongkim, a Thai nurse, talk with an American soldier wounded in the Vietnam war, February 1966. The nurses work in the Navy hospital in Saigon. U.S. Navy photo, ID 558528. Photo courtesy of the National Archives in College Park, Md.

FLIGHT TO JAPAN

The rest of the morning was routine for the patients. The nurses were busy, though. We were informed that most of us, the patients, would be leaving this hospital and going to other military hospitals. We had lunch and the staff began moving patients. The guy next to me, the one with the shrapnel, was the first guy taken out of our ward. There were only a few guys left when they transferred me onto a gurney and wheeled me away. We were loaded onto a bus and, after the bus was filled with patients, we were taken to the airport where we were loaded onto a C-141 military jet. From my recollection, there were 80 patients on the plane, all in litters. We were stacked four-high, two-wide down the center of the plane. We were loaded on from the rear of the plane. I was the second from the top on the last litters on the plane. It appeared that I was the only patient lying face-down.

The guy they loaded under me was an older man who apparently had a spinal fracture. His litter was made up differently than the rest. His feet were bound together and had a small cable over a pulley with weights holding his feet rigid and taut. He had a metal frame around his head and secured to his chin. A metal pin went through the frame and into his skull on each side of his head about one inch above the ears. A cable was stretched over a pulley with weights holding his head taut. No one was loaded into the space under him.

We were told that we would fly to a hospital at an
Air Force base in the Philippines, and we would stay there
overnight. The flight would take about six hours.

We were all securely strapped onto the litters. When
the plane took off, there were three nurses tending to the guy
with the spinal condition. Once we were high enough to level
off, two of the nurses went about other business.

An hour into the flight, the plane apparently hit an air
pocket. It dropped vertically down a considerable distance.
Initially, I thought we were going down. It sent a frightful chill
through me. I'm sure I was not alone. As soon as the plane
stabilized, two nurses came to aid the nurse on the guy below
me. I could see the nurses could use more room, so I volunteered to sit on one of the benches to the side of the plane.
They were happy to have the extra space. Later on, one of the
nurses told me the plane had hit an air pocket and fell about
700 feet before stabilizing.

The bench was hard wood and, because of the wound
to my buttock, I could only sit on the left half of my butt. This
was okay for about an hour but became strenuous as time
wore on. There were loop straps above our heads to hold onto.
I stood up and looped my arm through a strap to give my butt
a break. I alternated standing and sitting for the next three
and a half hours. We hit another air pocket, but it was barely
noticeable.

Twenty minutes before landing, a nurse said I had
to get back into my litter. She helped me crawl onto it, and
strapped me down. We landed and, as soon as the plane
stopped moving, the back gate was dropped. There were
numerous military ambulances waiting to haul us away. The
guy with the spinal problem was the first off the plane, and
he had an ambulance to himself with two nurses. I was loaded

onto an ambulance with three other guys. All we got was a male medic who rode in back with us. He wasn't even cute.

When the ambulance pulled up in front of the hospital and the door was opened, the first thing I noticed was a paved driveway with concrete curbs. There were concrete sidewalks and mowed green grass. There was a flower garden in the center of the driveway turnaround. This was the first I saw like this since leaving the States. It was like taking a step out of the past and into the future. It was inspiring and beautiful. Being removed from such order for the past three months allowed me to fully appreciate this scene now. From that day on, I would appreciate many things more that we often take for granted.

My view of the scenery was short-lived. I was put on a gurney and wheeled into the hospital and onto an elevator that stopped on the third floor. I was put into a hospital room. A doctor looked me over and told a medic to remove all the bandages. A medic removed the outer bandages. There was a porous gauze strip embedded into my open back and butt wounds. The seepage had come through the gauze and was now dry, binding the material to the raw flesh. The medic was soaking the gauze and slowly removing it a fraction of an inch at a time. Each time he pulled it felt as if he were tearing a chunk off my back. Ten minutes later he had removed only a short strip. The doctor came in and looked it over. He asked me a question and as I was answering he yanked the gauze off with one quick motion. It felt like he tore my insides out. I tried to crawl through the mattress. A few seconds later the shock left and the pain subsided. He tore the gauze off my butt. This felt like he was petting me compared to what he did to my back.

The medic cleaned off the fresh blood, washed the wounds and redressed them. I fell asleep as soon as I was left alone. The nap was short because supper arrived. Supper was a large hamburger on a bun, French fries, raw onion, green beans, and ice cream for dessert. This meal hit the spot. Everything was beginning to feel American. I suppose we take a lot of things for granted if they are available any time we want them. This type of junk-food meal was a real treat for me.

I had a room to myself. After eating, I got up and went to the window. I could not see too much from the room window, so I went out into the hall. At the end of the hall was a window that faced the front of the hospital. I could see an overview of the entrance driveway, the sidewalks, the grass and multiple flower beds spread around. The sun was setting and everything drifted into shadows and dark shades. I stared and watched until everything beyond the street lights was in complete darkness. I went back to my room. I was tired, but before I fell asleep a male nurse came in and gave me a penicillin shot.

It seemed as if I had just fallen asleep when I was awakened for breakfast. The sun was shining and a new day was under way. Shortly after breakfast, I was carted out to an ambulance and, along with other patients, was taken to the airfield for the final leg of our journey to Japan. The older man with the spinal fracture was not on this flight.

The flight from the Philippines to Japan took about six hours. It was a dull and boring flight. After a few hours, the drone of the engines became an almost unbearable sound. The planes were not as sound-proofed as commercial flights. I was on a bottom bunk. Three times during the flight I got out of the bunk and sat on one of the benches along the outer cabin corridor. Once the plane landed, everyone seemed happy to get off. Our cots were loaded onto military buses and we were transported to hospitals. Certain patients were taken to a hospital near Yokota. I was on a bus that took us to the 7th Field Hospital at Johnson Air Force Base near Fujisawa.

Fujisawa is a suburb of Tokyo. On the trip from the airport to the hospital, we went through the town of Tachikawa. Along the road there were a series of heavily fortified concrete towers, standing about 40 feet high, with old anti-aircraft guns mounted on the upper base platform. There were at least 10 of these towers, most likely a standing tribute as a World War II memorial.

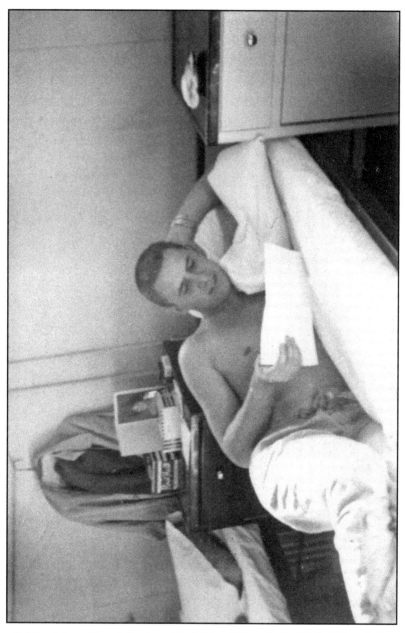

Bob Kunkel, reading a letter from his girlfriend Eileen, in the 7th Field Hospital in Japan. He is wearing the watch his girlfriend Eileen sent him for Christmas while reading a letter from her. Her photo is on the nightstand behind him.

7th FIELD HOSPITAL

The trip from the airport to the 7th Field Hospital took more than an hour. By the time we arrived, nighttime was settling in. As soon as I was installed in my room, a nurse came in and began removing bandages. She had a distinct New York accent. I asked her what part of New York she was from. If I remember correctly, I believe she said Yonkers. I told her when she got to the gauze that was sticking to the wound, to just rip it off. As it turned out, the gauze came off with very little pain. A doctor came in and looked at the wound and went over my chart. Apparently, I had an infection in the wound that had started at the time I was shot. This is why I had the heavy doses of penicillin. The doctor gave instructions and the nurse went to work soaking and washing the wounds. She scrubbed the back wound for a long time but gave the butt wound cursory attention. By now the stitches in my head wound had an itch; this is a good sign of healing.

There was another bed in my room but it was unoccupied. Supper arrived and I was famished. I don't remember what I had, but the food in this hospital was very tasty. After supper, I slept for a couple of hours. The nurse came in and woke me to take my vitals: temperature and pulse. Since I was lying on my stomach, I sat up. I spent the next couple of hours thinking about our platoon and company back in Vietnam. I said a few prayers for them. I was happy to be out of Vietnam but had a feeling of guilt for not being there with the guys I had come to know so well. These thoughts weighed on me quite often while I was in the hospital. Sometime after 10 p.m., the nurse came in and scrubbed my back and butt wounds again. The first night in the hospital I was awake more than asleep. I had a hard time adjusting to the hospital mattress. I think it was too comfortable. At least every two hours a nurse would stop in and take vitals. The night nurse was a very tall redhead from Columbia, South Carolina. She had a very distinct, pleasant and almost dreamy southern drawl. I would ask her questions just to hear her talk. In a sense, I fell in love with her. In fact, the way the nurses treated me, I fell in love with all of them. During my entire stay in the various hospitals, I felt I was always treated special by the nurses. I'm sure they treated all the wounded GIs with a special interest.

After breakfast the next morning, the day nurse brought a Japanese nurse's aide into my room and demonstrated to her how to clean and scrub my wounds. From then on this same nurse's aide took care of scrubbing and redressing my wounds.

When redressing the wound on my butt, I had to kneel up so she could wrap the wound around my upper thigh. She had to reach blindly around my inner thigh to retrieve the gauze roll. On one occasion she grabbed my penis. I had an instant erection. She said she was sorry and giggled. I told her, "You got it up, now you have to get it down." She giggled some more and said, "I can't do that." I told her that was a hell of a condition to leave a patient. Of course I was joking with her, and it made her giggle more.

Late that afternoon I got a roommate. When he was brought in, he was as pale as a ghost and wired high with tension. I told him he looked as if he saw a ghost. He said he damn near saw his own ghost. He said he was a litter patient on a C-141. When they were coming in for a landing, the landing gear would not come down. The plane circled the airport until ground crews could foam the runway. The plane had to make a belly-slide landing. He was sure he was going to die. I told him that he would have a hell of a story to tell his grandkids some day.

My roommate was with the 25th Division operating in the Mekong Delta when he was wounded. He had two gunshot wounds down his back. After his initial operation, he had a chunk of meat missing from his back about 4 inches wide and 8 inches long running up and down his back to the right of his backbone. His name was Brad Brugstad, and he was from New York City, either Long Island or Staten Island. It didn't take long for us to become good friends. We found a lot of things to BS about. He was from the Big City and I was from the country, yet we had many things in common.

There were two guys in our ward who had foot or leg injuries and were confined to using wheelchairs to navigate. They became very proficient with the use of these carts. They had races up and down the hallways. They could spin the wheelchairs around on a dime, and balance them on two wheels for long periods. They were constantly challenging each other to refine new tricks with the wheelchairs, similar to what the skateboarders of today do. In a way it was entertaining to watch them and, even though they could be menacing as an accident waiting to happen, hospital staff did not make too big a fuss. On occasion, though, the nurses had to shut down the escapades so they could do their work without interference.

There was a large bathroom for ward patients at the end of the hallway. If you weren't confined to your bunk, you had to use this bathroom. One time, close to a week after taking residence on this ward, I went into the bathroom. Some guy in the end stall was taking his first crap after having a hemorrhoid operation. From the sounds he was making, it was obvious that he was in extreme pain. He was moaning, whining, and calling on God for mercy and assistance. At one point he said he would never eat again. At the time I didn't know what was his problem, so I asked him if I should call staff to help him. I don't think he knew I was there until I talked to him. He said he didn't need help. He had to get through this on his own. I left the bathroom and went back to my room. I stood in the doorway, watching to see who would come out of the bathroom. About 20 minutes later he emerged from the bathroom. He looked pale and weak as he made it back to his room. I made a note of what room he went into and intended to talk with him later.

Later in the day I made it to his room and introduced myself. I told him I was the one who was in the bathroom when he was in his agony. This is when he told me about the hemorrhoid operation he had. He was from Boston, and his name was Tom Hennessey.

I spent about 30 minutes with him. He was a little bit on the quiet side but seemed very intelligent. Later on in the day, he found me in my room and we talked again. I introduced him to my roommate Brad. From that day, and for as long as we were together in the hospital, we were good friends. Over the years I had many good thoughts and memories of these two people who entered into my life for my stay in the hospital.

The next five weeks dragged by slowly. We got to know most of the patients on our ward, and played cards often. We played poker for payday stakes. I was a big winner, but I knew I would never see the money. None of us got paid while in the hospital. If we wanted money, we had to write home for it, or write to friends we left back in 'Nam. I wrote to the company clerk to have him send me my wallet. I had around $120 in my wallet when I got shot. I also wrote home and asked Mom to send me about $40. I figured that, with the money in my wallet and the $40 from home, I should be able to take care of my stay in the hospital. I received the wallet with the bullet hole from when I got shot in the head. It had old dried blood on it and it was green/gray with mildew. There was no money in it. Close to the same time I got the $40 from home. I wrote home for more money when I realized I would be a little short on cash with the loss of my money in 'Nam.

For a change while resting, I discovered it was fairly comfortable for me to sleep on my left side, close to the edge of the bed, right arm extended out and down at the elbow, and hanging over the edge of the mattress. I propped my left arm up and supported my right arm in the cradle of my palms on the high side of the elbow.

Around Thanksgiving, the hospital began playing Christmas music over the speaker system in the hospital. The music seemed okay at first, but after hearing it day-in and day-out it started to stir up homesickness. Elvis Presley came out with a new song called, "[I'll Have A] Blue Christmas Without You." This song was played two or three times every hour. It got so I couldn't stand it. In fact, all the Christmas music wore me down so much that I still don't want to listen to it some 50 years later.

On or about December 8, I got a letter from Ray Judy. He had to tell me about the firefight B Company got into December 1st. He listed the people who were killed. There were three from 2nd platoon. One was Dennis Benedetti, the machine-gunner who worked with our squad most of the time. It took a long time for me to put it in my mind that he was actually dead and that I would not be seeing him anymore. I considered him one of my best friends along with Ray Judy and Tom Gray. Two other guys from the platoon who died were Lewis Albanese and Xavier Fernandez. Albanese jumped into a trench that had about eight gooks in it; they were about to catch B Company in crossfire as they moved forward. He worked his way down the trench killing all the gooks until he was killed himself. When they found him, he had his hands wrapped around the throat of a dead gook, apparently choking him to death. Albanese had multiple gunshot and stab wounds to his body from his close encounter with the enemy. He subsequently received the Medal of Honor for his actions.

According to Judy, the gooks were setting up a mortar to use against the company. One of the squad leaders called the information to Capt. Hitti. Using the squad leader's position as a reference point, he called in artillery on the mortar position. The round came damn close to dropping in the muzzle of the mortar sending the mortar catapulting into the air, and disintegrating at least four bodies.

Judy wrote that Joe Gonzales was a machine-gunner. He opened up on a gook machine gun position, knocking it out. In all, the gooks had five different machine guns to use against the GIs. Firing that many rounds, Joe's machine gun got so hot that the receiver did what they call a hot-freeze: the machine gun would not stop firing until it ran out of shells. Once it stopped firing, it was unusable. He yelled for all the rounds in the platoon. Everybody except the radioman carried at least 100 machine gun rounds on their person. Some carried 200 rounds. GIs started throwing their ammunition belts to the next guy until it was relayed to the ammo bearer, who then linked it to the belt feeding through the gun. The gun barrel became white hot, actually bending downward with the heat. Joe had to raise the barrel on his targets. Every fourth round for the machine gun is a tracer round; you use the tracers to guide your aim. Judy wrote in his letter that Joe fired over 5,000 rounds taking out all five enemy machine guns.

Fernandez was wounded, but couldn't move. He was calling and even begging for help. The gooks were so close to the GIs that, when they ran out of ammunition, they threw rocks at the soldiers. According to Judy, Capt. Hitti called artillery almost directly on the company's position because the enemy was so close. Our artillery is what eventually killed Fernandez.

Eugene Feldkamp was wounded during the firefight. It was after dark and someone shot at him, wounding him. He jumped into a trench with gooks in it and he lost his rifle. They shot him again. He yelled so they shot him again. This time he played dead. The gooks left him alone and eventually crawled out of the trench to make their escape. Feldkamp crawled out and went the other way. Once he was safely away from the trench, he called and said who he was and that he was

Joe Gonzalez, machine-gunner.

coming through the lines. He had been shot five times. He was happy that he found his rifle before coming back. (Feldkamp was the guy I found crying on the ship when we were en route to Vietnam, and the same guy who almost threw Sgt. Inez overboard on the ship.)

Benedetti was killed when he was crawling forward to transfer a LAW to Sgt. Nehr. A LAW is a hand-held rocket used

Dennis Benedetti on the ship USS Hugh Gaffey.

to blow up bunkers or other fortified enemy positions. He came to an area that had no cover. It was possible that he could have thrown the LAW to Nehr. Instead, he chose to roll across the open area. He was shot in the neck and head.

After Benedetti was killed Walter Zimmerman, the assistant machine-gunner, became the main gunner. As the battle carried on he ran low on ammunition. Each time he had to fire he was conservative with the number of rounds he fired. As darkness settled in, he had four rounds of ammo left on the belt; he was saving this for a last stand. He was close enough to the enemy that he could hear the gooks breathing and whispering to each other. He was sure that he was going to die as he was somewhat isolated from the rest of the platoon. It was fairly dark as a hand came up over the bank on which he had the gun resting; that hand grabbed the barrel end and started to pull the gun. Zimmerman let loose the last burst of ammo. He heard a scream followed by the sound of someone crawling away from his position. Now, without any ammo left, he was more sure than ever that he was going to die.

About this time artillery rounds started coming in. They were landing very close to him. He pulled down his head and lay as flat as he could to the ground. He could hear chunks of metal sailing over his head. He had the bank of ground to his front but no cover from behind. The artillery finally stopped and everything was quiet. After a time, he decided to pull back and try to locate other members of the platoon. He came across another person going the opposite direction. He was going to tell him he was going the wrong way when he realized it was a gook. He watched the gook until he disappeared into the darkness, and then he continued on his way until he heard American/English conversation. In a low tone, he called out stating who he was and that he was coming in.

(This information about Walter Zimmerman I learned when he attended the 50-year reunion of the 5/7 Cav in August 2016 in Colorado Springs, Colorado.)

I read Judy's letter a couple of times. I started to tell my roommate Brad about the firefight. I had a hard time trying to explain, so I gave him the letter to read for himself.

My mind was full of mixed feelings about the letter. I felt sad for those who died, proud of those who fought, and I felt guilty because I wasn't there. I got the letter late in the day, and I didn't sleep very well that night.

On or about December 10, three doctors came into my room to check on my back wound. They were discussing how they would put me back together. They wanted to sew my back together instead of patching it with skin grafts, as was the normal procedure with a wound like mine. After their discussion, one of the doctors explained to me what they wanted to do. I did not like the idea of having skin stripped from my thighs and grafted onto my back. I also didn't like the idea of having the trough running across my back, as would be the case if they grafted the skin as opposed to pulling the wound shut and stitching it together. This would be a new procedure so they needed my permission to do it. They had it. I didn't get any supper that evening and had to refrain from drinking any water after midnight.

At about 7 a.m. the next morning, I was loaded onto a gurney and taken to the operating room. An IV was hooked up, and the next thing I woke up feeling like a twisted-up knot.

I had a harness made of sheet-like material around my shoulders and around my hips. My hips and shoulders were pulled together, and a winch was made from the wraps to put a severe arch in my back. The pain was almost unbearable. As soon as I tried to stir, a nurse gave me a shot of morphine.

I got the shot on a regular basis after that for at least the next 10 days. I could not keep track of time as I was always sedated. For the first week, I couldn't get out of bed. Apparently, the doctors didn't want me to move for fear I would tear the wire stitches in my back. Since I was heavily sedated with morphine, I slept a lot, and the days went by in a blur.

Six or seven days later, the doctor took a little pressure off the knotted winch. Then each day he took a little more pressure off. The 10 days on morphine were a blur: I was conscious of what was happening, but the entire time my mind seemed to be in a displaced state. One morning the doctor decided that I had had enough morphine. He put me on another painkiller of some type. The next two days were a hell for me as I went through withdrawal. I yelled at and threatened the nurses because they wouldn't give me the shots. It's a good thing I was in no position to carry out the threats. I told the day nurse, the one from New York, that I would kill her the first chance I got if she didn't give me the morphine. I had full recollection of what I was saying, and the only thing that mattered is that I needed another shot. I now know what an addict goes through. It's not a pretty picture. It took at least two full days to withdraw from the morphine. Once I was stable, I had a good memory of what I had said to the nurses. Once my mind was straight, I apologized to each of them. They all understood and were pleased that I had apologized.

My girlfriend then, now wife, Eileen sent me a package. In it, she sent a Bulova wristwatch and a photo of herself. The photo showed near-cleavage and a lot of shoulder. Besides that, she had the prettiest face. After holding it for a time, I placed it on a small credenza on the wall next to my bed. I received many compliments on how beautiful she looked. The doctor, who otherwise seemed to be a matter-of-fact guy, even commented on her beauty. I was proud of that photo.

A couple of days before Christmas, a nurse told me that I had a phone call. She directed me to a phone and, once I informed the operator that I was on, she put me through. Eileen was on the other end. I was still on some pain medication, so I don't think I seemed very excited about the call, but I was happy she went through the effort and expense to make it. While we were talking, I began to think how much this call was costing her, and I felt guilty about it. I believe I may have mentioned this to Eileen and figured I should keep the conversation short so the bill didn't get too big.

Christmas came and went with little fanfare other than the traditional turkey dinner. Some Red Cross women came through and talked briefly with each of us, handed out some wrapped chocolate candy and peanuts, wished us a Merry Christmas, and moved on to the next room.

The music continued to edge our sanity to the left of center, and they must have worn out at least three "Blue, Blue Christmas" records.

CONVALESCING

The day after Christmas, the doctor came through and told me that I was going to be moved to an open ward in another part of the hospital. I gathered my personal effects and was guided by a nurse assistant to the new ward. On the way, he showed me the cafeteria and the canteen. There was a barbershop as part of the canteen. Haircuts were 50 cents and I needed one. I was shown to a bed that had a locker and a small vanity beside it. There were 30 beds in the barracks and most of them were in use.

The first guy I recognized was James Underwood. As I was getting situated, he stopped by my bunk and we talked. I also saw the two guys who were among the wheelchair Olympians.

One of them called me Comanche. I told him, "Not for long." I still had the misfit haircut. The hair on the left side of my head was about two inches long or longer, and the on right side it was still less than an inch. Uncle Sam was not about to waste any money on giving one of their finest a free haircut. It was close to noon and Underwood and I went to lunch together. The food was good. The dining room had one rule, take all you want, but you have to eat what you take. This was a mistake for me. All I could think of was the many times I had gone without food or had too little food while in Vietnam. I filled my plate. I had a hard time finishing it, but I managed.

Lying around for about seven weeks with nothing to do but rest, then walking the hallways of the hospital transferring to another unit, and then filling my stomach past capacity made me tired. I got back to the ward, flopped on the mattress and fell asleep. After a good hour, I got up and went to the canteen to get a haircut. The barbershop was closed. I was told the barber only cut hair in the morning and I should come back the next day.

I walked around the hospital, checking it out. I wandered into another ward with rooms similar to where I had spent my first seven weeks. I was checking the rooms to see if I knew anyone. In one room, the guy from the 4th Division who was in the bunk beside me in Qui Nho'n was lying in his bed. The first thing I noticed was that he had one leg missing. I stepped in and talked to him. He was in a depressed mood. He told me that he wished he had died. He seemed okay with me being there, so I stayed and talked for at least an hour. He still had not written home to tell his family what had happened to him. He broke down and cried when he told me this. I just didn't know what to say to him. I believed that if I had been in his place, I most likely would have felt the same as he did. He said as soon as he was in good enough shape, they would ship him State-side. He said he wished he could go back to 'Nam and get it over with. I knew he meant to go back and die. I tried to cheer him up, but the way I felt for him I was feeble at best in my attempt. I talked with this guy twice more before he was shipped State-side. There was little or no change in his mood.

About three days after Christmas, the walking wounded were invited to a community-like day room close to the hospital to see and listen to Charlie Walker and his band. Walker was a Country Western musician who had some songs that made the elite record charts. Underwood and I went together. The band sounded really good, and it was good to hear something that wasn't Christmas sounding for a change. The band let patients who had music ability play along with them, or sing by themselves. One GI took up the guitar and sang a solo of "It's Suppertime." Another one said he played lead guitar for a band back in South Carolina. He played while the band accompanied him and he sang. I forget the song, but it sounded very good. The way he picked those strings, it was evident that he had done it a time or two before. When the song was over, Charlie Walker told him he would hire him on the spot. He made some joke about his lead guitar player needing more practice or something. At any rate, he gave the guy a card and told him to give him a call once he got out of the service. He said that he would hook him up with some people who could get him in with the right people to make some money in country music.

A 1st Lieutenant played the piano. He played a few songs with the band. He also had the knack for listening to a few chords of music for a song and then jumping in and

playing along, even though he had never played the song before. I guess when you get a cross-section of people as those in the armed services, you get a good cross-section of talent as well. That's even more evident in the music field.

About mid-morning the following day, the doctor came into the Ward and looked at the wire stitches in my back. He said it was time for them to come out. He left and returned a short time later with a small wire cutter and a couple of different pliers. He cut all the wire stitches across my back and then began to pull the wires out through the meat. As he pulled each stitch there was a severe sharp and stinging pain. The two on either side of my backbone were extremely tight and would not come out as easily as those to the outer sides of my back. He initially tried them and all he managed to do was stretch the meat and skin, sending me into a blaring groan. With his knee in my back, and one hand compressed against my skin around the stitch, he finally pulled one wire through. As if this wasn't bad enough, the last wire stitch broke at the skin surface. The doc wrapped the pliers around the other side of the stitch and began pulling again. My scream must have been heard on the other side of Tokyo. It finally came out. He released his hold on me and I began to rise off the bunk. He pushed me down and said not to move for at least 15 minutes. I looked around the room and everyone was standing and looking at me, their faces serious and concerned. The doc gave me medical orders to go out on the town, find a Geisha house and get a full-body massage, then get drunk and get laid. He said it didn't have to be in that order either. I didn't follow the doctor's orders exactly. I went out with Underwood to the Johnson Air Force Base NCO Club and got drunk. I didn't have that much to drink actually but, being out of circulation for at least five months, a few beers did the trick.

The Johnson Air Force Base NCO Club is unlike any military club I have ever seen previously or since. It covered at least a large city block. It had a smaller lounge bar area that could seat about 150 people. The main lounge arena could seat at least 2,000. There was a dining room that could seat about 300 people. You had to go outside the lounge areas to get to the dining room. There was a small casino area between the two lounges, and there was a game room separated from the smaller lounge. Drinks were very reasonable. Falstaff and Black Label beer were 15 cents a bottle. Budweiser, Miller, and one or two other brands of American beer were 20 cents a bottle. Mixed drinks were 20 cents for a single mix, i.e. rum & coke, whiskey-7, brandy-sour, etc. Any multiple-mix drinks were 25 cents each.

Most nights there was a live band playing the smaller lounge. On weekends and for special occasions a popular-name band would play the large lounge. Every Thursday night was Bingo night. People would pack the large lounge to play Bingo. Blackout games, if completed within the minimum numbers called, would pay as high as $10,000 dollars. If it went beyond the minimum numbers called, it paid $2,000 dollars. The blackout games were played between the Johnson Air Force Base and the Yokota Air Force Base, which was about 20 miles away. Bingo was big in Japan for military staff. I played Bingo twice. The first time while playing a blackout game, I had every number on my card filled with the exception of one number: O-71. There were about five numbers to go before the minimum numbers were completed. The caller was calling from the Yokota Base. Three times in a row he called an "O" number. Three times my heart jumped into my throat. Three times I was disappointed. Bingo was finally yelled two numbers after the minimum numbers were called.

There was a Japanese woman who waited on clients in the small lounge area. She was about 28 to 30 years old. She spoke fluent English. After waiting on us a few times, I called her "Mama-san." She became upset and told me she was not a Mama-san. She said she was a Jo-san, (Japanese for girl or young woman). I apologized. She accepted it and became very friendly and protective of me. She sensed that I didn't have much money, so she wouldn't accept any tips. She told me to drink slowly so I wouldn't have to buy so often. I accepted her advice, and she seemed to take a special interest in me.

This was wintertime in Japan, same as in the States. However, since Japan is a large island surrounded by the Pacific Ocean and the South China Sea, it was a mild climate. On clear days, from the hospital we could see Mount Fuji to the west. In the early mornings and late at night, you might need a light jacket or at least a long-sleeved shirt to be outside for any length of time. But most days were mellow enough for short-sleeved shirts and shorts, if you preferred. On rare occasions it would snow, but this did not happen while I was in Japan. Nearly all of the buildings were compacted with one wall separating two buildings. There were no front or back yards. Flowers were growing where any little space provided. Even though things were tightly grouped, there was a neatness and order about it. Many residents rode buses to move around, and there were a lot of bicycles, but there were still many automobiles moving on the streets.

On New Year's Eve, Underwood and I went to the NCO Club early. It was expected that there would be a large crowd, and we wanted to make sure we had a table so we were in position to hear and see the band. We nursed a couple of beers until the main crowd started to arrive and fill the place. By 9 p.m. the entire NCO Club was full of people, celebrating the last day of 1966 and the beginning of 1967. An older couple came in and stood around looking for a place to sit. Since there was no other space available, we invited them to sit with us. We had to scrounge up a couple of extra chairs. Introductions were made and the gentleman bought us a drink. He told us to put our billfolds away because he was buying for us the rest of the night. He added one condition to his offer: we had to dance with his wife occasionally. The guy was a retired Air Force Colonel. He said he preferred to come to NCO Clubs because the Officers' Clubs had too many snooty people for him. His wife, for her age, was very good looking. She loved to dance. I danced with her at least six times, as did Underwood.

Our glasses never got quite empty before another one arrived. Our waitress was my favorite guardian angel of the bar. She accepted tips, very generous tips, from our benefactor. He pumped us for all the information he could get from us with regard to our stint in Vietnam. We had an exceptional New Year celebration.

The band sounded terrific. They played a lot of the popular and fairly recent rock. They were playing the Twist, and a black couple was on the dance floor right in front of us. The lady had a husky but attractive build, and she was wearing a thin-strapped, white floor-length dress with a slit up above her knees. They were really into the music and her left shoulder strap began to slide down her arm. Her breasts amply filled the top of her gown. Well, let's just say I had to admire the strength of the thread holding that dress together. When the strap slipped far enough, her bare breast jumped right out of her gown. I must say that it was a very admirable part of her anatomy. Without missing a beat or movement, she slipped it back in place and finished the dance. The rest of the night, I caught myself watching her to see if it would happen again.

The day after New Year's Day, I was transferred out of the hospital to a barracks next to the hospital. With this move,

I had to start following military procedure again. When we left the compound, we had to sign out. We still ate in the chow hall in the hospital. Roll call was taken every morning and every evening. Over the next three weeks or so, I missed roll call more than once. No one ever pushed the issue. During the rest of my stay in Japan, we had to go through a regimented exercise program to get back in shape to go back to Vietnam. At 9:15 we were to line up outside the barracks and march to a gym area. From 9:30 to 10:30 a.m. we would go through the standard military exercise program. From 10:30 until 11:30 we broke up into groups and played either volleyball or basketball; I usually played basketball. We had enough people in basketball to make up three teams. Two played and one sat out. The winning team played back-to-back games. Even though I had pains in my back and shoulders, it felt good to get the exercise. The afternoons and evenings we had to ourselves.

Saturday night after the New Year celebration, I was at the NCO Club with about $2 to my name. I was still waiting for money from home. The Sons of the Pioneers was the band playing in the large lounge area. Tables were arranged in a herringbone angle facing the stage. Between shows, I had to use the bathroom. When I came back from the bathroom, I walked past the casino/slot machine section. I dropped a quarter into the first slot machine. Three plums came up. It paid out $18. About the time the coins were falling in the tray, my favorite waitress was standing beside me. She said she would take the money and exchange it for bills for me. I told her that I never leave a winning line showing. I dropped another quarter in the machine, and the three plums came up a second time, again paying out $18. I threw one more quarter in the machine with no win, so I quit. She took the coins and exchanged them for bills. When she returned, she told me to stay away from the slot machines and to spend the money carefully.

By now Brad Brugstad and Tom Hennessey were out of the hospital and both ended up in the barracks where Underwood and I were housed. After lunch, we would leave post and walk around the Japanese city of Fujisawa to check out the shops and, more than anything else, the Japanese lifestyle. Space is a precious commodity in Japan, so the shops were compacted such that it was a tight squeeze for an adult to walk the aisles between the merchandise. If there were no other customers, the merchants came right with us. I'm not sure if it was out of distrust or that they wanted to be very helpful.

On the following Sunday evening, the NCO Club was rather quiet. Underwood, Brugstad, Hennessey and I were sitting in the lounge casually imbibing refreshments. My Japanese watch-guard, the waitress, came to our table and sat down for a few minutes. She spoke fluent English. I asked her if she took English lessons or if she picked up the language by association with the GIs. She said she had married an Air Force enlisted NCO. She moved with him to Detroit and lived there for about three years. She always longed to come back to Japan. Things weren't going very well in their marriage, so she divorced him and came back. She said she still likes to be around the American GIs. Hennessey was somewhat of a ladies' man and he found the opportunity to talk to her in private. He did not make it back to the barracks that evening. There were a number of other evenings he did not sleep in the barracks. When roll call was taken, one of us would tell the Day Sergeant that he was shacked up. Since this was common for many GIs, nothing more was made of it.

Most of the GIs talked about the bars in downtown Fujisawa, and how wild everything was. So one night Underwood, Brugstad and I went downtown. Every bar was just like the one we left. We must have hit at least 15 bars. There were live Japanese bands playing or attempting to play American country music. The bar girls pumped you to buy them a drink and, for a fee, they were available for sexual favors. This was the only time we went to the GI bar strip. I felt that, as long as I was in Japan, I would prefer to see the country as the Japanese do.

Brugstad, Hennessey and I befriended a medic by the name of Kuhler. He was from Iowa. We nicknamed him Kuhler-san. He worked until 8 p.m. He said that, if we waited for him, he would show us some of the Japanese bars. We went to two of these bars and had a couple of drinks at each. After socializing in the Japanese nightclubs, we decided to go to one of the restaurants for Japanese nourishment. As soon as we entered the door, we were greeted by the maître d'. We had to take our shoes off at the entrance and were escorted to a table built low to the floor with large pillows on each side for seats. We had just seated ourselves when a uniformed Japanese came to our table. He invited us to come upstairs with him to help celebrate their graduation from officers' training school. Kuhler had been in Japan for more than a year and he understood enough Japanese to interpret for us.

The upstairs was one large room with two rows of tables. There was a lot of bowing going on, and we shook hands with many of the officers. This party had been going on for some time already, which was evidenced by a few of the officers who were more than a little drunk. We were each given a small glass and sake wine was poured into our glasses. We toasted their graduation and drank the rice wine. Our glasses were filled again, and they did a toast to us. As long as this party was well under way, we helped ourselves to another glass of sake. Apparently, this was not in line with their custom. One of the officers, who seemed to be in charge, held up a board with large, bold Japanese printing on it. He said a few words in a loud voice to get the attention of the others.

About this time the maître d' came up the stairs and told us to go now. I protested, saying that the party was just starting to get good. He said, "You go, or there be trouble." So we left. We forgot about eating and went back to the barracks.

Every day a bus came on post and picked up anyone who wanted to go into Tokyo. The four of us – Underwood, Brugstad, Hennessey and I – decided to go. There was a lot of traffic on the roads. When he could, the driver drove the bus at what I guessed was 75 to 80 miles an hour. Japanese drivers kept one hand on the steering wheel and one hand on the horn. The horn was used often. It seemed the rule of thumb for driving in Japan was that, if you're bigger, you have the right of way. The bus was bigger than most anything else on the road, so the bus driver took the right of way regardless of the driving laws. We were on a four-lane, one-way highway and came up to a semaphore. The bus driver was in the extreme left lane. The light was red and there was a motorcyclist waiting in the center of the driving lane for the light to change. The driver tooted his horn, but the cyclist did nothing. The driver turned the bus to the right, nearly sideswiping a vehicle in the lane to his right. He got the nose of the bus inside the back tire of the motorcycle and swung the bus hard to the left, knocking the motorcycle off the road. The rider went down with the cycle. He got up and yelled at the bus driver, shaking his fist at him. The light turned green and the bus driver tooted his horn, waved, and drove on.

The trip to our destination took a little more than an hour. Our drop-off point was some type of recreational community center that was frequented by Americans and Japanese. The four of us walked around downtown Tokyo for about three hours, checking out the shops and the people. We found a street deli, or whatever they call them in Japan, and had hamburgers for lunch. We got back to the recreational

community center and had nearly two hours to kill before
the bus was to pick us up for the return trip. There were a
number of pool tables and ping pong tables in the commune.
Hennessey and Underwood teamed up to challenge two other
guys at pool. There was an empty ping pong table, so Brugstad
and I began playing. Brugstad was not much at ping pong so
he said he had had enough. Immediately a young Japanese
man challenged me. I stayed close to him for the whole game,
but he beat me in the end. We played again, and by the end of
the game I figured he was toying with me. I beat him. He then
wanted to put some money on the game. I told him no. I also
told him that I thought he was a better player than what he
had demonstrated so far. Actually, I told him I thought he was
trying to sucker me into a game for money, but I didn't have
enough to make it worth his while. We played one more game.
Although I scored about 10 points, it was evident that he was
the far superior player.

In another area of this recreational center, there was
a mini railroad setup. It was the larger-scale track system. It
had two tracks to carry the railcars and an inside track that
conveyed the power for the railroad engines. There were eight
different sets of engines and cars and eight different tracks.
The track system went around the entire room, rising on a
slow incline over the top of the entrance door. The room was
about 30 feet wide and at least 50 feet long. The tracks had
areas for the railcars to transfer from one track to another.
When one train was crossing at an intersection, a mini rail
arm came down. If another train was within a foot of the
intersection, the arm switched the power off on the train
approaching the intersection. It was designed so the trains
would never collide on the tracks. The trains were numbered
one through eight. Near the center of the room was a narrow
table that held the handsets for the trains. Each handset had
a length of cord that allowed you to move around enough so

you could visually see the train you were operating. If you wanted to play, you simply chose one of the handsets, flipped a switch, and followed by eye the movement of the train. If all eight trains were in use it could get a little congested around the power source table. I secured one of the handsets and played for almost an hour. It sure would have been nice to have a scaled-down version of the setup in a recreation room of my own.

Johnson Air Force Base had a 24-lane bowling alley. On a Sunday afternoon Brugstad, Underwood and I went bowling. The place was packed. Bowling was very popular with military personnel and their families. While we were waiting for a lane to open, we were talking to two young girls who were also waiting for a lane. They were about 16 years old and were the daughters of Air Force officers. When our name was called for a lane, we asked them to join us. We bowled a total of five games. I had the most phenomenal day of bowling in my lifetime. I forget the scores, but I remember one being 290. I could have taken the total of any three games I bowled and had a 700-plus series. People had gathered behind our lane to watch. I'm sure much of it had to do with the power of concentration and being intent on what I was doing. For three months in Vietnam, there was no let-up. The body and mind were tense and concentrated almost all the time.

By this time, I knew I was going back to Vietnam from the hospital. My mind most likely had already prepared for the concentrated intensity upon my return.

I was having a lot of trouble with the wisdom teeth in my right jaw. I made an appointment with one of the Air Force Base dentists. He looked in my mouth and said that the teeth had to come out. He injected novocaine in the jaw around my teeth and when they were numb, he took his big extraction pliers and began pulling the teeth. I should say more accurately that he began ripping the teeth from my jaw. The top one came out first. When he began on the bottom tooth, it was much more difficult. He twisted and pried and finally crawled up on the chair, put his knee on my abdomen, and twisted and pulled until the tooth broke loose. When he pulled it out, there was what looked like a chunk of the jawbone hanging on the root. He held it up in front of me and said it was as big as the tooth of a horse. I refrained from telling him a horse would have been treated better than I had. He had to put a few stitches in to pull the gums back together. He told me that I should get the wisdom teeth on my left side pulled also, after my jaw was healed.

He gave me six Darvon, pain pills. He said that I would have a little pain when the novocaine wore off. About three hours later the novocaine wore off and the pain was almost unbearable. I took one Darvon, then another. Within the first eight to 10 hours I had taken all six Darvon. I went to the hospital and talked to the night nurse. She arranged to get me a two-day supply of additional Darvon. It took the next two days for the severe pain to subside. I had a sore jaw for at least six more weeks.

One Saturday evening, Brugstad and I decided to go to the NCO Club dining room and have a steak dinner. We got a large 16-ounce rib eye with potatoes, salad, and all the trimmings for the outrageous price of $1. Drinks were extra. While we were waiting for our steak, a waitress delivered a large plate of spaghetti and meatballs to a table behind me, but within view of Brugstad. He was looking past me and with a surprised look on his face said, "God, look at that!" I turned around just as this very large (I would guess in the 300-pound range) lady was shoveling a fork-full of spaghetti into her mouth. I looked just as she opened her mouth. She was at the table directly behind me and sitting across the table so I could see down her throat as she opened it to receive the offering. I don't know how she got that much spaghetti on her fork, but it was a pile. The spaghetti went into her mouth and she sucked in the straggling noodles. I busted out in a gut-wrenching giggle before I could get turned around. Brugstad was laughing so hard, both at the fact that he caught me by surprise, and also because he found it as funny as I did. He said it looked like the Lincoln Tunnel swallowing a train. I couldn't bear to turn around again, but Brugstad said she was giving us an evil stare.

Through most of the month of January Brugstad, Hennessey, Underwood and I bummed around the streets of Fujisawa during the afternoons and frequented the NCO Club at night. Every so often we would go out to eat in one of the Fujisawa restaurants.

Somewhere around January 22 Underwood and I got our orders to go back to Vietnam. The orders read to return to the 1st Battalion, 2nd Cav, of the 1st Cav Division. Since we were with the 5th Bn 7th Cav, the orders seemed not correct. We talked to one of the people in logistics, and he was not about to cut new orders. He told us to take it up with the placement services when we get to Tan Son Nhut Air Base near Saigon.

Our departure time was around 0900 hours on January 24. We found the bus schedule that would put us at the airport very close to the time of departure. The plane we took was a TWA 707. Our total flight time was close to eight hours. However, as we headed west, we gained time. We landed at Tan Son Nhut between 1400 and 1500 hours.

Bob Kunkel at the 7th Field Hospital in Japan returning to Vietnam.

BACK TO 'NAM

On the flight from Japan to Vietnam, Underwood and I discussed the possibility of not changing our orders, returning to the 1st Cav, and setting up shop as a battalion of the 1st Battalion, 2nd Cav. Since I had more time in grade, I would be the Battalion Commander and immediately promote myself to the rank of Lieutenant Colonel. Underwood would be the Battalion XO and he would be promoted to the rank of Major. After discussing the possibility, we tried to figure how we could get orders cut to send us home. We decided that we would need one good battalion clerk who knew his way around the paperwork. We dismissed the idea as just dreaming. Knowing how the military works, though, I believe we could have pulled it off.

When we stepped out of the airplane, we were greeted by an immense blast of heat. The plane was air-conditioned and the weather outside was probably around 110 degrees. As we descended the steps, a Corporal started yelling commands on where to line up. The F-word came out of his mouth every third or fourth word. I walked up to him and told him to settle down, and that I was in Vietnam before he got busted to a Corporal. I must have hit the nail on the head. He looked at Underwood and me and decided not to mess with us. One thing I learned: if you were seasoned infantry, people didn't mess with you because you just didn't give a damn. The worst they could do is bust your rank and send you back to the field. We were headed there anyway.

The Corporal assigned everyone to one of the many Quonset hut barracks, used as temporary housing for incoming troops, located near the airfield. After we were situated he told us that, at least two or three times a week, the gooks send mortars into the base. He said, "If this happens, you would hear a loud siren. If you hear the siren, you are to grab one of the M16 rifles in the rack in the barracks and a couple of extra M16 magazines, and head for the bunkers on the perimeter of the airfield." He then showed each barracks their area of responsibility.

Sure as shit, that night shortly after midnight there were a few explosions and the siren sounded. This was our welcome-back-to-Vietnam party. We sat on the perimeter for at least two hours and then were instructed to head back to our barracks. I asked Underwood if he thought these might be war games the airfield cadre were playing for the benefit of the new guys who just arrived. He was thinking the same thing.

The next morning, right after breakfast, Underwood and I found the placement officer. We showed him our orders. He took his pen, crossed out the 1st Bn 2nd Cav, and wrote B Company 5th Bn 7th Cav. He told us that we had about one hour to get our gear ready because we were flying out with a plane that made a stop at Camp Radcliff, home of the 1st Cav. We jumped on the designated plane and, after four stops at various locations, we landed on the airfield at Camp Radcliff.

From the airport at Camp Radcliff, we hooked a ride with a jeep that would take us to within a couple of blocks of our battalion base. As soon as we arrived we checked in with the B Company clerk Rodney Salvi at the Orderly Room. He sent us to the battalion supply tent to get field gear, weapons, and ammunition. I asked the supply clerk if he still had my gear from when I got shot. He said I could go in the back and look. It took me about five minutes to find a bundle with my name on it. I pulled out the helmet. It had dried crusty mildewed blood in it. I brought the helmet out front and told the clerk I wanted this helmet. He told me that they were not allowed to hand out damaged equipment. I asked him who I had to see about getting this helmet. He told me that the supply officer was in town and would be back in the morning. I told him I would keep the helmet in the meantime. He refused my request. I started to raise hell and he called for Sgt. Wilbur who was the battalion orderly. The Sarge told me I couldn't have the helmet.

Then Wilbur said, "As long as you're here, I will send you two out to help with green-line duty tonight." Green-line duty was securing the perimeter for the division. Base Camp Units had to supply extra staff to help with security each night.

Underwood and I went back to the B Company Orderly Room and asked Clerk Salvi where B Company was located. He said that they were assigned to green-line duty and were located on either side of the north entrance road leading into and out of the compound. The gate was about three-quarters of a mile from the 5th Bn 7th Cav compound. I told Underwood that I was going back to my platoon. He asked, "What about Wilbur's orders?" I told him, "Wilbur assigned us green-line duty, that's where we are going."

BACK WITH THE PLATOON

Underwood and I walked out to the north entrance gate and crossed the bridge going across the An Khê River. Sitting up the bank from the bridge was a large generator. The generator was about the size of a reefer truck box and would handle all electrical needs for Camp Radcliff. The generator arrived by ship and was trucked from Qui Nho'n Bay to where it now sat. After bringing it this far, the engineers realized that the bridge was not strong enough to support the weight of the generator. This was no big deal. The Cav had a couple of CH-54, giant helicopters referred to as flying cranes, that were used to transport heavy equipment such as tanks, personnel carriers, the large 14-inch artillery guns, and whatever else was too heavy for the smaller helicopters to carry. The only problem with this monstrous generator was that it was too heavy for the big helicopter to lift. So here it sat collecting rust.

Underwood and I walked up to the tower by the gate and asked the soldier manning the tower where the 2nd and 3rd platoon headquarters were for B Company. He said 2nd platoon was the big bunker about 200 meters to the east of the gate. We could see the bunker from where we stood. He said 3rd platoon was about 600 meters or more to the west. At this point, Underwood and I split up. He headed for the 3rd platoon and I headed for the 2nd.

As I approached the bunker I could hear those inside talking. I stepped into the entrance and everyone stopped talking for a second. Then came an overwhelming "welcome back" from the old guys who remembered me. Nearly half the people who were now in the platoon were new to me. I was introduced around to the new troopers. 3rd squad had a new squad leader by the name of Hutnam. He was only a Spec-4 the same as most of us, but he had someone sew acting jack stripes on his shirtsleeve. My first impression was: super soldier, and dangerous. Ray Judy told me that he was taking out a patrol that night and asked if I would walk point. I told him I would go along, but let someone else take point until I get accustomed to the surroundings again. I was introduced to John Albanese, no relation to Lewis Albanese. He came to the platoon right after I got shot. He was the point man for many of the night patrols in my absence.

After evening chow we got ourselves ready. Being back with the platoon and getting back into the war scene actually felt good again. Just a couple of days earlier, I was dreading coming back to 'Nam. As soon as it was dark we headed out. Albanese took point and I walked second. We took a trail that led from the compound and into old An Khê. It was close to a mile walk. We walked through the village and stopped at a hooch on the far edge. We were invited in. One of the guys had a girlfriend who lived at this hooch, so that is why we were there. Judy called in the first SitRep (Situation Report). Before I was shot, our radio handle was Comanche Brave-2-3. Now Judy used the handle of Cold Steel-2-3. I said, "Another change." We were supposed to call in five different SitReps, from five different locations. We stayed in the hooch all night and Judy made all the calls from the one location. Some of the GIs lit up joints and were passing them around. I didn't take any. Things seemed far too lackadaisical from what it was three months earlier. I'm sure we took the same trail that night as they did every other night. This makes it easy for an enemy to set booby traps. Not covering the ground we were supposed to cover could allow an enemy to get in closer to camp and pull a surprise attack. The patrols were to give the main force information and advanced notification if something was about to happen. My thoughts were, "This is not good," but I didn't say anything.

The next morning we sat around the platoon head-quarters bullshitting and catching up on what had happened in the last three months. One of the topics of the BS was, a few days prior, when Sgt. Crockett shot up a jeep. The gate to the north entrance of the compound gets closed every night at 1800 hours. If anyone is off post, they are supposed to use the south or main entrance gate, which is at least two or more miles from the north gate. It was after 1800 hours and the gate was closed. A jeep pulled up to the gate with two GIs in it. The passenger jumped out of the jeep and came up to the gate to open it. Crockett told them they would have to go to the south entrance. The passenger ignored him and started to open the gate. Crockett opened a volley of machine gun rounds on the spare tire and water can attached to the back of the jeep, shooting right past the driver. The passenger threw the gate shut and they left.

They also talked about seeing the Bob Hope Show. They were out in the field humping and had to walk in from the field for the show. The show had already started, so when they came trooping in with their full military load, they were invited to come down to the front and take ground seats right up front. A couple of the guys got to be in the show when they were called out of the audience to come up on stage.

The new platoon leader came out that morning. He was a small guy and seemed very unsure of himself. He admitted that he was not infantry, but they gave him a position as an infantry platoon leader. He said that he did not know anything about what was going on, so he was going to rely on the old guys to keep him out of trouble. He said that he did not want to be a hero. He was an exact opposite of Lt. Frank. He also said that he had requested a transfer back to his previous MOS. I'm not sure what it was, but he sure seemed out of place in the infantry. About a week later he was gone.

Since basic training, my pay had been screwed up. I never got my whole monthly pay like everyone else. The paymaster told me when my first monthly payment was wrong, "They will never get it straightened out before you get out of the service." He knew the Army very well. The Lieutenant was heading back to battalion headquarters. I asked if he could give me a ride because I needed to go Division Finance to straighten out my pay. He gave me a ride to the door of Finance, waited until I completed my task, and then gave me a ride back to the platoon bunker. He seemed like a friendly, likable guy, but out of place as an infantry platoon leader.

During the day, there only needed to be a skeleton crew to man the machine gun towers around camp. Between the machine gun towers, there were about four ground positions. That afternoon some of the platoon went down to the swimming hole just west of the bridge, and some went into new An Khê. I went with the crowd into town. An Khê is divided into old An Khê and new An Khê. The new An Khê developed after the military base set up. It was like a large carnival setting. There were many open-front shops made up of scrapped material from the military compound: cardboard and old cans and barrels pounded flat. Five of the bars had back rooms, if you want to call them rooms, for privacy. The prostitutes were not shy about selling their wares. If you walked in the door, a prostitute would grab you by the crotch and say, "Buy me a drink and we bang-bang [term for amorous encounter], 500 P," (P=Piaster, Vietnamese money). Of course, they took GI scrip.

When the battalion first arrived in Vietnam, the price was 400 P. Wartime inflation.

Out in front of one of the shops I was dickering with one of the merchants on an item. I forget what the item was, and I didn't purchase it. The kids would come around in hoards looking for handouts or trying to sell their number-one sister for sexual favors. You were a number-one GI until you told them to scram. Then you were number-10 and they hoped the Viet Cong would kill you. I pulled out a $20 scrip note and was waving it in front of the merchant. A kid of about 10 years old snatched the $20 from my hands and ran off into the crowd. I told some other kids standing right there, "You get me that $20 back, and I will give you half of it." They took off. I figured I lost 20 bucks. About 20 minutes later here come three kids with the $20. I took a $10 scrip out of my billfold and held it up. I said, "The 20, first." As soon as I had the $20, I gave them the $10.

That evening I was assigned as one of three people to man the machine gun tower by the north gate. Each person covered two, two-hour shifts, except the first man. We would cover the position from 1800 hours to 0700 the next day, 13 hours total. The first guy pulled a three-hour shift so the numbers came out right. I took first watch. About 20 minutes after 1800 hours, a jeep pulled up to the gate. The driver got out and walked up to open the gate. I told him he would have to go around to the south gate to get into camp. He said, "Bullshit," and grabbed the gate. I pulled the bolt slide back on the machine gun and let it fly toward. He froze in position. He said, "You sure the hell ain't gonna shoot me." I told him, "There's one way to find out." He said, "You guys are crazy." He got back to the jeep, turned it around and left.

The next day our battalion was pulled from green-line duty and replaced by another battalion. The 5/7 Cav was headed back to the field. We went back to our battalion area and got our gear ready for the move out the next day. After our supper chow settled, a number of B Company soldiers went to our EM Club. We had a few cans of beer. Our EM Club was very small and the place was wall-to-wall people that night. Some of us decided to go down to the 8th Engineers' EM Club. There were probably about 25 5/7 Cav troopers in our group headed there.

The EM Club for the 8th Engineers was fairly busy when we got there. They had the slot machines, and all were in use. We each ordered a beer and stood around the club bull-shitting. A big black guy was playing on one machine and he ran out of money. He walked away from the machine. A medic from the 3rd platoon, nicknamed Red Dog because his hair was an orange/red color, began playing the machine. About 10 minutes later this big guy returns and wants to get on the machine again. Red Dog told him, "When I'm done with it, you can have it." The big guy said that he had dibs on the machine; he had only left to get more money and, now that he was back, he wanted the machine. Red Dog told him to get lost. The guy pulled a switchblade out and stabbed Red Dog in the back, up in the shoulder area.

Someone from the 2nd platoon was standing near the encounter and saw the stabbing. He punched the guy with the knife, hitting him in the back of the head at the neckline, knocking him down. He then kicked the guy in the ribs and kicked the knife away from him. Someone from the Engineers jumped in and punched the soldier who kicked the stabber. Then the whole club erupted into a fight. I stood there looking around to make sure no one hit me. I was trying to stay out of the fight this time. Someone slammed into my back. I turned around and punched him; the guy had just got punched by someone else and was knocked into me. Kloemken got pushed

294

into the back of Ray Judy; Judy turned and let loose with a punch, hitting Kloemken. A few people tried to settle the fight down but only ended up in the middle of it as punching bags. After what seemed like 10 minutes, a Major from the Engineers came in and put his hands up in a gesture for everyone to settle down. He yelled that the 7th Cav troops should leave and go back to their unit area. As he was talking, someone took a swing and knocked him down. The fight had been dwindling down but, when the Major got hit, it started all over again.

There was a pile-up of soldiers by the front door. They were wrestling and punching each other. It was hard to tell who was with which side. Someone was pushed into the door. The door was actually a double door, with one side open and the other side closed. When the guy hit the door, both doors collapsed outward, leaving a six-foot gap. By now the Engineers had gotten support from some of their troops who were not initially at the EM Club. Apparently, the MPs were called. They showed up a few minutes later. Eventually, everyone was herded outside. There was still a lot of turmoil, but the fighting stopped. The MPs told the 5/7 Cav troopers to go back to our unit and this would be the end of it. We wanted to know where Red Dog was taken. After the fight started, he had disappeared. The Major, now with a sore jaw, said that he was with the medics and that they were taking care of him.

We headed back to our battalion area. It was still early, so we stopped at our EM Club. Everyone was standing around replaying the fight and their role in the melee. We were just getting into our second beer when a guy by the name of Sully showed up. He was from the 1st platoon. He didn't have any clothes on. He apparently got dragged away from the group by some of the Engineers and was worked over pretty good. They took all his clothes off him and sent him on his way. He wasn't hurt too badly, and he was laughing. Some of his buddies wanted to go back to the Engineers and get it on again. Most of the group decided this wouldn't be too smart. Someone gave him a shirt, and someone else took off his undershorts and gave them to him. He helped us close the place.

While I was in the hospital, B Company got a new First Sergeant. His name was Clarence Baldwin. He was much too old for field duty. The rumor circling around was that he was getting ready to retire, but he still did not have his CIB (Combat Infantry Badge).

To get the CIB, a soldier had to have served for a 90-day period of time in a combat zone or had to have been involved directly in a combat battle. Baldwin wanted a CIB before retiring. He was well over 50 years old, overweight, and out of condition. He walked as if he was trying to keep the weight and pressure off his right leg. When he was standing, he leaned so the left leg carried more of his weight. He was the exact opposite of our former and deceased First Sergeant, Dayton Hare.

The following day, we were flown out to some artillery LZ. We set up a security perimeter for the LZ. The temp was pushing 110 degrees. The heat was helping me to get acclimated to the conditions again. That evening Ray Judy led out a patrol for the LP (Listening Post). In essence, you are out far enough to intercept the enemy before they can converge on our main force. If you get hit, everyone else will be alert and ready; only you will be SOL (Shit Outa Luck). I went out with the patrol.

The LP squad left before dark and selected our site for the night. We split into two groups, 100 meters from each other. As a rule, whenever we set up LPs, it was always done after dark so that the enemy would not know our location, in case they had eyes watching us. Before dark, we set up in some heavy brush at the edge of an open valley. Maybe it was only my mind because I had just come back from the hospital, but I had that, "I don't like this" feeling about our situation. I was disturbed that we did not wait until after dark to set up. I didn't say anything then, but I intended to talk to Judy sometime when we were alone about the lackadaisical habits that had developed in the past three months.

Darkness started to settle in right after we were in place. For some reason, I was all tensed up. I thought it just might be me, but everyone else seemed to be on high alert and tense. About two hours after dark we heard short and quiet rustling noises out in front of our position. There would be one sound to our front, a few seconds later another sound at a slightly different location, and then another sound from still another location. It appeared that we had gooks moving in on us. One of their tactics was to move one person at a time so there is not too much noise that will give them away. Judy got on the radio and talked, in a low tone, to Kloemken who was with the other group. He asked if he was hearing any noises out to his front. Kloemken said there were noises coming from his front and his right side. Ray told him to get his group ready to move. In 30 seconds they were ready to go. He then said everyone will throw one grenade and we were to run back to the sharp incline we came down earlier, and regroup there. We all stood up and threw grenades, scattering them, and ran like hell for about 200 meters back toward the incline.

We had one M79 grenade launcher with us. As soon as we regrouped, we fired about 20 grenades back into the area we just left. Prior to this, Capt. Hitti had called asking for a Sit Rep. After firing the grenades, Judy got on the radio and reported what had happened. Judy also requested that we be allowed to come in. Capt. Hitti told us to take up defense positions and stay put, he was calling for artillery on the position we left. A minute or two later a barrage of artillery was coming in close to where we had been earlier. Hitti had to call the artillery from another artillery battery because the one we were securing was too close to the enemy objective. After the artillery barrage was over, Hitti said they had movement out in front of their perimeter earlier, between our position and the LZ. I thought, "Oh, great! We've got gooks on both sides of us." By now we had crawled to the top of the incline. It went up at a sharp angle about 25 feet and then leveled off. We found cover and set up for the night. About 20 minutes later, small arms fire began at the LZ perimeter. In the quiet of the night, it sounded much more intense than it would during daytime. It lasted for about five minutes.

After the shooting frenzy on the artillery perimeter, everything became quiet. About three hours later, we began to relax. I drooped my head and apparently began to doze. I jolted awake, yelling, and I lost my helmet. It toppled down the incline, bouncing off the rocks. I must have had a dream. Judy said to be quiet. I told him I was sorry, but dreams were hard to control. I started to get my helmet, but he said to wait until after daybreak, which made sense. I sure felt naked without that helmet, though.

After daybreak, I retrieved my helmet. I asked Judy if we were going out to see if we got any gooks. He said, "The hell with it! They'll probably give us 10 or 15 kills, why should we prove them wrong?" We headed back to the LZ, calling ahead and informing our company that we were coming in. As we came up to the perimeter, we were directed to make a sweep of the area out from their line. We were looking for bodies or evidence of dead bodies. Nothing was found that could substantiate that there were any dead. There were tracks made by Ho Chi Minh sandals (sandals made of old tire treads and tied to the feet), and weeds and small brush that had been trampled.

Judy made a detailed report of our contact and the estimated numbers to Capt. Hitti and we went back to our platoons to wait for the chow chopper. Talking with the other troops, it seems that everyone was having that sensation of enemy troops all around the area before we heard them. It was nice to know I still had that sixth sense, as they say.

ꙮ A GUNG-HO ACTING JACK

The line soldiers, most of the time, were never sure of what was going on until they were ready to do it. It seemed that everything was on a need-to-know basis. Shortly after 1200 hours, we were told to saddle up; we were getting air-lifted to another location. Our new platoon leader's request for a change back to his old MOS came through. I believe Capt. Hitti had a hand in it to see that it did. He was not infantry material. And he was one happy man.

We were told that we could expect a hot landing coming in. 2nd platoon would be the first one in. Being back with the troops all of a sudden didn't feel that good. We came into a heavily brushed hillside with jungle as close as 100 feet on each side of the opening. The door gunners were doing their job, spraying the edge of the jungle with ammunition. No one shot back. The brush was too heavy to land, so we had to jump from the helicopters while hovering six feet off the ground. We moved to the edge of the jungle and secured it for the next sortie.

Once everyone was down, Capt. Hitti told each platoon to send out two different patrols to make sure that we did not have any unexpected supper guests. 3rd squad, led by make-believe-Sergeant Hutnam, went down the hill and to the left of the LZ. I was walking point. Hutnam kept telling me to veer right or left. I finally turned around and told him, "I've done this before." I came to a used trail at the base of the incline. It had heavy foliation over the top of it. Of course, Hutnam had to stop and radio Capt. Hitti what "he" had found. We walked on the trail for about 200 meters and it opened along a rice paddy. There was a small hamlet across the rice paddy. We walked a little farther and a soldier, carrying a rifle and a web belt that appeared to have ammo bags hanging on it, came to the edge of the rice patty across from us. He was jumping up and down yelling, swinging the rifle over his head, and waving the ammo belt. We stopped and watched. Hutnam called Capt. Hitti and reported a Victor-Charlie-Sierra (Viet Cong suspect) across the rice paddy from us, and he wanted permission to go after him and bring him back for military debriefing. Capt. Hitti said to go ahead but to be careful.

Our patrol was comprised of five FNGs, along with Hutnam, Ray Judy and me. I looked at Ray Judy, waiting for him to say something. When he didn't, I told Hutnam that it was suicide going after that gook. I also told him that he's not a "suspect." The S.O.B. has got a rifle. That makes him an enemy. Judy then spoke up and told Hutnam that the gook was trying to pull us into the open so they could tear us all a new ass. Hutnam said, "We're going after him." I told Hutnam that I was not going. I also told the new guys that if they go out into the rice paddy, they're going to be dead meat tonight. Judy backed my assessment of the situation. He said that the gook is baiting us to come after him. Judy wasn't going either. Hutnam called back to Capt. Hitti, reporting that he had fellow soldiers disobeying a direct order. Capt. Hitti asked who was on patrol with him. He gave Capt. Hitti Judy's and my line numbers. Capt. Hitti said to put Line #78, Ray Judy, on the radio. Hitti asked Judy to brief him on the situation, which he did. He then told Judy to assume control of the patrol and come back to his location. He wanted to see Hutnam, Judy and me. Hutnam's ego deflated. I was going to take a few shots at the gook before we left, but he had already disappeared. They would have been long shots anyway.

When our patrol got back to the LZ, Hitti came to meet us. He asked me what we came across. I explained the situation from my perspective. Judy echoed my every word. He asked Hutnam how he saw it. Hutnam had to admit that what we said was correct. Capt. Hitti reached out and tore Hutnam's stripes off his shirt. He told him that in the field these are not needed. He also told him that he was relieved as a squad leader.

The 5/7 Cav had a new Battalion Commander, Colonel Hanahan. He did not like perimeter settings. He wanted the troops to set up in strong point positions overnight. He wanted the points spread apart at least 100 meters. His philosophy was that the further apart we are scattered, the better chance we have of making contact with the enemy, and the more enemy dead we should have. The flip-side of this coin is: the more KIA we will have among the troops. If a strong point makes contact with the enemy, that point is on their own. The next point on either side of them is too far off to be of assistance. It was a dumb idea at the time, but no one ever said that all officers were intelligent.

We knew we had gooks in the area. We didn't know how many, but the feeling was that there were more than we wanted to know about. We still set up in strong points but, instead of the two-man point as usual, we set up in squad-sized points. Judy was now our squad leader.

Hutnam stayed with Company Command. Prior to dark, we found a washed gully in a now dry stream coming off the hill. There was heavy foliage on the hillside above the gully, as well as on the downstream side. It was about six feet wide at the widest spot and tapered down to a thin stream again about 40 feet downstream. The gully was fairly flat and was about three feet deep from the ground on either side of it. It was a natural trench-like bunker. This is where we chose to set up for the night. Our squad left the site and went back to our platoon area. As soon as it was dark enough, we returned to our strong point. We had no idea where the next, or closest, strong point was located. With the exception of where we landed, and the rice paddy and hamlet we found earlier in the day, the terrain was heavy jungle.

The next morning, for breakfast, we found ourselves eating C's. We were told that we would be scouting the hamlet we saw the day before. This time we would be doing it with A Company instead of an eight-man squad. 2nd platoon took the lead and 3rd squad led. I walked point. I figured that we were going to hit the shit today. At least we were not going to approach it from the open rice paddy. We worked our way up the valley and crossed to the other side where it seemed the most narrow. We crossed the valley with 30-meter intervals between us. If the shit hit the fan, at least we would not have as many soldiers exposed at one time. 3rd squad crossed, scouted the immediate area, and spread out and up the steep embankment into the jungle to better secure the area. Once we were in place, the rest of the company crossed.

First Sgt. Baldwin stationed himself toward the rear of the company movement. After crossing the rice paddy, he had to climb the ridge we were on. He was having a difficult time of it. He fell a couple of times, sliding backward. Eventually, a couple of soldiers helped him. We began to work our way along the valley toward the hamlet. Because of the thick terrain, we moved back into a column and spaced about four to five meters between each man.

It took almost two hours working our way through the jungle terrain and walking sideways along the steep ridge to cover what may have been a mile. As we approached the hamlet, the ridge gave way to a gentle slope. As soon as the hills mellowed out, we found a trail. We stayed off the trail but followed alongside it until we could make out the village. Then we spread out on line and slowly worked our way in. When we saw the women and kids watching us, I felt relieved. Usually, if the shit is coming, they'd have disappeared.

This was the longest trek I had walked with field gear since coming back from the hospital. My legs felt tired, but they would work in shape. With full gear on, my back was killing me. After clearing the village, I took off my rucksack and slung it over my left shoulder and carried it.

We worked our way down the valley and searched two more small hamlets. At the end of the valley, the ridge rose to about 800 feet at the highest point. It was a steep incline going up with heavy jungle. Once over the top of the ridge, the decline was not as steep. From the high point, we walked two more klicks and came out of the jungle in a high grass opening. Capt. Hitti ordered a security perimeter and called for a pick-up. B Company was air-lifted to LZ Hammond. Our company had an easy night in LZ Hammond: no patrols, no security.

Near An Khê, men of the 1st Cav. Div. pause on top of a huge boulder on patrol in the An Lào Valley during "Operation Pershing," circa 1967. U.S. Army photo, courtesy of National Archives and Records Administration No. 639914.

MOVE TO LZ ENGLISH

The next morning after breakfast, we got our grit together and were standing around the tent area waiting for orders to move to the helipad. There was a company of ARVN (Army of the Republic of Vietnam) soldiers about 150 meters from our location. They too were standing around waiting for transportation. They had their rifles stacked in groups in an orderly line. There were four or five Vietnamese women standing under some trees near the ARVN soldiers. Two ARVNs started to yell at each other. Apparently, they had a dispute relating to one of the women. They began to wrestle with each other. One of the combatants was knocked to the ground. He jumped up, ran for one of the rifle stacks, pulled a rifle out, shot and killed the other ARVN. Another ARVN took the rifle used to kill the dead ARVN and, with help, re-stacked the rifles. When the one rifle was pulled from the stack the other rifles fell. From what we could tell, this seemed to be business as usual.

Eventually, we were instructed to move to the helipad area. Once there, we stood around some more. We were waiting for the Chinook helicopters that would fly us to our new destination. There were two new generators bolted to wood pallets sitting to the right front of the helipad depot building. We were standing fairly close to the generators. Lt. Merten from the 3rd platoon came over and said, "We will need at least one of those generators when we get to LZ English." I just requisitioned it. He pointed to me and three other GIs and said, "You are the requisitioning committee. When we load on the helicopters, you each grab a corner of the generator and carry it on board with you."

He went back to his platoon and moved them in a group so they blocked the view from the depot building. When the first Chinook arrived, we did as instructed and his platoon moved along with our movement, blocking the view of those inside. These were not small generators. By the time we set the thing down, my body seemed as if was locked in a left-sided bend.

LZ English was a series of small rolling hills about 10 miles west of Bong Son, in the Bong Son Plains, a flat, level, very large area which at one time contained thousands of rice paddies. The rice paddies were not now in use; they were full of bomb craters, many of which were left over from the French. I'm sure that the U.S. claimed some as their own too. Flying over the plains was a sight to behold. Looking at the massive number of craters, one had to wonder why would they bomb this area when there is no place to hide. I'm sure the bombing was to destroy the crops. A deep hole in the middle of a rice paddy will allow the water to settle below the level needed to grow rice. It may have also disturbed the deeper landmass so the paddies would drain instead hold the water.

There were three small hamlets on three sides of the LZ. On the northwest end of the LZ there was a hill, or what we called a finger, protruding out into the rice paddies. One hamlet was at the base of this finger. Almost directly south and across this hill to where it descended into the rice paddies again was another small hamlet. A road coming from Bong Son to the LZ ran right past this hamlet. There was another hamlet to the northeast, beyond the airfield. In all, the LZ covered at least 250 acres. It was longer east-to-west than north-to-south. Our area of operation was the west end of the

LZ, to include the helipad. This was our forward base camp. All supplies for field operations would come from this location.

The flight to LZ English took about 30 minutes. LZ English had been around for about four or five months. We were expanding it. Headquarters had tents pitched. The kitchen staff had a very large tent set up for the cooking. As soon as we arrived on the LZ, we were assigned an area to build defense bunkers. Some had to help build the supply bunker. This needed extremely thick walls and ceiling because ammunition would be stored in it. It had to have a divider so that Sgt. Nuss, the company supply sergeant, would have private accommodations. Others had to help build a bunker wall around the medical station. The first two days we worked our butts off. By noon the third day, we were told to relax. With the arrival of the new day, we were going to be humping in someplace called the An Lão Valley.

Because of my back injury, I knew I wouldn't be able to carry a rucksack any longer so I emptied the contents from it to see what I actually needed. I removed the back straps from my web belt. I rolled my poncho extremely tight and, before making the final roll, laid my web belt in the poncho and rolled the poncho tight, securing it with Como wire. I discarded gear. I normally carried three water bottles; I shrunk that to two. I usually carried four grenades taped to my shoulder harness; I now taped them to my web belt. With the bayonet scabbard, my web belt was completely filled. I strapped the belt on. It fit okay. I walked around for a while with it on to see how comfortable it would be. My biggest concern was that it might slide down without the shoulder harness. I guess my ass was big enough so this was not a problem. I always carried my ammunition in a Claymore bag with the strap wrapped over my shoulder. As a rule, I kept two ammo magazines taped back-to-back, offsetting enough so they still slid into the magazine slot of the gun. I could squeeze 22 magazines into the Claymore bag.

I hadn't fired an M16 since I got shot, so I decided to take a little target practice. The M16 I had fired one round and jammed. I cleared the jam and fired again. The gun jammed again. I tried it one more time with the same results. Now I was really pissed at battalion supply. They had given me a weapon that was not reliable. I had carried that rifle for a few days when we had gooks all around us. I went to see Beaupre, our field armor. He worked on the gun for some time and said the extractor was worn. He came out with us and had to set up a bunker-type shop. He was going back to An Khê to get his supplies the following morning. I told him I could not go in the field with that weapon. He gave me his to use until he got mine fixed. He said that without his gun, it might be a good excuse to get out of pulling duty on the line overnight.

AN LÃO VALLEY

Following our breakfast in the morning, we got ourselves ready and hiked up to the helipad to wait for the birds (helicopters). Sgt. Nehr was back with us. He was acting as a temporary platoon leader in the absence of having a real Lieutenant. He was mentally equipped to handle the job more so than any Lieutenant. The An Lão Valley was supposed to be a major operation area for a Division of the NVA. When Nehr gave us this info, Tom Gray said, "Well, they were there first. Why can't we let them have it and we go find our own valley?" As a rule in a military organization, the next-highest in grade assumes command in the absence of a leader. Normally this would have been Sgt. Inez. But thank God he was on leave somewhere. In fact, there was rumor going around that he knew when the shit would hit the fan. Just before any major military battle, he would leave the field. The next day we would get hit. I don't believe anyone actually believed this, but with the likes of him, we wanted to. The fact that he was on leave bothered us.

The An Lão Valley carries the An Lão River from the North Central Highlands east to southeast toward the ocean above Bong Son. There are hundreds of small valleys stemming off from the main valley into the hills.

The choppers took us into the An Lão Valley. We were dropped on a hilltop not far from a village. We were setting up for the night right where we got dropped off. The Army seldom tried to cover where they were at when the force was large enough and the advantage was theirs. We went out on patrol as usual. 3rd squad headed straight for the village. The village had a lot of activity for as small as it was. There were open shops with food, tools, clothing, and other goods. It was an exact opposite of New An Khê. There were kids around, but they were not begging for money or trying to sell their sisters. They did gather around to gawk at us, though.

We found a shop that sold beer. They had two kinds; both were Vietnamese brewed. One was in a bigger dark amber bottle called Tiger. We had it before and we referred to it as Tiger Piss. It tasted awful, but it was better than the other brand, Club 33. We selected the bottle and made sure it had the fizzed "pop" when opened. We didn't take any chances of getting beer spiked with something. The bottle was about 20 ounces.

In front of a shop, a Vietnamese had his barber chair set up with a standard barber pole. After lubricating our innards, I decided I needed a haircut and a shave. Kloemken asked me if I was going to trust this guy with a scissors and razor working on me. I told Kloemken that I expected he would watch the guy to make sure he didn't slip. I asked the barber if he was a VC. He shook his head and said, "No VC. No VC." I asked him, "How much for a haircut and shave?" He said, "400 P." I told him, "Too much. I pay 200." He said, "No. 400 P." I told him again, "200." He finally said, "300 P." I said, "If you do a good job, I give you 300 P. If you screw up, I pay you 200 P." I'm not sure he understood, but he shook his head up and down. I told him, "Make sure you don't slip." I pointed to Kloemken and told the barber, "This old boy is going to watch you. If he sees my blood, he shoots you. You understand? Shoots, like Kau-Ke-Dau" (Vietnamese for "to kill"). I think he got the meaning. He did okay cutting my hair. But when it came to the shave he was shaking. I grabbed his hand that held the razor and I told him to settle down. It seemed to help. I never had a shave with a straight razor before and it was pretty good. Then he took a large cotton swab for my ears. It must've been the shave, haircut, and ear-cleaning special I ordered. I pushed his hand away and waved him off. He had a mirror on a post. I looked in it to see what kind of a job he did. The shave was okay, but the haircut was awful. I told him he was a good sport, so I gave him 400 P. Then I asked, "You sure you not VC?" He said, "No VC. No VC." When we left, Kloemken said, "There is no way I would let a gook give me a shave with a straight razor." I told him the barber was more scared of cutting me than I was of getting cut.

Our patrol browsed around the village for another hour and headed back to the company CP. 2nd platoon had moved to another hill about 400 meters up the trail or away from the village from the company CP. We joined them.

The next morning we headed out on patrol. We would go into the feeder or branch-off valleys, go through the hamlets searching for gooks, weapons, and ammunition, or any other evidence of enemy activity. This never produced as much as hoped for. The only people in the hamlets were women, children, old men, and occasionally a Dinky Dau. Smitty was walking point. His name was Jerry Schmitt, and he was from the Tennessee hills. He came to the platoon when I was still in the hospital. He was a thin, wiry guy who had a gift of gab. He liked to joke around. Smitty also had asthma. How he got into the service, much less in the infantry, was a mystery. He carried inhalers to cope with his asthma. He liked the field, and he liked walking point.

When we walked through the hamlets, the locals would smile and wave and nod their heads up and down, which was supposed to be a gesture of friendship. I'm sure they were wishing we would leave. There was nothing that we were going to do that was going to make a difference for the better for these people. The fact that none of the men were around was evidence enough we had disrupted their lives from normal living. The men, if they were not in the South Vietnamese Army, were considered VC suspects. If we found any, we either killed them, or we detained them and sent them back to re-education camps. I guess if I were in their shoes, I would be damn sore at us.

We came to one hamlet set at the end of the valley. The terrain went uphill from here or back out into the valley. We found an old French rifle and about 10 rounds of ammunition for the rifle. This hamlet had at least 50 banana trees just where the level ground began to rise into the jungle ridge. The trees were hanging full of bananas, mostly too green, but some ripe enough to eat. We were told to destroy the food, so someone brought out their machete, and we took turns whacking the trees down. We were competing to see if anyone could take one down with one swing of the machete. Banana trees are comprised of soft plant growth rather than wood and bark. As we dropped the trees, we picked off the fruit that was ripe enough and ate bananas. They were small, only about four inches long, and very sweet. A few people ate too many and got sick, throwing up as we were humping afterward.

In one hamlet, between two hooches, there was an underground bunker. No one else wanted to go into it, so I crawled in. It seemed fairly tight. I got in okay and there was an opening at the far end of the bunker with another tunnel that went into another leg of the bunker. I crawled partially through it. It seemed tighter than the opening. I tried to back out. My clothes pushed up against me and I couldn't move backward. I had to crawl into the next section to turn around. I tried to turn, but my body was too large to turn around.

I started to lose it. I twisted my body again putting all the pressure I could on it to bend around. My shoulder was digging into the bamboo slats. My butt and hips pressed against the bottom side of the bunker. I was panicking. I pushed with everything I had to get my shoulder turned around to go the other way. It seemed as if I were crunching my ribs and backbone closer together to get more room. Finally, my shoulder came around with a pop. I crawled out of the bunker with a stiff back, sore hips, and a heavily bruised shoulder. I was panting, gasping for air. Doc sat me down and waved smelling salts in front of my nose. It took another 10 minutes for me to settle down enough to continue. I would never go into a bunker or any other tight space again.

One morning we came into a hamlet that was more like an island in the middle of a valley full of rice paddies. There was a main trail leading from the mainland to this island. There was one large hooch on this island. There were six older women and one old man in the hamlet. I'm sure the children were hidden off somewhere. One theory was that the gooks had them, as protection against the locals ratting them out. That's what some GIs wanted to believe. When we arrived, the women were all outside the hooch. The old man was squatting in the doorway of the hooch with a smile as wide as his face. His teeth were black and worn down to the gums. I doubt he weighed 75 lbs. We checked the area, and I walked past him into the hooch. There was no evidence there had been any heavy activity. We would look for anything that might give away the presence of more people having been there recently. Occasionally we would find an under-the-ground hole for storage of weapons or even people. This happened rarely. The old man never moved when I went past him. I thought he was rooted to the ground. I looked carefully all around him to see if he was covering up something. He didn't cover enough ground to hide anything. He just sat there and smiled. He was probably just playing with our minds.

After the search of the hamlet, we moved up the valley on one side of the rice fields and came back on the other side. At least six hours later, we came back to this same one-hooch hamlet. Everything was in the same order as we had left it that morning. The old man squatted in the same position with the same smile on his face. The women hadn't changed the order in which they stood outside the hooch. One of three things was going on: they hadn't moved all day, they were very ritualistic about what they did when company came, or they were playing one hell of a mind game with us.

As a platoon, we cleared a few more hamlets before our search-and-destroy came to an end for the day. In one hamlet, we found three large watermelons. They were the long non-striped type. We bartered with the owners for the watermelons. They were willing to barter but kept trying to tell us something about the melons. Sgt. Nguyen, the company interpreter, was with Capt. Hitti and another platoon. We thought they were holding out for more exchange items. Since we got our cigarettes free, we gave them at least a carton of cigarettes and a number of C-Ration meals. C-Rations were an excellent trade item when bartering with the Vietnamese. Eventually, we got to the bowing stage and we left the hamlet, carrying the melons with us.

First Sgt. Baldwin would be with us one day, and back in camp the next day. I believe Capt. Hitti sent him out of the field when it was apparent we would be doing a lot of humping. He was with us this day, and we had done a fair share of humping. We were setting up that night on a ridge overlooking the valley. The ridge was extremely steep as it left the flats along the rice paddy. At the very base of the ridge, there was a straight-drop incline bank close to six feet high. Coming out of the rice paddies we had to climb the bank. Above the bank a person could stand; however, the ridge ascending the hill was steep. Our company was going up to the top of the ridge. Baldwin could not climb the bank. He tried at least four times but fell before cresting the top edge. A rope was tied around him, and some soldiers pulled him while others pushed him up the bank.

There were no large trees in this immediate area, but a lot of small undergrowth. This was good camouflage to conceal our position. Once we were set up, we cut open the first melon. The fruit inside was still a pale green. What the hell, we could each eat a little green melon. The first bite told us what the locals were trying to tell us. These were not melons at all. They tasted like cucumbers. We had bartered for huge cucumbers.

Kloemken and I were teamed up together. Since I always had a hard time getting to sleep, I always pulled first watch. After two hours or more, I woke him and he pulled his watch. I was sleeping and was startled awake by something in my ear. It was burrowing into my inner ear. I reached up and grabbed it. It was a sand leach about the size of my little finger. It had slithered into my ear and was just beginning to work on the inner lobe for blood. I pulled the leach out. It had already had a slight hold on the inner lobe, but it broke free easily. I squished it with my fingers and threw it away.

The next day we finished clearing the valley we were in and moved to another. The next area was declared a free-fire zone. There were supposed to be no civilians left in the area. We were going to set up on the far side of the valley overnight, but we did not want to get there much before dark. We stopped at an empty hamlet for a break. There was a clear, fresh stream coming off the ridge at the far end of the valley and running just out in front of the hamlet. Capt. Hitti had us set up a circumference as if we were setting up for the night. He said that we could take a swim in the river, as long as we have our backside covered for security.

It was a hot day. We were sweaty, and a swim sounded good. Guys even washed out their clothes and laid them out to dry. We found an old bike with the back wheel missing. Tom Gray braced the bike so it stood up. His clothes were drying out. He was birthday-suit naked. He slung two 100-round machine gun ammo belts over each shoulder in a Mexican bandit style. He took his helmet liner out of his steel pot, and put the pot on his head, strapping it under his chin. He took an M60 machine gun, slung the sling over his shoulder, and pointed the gun to the front under his right arm, like Sgt. Rock. The medic had a watertight bag for medical supplies. He also carried a small 35mm camera in the bag. Gray told Doc to snap a couple of photos. He wanted to send one home to his family. This got everyone to laugh. Even the serious and stoic Capt. Hitti had a good laugh. We had a few cut-ups in our company, but I don't think any were as funny as Gray. He came off the wall with one-liners that always got a good laugh. He was an upbeat, happy-go-lucky guy. He was also a good soldier who knew when to be serious.

Tom Gray on a bicycle he comandeered.

The old and the young flee Tet offensive fighting in Hue, managing to reach the south shore of the Perfume River despite this blown bridge, 1968. U.S. Information Agency photo, ID 541870. Photo courtesy of the National Archives at College Park, Md.

THE TET NEW YEAR

We were approaching the Tet New Year. There was talk of a ceasefire for the Asian holiday. A rumor was flying around that the gooks were going to fight us up until the Tet holiday, and then call it quits. I believe the gooks thought we would honor their holiday and take it easy. Instead, we loaded up in helicopters, circled the hamlets, landed, and hit the hamlets from two or three sides. As soon as we cleared one hamlet, we would load up in the choppers again and hit another hamlet in an adjacent valley much the same way. We caught some of the gooks, literally with their pants down. 2nd platoon had landed behind a ridge and worked our way on foot along the ridge to where it came to a point. Over the ridge was a hamlet. 1st platoon landed on the far side of the hamlet. By now we had made our way to the top of the ridge above the hamlet. When 1st platoon landed, four gooks ran our way. When they saw our platoon, they turned and ran south, through the rice paddies. I knelt on one knee, pulled up to shoot but pulled my gun down. Kloemken ran up beside me and was aiming his rifle at them as they fled. I grabbed his rifle and pulled it down. He yelled at me, "Why the hell did you do that?" I knelt there, dumbfounded. I didn't have a clue why I didn't shoot, or why I pulled his rifle down. My actions were impulsive and puzzling.

In one of the airlifts, we were put down in a rice paddy about 50 meters out from some hooches. The pilot was not experienced in holding us steady in flight so we could jump out while it was still hovering. The chopper would come down to within six feet of the ground and then ascend again to as high as 15 or more feet. The rice paddy had at least eight to ten inches of water over the soil. From experience, I knew it would be murky and soft. On about the third try, the pilot got the chopper about five feet over the top of the rice stems. I was the first to jump out. As soon as I jumped, the chopper ascended upward about 10 feet. I was already in the jump motion as the chopper began to rise. The chopper was about 12 feet off the ground when I went out the door. I sunk into the muck of the rice paddy almost up to my knees. I couldn't pull my legs out. They were sucked into the mud.

The chopper came down again over the top of me. I had to sit down and crunch my body forward to keep the skids from hitting me. A couple of other soldiers jumped out and it went up again. One of them motioned the chopper forward to get away from me. He and the other soldier pulled on me and pushed me back and forth until my feet became loose enough so I could pull them out. It's a good thing this wasn't a hot LZ. The rest of the soldiers finally made it out of the helicopter and we fanned out and went into the hamlet. As soon as the search was complete, we directed the pilot to set the chopper on a two-foot-wide dike. Once he had settled it on the dike he could hold it steady and still keep a little lift momentum so it didn't topple off the dike.

Our company made at least 20 separate airlifts that day. We killed close to 20 gooks and captured half that many. We confiscated a number of weapons, ammunition, and a few explosive devices for booby traps. It was a good day. I was kicking myself in the ass for what I did with allowing some gooks to run free earlier.

In our first 10 to 12 days in the An Lão Valley, we did not have a casualty. We were sniped at, often enough, but we just had a run of good luck during this time. A, C, and D

Companies did not share our good fortune. They hit booby
traps and took injuries from the snipers. There were enough
gooks around, but we were lucky to avoid the injuries.

On February 11, we set up for the night in a large
hamlet along a large rice paddy layout. We moved all the locals
in the hamlet into a couple of the hooches. Capt. Hitti chose
a large hooch along the main trail that came into the hamlet
and went out the other side. As usual, we were set up in strong
points. Ray Ascher and I set up a position right along the main
trail. We were sitting right at the edge of the rice paddy and
along the moat that ran around the hamlet. This moat was
used to flood the rice paddies after planting. It was about six
feet wide and almost that deep. There was a dike between the
first rice paddy and the ditch. Right after dark, Capt. Hitti
came from the CP and said that there were a lot of gooks in the
area. He added, "Please stay alert, I don't want any surprises.
I'm counting on you two to keep the CP alive." I told the
Captain that we had him covered.

Ascher was exceptionally tired. Of course, he was
always tired. I told him that I would pull first watch, and go
until I couldn't keep my eyes open any longer. Then I would
wake him and he should do the same. I managed to let him
sleep for at least three hours. I even stood up a few times to
circulate the blood, so I could handle the tiredness. I was
getting ready to wake him to cover for me, but I heard a noise
off to my right, around a bend in the hamlet perimeter. Something or someone was walking in the rice paddy and coming
toward me. It was moving very slowly but did not seem too
concerned about being quiet. I could see the water rippling, as
it was about to come from behind the point to my right beyond
the hamlet perimeter. I slipped the safe off and waited. I pulled
the gun to my shoulder and just as it rounded the corner, I
was ready to squeeze the trigger. As it stepped out beyond the

point, I could see it was a pig. It was the biggest damned pig I believe I ever saw. The thing looked as if it stood four feet above the water line. He must have sensed that I was there. He gave a loud grunt and sloshed away from me with a fast walk.

After allowing Ascher to sleep for more than three hours, I felt he should be able to handle at least two hours taking his turn. I woke him up. I told him about the pig, and not to shoot it. I made sure he was fully awake, and then I crawled below the bank I sat on, pulled my poncho over my body and slept. Some time later, I awoke. Usually, when in the field, if I wake on my own, it's because of a noise, or I got more than the usual two hours of sleep. I listened first before moving, and then slowly pulled the poncho down off my face. I lay there for a minute or more before moving. I could hear a faint moan or groan. My first thought was that someone got to Ascher and he was dying. I looked at the back sky over the hump I was behind to see if I could see any movement with the sky in the background. There was nothing there. I could still hear the moaning, but very faintly. I slid the poncho off me, got my rifle in the ready position with the safety off, and crawled up on the mound. Sitting hunched over, wrapped in his poncho with his head down and snoring was Ascher. The son-of-a-bitch fell asleep. I stood up, got directly behind him, and kicked him in the middle of his back and into the moat. He went under and came up gasping. He probably swallowed some of that feces-infected water. I told him to keep the noise down. He crawled to the bank and scratched his way up it. He said, "Why the hell did you do that?" I told him, "The next time you fall asleep on me, I will kill you, you son-of-a-bitch."

I checked my watch. I had slept for more than three hours. I felt fully rested. Ascher was shaking now. I told him to wrap up in his poncho. About two hours later, I was thinking of waking Ascher again. You could just make out a lighter sky to the east. I didn't think I needed more sleep, but a person should get more than three hours a night.

There was a sudden volley of shots coming from the north to my left. I yelled at Ascher to wake up. He heard the shots also. Capt. Hitti came out of the hooch along with the rest of the CQ group. I was looking down the line to the north, and someone yelled, "There they go!" You could make out about eight gooks running full-tilt toward a hamlet across the rice paddies. There was a bomb-damaged church in this hamlet. Capt. Hitti called in artillery strikes on the hamlet. The hamlet was unoccupied.

Colonel Hanahan got on the radio, intercepting the air strike calls. He wanted to know what was happening. Hitti told him of the situation. Hanahan asked if the enemy used artillery against us. Hitti responded in the negative. His reply was, "If they don't use artillery then we shouldn't use it. We should go after them on foot." I had never seen Capt. Hitti really upset before. I may have seen him bothered but, before today, nothing else seemed upsetting by comparison.

Zachery, who was one of the two soldiers in the position to our left, was calling for a medic. Doc, Hitti, and the Company RTO responded. Tracy Jones had intercepted a squad of gooks who were moving from west to east, toward the hamlet across the rice paddies. According to what his partner said, he heard Tracy yell "Halt!" They immediately opened up firing, killing Tracy Jones. If you knew Tracy, you liked him. He was a tall, athletic kid with a quiet, mellow disposition. He probably didn't have the killer instinct in him. That is probably why he yelled "Halt!" instead of shooting right away. Everybody in the company felt it. Capt. Hitti had to fight back tears as he dictated a short letter to Tracy's parents and family. Doc, the medic, wrote the letter as Hitti dictated.

As a company, we followed the path taken by the gook squad through the hamlet. We made a thorough search of the hamlet before moving on. We knew we would not catch them unless they wanted us to. Then they would have many more men and be ready for us. That thought was not inspiring.

After doing what the higher command expected, we went back to the search-and-destroy routine like we had for the past couple of weeks. We pushed hard all day with little break time. I think Capt. Hitti was trying to work the aggravation of the morning's events out of his system. It was nearly dark before he decided to set up for the night. He said we will still set up on strong points, but from now on we would tighten them. He wanted no less than three men in each position. Tom Gray, Ray Judy and I hooked up together. Hitti told us to be ready for trouble, and he wanted to see bunkers for cover. Again, this probably had a lot to do with what happened to Tracy earlier in the day.

While we were setting up, I found a stump partially embedded in the ground. Gray and I worked to free the stump and use it as part of our bunker. The stump resisted. We were on a fairly sharp hillside. Gray worked on the bottom side of the stump, and I pulled from the top side of the stump. I gave it everything I had. The stump broke free, and the muscle in my shoulder snapped. I pulled the muscles in my back on the right shoulder. It originated from the shot and scar across my upper back. It must have been a pretty good tear because a minute later the muscle was still fibrillating when Doc looked at it. He fixed me a sling, and said to keep it immobile; he would look at it again in the morning. He asked if I wanted something for the pain. I was tempted to say yes but thought I needed to be alert and pain medication dulls the mind. He gave me a couple of painkillers anyway, and said, "If it gets too bad, you might want these."

The next morning my shoulder was sore as hell. It throbbed all night. Doc and Capt. Hitti looked at it. Hitti looked at the scar across my back and said, "Why the hell did they send you back to the field?" He added, "They should have sent you home." He asked me why I didn't carry a pack. I told him, any weight hanging on my back irritates the hell out of it. He told me I was going in with the breakfast sortie. Doc wrote up his medic's note and told me to give it to the Battalion Aide at LZ English. When the helicopter lifted off, I sure felt good about getting out of the field again, and at the same time I also felt shitty about leaving.

Back at LZ English, I went directly to the aid station. I gave a Spec-4 Doc's note. He took my name and company information and told me to have a seat. I sat there close to an hour. I believe I was their only customer. After nearly wearing out an old folding chair, a medic with Spec-5 rank came from behind a flap and talked to me getting the particulars. He jotted the information down on the appropriate military form and disappeared behind the flap. I could hear mumbling in the background. After another 20-minute wait, the medic opened the flap and called me behind it. Our battalion doctor was sitting beside his table. There was a gurney off to one side.

The medic directed me to sit on the gurney and take off my shirt. The doctor picked up the form the medic had filled out and he looked at it. I'm sure he looked at it before, but I believe it's appropriate to do so in front of the patient. He looked at my right shoulder, front and back, and asked how it felt. I told him my perspective of the pain. It was not throbbing as it did during the night. He said, you most likely tore a muscle and described which one it was. He added, we have to watch it. If it doesn't get any better, or if it gets worse, we'll have to send you back to An Khê for X-rays.

He wrote something on the chart and I was dismissed for light duty details. Light duty details amounted to filling sandbags and loading them onto mules for displacement elsewhere. How fast or slow you worked at it determined how light your duty was. There were about seven or eight people on light duty status filling sandbags. It seemed like I was the only guy who worked at a steady pace. A few told me that I work too hard. They said I would work myself out of a job. They were milking their status and wanted to stay on it as long as possible. I had no inclination to work with the pogues for any longer than what was necessary.

While I was gone, the 2nd platoon had a run-in with some gooks. Ray Olin was the platoon RTO at this time. When it came to military procedure and discipline, Olin was a screw-up. When it came to the war in the field, however, you'd want him with you. He was a good field soldier. Ray knew the procedure for calling in artillery. He knew the coordinates, and the pre-designated aim bearing points. Procedurally an officer is the only one who should call in artillery. After six months in Vietnam, there were not enough officers to go around, so NCOs would call in the artillery. An enlisted RTO, usually a Spec-4 who had been on the job for some time, was probably better versed and qualified for calling in artillery than many officers. Olin called in artillery on the gooks. Colonel Hanahan broke in on the call to find out what was happening. Olin came back on the radio and told him to stay the hell off the air when he was calling in artillery. Olin added that we need artillery now, not later. The Colonel wanted his name. He told him to get it from his Captain but to get the hell off the air now. Olin got his artillery. Olin got busted from a Spec-4 to an E-2. Three days later he was back to a PFC and three weeks later he was back to his Spec-4 status. Olin thought this was a small price to pay for telling off a Colonel.

While on light duty, Sgt. Nuss told me I had to catch a helicopter going out to some artillery LZ in the An Lão Valley. He said the Brigade Commander was going to be there handing out awards and I was to receive one. I had no knowledge of such an award. I found Terry Olexy and asked him what he knew about the award. Olexy was in our 2nd platoon and got wounded on November 1st. He did not go back to the field. He was given the job of shuffling reports from the forward base camp to battalion, brigade, or division as assigned. Part of his job was to write up recommendations for military awards. Olexy said he was not in his present job when the recommendation for an award for me was submitted. He wasn't sure of what it was about, but he knew I was going to get the Bronze Star with V device.

There was another GI up for an award from another company of the 5th Bn 7th Cav. He and I loaded onto a helicopter and were flown about 15 minutes out to the artillery LZ. A Sergeant from the artillery organized us in a semblance of order on the side of the hill below the artillery gun placements. He made sure we were in the order that we would receive the awards. One of the GIs receiving an award was Sgt. Peyton, my old Basic Training Platoon Sergeant. For some reason that was only a year before, but it sure seemed like a lot had happened since that time, and it did seem much longer than a year.

After we were in line, Colonel Harold Moore and a few other officers came down the hill to our location. As he approached, the artillery Sergeant called us to order. Col. Moore told us to stand at ease. He then gave a speech about pride, discipline, sacrifice, bravery, duty, and whatever the military stood for. He commended us as a group for living up to and exceeding the standards of ordinary men, and a few other blah-blah-blahs. Then, one by one, they awarded the medals as an assistant read what each medal was for. I kept asking myself why I was with this group. I did not recall doing anything so dramatic as what these other men had done.

Then it came my turn. The custom was that when it came time for your individual award, you snapped to attention and stayed that way until the Colonel moved on. At that moment, a fly landed on my face and began crawling around on it. It was extremely irritating, and I wanted in the worst way to slap it off. Colonel Moore apparently saw my face twitching and brushed the fly away. As the assistant read the what for, I was asking myself, "Where was I when this happened?" In the end, it was in the perception of how each individual saw it. I was crawling for my life, while others saw me as trying to save a mortally wounded buddy. As others saw my attack with the M79 I took from Ascher, in reality I was pissed off and mad as hell. The round in my butt stung like hell and insulted my dignity. In the end, I thought someone had exaggerated the event to better fit the award.

After the ceremony was over, I talked with Sgt. Peyton. He remembered me well. I told him that I expected him to have me drop and give him 50 (push-ups) right there. He laughed. He told me that I was the best soldier in his platoon. He said that he knew I could handle all the extra harassment and the push-ups. So he used me as an example to show the rest of the platoon that it could be done. He said, "When training, I always look for the one soldier who could take the harassment. You were that soldier." He also said, "From what I saw, you had a lot of fun with the extra harassment and seemed to enjoy it." It felt nice hearing that from him. Sgt. Peyton and I talked until the choppers took the guy from C Company and me back to LZ English.

While I was gone from the field, the company had a run-in with some gooks. They killed a few and captured one with a wounded leg, and a female nurse. The wounded gook had a bleeding femoral artery and was losing blood fast. Capt. Hitti told Doc to patch up the wounded gook. Aragon said he was bleeding so much, it would be wasting good bandages on someone who was going to die anyway. Hitti ordered Aragon to put a tourniquet on the gook.

Hitti and Sgt. Nguyen interrogated the nurse. She was not cooperating and wouldn't say anything. Sgt. Nguyen tore the top gown off the nurse, grabbed her by the breast, stuck his knife in her breast far enough to draw blood, and told her that he would cut it off if she did not answer the questions. She became very cooperative, talking so much that she told them things they weren't even interested in.

Capt. Hitti asked Aragon if he had put a tourniquet on the wounded gook. Aragon said that he did. He asked if they could talk to the wounded gook. Aragon said no, he wouldn't be talking. Hitti asked what he did to the gook. Aragon said he put the tourniquet on and now he won't talk. Hitti asked where he was. Aragon told him he was just over the bank. The company was located above a sharp-drop bank. Aragon had tied a rope around the base of a tree and put a wrap as a tourniquet around the gook's neck, tied the rope to the wrap and then pushed the gook over the bank. His feet didn't reach the ground.

Three days later the pain in my shoulder was no longer severe. There was still some pain, but I could deal with it. I went back to the doctor and told him I was ready for the field again. He said that he was watching me and it was evident there wasn't much pain. He must have had a peephole in the tent from where he watched me. He sure didn't show himself around camp where we were working.

I went out with the evening chow run. When I got off the helicopter, Capt. Hitti asked why I came out. I told him the

Doc gave me the okay to come back in the field. He said, "You don't belong out here anymore. If you can't carry a backpack, you don't belong here." The chopper had already left. He told me I would be staying with the company CP overnight. He also said, "You will be going back with the breakfast run in the morning." I told him, "I don't care to hang around with the pogues. I'm too damn proud for that." He wrote a note for Sgt. Nuss, the field Supply Sergeant, and instructed him to give me an assignment with field supplies.

Sgt. Nuss was not elated with the note. He told me that he had one assistant and really didn't need any more. I told him that I'm easy. He told me to help Kampa until he finds something else for me. Kampa was the guy who caught the shrapnel in the butt when we were on the highway. He and I got along very well. Kampa had a mule assigned to him. He used it to transfer supplies, including the food and water from the post compound to the helipad for transfer to the field. He was happy to have someone helping him. Handling chow, water, ammunition, and any other supplies as ordered for four platoons was a big job. At least 50 percent of the time we were busy.

The next day was February 18. B Company hit the shit. It started at about 1300 hours. Sgt. Nuss was in contact with the field by radio. All orders came down from Battalion Headquarters. With the radio, as soon as the request was made for re-supply, we were already on it when Battalion got to us. We were listening to the radio when Capt. Hitti called for re-supply of M16 ammunition, M60 ammunition, two extra M60 barrels, a case of grenades, and extra water. By the time Battalion sent down the word, we had the supplies loaded onto the mule and were ready to head out. We verified the order to make sure there were no changes and headed for the helipad. We were standing by when the supply chopper came in. The chopper no more than settled on the skids and we had it loaded and ready for take-off again. Even if I wasn't in the field, I was doing something productive.

Kampa and I went back to the supply bunker and sat with Sgt. Nuss, listening to the radio. Soon after that the field armor Mike Beaupre and Larry Miller came in. Sgt. Nuss liked Beaupre, but not Miller. Miller was somewhat of a know-it-all, and you had to take him with a grain of salt. If you allowed yourself time to get to know him, he was pretty decent. After listening for awhile, Sgt. Nuss said, "It's getting too crowded; some of you guys have to leave." I volunteered to go and, since Kampa filled me in on Nuss's love for Miller, I conned him into going with me.

Sgt. Nuss was an American Indian. He had been in the service for 24 years and was due for retirement within the next two years. 80 percent of the time he was a pretty decent guy. The other 20 percent he was a bear. If he was in a foul mood, stay out of his way and out of his hair.

At about 1600 hours we learned that our Battalion Commander Hanahan had the command helicopter drop him and Lt. Alan Patrick into the battle area to take over ground command. Lt. Patrick was the formed mortar platoon leader assigned to B Company. He was now assigned to Division S-2 coordinating battalion operations with Division Command. Once on the ground, Lt. Colonel Hanahan and Lt. Patrick were struck by incoming rockets from our own helicopter gunships. This is known as friendly fire.

Lt. Colonel Hanahan had his leg nearly torn off, and Lt. Patrick was severely wounded.

All afternoon, while the battle was in progress, everything seemed very somber around Battalion. There was a real concern from everyone. Whenever there's a firefight, some people die. I tried not to think about who they might be. The evening chow was ready to go, but it was put on hold. Knowing how things went in the field, no one would be eating hot food tonight. Kampa and I went to supper. I wasn't very hungry, but I ate something. After supper, Kampa and I went back to the supply bunker. Sgt. Nuss was there by himself. I asked if there was anything new. He said that they haven't given out any line numbers of dead or injured yet. He said that he wanted some supper, but he hated to leave. I told him I would get him his supper. I'm not sure what Nuss thought of me, but I believe when I pulled Miller out of the bunker with me, and then brought him his supper, he began warming up to me. I was just happy to have something to do.

I was assigned to pull night security at the bunker on the main, south gate with Beaupre and Miller. I talked with them earlier and told them I would get there late, but I would get there. They had no problem with it since they usually played cards for a couple of hours each night anyway.

At about 2000 hours, the line numbers of the dead and wounded were called in. Dead were Johnny Burton, Sgt. Delmar Crockett, William Gould, Thomas Gray, Sgt. Pablo Patino, Charles Shaffer, and Jerry "Smitty" Schmitt. I had worked closely with Crockett and Patino. Gray was one of my two best friends. His name listed as a KIA hit me really hard. There were 40-plus soldiers who were injured. Two of the injured I knew very well were Ray Judy and Kloemken. By now it was nearly dark. Out behind the supply bunker was the squad bunker. I went behind the bunker and sat up against the sandbags and stared into the dark. I'm not sure if I was dumbfounded, shocked, or what, but I was having a tough time accepting Gray's death. I fought back the tears but eventually gave in to them. I said some prayers for him and all the dead.

A good 40 minutes passed before I got myself under control. I walked over to the bunker at the south gate. When I got into the bunker, Beaupre and Miller wanted to know if I had heard anything yet. I gave them the news. They weren't as close to Gray as I was, but they knew him well. Gray's humor touched everybody.

The next day, it was back to the war as usual. The events that had happened the day before were shrugged off, and not brought up again. That's the only way you could deal with it without losing your mind.

This was the first major battle for Sgt. Inez. He was conveniently out of the field for the other battles. He got shot five times. Two wounds came from one direction and three wounds came from a different direction. There was talk that someone from the 2nd platoon provided three of the wounds to Sgt. Inez. There was an inquiry from S-2 about his injuries about five days after the battle. If there was not a risk of reprisals, I'm sure many from the platoon would want to take credit for it but, as it was, no one said shit. Inez's wounds took him out of the field permanently. No one would miss him.

We learned later that Sgt. Crockett had picked this time to die. In the middle of the fight, he was located close to Sgt. Kanten. He looked over at him and said if I don't do it now, I may never get another chance. Then he jumped up and charged toward an enemy machine gun. Sgt. Kanten was a good friend of Crockett's. After he was killed, Kanten went into a deep depression and was unable to function. He had to be sent out of the field. I don't know if he ever went back out again.

A Marine takes cover behind a garden wall during the Battle of Hue, February 18, 1968. U.S. Marine Corps photo, ID 127-N-A190494. Photo courtesy of the National Archives at College Park, Md.

LZ SECURITY

After the battle of February 18, B Company had 28 soldiers left in the field. Two of them were walking wounded. They continued to operate as a company but combined to form a single platoon. For about 10 days, B Company continued in the An Lão Valley. They seldom made contact with the enemy during daytime hours. Frequently at night, there was some type of enemy harassment.

While pulling night guard in the field, snipers were shooting into the company perimeter. A FNG apparently pulled the pin on a hand grenade and then dropped it in his foxhole blowing himself up. The kid was in a foxhole, and his partner was trying to get some sleep outside and behind the foxhole. His partner was the same redheaded soldier who was with the complainer who shot himself nearly four months earlier. There was some speculation that the deceased may have intentionally killed himself, but his death was listed as an accidental casualty.

At LZ English things seemed to be laid-back. Besides working with supplies, Kampa and I worked with the sandbagging crew. We added sandbags around the medical station, the Battalion Command Post, the kitchen tent, and the perimeter bunkers. While we didn't have to work hard, we kept fairly busy. At night we pulled security on the perimeter. I teamed up with Mike Beaupre and Larry Miller. For three nights we would pull security at the main, south gate. Then we would switch with three other soldiers and take the outpost on the north end of the compound. At least we didn't have to look at the same dark spots every night.

Ten days after the February 18 firefight, Division Headquarters decided to pull B Company out of the field for a three-day stand-down. A stand-down is a short relief period to allow the troops a break and a chance to unwind. The whole company, including those back at LZ English, were flown to Camp Radcliff for the stand-down. It was obvious that everyone was happy to be out of the field for this short period.

Once everyone arrived at Camp Radcliff, I went to the company Orderly Room to request to go back out with the troops when they returned to the field. I figured they would want more help, as short as the company was after the battle on February 18. Capt. Hitti had the remaining platoon leaders with him to pass along his instructions. While I was waiting for a chance to talk to him, Major Bullock sent a runner to B Company headquarters with instructions for a full field inspection at 1500 hours that afternoon. Capt. Hitti told the platoon leaders and Sergeants to have everyone take stock of their gear and replace anything that was missing, and then authorize half of the remaining company to go into town and unwind today, and the other half could go to town the following day. He also said there would be no field inspection. The Orderly Room was a metal shed structure with an open-top divider between the Clerk's front desk and the back office. Anything said in the back office could be overheard in the front.

Rodney Salvi was the Company Clerk. That evening as we were unwinding at the 8th Engineers' EM Club, he told us that, when Major Bullock came to the Orderly Room for the inspection, he asked Capt. Hitti if he was ready to inspect. Hitti told him, "No I'm not." Bullock asked if he did not get the word for the inspection. Hitti said, "Yes I did." Then Bullock questioned him why he wasn't ready for the inspection. Hitti told Bullock that his men had been in the field for nearly a month without a break. He also told Bullock that he was responsible for his men, and his men needed to unwind more than they needed to be harassed by an inspection. So it was his decision to allow the men to unwind as they saw fit.

I never had a chance to talk with Capt. Hitti. I did talk with 1st Sgt. Baldwin. When I put in my request to go to the field, he asked for my name again. When I gave my name, he said no, I would not be allowed to go out in the field. I then requested at least to be allowed to go out with the artillery working with the battalion and pull security. He said he would talk with Capt. Hitti. I never heard from him again.

On the third morning of stand-down, the company loaded on trucks with all necessary gear and we were transported to the airfield where we boarded on Chinook helicopters and went back to LZ English where the company was assigned to pull security. That afternoon some C-130 planes landed at the airfield at LZ English. There were 100 FNGs on the C-130s. With all their gear they were marched from the airfield to our Battalion area. B Company got all 100 of the FNGs. They were then assigned to specific platoons.

B Company remained at LZ English for one more day before going back to the An Lão Valley. For a period of time there was no major contact with the gooks, but about every second or third day, B Company had one or more casualties, mostly from booby-trap explosives. It was almost always one of the FNGs that was getting wounded. There were so many of them, and I suppose the old guys knew enough to position themselves back away from the lead soldiers. While the regulars were not yet categorized as short-timers, they were already thinking of making it back home. In the first seven months, you did not think of going back home. You also realized your chances of making it back home were not very good. But with five months to go, it crossed your mind from time to time.

Larry Miller approached me one morning and asked me if I wanted to go along with him into the village of Bong Son. He said he had an errand to run. He also said there was a nice sandy beach along the Bong Son River where we could take a swim. During the daytime, the temperatures always went above the 100-degree mark. Even though we were now in the dry season, it still rained every day. We had limited shower facilities, so a swim in the river sounded good to me. Bong Son was about 12 klicks due east of LZ English. Once at the swim site, I put my helmet, web belt, rifle and ammunition on the back seat of the jeep. I walked into the river with my clothes on. Then I took them off and washed them without the aid of soap. After washing the clothes and wringing the excess water from them, I placed them across the hood of the jeep so they could dry in the hot sun. I went back in the river for the swim.

A couple of Vietnamese women and seven or eight children came down to the river. They parked themselves and squatted side-by-side about 15 feet in front of the jeep. The children were running around. I checked every so often to make sure they did not get near the gun or my belongings. After a few minutes, they left. When I came out of the river I put my clothes on and grabbed my helmet, rifle and web belt. My billfold was lying under the helmet on the back seat of the jeep. I kept it wedged up in the helmet liner webbing. I had at least $80 in scrip in my billfold. Now there was only a $20 scrip note left in it. Everything else seemed to be in order. I believe the women and kids were a distraction while someone else pilfered my billfold. There was damn little I could do about it.

Being low on money I decided that I needed to straighten out my affairs with Finance again. I talked to Sgt. Nuss and requested to go back to Camp Radcliff to the Finance Section and try again to get my pay squared away.

Two days later, I caught a helicopter that was heading that way and hitched a ride. Finance was in a cluster of metal shed structures in the middle of the post. I went directly to a building that was labeled Division Finance. There were board-walks along the dirt roadway, and leading up to each Quonset building. I walked into the Finance building and initially talked with a Clerk. As I was talking with him, someone behind him yelled "Bob!" I looked up and there was Jerry Theisen. His dad was a long-time bartender at the Sportsman Bar and Café in St. Cloud. He had leased a lake lot from my dad when I was much younger. Jerry was the oldest of three boys. He and his brothers Jim and Delroy spent a lot of time with my brothers and me at the home farm when we were younger. After explaining my situation, Jerry helped me out. I took about $120 and the rest of my pay was sent home.

I left the Finance building and was walking back to our battalion area. I approached a jeep that was parked along the boardwalk, facing the wrong way by driving standards in the United States. Sitting in the front passenger seat was an officer, Major by rank, who was very much overweight. As I was walking toward the jeep he had his eyes glued to me. As I passed the front of the jeep, I feigned a salute but instead scratched the side of my head. He saluted me. I said, "Gotcha," and walked by. He yelled, "Hey you!" about three times and then called for his driver. I kept right on walking.

A gravel truck came by fairly slow and I jumped on the running board. I told the driver where I was headed and he said he would pass our battalion within a couple of blocks. I told him an officer was looking for me and I needed to duck out of sight. He told me to jump in the back. I told him to honk the horn when he approached the closest area to our battalion and to slow down. I would jump out of the truck and duck into the bushes. If the Major pursued me, he wouldn't find me.

As soon as I got back to the base camp, Sgt. Milbur told me to change into clean clothes since mine were stained with red clay. Rules were that anyone coming out of the field was to change into fresh uniforms before going anywhere on post. My business was done, so I saw no need to change clothes. Besides, the red-stained clothes acted as camouflage, and it also told people you didn't know that you had been in 'Nam for some time and you were a seasoned soldier.

Milbur also told me I would be pulling guard duty on the perimeter that night. I told him it was my intention to go back to LZ English that afternoon. He said there would not be any choppers heading back to LZ English until the following day and that I would be pulling guard duty on the perimeter overnight. I was to report right after evening chow.

I ignored changing clothes, ate an early supper, and went to the battalion EM Club for some beer. I ignored Milbur's orders for guard duty. I figured these guys in the rear could pull their own weight. This one night away from LZ English I was going to relax, unwind, and have some beer and fun. The next morning I ate breakfast, caught a ride down to the airfield, and within a half hour caught a ride back to LZ English.

Larry Miller and Olexy were having a conversation about whether Miller was entitled to a purple heart. Shortly after expanding LZ English, it was decided that the locals in the hamlet close to the south main gate had to leave their homes. The locals were loaded onto helicopters and taken to one of the education camps. The security people at LZ English had the job of clearing the hamlet and destroying food and huts. Larry Miller put a grenade into or onto some item to destroy it. After pulling the pin he ran and ducked behind a tree. His butt was apparently too big to get fully protected. The grenade went off and he got a shrapnel sliver in his butt. Miller felt he was entitled to a Purple Heart for that. Olexy argued that it was his own grenade, and it was not a hostile action that caused the injury. He also said that if his ass wasn't so fat, he would not have gotten the sliver of shrapnel. Olexy added that Miller was not even injured. Larry argued he had to have the doctor look at it. Olexy responded, but he didn't do anything with it. He also said, "How the hell am I supposed to write up your injury so it doesn't insult the rest of the 5/7 Cav troopers?" They went back and forth for quite awhile. They were doing it in fun, but I believe Miller really wanted that Purple Heart. I'm not sure if he got it.

There was a large fuel dump about 200 meters east of our battalion area. The fuel dump was a bladder made of heavy rubber and canvas binding. It was about 100 feet long, 40 feet wide and, when full, about 12 feet high at the high mid-crown. The bladder was dug about half-way into the ground. What was above ground had sandbags about 4 feet wide stacked as high as the bladder all around it. The fuel bladder was on a hillside. On the bottom side of the bladder, there was an approach dug down below bladder level. The approach had sandbags stacked in an L-shape out from the sandbags surrounding the bladder. Whenever someone wanted to fill the tank on a vehicle, the vehicle was backed into the approach and, with the aid of a hose with a nozzle, gravity would supply the pressure to fill the tank.

Around the perimeter at LZ English, Claymore mines were set out in strategic locations in front of the security bunkers. Every so often someone would discharge one of the Claymores during the night. They usually said they saw someone, or heard someone, out in front of their position. Major Bullock put out the word that no one could set off a Claymore mine without first getting permission from Battalion Headquarters. Como wire was strung from Battalion Headquarters to every bunker that had a Claymore-triggering device. A land phone was put in each of the bunkers. There were three Claymores out in front of our position at the south gate. This gate was considered a crucial security site. One night the gooks decided to send some mortars into LZ English. Most of them were designated for the airfield. A few landed in the vicinity of the fuel dump. At least one of every four mortar rounds were duds. You'd hear the round whistling in and then hear a thud with no explosion. You could tell when a dud round hit the airfield. The airfield had interlocking perforated and ribbed metal plates spread out for the landing field and to where the planes and helicopters were parked. When the dud round hit, it made a metallic thunk sound instead of the thud when it hit the ground.

When enemy mortars landed, especially at night, you had to be prepared for the possibility of an enemy ground assault. Often times after the mortars, the gooks would attack in massive numbers and attempt to overrun the camp perimeter. As soon as the mortaring stopped, our own mortar platoon would send up flares. A flare lights up an extremely large area as bright as daylight for about a minute.

When the mortaring started, I was the only one awake on guard duty. Beaupre and Miller were sleeping. When the first flare ignited, there was a gook out in front of my position just beyond and to the left of the gate. As soon as the flare lit, he dropped down in the weeds and brush. I thought he was fairly close to one of the Claymores, so I hit the triggering device and discharged the Claymore. This woke Beaupre and

Miller. They asked what the hell was happening. I told them. Beaupre said Bullock was going to be pissed because I didn't get permission to blow it. I grabbed the Como wire and gave it three hard yanks. I told him the phone was out of working order and I couldn't get permission. I then tried calling Battalion Headquarters to make sure the phone was out of order. Headquarters could not be reached. About 15 minutes later I heard someone coming from bunker to bunker asking if they had set off the Claymore.

Bullock came to our bunker and asked if we had set off the Claymore. I told him that I did. He asked why I didn't get permission. I told him that I tried but the phone wasn't working. I also told him that I saw a gook just outside the gate with a rifle, so I didn't wait too long to set off the Claymore. He wanted me to go out and see if I got the gook, and I told him it would have to wait until morning. I wasn't going outside the perimeter during the night. About that time another flare lit up the sky. Major Bullock was standing outside the bunker, looking in. Shortly after the flare ignited, someone took two quick shots at the Major. He ducked into the bunker and that is where he stayed until daylight. He made all three of us stay awake for the rest of the night. I missed my sleep again.

Working detail assignments during the day and pulling security watch at night became routine and somewhat boring. Many people looked for something to spice up their situation. One night Larry Miller lit up a joint. I gave him some shit about it. A lot of GIs in Vietnam smoked marijuana. He handed the joint to me and said, "Don't knock it until you tried it." I told him I wasn't interested. He prodded me a little, so I said, "Okay, I'll give it a try." He told me to inhale it and hold it in as long as I could, and then let it out slowly. He said it has better effect when you do it that way. I did as he instructed, and found no sensation at all. I told him it tasted like a cigarette someone had pissed on. I didn't get loopy or high. I told him I would stick with my beer. At least that had some taste to it.

The following night we switched with the crew that was on the outpost bunker on the north end of the compound. A night scope had been installed in this bunker. Looking into the scope was like looking through a pair of binoculars. The outer end of the scope was about 10 inches in diameter. During daylight hours the scope had to be covered to protect the lens. There was a locking shield over the outer end of the scope to make sure it was not exposed to sunlight. The scope had a switch to activate the night lens. There was a hamlet about 200 meters down the hill from the bunker. Even in pitch blackness, when you focused the scope on the hamlet, you could see anything going on in it. All structures and people had a green glow. We would direct the scope out past the hamlet to see if any visitors came in after dark. At least we had something to see while sitting in the dark at night.

This bunker sat out about 150 meters beyond the rest of the compound perimeter. If anyone came out to the bunker after dark, they were supposed to give us fair warning that they were coming. This was to prevent anyone from shooting our own people. We seldom got any visitors, but on occasion one of the officers came out to check on us. One night while I was on guard, I heard a shuffling noise behind the bunker. I challenged the intruder. No one answered me. I shook Beaupre awake and told him of the noise and said I was going out to check it out. I stepped out of the bunker and heard a rustling noise coming my direction. I was about to yell "Halt!" and was ready to fire. A small deer, running full-tilt, hit me in the shins. The deer gave a squeal, spun around and ran off. It damn near took my legs out from under me. The next day I had bruises on both shins. The deer in Vietnam were a little larger than a Minnesota jackrabbit. Running full-tilt he packed a good wallop.

Quad-mount M2 .50 caliber machine guns firing in support of D Company 1/7th Cavalry 1st Air Cavalry Division during Operation "Pershing," 1967. Photo courtesy of *www.armyheritage.org*.

B COMPANY TO GET A NEW LEADER

Word came down that Capt. Hitti was going to be replaced and that he was leaving the field to be assigned to Division, S-2, which is Military Intelligence. He had a chance to leave the field after four months but turned it down to stay with the company. Every month after that he was given the same option. He always turned it down. The Division took the option away from him and he was now going to be replaced. He requested to spend three additional days with the company to orient his replacement on the men under his command before leaving the field. I made up my mind to be in the field for Capt. Hitti's last day. I felt close to him and had a lot of respect for him. I wanted to be with the company on his last day.

Sgt. Nuss, the Supply Sergeant, had to turn in the roster each day for those from B Company who were stationed at LZ English. I cleared it with him to go out in the helicopter with the morning chow. I got my field gear together and helped Kampa with the chow run. When we loaded the chow on the chopper, I got on with it. As soon as it landed and I got off, Capt. Hitti asked why the hell I came out. I told him my reasons and he accepted it. He told me, "When I leave this afternoon, you will leave with me." He introduced me to the new Company Commander, his name I don't remember. Hitti told me to stick close to the Company RTO for the day. The RTO usually walked about 10 meters behind the company

Commander. Things seemed normal for the company until about 1400 hours that afternoon.

The point man, a fairly new guy who I didn't know, was walking about 15 meters to the front of the second man. Everyone else was spread about the same distance apart. We were sweeping hamlets along the edge of some rice paddies below a heavily foliated ridge. There was a trail running along the rice paddies toward a hamlet. Capt. Hitti and his replacement were walking with about five meters between them, and fifth and sixth in column behind the point man. There were at least 75 meters between the point and Hitti. The point man rounded a curve in the trail and the trail exploded shaking the ground and sending dirt and debris 100 meters in the air and out beyond 100 meters. I was at least 10 meters behind the RTO and we both ended up on the ground. I don't know how I ended up on the ground but it seemed like the place to be at the time.

When the dirt and dust settled, the point man and the man behind him were gone. They disappeared in the explosion. The third soldier in line was killed, and the fourth was severely wounded and not expected to live. The new Company Commander was lying on the ground and severely injured. The two enlisted GIs were not expected to live. The new Captain was injured with fairly severe wounds. The shrapnel caught him in the thigh and shoulders. He had other minor injuries. Capt. Hitti had injuries to his right arm and shoulder, which were not severe but bad enough.

Aragon was still the medic. He fixed up the wounds with help from a few other soldiers. Doc brought out the body bags and soldiers searched the area, picking up body parts and placing them in the bags. There was no way to tell which particles of flesh belonged to which deceased soldier. The only way we knew two people were killed, was that we found three shoes with foot parts still in them. When we were done picking up body parts, we didn't have more than thirty pounds of meat between the two bodies. What gear was found was also placed in the body bags. What seemed strange to me was that, since I didn't really know these guys, I had no feelings about their death or that I was handling chunks of their dead meat.

It was thought the booby-trap mine was actually one of our dud 500-pound bombs that had not exploded when it was dropped. The gooks set their own charge in the head of the bomb and rigged it to a trip wire.

A medevac chopper was called for the wounded. I talked with Capt. Hitti before he left, and so did others. He told me to be sure and get on the chow chopper when it went back to LZ English that evening. With that explosion, I had my fill of field duty. I was no longer anxious or wishing to go back to the field. It probably had more to do with Capt. Hitti not being there, and most of the people I went over to Vietnam with were gone, either dead or wounded. I was also looking at having fewer than five months before I went back to the world, meaning the United States.

A black Lieutenant, who was the platoon leader of the 1st platoon, took over as the Company Commander until a replacement was found. His name was Bronson. Bronson was the type of officer who did not draw attention. He seemed laid-back and more reserved. Initially, many of the troops under him did not see him as a leader. When we got to Vietnam, this quickly changed. When he got in the field, he learned quickly. He was the only officer who went over with the company that was still left in the field. He was dependable, thorough, and did not take unnecessary risks. The troops liked him.

Bronson's tenure as the acting Company Commander lasted about one week and then B Company was blessed with Capt. David Gibson. Gibson was a West Point graduate. He was

Gung-ho and glory-hound crazy. He wanted ribbons as a war epithet. He lasted 14 days in the field before getting himself killed.

To demonstrate his search for glory, I will relay a few of his dramatized accounts. A couple of days after his arrival, 2nd platoon received sniper fire from some rocks in the hill above them. Sgt. Nehr was running the platoon. He organized a two-team squad and moved up the hill, pinning the gooks down with heavy return fire and killed both gooks. The gooks did not have enough cover and were unable to escape because the return fire was too heavy for them.

When Capt. Gibson heard of the skirmish he had the bodies placed back in some cover and he staged himself as an Audie Murphy replica and, with fixed bayonet, charged the dead gooks firing his M16 rifle into the cover. When he approached the dead gooks he ceased firing and charged in and stabbed them with the bayonet. He had his RTO record this action on film with a series of still shots from his camera. He sent the photos home to his wife. Unknown to the field troops, he put himself in for a Silver Star for his heroic actions. Olexy is the person who was supposed to forward the recommendation for the award. When he learned what really happened, Olexy conveniently lost the paperwork.

In another incident, B Company was setting up positions for the evening. 2nd platoon was on a hill at one location. Capt. Gibson was with 3rd platoon on another hill about one klick distance from 2nd platoon. Greek was setting up a Claymore mine out in front of his position on the side of a used trail. He was bent over the Claymore and heard someone coming up the hill on the trail. They were talking in Vietnamese. Greek waited in the brush until they were within 10 feet of him. He put his M16 on full automatic, squeezed the trigger and killed both gooks with a full clip of M16 rifle fire.

Capt. Gibson was shaving at the time. He was bareback and had just put shaving cream on his face. When he heard the shots he requested his RTO to find out what happened. When he heard the news of the dead gooks, he took off running from his location to where the 2nd platoon was located. He still had the shaving cream on his face. He wanted to congratulate Greek for the heroic action.

This was also verified by the medic "Doc" Aragon who was at both events. Even though I was at LZ English, information flowed freely on what was going on in the field. Troops were always coming and going. Although I am relaying the info second-hand, there were enough sources relaying the same account to verify reasonable accuracy. In my mind, Capt. Gibson was a danger to the people he commanded.

I still wanted to go out to the artillery LZs and pull security around them. This would put me in the field but I wouldn't have to hump. I ran my request through Sgt. Nuss. He said he would check on it.

Catholic chaplain Cpt. Bruno Massoti conducts services for troops during "Operation Van Buren," a combined operation of the Republic of Korea, Republic of Vietnam, and the U.S. Army 101st Airborne, January 23, 1966. Credit Robert C. Lafoon. U.S. Army photo. NARA 111-CC-33194. Photo courtesy of the National Archives at College Park, Md.

EASTER 1967

As long as I was at LZ English, there were no church services. We didn't keep track of the day of the week; one day was like all the rest. We were going to have a priest, Army slang "Sky Pilot," come out for Easter. He actually came out on Holy Saturday.

A small tent was stretched out next to a large bunker complex in the battalion area. An OD green sheet was stretched out from the back wall, and a chair was placed on each side of the sheet. This was set up so the priest could hear confessions. The priest took one chair and the one going to confession took the other chair. An hour after confessions were completed, the end of the tent was opened and an altar table was placed in the center of the tent opening. The priest then said Mass. There was a fairly large crowd for the services. I went to confession and, of course, attended the Mass. Since coming to Vietnam, this was my first time going to confession one-on-one. The priest had to be back at Camp Radcliff for services later that day, so as soon as services were over he hopped on a chopper and headed out.

B Company was clearing an area for an LZ. The call came in that they needed 10 cases of Bangalore torpedoes. Bangalore torpedoes are tubes of steel, two and a half inches in diameter and five feet long. They are hooked together on the end to form a line as long as you want to make it. A trigger device is hooked up to the end of the torpedo line and set off by squeezing the triggering charger, the same as you would for a Claymore mine. When the torpedoes explode, they shred and clear out of the way all brush and small trees up to an inch and a half in diameter. Once detonated, the Bangalore torpedoes will clear a path about 60 feet wide. The company had strung out about 50 of the torpedoes on one line.

A soldier by the last name of Schreimf was hooking up the charge wire to the end of the first torpedo. Either static electricity or a crossed wire caused the torpedoes to go off prematurely. He was on the end of the torpedoes and they blew out sideways shredding everything in the way. When the dust settled, Schreimf was standing on unsteady legs, covered from head to toe with black dirt and explosive debris. He was disoriented and in shock. There did not appear to be any external injuries. A medevac was called and he was flown to a field hospital. I do not believe he ever came back to B Company.

MONKEYS, DOGS, AND FIRE

Someone came in from the field with a monkey. He was on a leash and quite domesticated. He became our temporary company mascot. We could release him and he would hang around, sometimes mimicking us when we were goofing off.

There were a number of dogs in the compound. I think they came from the nearby hamlets. They got better food from us than they did in the hamlets. They were all skinny when they came, but put weight on as time went by. We kidded that the gooks sent them into the compound to fatten them so they could eat them later on.

One evening before dark, we turned the monkey lose among the dogs. The dogs took an immediate dislike of the monkey. There were five dogs and the one monkey. The dogs attacked the monkey. They would rush in on him and try to bite him. He would jump on their backs, bite them in the neck, and pull them over on their sides. The monkey was much quicker than the dogs and seemed to be enjoying the confrontation. The more he messed with the dogs, the madder they got, and the harder they charged. The result was always the same. At one point all five dogs converged on the monkey at the same time. He jumped on one's back then the next and the next. A dog would jump at the monkey landing on the dog the monkey had been on. Eventually, he had the dogs fighting with each other. We let this go on for at least 20 minutes, then caught the monkey and took him back to the company bunker next to supply.

We rigged up a little sandbag bunker against the big bunker, just outside the entry to the bunker. We tied the monkey's leash to a stake, and he was content with his home and surroundings.

One particularly hot day, a bunch of us were sitting around trying to catch some shade. Someone brought out a can of warm beer. We took an empty can of C-Rations, dented the bottom in to form a shallow basin, and poured some warm beer in it. The monkey drank the beer. More beer was put in the can and he drank it. The monkey drank about half of the can of warm beer. He started to show signs of inebriation. He had glossy eyes, a grin on his face, and he would slowly lean sideways until he fell. He staggered around, falling as he tried to walk. We watched him for about 15 minutes and he dozed off. His leash was tied to the top of the bunker and that is where he fell asleep. We eventually forgot about the monkey and were making idle chatter sitting in the shade. Someone noticed he was no longer lying on the bunker. His leash was draped over the far side of the bunker. We walked around the bunker and found the monkey hanging by its leash. He was dead. Normally he would have climbed back up the side of the bunker, but in his drunken stupor, he probably could not coordinate his actions for that simple task.

After picking up the empty chow and liquid containers from the helipad one morning, Kampa and I were heading back to the kitchen area with the mule and the return canisters. The road from the helipad ran into the main road coming on post at the south entrance. Just before the road left the compound, a trail made by the engineers led up to 5/7 Cav compound area and eventually to the kitchen area. Close to this intersection was an area where rubbish was piled for burning. Powell, from

B Company, was the designated shit-burner. So he also had to take care of the rubbish and burn it.

As Kampa and I were coming down the road, we saw Powell throwing J-4 (the military term for gasoline) onto the rubbish pile. As we neared the intersection he lit a match and threw it on the rubbish. He apparently spilled gas on himself. The rubbish ignited with a gushing explosion as gasoline fumes do, and he was too close to the fire. His clothes caught on fire. He immediately dropped to the ground and began rolling around. Much of his clothes were in flame. I jumped off the mule and grabbed the first liquid canister I could reach. It was last night's coffee from the field. I ran over to Powell and poured the coffee over the flames. He had his shirtsleeves rolled up and the shirt was on fire. As soon as the gush of cold coffee hit him, the skin on his arms cracked open and exposed the meat inside. By now one of the cooks came running over. He told me I should never pour cold liquid over burning skin. We threw everything off the mule, loaded Powell onto it, and transported him to the medical station. About 15 minutes later a medevac chopper came in and hauled him off. That was the last we saw of Powell. Powell was the same guy who drove the cigar down Sgt. Inez's throat when Inez took it out of a package Powell had received from home.

Luis "Doc" Aragon showing off his Bronze Star.

Dennis Benedetti at Fort Carson, Colorado.

INCOMING

Right after daylight one morning, while Kampa and
I were loading the mule for field request for B Company, Sgt.
Nuss told me that B Company was going to an artillery LZ near
Dak To. He told me to get my field gear and I could catch the
supply chopper to fly out with it. The chopper landed at an LZ,
but there were no artillery guns around. We unloaded supplies
and I asked one of the soldiers where the artillery was located.
He said it was about two klicks due north. Dak To was close
to one klick from the LZ where we were located. There was a
well-used dirt road, which ran south to north past the LZ and
into and through Dak To. One of the soldiers said that he had
to truck some of the supplies to the artillery LZ and I could
ride along. When I got to the LZ, I located 2nd platoon. There
were only a handful of the regulars who had come over on the
boat. Sommers, Walters, Holcomb, Callister, Dalton, and Joe
Gonzales I could remember. None of them were members of
the 3rd squad. I was the only original member of the 3rd squad
left in the field at this time. I would only be here until they
went into the field again. Just the same, it was good to be back
with the platoon.

The word was that we could expect to get mortared
during the night. The rule of thumb was that the GIs control
the days and the gooks control the nights. I teamed up with
Walters and Sommers. At about 2300 hours the mortars began
arriving. The LZ was on a hill with the artillery guns on either
side of the crown. There were fortified bunkers around the

entire LZ, scattered in the midst of the guns. The artillery rounds and powder for the guns were stored in heavily fortified bunkers to prevent premature explosions in the event that a mortar round was lucky enough to get a perfect landing. Most of the mortar rounds were short and didn't get close to the LZ. A couple landed within 50 meters of the perimeter. About 15 mortars exploded and it was over. As soon as the mortars stopped, artillery flares were shot overhead to light the area in case the gooks tried an attack. This didn't happen. This apparently was a nightly routine at this artillery site.

A river ran past the village of Dak To. Below the bridge crossing the river was a fairly decent swimming hole. The next day as the sun got higher in the sky, the heat became nearly unbearable. It was probably hitting the 110-degree line on the thermometer. At least six soldiers from 2nd platoon decided to go to the river for a swim. While we were swimming a couple of women came down to the river carrying a basket that had eight bottles of Tiger Piss (beer). The first thing I did was to grab my billfold. I wasn't going to lose money again. We didn't have any swimsuits and we never wore underwear, so we were swimming in the nude. This did not seem to bother the women. Since we were used to living in a crude world, it didn't bother us to be seen naked. They sold all their beer and left. After the swim, we walked into Dak To and we each bought another bottle of Tiger Piss before going back to the LZ.

Back at the artillery LZ, most of the GIs had found shaded areas to relax out of the sun. No one felt like doing anything until the heat of the day passed. About mid-afternoon it rained, cooling the air. Instead of getting out of the rain, most of the GIs stepped out in it to cool down. The rain lasted about 30 minutes. As soon as the rain quit the sun came out again, as hot as before. Toward evening the temperature slowly came down and things started to buzz again.

After the evening chow, two patrols went out. As dark settled in, GIs got into their perimeter bunkers. I again teamed with Walters and Sommers. At close to 2300 hours, one of the squads had contact with a gook patrol. They were out from the artillery LZ a little over one klick. There was a heavy volley of shots for about two minutes. The gooks broke contact and fled. We didn't get mortared that night. The next morning after breakfast, B Company was going back to the field. I hopped onto one of the choppers that brought out breakfast and went back to LZ English.

Soldiers from the 101st Airborne Division duck for cover during a firefight.
Photo courtesy of *www.armyheritage.org.*

ONE HELL OF A FIREFIGHT

On April 8th, around 1300 hours, word came in that A Company of the 1st Bn 7th Cav was involved in a heavy firefight with a large NVA force. The company was surrounded and had already taken heavy casualties. There was a trooper from our 2nd platoon who was transferred to the 1st Bn 7th Cav. He was in the company that was surrounded. His name was Frank Childs. Childs had a severe drinking problem that went unnoticed until he got to Vietnam. We did not have much chance for booze, and this drove him a little insane. When he had the chance, he would buy large bottles of Vitalis hair tonic, cut it with water, and drink it. Vitalis had a substantial amount of alcohol among the ingredients. When the problem was evident, he was removed from our platoon and most likely sent somewhere for drying out. When he came back he was transferred to the 1st Bn 7th Cav.

The 1st Cav Division had a number of battalions working in fairly close proximity to where this battle was taking place. At least two full battalions responded to this site. They were supposed to move into position and surround the NVA force so that they could not escape, and wait for additional support to move on the NVA.

B Company of the 5/7 Cav was the earliest responder. Orders were to cross a river, move in at least 100 meters from the river, form a blocking line and wait for support. Capt. Gibson ignored the "FORM A LINE" portion of his assignment. He led a charge into battle. Of course, he had to be out in front of the battle line and on a dead run. He had his RTO Charles Heaps with him. They were out in front of the rest of the troops. They were cut down by the gooks. Lt. Bronson assumed control of the company again. Everyone else took up positions according to plan, dug in for protection, and waited. No one could get to Capt. Gibson and Heaps to help them. They were too close to enemy positions, and any move on them would have been suicidal. The rest of the company was involved in the battle attempting to form a good blocking line.

The balance of the afternoon more 1st Cav troops moved into position to successfully close up any escape routes for the gooks. The gooks were trapped in their own ambush. This was not good for the trapped company of the 1st Bn 7th Cav.

Kampa and I were busy loading ammunition, grenades, C-Rations, and water on a mule for the call when it came. A helicopter landed on the helipad and Ray Judy got off. He was back from his wounds on February 18. He came into camp, and we told him what was happening. I told him to get lost for a while. Instead, he quickly got all his gear together so he could go out with the re-supply chopper. The call came for supplies. He rode with us to the helipad, helped us load the chopper, and jumped on. I didn't even have a chance to bullshit with him. But I had a lot of admiration for him. He could just as easily have avoided going back to the field at this particular time, but that wasn't like him.

The 11th Armored Cav was operating somewhere in the Central Highlands near the Cambodian border. Since we were in the dry season, moving heavy tanks was possible. The Armored Cav was summoned for the clean-up battle. It took two days to move the tanks across the hilly terrain and into position. With numerous rivers, hills and ridges that were too steep to scale with tanks, 40 to 50 miles was more like over 100 miles.

The tanks eventually made their appearance. Three hours later the battle was over. As the tanks moved in, the troops fell in behind them. They pushed right through all resistance, killing hundreds of gooks in the process. Some of the gooks broke out and ran but were cut down as they ran.

Near the end of the battle, a single gook was running straight away from a tank. The machine gunner put his sights low on the gook and began firing behind him. He very slowly walked the tracer rounds up on him and held the line of fire on his heels for awhile, trying to get more speed out of him before running it up his back.

Another tank took after a gook who was on the run. The tank knocked the gook to the ground and ran him over. The gook went between the tracks and was only injured. The driver came back, ran a track over him and then ground the tank back and forth on top of the gook tearing him apart with the tracks.

I don't understand the psychological terms for it, and it doesn't happen to everyone, but once a person kills, there's a vicious quality or character comes out. During wartime, that viciousness can flow freely without consequences. It's scary and dangerous.

In the end, more than 400 gooks were killed that day. The company from the 1st of the 7th Cav, which was pinned down, lost close to 40 GIs. Childs was one of them. I don't know how many from other companies and battalions were killed. The following were killed from B Company 5th Bn 7th Cav: Billy Carver, J. Geyer, Capt. David Gibson, Charles Heaps,

Dorsie Register, Lloyd Stearns, and Vincente Sandoval who was killed by one of our own FNGs.

After the first day of fighting, when night had settled in, Sandoval, now a Platoon Sergeant, was checking on the troops in his platoon. He moved from position to position making sure that they had enough ammunition and grenades, and he gave them the requisite "hang in there" encouragement. At one position he stepped out in front of it and was taking a leak. A young kid in the next position saw movement out in front of the position beside him. He opened fire and killed Sandoval. This kid had been in the field for three days; he was most likely frightened because of the intensity of the situation. Sandoval was a well-liked guy. Most people didn't blame the kid, but a few who were really close to Sandoval had a hard time accepting his death the way it happened. After this battle was over, the kid was transferred to a different company.

After the battle, B Company spent the next day with clean-up, hauling dead bodies, checking paperwork, and whatever information that could be gathered for Army Intelligence. The company from the 1st Bn 7th Cav went back to Camp Radcliff for a three-day stand-down. The 5th Bn 7th Cav went back to sweeping and clearing hamlets in the area they had left before the battle. Things seemed much more at peace in the An Lão Valley after this battle. There were fewer night mortars, fewer booby traps, and less enemy harassment in general.

CAPTURE–ESCAPE–HERO

The following story comes out of D Company. It was verified, and it probably saved many GI lives. I am telling the story as I heard it and remember it.

D Company was going to make a move and they gathered on a landing zone to wait for the choppers. There was one soldier in the outfit who was sick, possibly with malaria. He was told to get on the last sortie and stay on when they were dropped off and to go back to the Aid Station at LZ English. He walked off to the side and lay down in some high grass. He left his gear stacked where others had stacked their gear. One sortie came in and picked up some troops. The second sortie came in and picked up the rest of the troops. The sick soldier was still sleeping. Someone saw the unattended gear and figured someone left it behind. Another soldier grabbed the gear and put it on the chopper.

After a sound nap, the GI awoke and found he was alone without any weapons, food or water. He knew he had to get back to LZ English, so he took off walking in the direction he thought LZ English would be. Just before dark he found a small creek and drank his fill of water. Walking along the creek was pretty easy walking, so he followed the creek for a while. He was down in the gully of the creek when a small platoon of gooks spotted him from the bank above. Without any weapons, they had an easy capture. He was bound by the hands and led along until the gooks came to a cave. It was almost dark when they arrived at the cave. He was led into the cave where they tied his feet as well. The gooks made some rice but didn't offer him any. After catching some sleep, the gooks left the cave. There were three walking-wounded gooks. They were left behind to guard the prisoner. The captured soldier fell asleep.

When he awoke, the gooks were playing some type of card game. He worked his hands until the binding was fairly loose. After a while, the gooks began arguing among themselves. Two of the gooks went to the front of the cave. The other gook looked at the prisoner and then sat back, eventually falling asleep. The GI pulled his hands free, loosened the bindings on his legs, found a rock and crushed it over the sleeping gook's head, killing him. He took the gook's rifle, made sure it was loaded and figured out how to operate it, then sneaked his way to the front of the cave. He found the other two gooks sleeping just outside the cave entrance; he killed both of them. He had seen an old leather folder with paperwork in it inside the cave. He went back and retrieved the folder. He broke the stock off one of the rifles, and took the other two with him, along with plenty of ammunition.

He walked in the general direction of east to southeast, where he thought LZ English was located. He walked continuously the first day and found a concealed place to sleep during the night. The next morning he began walking again. He walked all day, and late in the day he saw a helicopter land and take off again at a location about 2 klicks from where he was located. He headed in that direction and came upon A Company from the 1st Bn 12th Cav. When he told them his story, it sounded almost too unbelievable to be true. With the paperwork he had and the guns he was carrying, it was hard to refute what he said. The Company Commander got in touch with Command at LZ English. They had the guy listed as

370

AWOL. He stayed with the 12th Cav that night and got on the morning chopper run the next day back to LZ English with his captured paperwork.

After translating the paperwork, it was learned that the gooks were planning to attack LZ English. Their plan called for gooks to move in small numbers and congregate in and near hamlets in the Bong Son Plains until they had a whole division amassed so they could strike the compound in force and by surprise. The attack was supposed to come within the next three weeks. With this knowledge, division pulled three battalions back to LZ English and began sweeping-and-clearing operations from LZ English and outward. All the hamlets and villages were cleared of people. As always, we only found women, children and old men in the hamlets, but these people were rounded up and flown by helicopter to education camps.

The 5th Bn 7th Cav was pulled back to LZ English. Ray Judy had married when he went home on leave before coming over to Vietnam. He had gotten word by the mail that his wife was pregnant. When he got back to camp, he had some mail. He opened a thick envelope from his wife and in it was a letter announcing the birth of a baby girl along with a photo of the baby. He was so high with joy it was like he was in another world.

Everybody had to look at the photo once, and some a second time. The entire day that was all he could think of or talk about. We were all happy for him. I wanted to tell him that he had to take good care of himself and be sure to make it home to be the father of the girl, but I didn't want to jinx him. Something told me he did not need to be told that anyway.

While the company was at LZ English, Kloemken and a guy by the name of Oblad came back from the hospital. They both had been injured in the battle on February 18. Oblad went to 3rd platoon. Kloemken joined the 2nd platoon. Oblad had been shot through the head but miraculously escaped serious injury. During the fight, a gook in a tree fired at him. The bullet went under his right ear and came out his mouth. He had two teeth knocked out and his upper gums were torn up. The bullet passed through the rest of the head without hitting anything other than internal flesh. He was one lucky soldier.

Many soldiers were in need of replacement jungle fatigues. They literally wore them so long until they began to shred off their bodies. The only fatigues available were the extremely large ones. Some of the soldiers were walking around with shreds of fatigues pulled together with Como wire, or strands tied together. When the legs of the pants got bad enough, guys would tear off the pants legs and wear them as shorts. Even the shorts were in bad shape. There was a lot of bitching, and someone finally raised holy hell with supply. Finally, some fatigues arrived that were reasonably close to the right size for most people. The smaller guys had to make do with larger-sized clothes anyway. The story came out of supply that it was hard to get replacement fatigues because of the buildup of manpower that was happening on a regular basis.

Every so often, along with the evening chow chopper, the field soldiers would get cold beer. It was stored in a plastic barrel with ice. When it came, each soldier was allowed two cans of beer. Word came down that a truckload shipment of beer that left Cam Ranh Bay was hijacked and stolen. For at least three months, there was no beer for the field soldiers.

MISSING FUNDS

After clearing the area around LZ English, B Company went back to the field. Sgt. Nuss told me to fly back to Camp Radcliff. I was on R & R. I caught the first helicopter heading back in that direction. As soon as I got back I went to the Orderly Room and talked with Salvi, the Clerk. He said that I had five days of R & R and I had to be back on the sixth day. He gave me the dates, but I don't remember them now. I located my khaki uniforms. They were clean but smelled of mildew. I got some clean water in a pan and soaked the uniforms. I hung them in the sun to dry. I took a receipt I had in my belongings for $300 I placed in the company supply safe just for R & R then I went to see the Supply Clerk, Mears. I showed him the receipt he gave me when I placed the money in the safe. He looked and said there was no money in the safe. I pointed to the receipt and told him if I put it there why isn't it there now. He said that quite a few soldiers had lost money for various reasons. I was starting to get pissed. I told him that someone stole at least $120 when I got shot and went to Japan, and now he's telling me someone stole my R & R money. I guess I started to yell at him. I asked him how the hell money could disappear from the safe. He said there were at least five or six different people who had keys. I asked him why so many. He gave me a spiel that he wasn't always around so someone else had to have access to the safe. Then he added that sometimes the safe is open when he goes to lunch, and anybody could come in and get in the safe. I asked him what the hell is the use of having a safe if you don't lock it. He didn't have any good answer. I asked him who all had keys. He said he had one, John Petters had one, Sgt. Nuss had one, some rear Lieutenant – the name I don't remember – had one, and he gave another name of someone who had one, but I don't remember that name either. As soon as he said John Petters had one, I lost interest in anyone else. Then I asked him why Petters had one. He said he had been helping out with supplies and sometimes he is the only one around, so he figured he should have one.

I left the supply building and looked for Petters. About an hour later he came walking into the battalion area. I called him over and led him around the backside of the B Company barracks. I grabbed him by the front of his shirt and asked him where my R & R money was. He said he didn't have any idea what I was talking about. I told him that, if I get my money now, that's all that will be said about it. I told him that, if I didn't get the money, I would beat him to within an inch of his life, and as soon as he healed I would do it again. He was scared shitless but swore he didn't take any money. I asked why he had a key to the safe. He said Mears gave him one. I believed Petters was being straight with me.

I went back to the supply building and asked Mears how he is going to come up with $300. I reminded him that I still had the receipt and it's good for $300, so he'd better start looking. He asked if there is no money, how can he come up with it? If I had to do it all over again, I would have pulled him outside and beat him until he was willing to come up with the money, but I didn't believe that he was the one who took the money. I asked him who I could contact to investigate this. He said the Division MPs have an investigation unit. I told him to dial the number and give me the phone. He was very helpful, maybe too helpful when I think back. I explained my problem to whoever answered the phone. The guy said they do not have the time to investigate thefts. He added that, if it's anything less than murder, they don't get involved. They are just too busy. I tried some more snooping around, but it was just a waste of time. I was out $300 and I wasn't going on R & R. They had just started to allow soldiers to go to Australia. I had planned to go there for R & R.

A little later I went to the mess hall to eat supper. I was sitting at a table by myself when Sgt. Milbur came in. He came over and said that he needed more bodies for night security on the green line. I told him I was on R & R, and not available. He let it go at that. After eating I went back to the barracks and tried to take a nap. I was mad and frustrated, and I couldn't sleep. I went over to the EM Club to drown my sorrows. A couple of other GIs came in. I knew the faces, but I don't remember the names.

After a few cans of beer, we decided to go down to the 8th Engineers' EM Club. Our EM Club was a little rattrap. The Engineers had a much nicer Club, so we headed out. I tipped too many cans that night. I think I remember going back to the barracks, but the only way I could be sure was when I woke up. The next morning, I was in our company barracks with the biggest hangover I had in Vietnam. I managed to catch the tail end of breakfast. I was not a heavy coffee drinker, but I drank my share that morning. I went back to the barracks and tried to get more sleep. The coffee rejected that plan. Since misery loves company, and it was getting extremely hot again, I took a walk down to the swimming hole by the bridge. There was a lifeguard on duty. They had rules, and I couldn't swim in the nude.

The lifeguard was pumping iron. He had a standard set of barbells with weights of all sizes. He was a humongous black guy. The weights were in a small shelter at the top of the bank. He could see the swimming hole while he pumped iron. His arms looked like 8-inch howitzers, his abs looked like an airfield landing strip, and his legs looked like culverts. He was one big boy. No, I mean man. I don't believe he would take kindly to being called a boy. We bullshitted for some time and when he was done with the iron, I tried it. I couldn't lift the barbell off the ground. He helped me change weights and I started pumping something more my size. He said I had a weightlifter's body and, if I worked at it, I could develop my muscles for bodybuilding competition. After pumping iron for a while I began sweating profusely. It was just what I needed for the hangover.

I started walking down to Division Headquarters. I didn't go far before a truck came by. I stuck my thumb out and the driver stopped. If you ever needed a ride somewhere, the next vehicle along was your ticket. If he didn't take you to your location, he got you as close as he could, and then the next vehicle was your ticket for the final leg. No one ever drove past someone walking. I thought I would look up Jerry Theisen at Finance. He wasn't around. I walked around the Division Headquarters compound and realized there were too many officers coming and going. On base camp, you were expected to salute them. I started to walk back toward our battalion area and caught a ride with a Lieutenant driving a jeep. He got me as far as the road leading past the 8th Engineers. It was only a few blocks away, so I could walk that far. The EM Club had just opened, so I stopped to quench my thirst. After a couple cans of beer, I walked back to our battalion area.

The first guy I saw was Sgt. Milbur. He asked why I wasn't on R & R. I told him someone stole the money I had set aside for the trip. He said the battalion would loan me the money I needed, and then I could sign a voucher so they could take it out of my wages to pay it back. I told him I decided to forget the trip to Australia and just hang out for a few days. He asked if I wanted to pull green-line security. I told him no, I was on R & R, and I was just going to relax. I told him I would probably head back to LZ English the following day which I did.

When I got back to LZ English, I talked with Sgt. Nuss about the stolen money. He told me there should be only three keys for the safe. He had one, Mears had one, and the supply officer had one. Then he said they are looking for help on an artillery LZ somewhere in the An Lão Valley. He said Oblad was going out with the afternoon chow run. I told him I would go along.

There were eight 8-inch Howitzers on this LZ. It was located on a rather sharp, open hill. There were dug-in positions around the perimeter. We did not have sandbag positions. If we wanted more cover, we had to get a shovel and work at it. We borrowed a shovel from the artillery and made our position deeper and more comfortable. Since we didn't have a permanent roof, we trenched the foxhole so water would run out and down the hill. The hill was steep enough so digging the trench was not too great an effort. At about 1600 hours on day two, the artillery got a fire mission. The guns were firing directly over us. There was one gun that was about 25 meters behind us. The barrel was pointed out over our perimeter position. When it fired, the percussion was at its maximum strength right in line with our position. A single shot made you go deaf. You could feel the percussion. It would literally move your body. When the gunner yelled, "Find a hole!" we would cup our ears, hold our mouth open, and yell as the round went off. This relieved the pressure on your head and body. The gun would fire about once every two minutes. The support fire lasted for more than an hour. When it was over, I had a pounding headache.

FROM PRIESTHOOD TO GENERAL'S AIDE

Three days on this LZ and we headed back to LZ English. When I got back I had mail from home. Mom said I should ask for leave to come home for Chuck's Ordination to the priesthood. Chuck was Charles Kunkel, my brother. I knew I would never get that request granted. I played with the idea of whether I should ask or not. As a rule, if you make waves for going on leave, you eventually get shit on for being a pest. I was sure I would never get the request granted, so I didn't even try for it. Besides, it would have been damn hard to make the trip back to 'Nam after going home on leave. I wrote a letter home telling Mom that I tried to get leave but was turned down.

My dad being the diplomat that he was, decided to contact Senator Eugene McCarthy (who grew up in the next town over from my hometown) to see if he could swing his weight to get me home for the Ordination. One day I got a call to go to the S-1 bunker. When I got there, a Major showed me a letter they received from Senator McCarthy. My immediate thoughts were, "Oh shit, here come the shit details."

I told the Major that my parents wanted me to make it home for my brother's Ordination. I also told him that I had told my parents that I couldn't make it, and I explained how I handled it. Then I explained to him what my father most likely did on my behalf without my knowledge. I told the Major that I had nothing to do with contacting the Senator and I sure hoped this didn't put me on the battalion shit list. As I explained it, he didn't think it would. Senator McCarthy was labeled a dove in political circles, and doves did not sit well with the military.

A couple of days later, Sgt. Nuss told me I had to go back to Division Headquarters at An Khê to meet with the Division Sgt. Major for an interview. He told me Capt. Hitti recommended me for the position as Aide to Major General Tolson, who was the Division Commander of the 1st Cav. At first, it was sort of a shock and then I got to thinking that this is something Capt. Hitti would have done. I wasn't sure I wanted the position. I was sure it would have meant an easy street for the balance of my tour in 'Nam, but hanging around and trying to stay out of the way of all the high-ranking officers, was not for my personality type.

It would have been military suicide to blatantly turn the position down, and I guess I wanted to see where it took me. So I caught a chopper from LZ English back to Camp Radcliff. As soon as I got to our battalion base, I went to supply and got outfitted with clean uniforms. I dodged Sgt. Milbur so he couldn't put me on green-line security. I reported to the Orderly Room and talked with Salvi, the company clerk. He had what information I needed. At 1300 hours the next day, Division would send a jeep for me. I would be going to talk with the Division Sgt. Major. The interview would last about an hour. Salvi was not too busy, so I sat around and BS'ed with him for the next half hour.

I stepped out of the Orderly Room and next to the dry food storage shed for the mess hall was a group of GIs standing around in a circle laughing. I walked over to see what was so funny. There was a cage that had two monkeys in it. One was a female the other was a male. The female was the horniest thing on two – or is it four? – feet. She was playing with the male monkey's penis until it became erect. Then she would jump on him, straddling his hips and work it into her snatch. She would rock on him until she got her rocks off. Then she would scream and jump up and flip around until she settled down. Then she would play with the male monkey's penis again and do it all over again. I watched her do at least three repetitions of this act and began to feel sorry for the male monkey. He looked as if he was done in. He put nothing into the act, but just sat there sort of in a daze.

I left this scene and disappeared from the main battalion area until suppertime. I went into the dining room, filled my plate, and went back to the 2nd platoon tent to eat. I didn't want to take a chance on Milbur seeing me. I'm sure he would remember me for not showing up for green-line duty at previous times. After eating, I took a short nap and then walked over to the EM Club. I nursed down four or five cans of beer and went back to the platoon tent, talked for about 30 minutes with a couple of other guys, and then went to bed. I slept for about two hours, woke up, fidgeted around for another two hours, then fell back to sleep. I was awake more than I was asleep that night. I was used to interrupted sleep, but I was also a little nervous about the interview.

The following morning, time seemed to stand still waiting for the ride to Division Headquarters. I had an early lunch but, because of a nervous stomach, did not eat much. At about 1230 hours I was at the Orderly Room waiting for the jeep. It didn't show until 1310 hours. On the ride to Division, I asked the driver if he knew Capt. Hitti. I was hoping to have a chance to talk with him while I was at Division. He did not know Hitti. The jeep pulled up in front of a metal building marked "1st Cav Division Headquarters." There were Division signs all over the place. Each building had a different title.

The driver told me to go inside and report to the Clerk. I did as instructed and was told to have a seat.

About 15 minutes later, the Clerk got my attention and told me that the Sgt. Major would see me now. He opened a door to a back office and I went in and reported in my finest military fashion. He told me to stand at ease and then he told me to take a seat, indicating a chair to the left front of his desk. He introduced himself and then he took out a form, I'm sure with questions. He told me that I came highly recommended for the position as an Aide to the Division General. He asked me a few opening questions to put me at ease, such as where I lived in the States, what I did before entry into the Army, where I went to school.

Then the Sgt. Major got into my short military history. I don't remember the questions, other than where I took basic and other training I had. I'm sure he had it all in front of him but he wanted to hear what I would say. Then he asked if I ever had any problems since coming into the service. I initially told him, no, and then corrected that by mentioning the altercation I had on New Year's Night with the fight at the PX Club. I don't know if there was any information available about that night, but I didn't want it to look like I was covering up anything. About a half hour into the interview, he told me that I was selected to be General Tolson's Aide on the condition that I extend in Vietnam for the balance of my military time in the service. I told him I was willing to extend for 30 days since this would get me immediate discharge upon my completion of service in Vietnam. He said that was not good enough, I would have to extend for the balance of service time, which would take me through the month of November. I told him I couldn't or wouldn't do it. He was very cordial and understanding with my decision. This concluded the interview.

I stepped outside and the driver gave me a ride back to our Battalion Headquarters. Frequently over the years, I questioned myself on whether I did the right thing. I believe I did, but I can't be sure. Later that day I was talking with Salvi and mentioned Capt. Hitti. He told me he was no longer a Captain. He was promoted to Major. I never saw Hitti again. I still wish I would have looked him up to at least thank him for what he had done for me and trusting in me so much.

I dodged Sgt. Milbur that night. I stopped at the EM Club and had a few brews, then went back to the barracks and slept fairly well. I was the only person in the barracks. Everyone else must have had to pull green-line security. The next morning after breakfast, I caught a ride to the helipad and got on the first chopper going out to LZ English. As soon as I reported in, Sgt. Nuss said Oblad and I would be flying out to another artillery LZ in the morning. He said we would probably be there for some time, so take whatever gear we would need for the longer stay.

The M-102, 105 mm Howitzer fires at suspected Viet Cong position after receiving fire mission from the airborne command post, July 6, 1966. The An/Arc-122 radio console set is used in UH-1D helicopters by the 1st Cavalry Division (Airmobile) at division, brigade and battalion levels to coordinate any form of mission with his entire ground force. U.S. Army photo, originally from the Records of the Office of the Chief Signal Officer. Photo courtesy of the National Archive at College Park, Md. Robert C. Lafoon, photographer.

LZ SECURITY IN THE MOUNTAINS

This LZ was a long narrow ridge that dropped off on both sides at a very sharp decline. Again, there were eight 8-inch Howitzers. The ridge was probably 2,000 feet high from the valley floors on either side. The LZ started at the helipad at the lowest end of the ridge. It gradually rose from the helipad at least another 120 feet to the highest point. Again, the guns were placed four on each side of the ridge. At the highest point, there was a large bunker for security. The ridge dropped off for about 60 feet and then came up again to a slightly higher rock point on which we constructed another bunker. This bunker sat out away from the rest of the LZ at least 200 meters. From this point, we could look down into the perimeter of the LZ. The artillery soldiers wanted this point manned at all times so no enemy could get on the hill and shoot down on them. This made good sense. During daytime hours one or two GIs were in the bunker. At night, we always had four people in the bunker. Oblad and I took our turns during the day hours, and at night this is where we usually sat. With four people, we could divide the night into four increments of time so you only had to pull one guard. Each day we made improvements on the bunker until we were satisfied that we had it as comfortable as we possibly could make it with the resources we had.

We had a set of binoculars to use in the outpost. While we were sitting in the bunker, we were supposed to scan the ridges and hillsides across the valley for movement or anything that would give away the enemy positions. In the west, we could see the An Lão Valley. It was fairly wide at that location and there were many rice paddy fields. If it hadn't been for the war, this was a breathtaking natural wonder.

Every night, gooks tried to mortar the LZ. Because the hill was so sharp and the width so narrow, the rounds either fell short or, when the aim was adjusted, the round went way over the top and down into the far valley. It appeared that all the mortars were coming from the south.

Two days after we arrived, a Chinook helicopter brought in a Quad 50 machine gun unit along with a gunner to operate it. It was mounted on the edge of the perimeter facing south. A bunker was built to one side of the Quad 50, about six feet above the ground level. Someone was to man this bunker with a set of binoculars and look for movement of gooks in the distant ridges. Around the fourth night, the gooks were intent on causing us some damage. They lobbed at least 30 mortars at us. They were trying to hit our outpost with many of them. They tried walking them up the hill toward our position. We did not have a sand-bagged roof on this position. All we had were ponchos stretched out to keep the rain off. One round came in with the descending whistle that indicated it was going to be close. When the whistling noise stops, you pull your head down and pray it's not a direct hit. The round landed about 20 meters below our position. When it exploded, you could hear the shrapnel whistling over our heads and hitting the ground just outside the bunker. The next round went over the top of us and landed about 30 meters on the far side of the bunker. They were getting pretty close. It would only be a matter of time before our luck ran out.

The next day we stepped up our vigilance. Based on how they walked the mortars up the hill, we assumed the rounds were being fired from a location to the south/southwest. There was a large ridge with nearly straight-walled cliffs. About mid-day, Oblad was scanning that ridge with the binoculars. I had just begun walking down to the LZ to get some C-Rations for lunch. I was about halfway between the outpost and the LZ when he called me back. When I got back to the outpost, he gave me the binoculars and pointed to a distinguishable mark on the side of the mountain. He said, "Train the binoculars on that position and tell me what you see." I looked where he directed and could make out what appeared to be a hole in the side of the cliff. While I was watching it, I saw a gook step out of the hole. I gave the binoculars back to Oblad and he looked again. The gook stood there for a short time and then went back in the hole. I went back to the LZ and talked to a Lieutenant and told him what we saw. The Lieutenant went with me back to the outpost and watched the spot we indicated. After about 15 minutes he saw a gook. The Lieutenant went back to the LZ.

About an hour later, a bubble-top helicopter flew over the top of the far ridge and swooped down into the valley. He circled back and flew along the ridge. Another hour went by and F-100 jets came in. They were carrying what we believed were 250-pound bombs. The jets would fly right at the side of the ridge. Just about the time you thought they would crash into the ridge the jet's nose came up sharply and a bomb would spit out of the undercarriage into the side of the mountain. There were six jets with the first sortie, and shortly after them came a second sortie of six jets. Each jet made four runs at the ridge and then they headed back to their airfield, probably Da Nang. They would load up again and come back for another run of four bombs. This went on for at least two full hours. There had to be at least 100 bombs dropped, if not more. If the bombs didn't kill the gooks, they were probably all stir-crazy afterward. We didn't get any mortars thrown at our outpost that night although the gooks still tried to drop mortars on the main LZ.

A couple of days later, someone was sitting on the bunker beside the Quad 50, scanning the forested valley and ridges due south of the LZ. He noticed some movement at least two klicks out. He called one of the Sergeants over and had him take a look. The Sergeant passed the binoculars to the Lieutenant, and then someone else. I even got a chance to check it out. In amongst the brush there was an opening. There were at least three gooks moving around that I could see. The gunner for the Quad 50 got into the seat of the Quad. He adjusted the barrel height to where he wanted it and lined the sights left to right or vice-versa. The Lieutenant asked him if he thought he could hit the spot at this distance. He said he would know in a few seconds. He engaged the trigger and the Quad kicked in spitting out rounds from each gun. Every fourth round of every barrel was a tracer round. You could follow the tracers to their mark. The Lieutenant was watching through the binoculars. The rounds were right on target. He did not have to adjust. He drilled at least 400 rounds into the area.

The Lieutenant called base camp with what we had. In about a half hour, a bubble-top spotter helicopter flew over the area a few times. Another half hour after that, here came the F-100 jets again. This time there was only one run of six jets. They dumped Napalm bombs, scattering them in the area of where we saw the gooks. I think that eliminated our harassment problems. Oblad and I stayed on the LZ for three more days. We did not get mortared during that time.

The night after the Napalm bombing, there was a skirmish down in the valley to our west. It started around midnight. You could see red tracers firing south to north and green tracers firing north to south. The American soldiers used red tracers and the gooks used green tracers. The firing went on for at least 20 minutes. Then someone got wise and called in artillery. From the area where the green tracers were coming, there were a number of explosions from the artillery rounds. In all, 30 to 40 rounds came in. The firefight ended after that. The artillery unit we were with was too close to the fighting and could not be used. The rounds had to come from another site at least four or more miles distance from where they were dropped.

Three days later, Oblad and I were summoned back to LZ English. As soon as we arrived, Sgt. Nuss told us that we would be going out with the evening chow run to another

Napalm bombs explode on Viet Cong structures south of Saigon in the Republic of Vietnam, 1965. Photo courtesy of National Archives at College Park, Md. U.S. Air Force photo ID 542328.

artillery LZ where B Company was located. This artillery LZ was located in a low, rolling hill location and was spread out considerably more than the last two where we had been. The perimeter was lined with huge sand-bagged bunkers with roofs on them. We were told that, after dark, we should be in the bunker because mortar rounds came in unannounced at any time after dark.

Sgt. Carter was the Platoon Sergeant for the first platoon. I never saw a platoon leader, so I assumed 2nd platoon didn't have one. Lt. Bronson was still the acting Company Commander. Ray Judy was now a Sergeant and squad leader for the 3rd squad. Ray Kloemken was still with the 3rd squad. Oblad went with the 1st platoon. There was something about this place that made everyone feel uneasy. The LZ was spread out too much, the perimeter was too close to the jungle line surrounding it, and there were a lot of depressions in the earth inside the perimeter, depressions made by mortars. This meant that the gooks had found their mark and were exploiting it.

Sgt. Carter had to put together a squad to go out that night. One of the other platoons had to send out a squad also. Carter told a guy named Felling that he had to take the patrol out. Felling refused to do it. He said he thought it was suicide to go out. He also said that he had never taken a squad out on his own before, and he was too short to start now. In the end, Felling did not take a patrol out. Ray Judy ended up taking a squad out. I told him to be damned careful.

Kloemken and I, and a fairly new guy named Jungers, took a bunker that had an M60 machine gun mounted in it. There was only about a 50-meter clearing between our bunker and the jungle. I took first watch. I was just coming to the end of my watch; it must have been close to 2200 hours (10 p.m.) when the mortars arrived. They were dropping all over the place. Many landed directly out in front of our position. Kloemken and Jungers woke up and took their rifles and got in position. We always expected an attack after the mortars.

One mortar seemed to have our name on it. I can't put my finger on why I could tell, but as it came in we could hear the whistling of the round and then the whistling stopped. This happened with all mortars that landed in the proximity of our location. Simultaneously, all three of us ducked down below the bunker wall. The round landed just to the outside edge and within two feet of the bunker wall. It shook the bunker, and the ground seemed to move. A few mortars landed inside the compound. At least 40 mortar rounds came in. When the mortaring ceased, flares were shot into the air to light up the area. The gooks did not come. After an hour of waiting, Kloemken and I tried to get some sleep. It took me an hour to finally doze off. I was sleeping for a short while and I must have had a dream because I woke up with a jerk. I was not going to get back to sleep. I told Jungers that I would finish his watch and allowed him more sleep time. I sat there for at least two hours and my eyes started to droop. I woke Kloemken and, when he was fully awake, I lay down to sleep. I dozed off for at least an hour and woke up again with a dream. I couldn't get back to sleep. I finally got up and told Kloemken to get what sleep he could and I pulled watch for the rest of the night.

After daylight, Ray Judy brought his squad back in. He said that they had a pretty easy night of it, but it sounded like us folks caught the shit. I checked the outside of our bunker and the sandbags were torn to shreds with gravel strewn around. After breakfast, I would have to find some sandbags and cover the torn ones with new bags of gravel to keep the bunker from deteriorating.

Patrols were sent out during the day to see if they could locate where the mortaring was coming from. They did not have any success. Everyone seemed a little tense waiting for the nighttime again. Mortars were good harassing tools, and the gooks were good at harassing us. That evening, we had just finished supper and were preparing for the long night. It wasn't completely dark yet and the mortars came again. It seems the gooks were varying their times to try and catch us off guard. The patrols had just left the compound and GIs were still milling around. As soon as the mortars started to arrive, everyone found a bunker. The rounds were again landing inside and just outside the compound. None came as close as the one did the night before, but you could hear the metal shards of shrapnel whistling through the air. When the incoming mortars ceased, flares were sent up to light up the area. Charlie still did not show.

The second night I was more accustomed to this shit and it didn't bother me as much. I was turning into a short-timer but I didn't want to think too hard about it. We were coming up to the end of May, and on the first of June I would only have two months left in Vietnam. A lot of people were keeping short-timers' calendars. To me this was too much anticipation, and when you started counting it made the time seem to pass by at a slower pace. At least I got more sleep this night.

For the past two days, the sky was overcast and we had rain off and on throughout the day and night. Today the sun came up with the new day. Spirits seemed to rise and everyone seemed in a more cheerful mood. Of course, with the sun and sitting in an opening between walls of jungle forest, the heat was more intense. There was no swimming hole to retreat to for cooling down. We just took off our shirts and made the best of it.

When I left Japan, I had a pencil-lead-thin scar across my back. With working the muscles, the stretching and the general hard living standard, the scar was now about a quarter-inch wide. I didn't notice it, but it would not stand any pressure strapped across it. Other people noticed the scar and commented on it. FNGs who came to the platoon in the past two or three months asked about it. At first, I didn't mind talking about it but, as the new GIs asked about it, I decided to put my shirt back on.

B Company pulled perimeter security for this artillery LZ one more night and then was scheduled to leave the next day. We got mortared again that night. This time the mortars came in around midnight. No one seemed to get excited about the mortars. All we had to do was stay in the bunkers, and duck as soon as the whistling stopped on an incoming round. You didn't want to take a chance on catching a stray piece of shrapnel.

The next morning Oblad and I got on the mess chopper and headed back to LZ English. We checked in with Sgt. Nuss and asked him where we were going next. He told us to relax and keep ourselves out of trouble for the present time. There wasn't much to do the rest of the day. Oblad played cribbage, so he and I played a few games without the aid of a cribbage board. We kept score on a sheet of paper by marking off points.

After supper that evening, Oblad went with the crew to pull security on the south gate. I went with Miller and Beaupre to the forward post on the north end. They still had the night scope. After we got settled in, Miller lit up a marijuana joint. He offered me a drag. I told him I wasn't interested. I told him I tried it once before and didn't care for it. He said, "You just didn't do it the right way." After riding me some more I said I would give it one more try. I did it just the way he told me. Pulled the smoke into my lungs, held it for as long as I could, and then slowly exhaled it. Then he told me to relax and let it work on me. After a minute or so, I asked him what I was supposed to do. He said by now it should be giving me a high. I told him I didn't feel anything other than a sour mouth. He told me to take another hit on it. I told him, "No, thanks. I'll stick with beer."

A couple of days went by with very little to do during the daytime. We pulled perimeter duty at night. I was getting bored. On the third morning after coming back to LZ English, Sgt. Nuss told Oblad and me to pack up all our belongings and head back to Camp Radcliff. We were being transferred. He didn't know where, but we were to check in with Salvi and he would have the information and assignment orders. Once back there, we were to get a new set of fatigues. Since we had been wearing the same fatigues for the past month or longer, we looked like part of the Vietnam dirt. We talked with Salvi and he said we were headed for Cam Ranh Bay, along the coast in the south-central part of the country. Everything I heard about Cam Ranh Bay was good. GIs went there for in-country R & R. It was supposed to be a choice assignment for Vietnam.

We weren't the only GIs making this transfer. There were 16 GIs from the 5th of the 7th Cav with transfers to Cam Ranh Bay. When we left the Orderly Room, Sgt. Milbur was on the prowl looking for us. He was expecting us to come in from the field. He said that we had green-line duty that night. I asked him if he really was going to stick it to us on our last night with the battalion, and I laughed as I said it. He said, "You shouldn't complain. Every time I assigned you for green-line, you managed to get out of it. Even though it's your last night with the battalion you will have to pull the duty." He laughed back as he assigned us. I thought, what the hell, this will be my last night; I guess I'll pull security and let him have his way.

After supper, we put on our gear and waited outside the mess hall for a ride to our duty location. Oblad and I left our grungy clothes on for two reasons: one, I didn't want to get the new fatigues dirty prematurely, and two, with the reddish-brown dirt-infused clothes, the man in charge should recognize that we just came in from the field and he'd probably go easy on us.

We were dropped off at a location about one mile from our battalion area. I figured we were on the west side of the Division compound. The 2nd of the 12th Battalion had a month on green-line duty and we were assisting them. A big Sergeant met us. He asked who was in charge. The senior ranking man was John Petters. He had almost six years in active duty but was still a Spec-4. No one said anything. He said, "Don't you idiots have any rank in your outfit. No wonder the 5th of the 7th Cav is so screwed up." Oblad told him to f--- off. He said, "This morning I was in the field. This is my last day with the Division, and I certainly don't need any shit from you." Somehow I wished that I had said it. He had a few of his troops with him and told them to split us up and place us in different locations with their troops. He told Oblad to get in the jeep and come with him. Once at my assigned post I volunteered to take first watch. If I pulled a three-hour watch, the other three would each have to pull a two-hour watch and we had the night covered. This set well with the other three guys.

I was just about to the end of my watch when the Sergeant drove up in the jeep. He asked if Kunkel was at this bunker. I told him that I was Kunkel. He asked when I was ready to be relieved. I told him in about 15 minutes. He said he was going to check on the other bunkers and that he would pick me up on the way back. I had no idea what this was about but, in the Army, this is not abnormal. I woke my relief and made sure he was awake. About five minutes later, the Sarge drove up. He told me to grab my gear and jump in the jeep. On the way back, he told me that I should have told him I had just come out of the field. I said, "You didn't ask, and I thought the dirty uniform would give me away." He said, "I guess I missed that one." Apparently, Oblad told him about me. He said in their outfit, people coming out of the field are not expected to pull green-line duty the same as the pogues. He said, "Your battalion is screwed up for sending you guys out." I told him that the guys in the field are okay, but we have assholes back at base camp. He said, "I guess we all have that problem." He told me it looked like it might rain so I would be sleeping under cover tonight. He said troops coming out of the field get treated differently than the butt-heads he finds in the rear. This was probably an apology for his earlier behavior, but I believe he was a good leader in the field.

The next morning we were trucked back to our battalion. Breakfast was just being served. Oblad and I had breakfast and then grabbed our new fatigues and headed for the shower. As a rule, the shower water was the same temp as the air temp. But at Battalion, they had a water heater and we had ourselves a warm shower. This was my first really warm shower since coming back from Japan.

We got our belongings together and waited outside for the truck that would take us to the airfield. I was feeling pretty much elated as I am sure was everyone else going to Cam Ranh Bay. No one had any idea what our assignment would be, but it sure would be better than what we had been doing. It was also one more step closer to home. Flights taking people back to the world left from Da Nang, Ton Son Nhut at Saigon, or Cam Ranh Bay.

It finally dawned on me that I was going to make it home. Prior to this, I was never sure. A mortar fired a slight fraction of degree differently could have landed in my lap. A gook with a lucky shot could have stopped my breathing. I had too many close calls over the past 10 months. Death and dying

A Sky Trooper from the 1st Cavalry Division (Airmobile) keeps track of the time
he has left on his "short time" helmet while participating in Operation "Pershing"
near Bong Son, 1968. Photo courtesy of the National Archives at College Park, Md.
Original photo from the Records of the Office of the Chief Signal Officer.
Photo ID 531453.

was a reality you couldn't ignore. Now it seemed to be over. It was a damned good feeling.

CAM RANH BAY

The C-130 landed at the Cam Ranh Bay airfield at around noon and the passengers were directed to buses near the airfield. There was another group of soldiers who had just arrived in Vietnam. The new arrivals filled three other buses and a few of them had to ride on the bus we were on. There was one E-7, Sgt. Harrin, who was in charge of our group. He was with the 3rd platoon in our B Company. Sometime during the previous three months, he was the Sergeant in charge when his platoon jumped out of choppers at a drop zone. The choppers dropped them in a fresh punji stick field. Immediately three or four GIs were injured. He was one of them. He told his platoon that if anyone else wants out of the field for a while, they can take a walk through the punji sticks. Rumor had it that a few soldiers took him up on the invitation and received injuries. In total there were about eight people who were injured by the punji sticks. The story got back to Battalion and there was an inquiry into the matter. As far as I know, nothing came of the incident.

The buses transported us to a placement company. After arriving, we stood around for at least an hour while Sgt. Harrin found out where we were to go. The new arrivals stuck with us. They were all infantry and would fill in as replacements someplace. While we were waiting, a Staff Sergeant came by and asked if any of us could weld. I told him that I grew up on a farm and held a welding torch occasionally.

One of the new arrivals said he took welding courses in trade school. The Sergeant asked the new guy his MOS (military occupational specialty code). He said he was an 11-B-1, which is infantry. The Sarge asked him if he would like to get it changed to transportation mechanic. He sure as hell wanted that. The Sarge told both of us to follow him. There was a mechanic shop next to the placement quarters. He wanted each of us to take a try at welding two pieces of metal together with a brazing rod. I bowed out of the competition. I told him I only stick-welded and I was not all that good at it. I added, if this guy has a whole year to do, let him have the job. It beats humping the field. The Sarge had the guy weld the two pieces of metal together. It was obvious that he knew what he was doing. He left a nice, even weld that held the metal as intended. Sarge told the guy to get his duffel bag, he had got a job with the mechanics. He also said that he would take care of getting his MOS changed.

Our group with the 5th Bn 7th Cav were told to get on the bus again with our duffel bags. We were transported to a compound in the middle of a flat sand dune away from the main area of the Cam Ranh Bay military compound. This was a signal company. We were attached there for living purposes only. There were two tents that housed only attached personnel. The Sergeants, E-5 and above, had their own living arrangement, separate from the enlisted men. It looks as if we were back to the military rank separation again. This was okay for the enlisted men.

We were assigned to a tent, and each of us picked an open cot. Kampa, Oblad and I slept on three separate cots on one end of the tent. A few other GIs took up the remaining empty cots, and the rest of the group went to an adjacent tent. There were other GIs in our tent that came from somewhere else in-country. Settling in was nothing more than picking a

400

cot, and a place to put your duffel bag. Each cot had one pillow, one pillowcase, one sheet, and one Army blanket. I put the pillowcase on my pillow and flopped the pillow on top of the folded sheet and blanket. I hadn't used either since coming from the hospital, and I didn't think I needed them now. I lay down to relax and fell asleep.

At around 1630 hours, Sgt. Harrin came to our tent barracks and called us and the group in the next tent outside. He said we were assigned to pull security detail for the main PX warehouse. This depot is where all PX merchandise is brought in, unpacked, stored, and made ready for shipment to other parts of the country. There was a lot of theft of PX items, and our job was to pull security to try and minimize the losses. We were given the information needed for transportation to and from the PX depot, where and when we ate, the general lay of the area, and expectations of behavior. We were also told that at 0700 hours the following morning we would all load onto a truck for transportation to the PX depot for an orientation and training in our duties. As soon as this meeting was over, we could go for supper.

None of us had eaten since breakfast that morning. Needless to say, no one hung back or scrimped on allowed portions. As a rule, we were allowed only the meat and the dessert portion served to us, but most other food items we could have extras. I took extra bread and vegetables.

Whether they cooked for the soldiers in the field, or they cooked for this signal company in Cam Ranh Bay, I have to hand it to the cooks we had in Vietnam. They took simple and standard food items and made them very tasty. There always seemed to be plenty of beef roast and round steak, but there were various ways to prepare the beef so it was not a mundane meal over and over. Chicken, ham, and hamburger were other meals we had fairly often. These, too, were prepared with various spices and trimmings to add variety to different meals. Hamburger would be served as regular hamburger patties, in sloppy Joes, and in meatloaf for variety. About once a week we would get pork, and once every two weeks we would get fish. There seemed to be only one kind of fish we would get, and usually it was baked. All in all, with the products the cooks had to work with, we were served what I would classify as excellent meals. I am sure not everyone would share this review. One only had to see what food there was to work with to understand how much effort the cooks put into creating a good variety of meals.

Because of the dry sandy soil and dust, the military powers would not let vehicles drive into the compound. There was a trail that ran around the compound, with sandlot parking areas scattered periodically so vehicles could get as close as possible to their destination without actually driving into the compound. The main road ran just south of this compound. There were no perimeter barriers for this area. The whole area was surrounded by sand dunes. Other than MPs patrolling the outer perimeter in jeeps, and the occasional patrols through the inner compound, there seemed to be no other security. I believe there was just too much open terrain to worry about any gooks attacking Cam Ranh Bay.

The next morning, we had an early breakfast and loaded onto the designated trucks for transport to the PX depot. The main road circled west away from the main military base, out through the sand dunes, and then north before heading back east toward the main base. At what appeared to be the edge of the military base, there was another cluster of tents similar to the signal company that we now called home. I believe this was the MP company's compound as well as the compound that was home to the permanent military assigned to the PX depot. Fourteen miles from where the road left the signal company compound, it intersected with another road that came north from the signal company area. It actually wasn't a road, although many jeeps traveled this trail to create what became a road. It was not graded smooth, so the big trucks would not drive on it. From the main road, it was two miles to the signal company compound on this trail. About five miles east of the intersection of the trail leading to the signal company, the road came to a "Y." The road to the right went into the main compound, and the road to the left went past the PX depot and down to the Bay of Cam Ranh. This is where the shipments for the PX came ashore.

The truck dropped us at the entrance of the PX compound. The entrance had a four-foot gate designated for pedestrian traffic. To the right side of this gate was an eight-foot by twelve-foot building used for the security guards covering the gates. To the right of that building was a large gate, approximately 12 feet wide for vehicle traffic. The building had doors on each side so the gate guards could have easy access for traffic coming and going, depending on which gate was being used. We walked in and Sgt. Harrin informed the Spec-4 manning the gate who we were and why we were there. He was expecting us and was glad to see us. There was a phone in the building and he made a call to the front office. We were directed to the front office and told to wait out front.

A few minutes later, a tall lanky Captain and a short husky First Sergeant came out. Sgt. Harrin called us to attention, saluted the Captain, and reported as ordered. The Captain told us to stand at ease. This was military procedure, as we knew it back in the world. It seemed strange here in Vietnam.

The Captain told us his role in the operation and gave a short explanation of the PX depot operation. He then directed the First Sergeant to fill in the details. We were again called to attention, the First Sergeant saluted the Captain, and the Captain went back inside. This was looking like the horse-shit side of the Army. The First Sergeant gave us a tour of the compound and gave a detailed explanation of the operation. He told us that they were experiencing at least a 50-percent loss of some merchandise once it came into the compound. He said that some losses happened in shipment before the goods got to Vietnam, but that there were substantial losses after the goods arrived. He added that most of the losses are the expensive items like cameras, stereo equipment, televisions, beer, and liquor. He also said that the merchandise is shipped in locked, metal Conax storage sheds. Sometimes they get a Conax off the ship that has had the lock broken, and the entire intended content is missing. He told us that our job was to stop merchandise from leaving the compound without proper authorization.

The PX depot compound was about 250 meters wide from north to south, and 300 meters deep from west to east. The road ran past the west side of the compound. The offices for the compound were in the northwest corner. Metal, pole barn-type buildings surrounded the compound on the north, east and south sides. Down the middle of the compound, running east to west, was a line of pole buildings that split two-thirds of the compound into two sections. The west side with the gate had, a 10-foot-high chain-link fence with two strands of barbed wire across the top. From all appearances, it looked fairly secure.

After the tour, the First Sergeant called a Sergeant E-5 to fill us in on the security procedures they had in place, and the new security procedures they were implementing for our benefit. We were to watch the gate to make sure that everyone coming into the compound had a government ID card and, when anyone left the compound, that they did not have any merchandise on their persons. This seemed simple enough. Some of our group would cover the gate and others would mill around the inside of the compound looking for anything unusual or suspicious. The first and second day we all worked during daytime hours to familiarize ourselves with the organization and the operation. The PX compound always had one of the assigned depot soldiers at the gate to check the paperwork and sign off whenever a shipment went out. They were also responsible for counting the number of the Conax shipments coming into the compound to see that they coincided with the numbers coming off ship.

I asked the Sergeant if anyone had recently checked the perimeter outside the compound to see if there were any tin panels that were loose or removable. He didn't think that anyone had ever checked outside of the buildings for openings. He thought it would be a good idea. He finished his procedural information seminar, and Sgt. Harrin divided us into four groups. One four-body group would cover the gates, one four-body group would patrol inside the compound, and two groups would be on break. Oblad and I volunteered to walk around the buildings outside the compound.

We started on the south side of the compound and walked east along the back of the buildings. The metal sheeting for the backs of the buildings was nailed in place. About two-thirds the way down the line, we found a panel that had missing and loose nails. I pulled the loose nails out and pulled the metal back. Oblad tried to squirm behind the metal and into the building. He was too big. He held the metal back for me and I tried to squeeze in. I could not quite make it. Someone just a little smaller than I would be able to squeeze through the opening. It was also big enough to slide merchandise out. Inside there were large boxes piled close to the outside wall. Since it would be difficult to tell where this loose panel was located from inside the compound, I paced the distance back to the fence at the west end. I turned around and paced it again the other way to make sure of my count.

Oblad and I then proceeded around the east side of the compound. We found a second spot with loose and missing nails on the east side of the compound. The metal would pull open about the same distance as the previous spot we found. Looking in we could see large boxes close to the wall. Again I paced the distance back to the southeast corner of the compound and back again. We continued around the compound and did not find any other loose panels. We went back to the gate and talked with the Sergeant in charge. We told him of our findings and he went with us to check them out from the inside. I paced the distance off from the fence and located the building we were looking for.

The buildings were a continuous line with partitions separating one from the next. The building we were looking for was the one where they kept the stereo equipment such as tape decks and power amplifier units, speakers, and turntables. There were crates and boxes stacked in front of the panel that was loose. Without moving some of the items, it was impossible to tell there was a problem from inside. After locating this hole, we moved to the other location. Again, I found out the width of the building, running west to east and calculated the feet and then paced off the distance to the next spot where we found the hole. This turned out to be the storage area for the cameras. Again we had to move some crates and boxes to expose the opening. The Sergeant organized a two-man detail from permanent staff to secure the holes again. Patrolling the outside of the perimeter was to become a timely detail in the future.

THE NIGHT CREW

The first two days all 16 of our group worked the daytime hours. This was still part of the orientation and training period. At the end of the second day, we were divided into two groups: eight would work the day shift and eight would work the night shift. The day shift came in at 0600 hours and worked until 1800 hours. The night shift would come in at 1800 hours and work until 0600 hours. There were two Sergeants in our group. Because of their rank, they both volunteered to work the day shift. Oblad, Kampa, and I preferred to work the night shift to avoid as much as possible the military procedural bullshit. The rest made their choices of when they would work, with the longest time-in-grade having first choice, and the shortest time-in-grade having last choice. Fourteen in our group were Spec-4s. The night shift group was issued M1 carbine rifles to carry, but we were not given any ammunition for the guns. I believe the brass thought with us just coming from the field, we might be a little too trigger-happy.

The only person in the night group with whom I had a hard time with was a guy named Crandall. He was with B Company but was one of those who dehydrated themselves to get sick and have to leave the field. Once he got out of the field, he managed to work his sickness to a permanent position. As time went on we also found out that Crandall was our company queer. He was arrogant and proud that he managed to keep himself unfit for field duty. It's one thing to be that way, and it's quite another to brag about it.

Sgt. Harrin was an E-7, so he was in charge of the day crew. As a Spec-4, I had the longest time-in-grade on the night crew, so I was put in charge. We divided the night crew into two four-man groups. Oblad was in charge of one group, and I was in charge of the other. We rigged up an area under some canvas coverings for one group to sleep while the other group pulled duty. Two people would work the gate and the other two would roam the compound. If you pulled gate duty the first watch, you roamed the third watch. This way no one could complain that they were getting stuck in one place too much. Roaming seemed to be the better duty. At least that is the way I felt about it. We began by pulling two-hour shifts, and after one night switched to three-hour shifts. This way you only had to pull two watches a night.

There was a Lieutenant who was permanent-party for the PX depot; he worked the night shift until approximately midnight. I believe he was supposed to work later, but you could never find him after midnight. Two other permanent-party Spec-4s worked the night shift. One was a good-sized boy named Mullins from Detroit. The other was your athletic-type named Ritter, from Portland, Oregon. These guys had an old ambulance they used to get from their compound to work and back. Shortly before 2300 hours, one would take our group on break to their Mess Hall for lunch. Right after midnight, the other would take the group that just got off duty to the Mess Hall. We usually ate very well.

During the daytime, there were about 150 Filipinos who worked in the compound. At night, there were approximately 50 Filipinos who worked in the compound. There were three large forklifts that were used to haul the metal Conax containers from the loading docks in the bay to the depot, and then take empty Conax containers back to the docks to be loaded back onto the ships. The docks were about one kilometer from the depot. Designated Filipinos drove the forklifts. Every morning at 0700 hours two large flatbed tractor-trailer trucks with four-foot sideboards would bring the Filipinos to the depot. They would get off the truck and come in through the four-foot gate. They carried their lunch and water with them. There was a faucet with fresh water located a short distance from the depot office building that the workers could use to re-supply their water. When they came in through the gate, they held a worker ID card in their hand. Security had to watch to make sure that everyone entering the compound had an ID card. There were no photographs on the IDs, so anyone who fit the look of a Filipino could pass as the worker.

At around 0730 hours, two deuce-and-a-half military trucks brought about 80 Vietnamese workers to the compound. They too had to have an ID card, with no photo, to gain entry into the compound. At 1700 hours, the Vietnamese workers would leave the compound and take the deuce-and-a-half trucks back to the village. At 1800 hours, the Filipinos would leave the compound and load onto the tractor-trailer trucks to be transported back to their compound. Their living compound was separate but fairly close to the village.

When the Vietnamese and the Filipinos left the depot, it was our job to make sure that they were not taking any merchandise out with them. When the trucks picked up the Filipino day crew, they dropped the Filipino night crew off. The night crew had to wait until the day crew left the compound before they could enter. There was considerable commotion and disarray between 1700 and 1800 hours each day. There were no weekends off. Everyone, including the GIs, worked seven days a week.

The Filipinos had a foreman for the day crew and another one for the night crew. A Sergeant would tell the foreman what duties he wanted to be performed and the foreman took over from there. Other than our patrolling and an occasional walk-through by the Sergeant in charge, the workers were unsupervised. The day crew foreman seemed to get more respect from his co-workers than anyone else. On one occasion, I noticed he forcefully clapped his hands and every worker in view stopped and directed their attention to him as he spoke. I didn't think too much of this at the time, but he did have control of the workers.

When we were still in orientation and all working the day shift, as the Vietnamese were leaving the compound, Oblad noticed one of the Vietnamese women walking with her legs tight together and taking small steps. He stopped her and told her to spread her legs apart. She acted as if she didn't under-stand. After repeating the order about three times, he walked around behind her and, with his foot, he pushed one of her legs away from the other. A can of pop fell to the ground. He asked the depot Sergeant what he wanted to be done with her. He said to take the pop and send her on her way. When the line was finished, there were two more cans of pop on the ground.

We discussed it afterward and surmised that the pop cans were probably a test to see if we would notice them. One had to wonder, what else had been removed by this method from the depot prior to our arrival?

Shortly after we divided into the day crew and night crew, the night Lieutenant called some of the night crew together for a bullshit session. He said he was from Chicago and, before joining the Army, he was in a car-theft ring. He said the money he made from the thefts paid his way through college. He said they usually stripped the cars and sold the parts, so it was not as traceable. After establishing that he

410

knew what the shady side of the law was like, he told us that he was the only officer in his outfit who did not have his own jeep. He told us that if one of us stole a jeep for him, he would give the guy $200 and a guarantee that he would get the guy upgraded to the rank of Sergeant. Warning flags went up for me immediately. The only way to get an upgrade to a Sergeant from a Spec-4 was by field promotion in war, or by way of the military review process. Lieutenants did not have the clout to circumvent either process. Crandall said it wouldn't be that hard to steal a jeep. He said they are sitting around with no one watching them all the time. I asked him if he was willing to risk his chance to go home on schedule for $200, and most likely a knife in the back from our friendly Lieutenant. I also told him the Lieutenant already told us that he was a car thief in Chicago. If it were that easy, why wouldn't he take the chance on his own? I don't remember Crandall's response, but it gave him food for thought.

One of the Filipinos, a forklift driver, was exceptionally friendly with us. He was actually nuisance-friendly. He had an excellent English vocabulary. I asked how he came by the English language so easily. He said that he lived in San Francisco for four years while he was in college and that he had graduated from college. Although he gave the name of the college, I don't remember it. I asked him why he was working here in Vietnam as a laborer instead of doing something related to his degree. He said that the money was better here.

His friendliness attracted our attention rather than disarming us as we suspected he was trying to do. Oblad was pretty sharp, and he's the one who thought this Filipino was pushing his friendliness out of proportion. About the fourth night working the security detail, we decided to stop him and his forklift at the gate as he left and give it a thorough searching. We found cameras, TVs, tape decks, and in total close to 50 items hidden in the housing of the forklift. We placed him under arrest and called the Lieutenant who in turn called the MPs. He was hauled away. The forklift was moved to the side and not used the rest of that night. We stopped the other two forklifts as they left and did a similar search. They had no merchandise in or on them. For the rest of the night, and the following night, we stopped each forklift as it left the compound. They were all clean.

Three nights after finding the stolen merchandise, the day foreman decided to work the night shift. The crew I was with worked until midnight and then went to lunch. It was around 0130 hours when we got back to the compound. One of the crew, who was roaming, said the Filipino foreman wanted to talk to all of us. We all walked out into the middle of the depot yard. There were some building supplies stacked in the middle of the yard, covered with plastic. He and six other Filipinos were standing in the shadows of a building on the far, east end of the compound. We stopped by the pile of building supplies and waited. I told the crew that we would wait right here in the lighted area, that he could come to us. A couple of minutes passed before anyone moved on either side. As a group the Filipinos came toward us; there were seven of them. I told everyone that, when they got close, we needed to get in front of the building supply pile so they could not get around behind us. I didn't know what to expect, but this whole scene was not in order.

They stopped about eight feet to our front. The foreman pushed his pith helmet back on his head and told us a little about his history. He said he was a wanted man in the Philippines. He had killed two police officers there and, if they got their hands on him, he would be imprisoned until they got around to hanging him.

412

Then he pointed to the crew with him. He said, "We are all wanted for crimes back in the Philippines." He added, "I chose these men because they are not afraid to kill if I ask them." He also said, "We are better organized than your Mafia in the States."

Then he said that we could have anything we wanted that was in the depot, all we had to do was ask. He said, "My men will steal it, and mail it to any address you give them." He added, "We will take all the chances. All you have to do is tell us what you want, and it is yours." He also said, "I know they won't give you any ammunition for your rifles. So we don't have to worry about you. But you have to worry about us, unless you cooperate." He looked directly at me and said, "If you ever catch one of my men taking any property out of the compound again, I will kill you." He added, "We can work together, but don't ever stop us again." He then held out his hand and said, "Let's shake on an agreement." I did not take his hand. Instead, I told him that there are two people at the gate and I would have to talk with them. I also said I needed to talk it over with everyone before I could give him an answer, and we would do that back at our barracks in the morning. He had the final word: "It better be the right answer!"

We went back to our hole under the canvas. I made sure no one else was lurking around. After this conversation, I did not trust any of the permanent crew working nights. I thought if we caught onto the thefts that quickly, the permanent staff were probably in on it, and could not be trusted. That was especially true for the Lieutenant.

The first thing I said was, "After all I have been through, there's no chink son-of-a-bitch going to threaten me and get by with it." Crandall asked what we could do about it. I told him we're going to talk it over first, but if it's up to me, we're going to turn them in. I also said, "I'm too damned short

to be taking chances on getting caught up in a theft ring."
Crandall said, "They are taking all the chances. Besides, what
has our government ever done for you other than send you to
this forsaken country and try to get your ass killed? Here's a
chance to get back at them." I asked everyone else how they
felt. Kampa said he's in favor of turning them in. Going around
the group, the rest felt as I did.

The only two people who did not have a say in this were
Oblad and his partner on the gate. I then shared my thoughts
on the permanent-assigned soldiers working the night shift.
We agreed not to say anything to them about our conversation
with the Filipinos or how we planned to handle it. When we
relieved Oblad and his partner at the gate, I explained the
situation. They were in agreement to turn them in. We also
agreed that we would demand to have ammunition for our
rifles before we worked again. I didn't know if we could get
away without working, but we would push the issue as far as
we could go with it.

The next morning, I was at the gate when the day
Sergeant came in. I asked him when the Captain would come
in. He said he would be at the office sometime between 0700
and 0730 hours. We were done at 0600 hours. I told the Sergeant
to tell the Captain to come and see me at the signal company.
I added that it was very important that he talk to me, and
that we talk away from this compound. The Sergeant told me
to give him the information and he would pass it on to the
Captain. I told him, "No, I will only talk to the Captain." I
again said that it was extremely important that I talk to him
away from the compound.

We went back to the signal company and I tried to
sleep. I was too anxious. I kept wondering if the Captain
would come to see me. I wasn't hungry, but I went to the
mess tent anyway. I took some toast and coffee and sat with

a couple of signal company soldiers who I had talked with on a previous occasion. After breakfast, I went out to the basketball court they had set up. It was nothing more than a platform of planking leveled off with posts and timbers under the planking. There were always a couple of basketballs laying around. I began shooting baskets just to kill time and try to occupy my mind. Kampa couldn't sleep and he saw me shooting hoops and joined me. He and I played a couple of games of 21, then switched to playing HORSE.

Kampa and I killed off an hour with the basketballs and then went back to the tent barracks. It was about 0900 hours. Oblad was awake. We were all wondering if the Captain would show up. I told them I don't want to go back to that damned place unless we have ammunition. We decided that, if the Captain did show up, we would request to clear post early for DEROS (Date Eligible for Return From Overseas), the term used for going back to the world. The military usually gave you three days to get a form signed off from multiple various departments. Since we were on attached status, we were only required to get three signatures for this form to clear post. We decided that we would settle for starting the DEROS process three weeks early instead of the usual three days. We really didn't expect to get this but, what the hell, we'd go for it anyway.

About three or four times a day a commercial airline would land at the airfield, and about that often one would take off from the airfield. As we were talking, one went overhead drowning out our conversation. Then we got to talking about the time we had left. We were down to six weeks. This is what I considered a short-timers space of time. We had heard previously that there was a swimming beach beyond the main military post. We decided we had to check that out soon. None of us had swim trunks, so we would have to go to the PX on main post to buy them. Basically, we were killing time waiting for the Captain to show.

Shortly after 1000 hours, a jeep parked along the circle trail near our barracks tent. It was the Captain of the PX depot. Oblad and I went out to meet him. He seemed pissed off and told us we should have waited for him that morning instead of making him come out to see us. He also said something like, "You'd better have something good to make me drive out here." The sun was beastly hot, and the ground was a light brown sand surface. He said, "Let's get out of the sun." We went to the next tent where the day shift called home. The side flaps were up and no one was in the tent. Since Kampa was with me when the Filipinos made their threats, I told him to sit in with us.

I explained the whole conversation and scenario that was played out during the night with the Filipinos. I told him that from now on we needed ammunition or we would refuse to pull security. Kampa was kind of quiet, but Oblad laid it on pretty heavy about the need for ammunition. The Captain said that he would get us the ammunition, but he would have to put together some post orders for using it. He asked why I didn't tell the Lieutenant about this. I told him that in the short time we were here, we found out how most of the stuff was being stolen. I said that anyone using a little common sense could have figured it out. So we had to believe that other GIs knew about it, and were probably threatened not to say anything, or maybe they were taking advantage of it. I told him that we just didn't know whom to trust. I also said that the Lieutenant was gone by the time the Filipinos talked with us, but I would not share the conversation with him anyway.

After filling him in on what we had, the Captain's attitude became more mellow and friendly. I then told the Captain that we would like to have three weeks to clear post for

DEROS. He chuckled. He said he didn't think he could get us three weeks, but he would see about letting us go a week early. I told him a week is better than three days but asked him to shoot for two weeks early. He laughed, shook his head, thanked us for what we did, and left.

After talking with the Captain, I felt a load was lifted off my shoulders. I didn't have the worry I had before. I'm sure some of the others felt the same way. We all seemed to be in a better mood. We sat around bullshitting for a while and then decided to form teams and play basketball until lunchtime. Even though the temperature was hitting the thermometer at about 110 degrees, doing something felt good. We were all conditioned for the heat; so as long as you could sweat it was bearable. We took a short break before lunch to allow our bodies to dry off and then went to the mess hall to eat.

I was hungry and ate a plate-full. Since I didn't sleep the night before, and after eating a full meal, I was tired. I went back to the barracks and sacked out, sleeping for almost three hours. When I woke Oblad, Kampa, Crandall and a few others were sitting in the tent bullshitting. They welcomed me back from the dead.

I was feeling grungy so I took a shower. Before coming to Cam Ranh Bay, I always slept in my clothes. After coming here I could have slept under sheets, but I preferred to sleep in my clothes. I didn't have another set of jungle fatigues so, even after showering, I had to put the old and dirty clothes back on. We were all in the same situation. Since we were attached and not assigned to the signal company, we could not get personal supplies such as clothes from them. After showering, I went to the signal company Supply and asked a Clerk how we could get a change of clothes. He said there were a couple of Vietnamese women who did laundry for the local GIs. He said they charged a reasonable fee. I asked him if they were around now. He said they usually come to their barracks in the morning. Anyone who wants their clothes washed will give them to the women and they usually get them back by early afternoon. It cost $1 to wash a set of clothes. Since they wash them by hand, I thought this was a fair enough price. He said he would send one of them to our barracks the next morning.

Since we had to be to work by 1800 hours, we had to eat supper as soon as the mess tent opened at 1630 hours. It was time to eat; I wasn't all that hungry but went to supper anyway. I didn't eat my normal ration of food this meal. After supper, I made sure all eight of our crew were there, and we walked to the road running past the south edge of the compound and caught our ride to the depot. When we arrived, the first thing I noticed was that there was no activity. All three forklifts were parked inside and to the right of the gate. Other than the day crew waiting for us, there were no other people around. I asked Sgt. Harrin, "Where is everyone?" He said that at about three o'clock a large troop of MPs came and rounded up all the Filipinos and loaded them onto trucks. From what he could gather, he said they were all put on a ship and they were all going back to the Philippines. He said they put cuffs on the foreman and three other guys, and they were hauled away in jeeps.

Shortly after our arrival, the night Lieutenant came to the gate with Spec-4s Mullins and Ritter. He gave us two ammo clips for each of the four M1 carbines we carried. He said we could load the clip in the gun but could not load one in the chamber unless we needed to defend ourselves or someone else. He gave a talk on gun safety. As a rule, he seemed to be an easygoing guy, but tonight he was very serious and stoic. He said the Filipinos would no longer be working in the depot. They were all on a ship and were to be sent back to the Philippines. I asked him what happened to the foreman. The

Lieutenant said that, as far as he knew, the foreman was using an alias name here in Vietnam. He and three of his friends are believed to be wanted criminals in the Philippines. They were placed under arrest and are being held temporarily in a local lockup until arrangements can be made to transport them back to the Philippines. He expected that would take place the next day. He also said that he didn't have all the information, but he believed that when the ship arrives in the Philippines the local police would board it and check all passengers to see if they are wanted criminals in their country before allowing them to disembark. He said that this was possibly the biggest roundup of criminals they would ever have at one time.

The next morning we were told that, before we left, the Captain wanted to talk with us. He had asked that we stick around until he arrived around 0645 hours. We were standing around the freight gate, bullshitting with the day crew, when a runner came and told us to come up to the office. Sgt. Harrin went with us. We were not marching in formation. As we approached the office, the Captain came out. Harrin tried to call us to attention and do the military procedure thing, but when you're not in formation, it doesn't work so well. The Captain waved him off and said we can get along without that this morning. The Captain then gave us a "job well done" speech and apologized for putting us in an at-risk, life-threatening situation by not trusting us with ammunition. He said that would never happen again. He also said that, because of what we did, he now had criteria to establish a more permanent security group. This was a request he had previously made, but it was turned down. He believed that he could now justify making another request and expecting more positive results. He then told us what was happening to the Filipinos. He confirmed that the foreman and a few of his henchmen were likely wanted criminals by the Philippine police, and they would only know for sure when they could be identified.

He said that he couldn't say too much about it, but they would be going back to the Philippines under guard. He added that he already has more soldiers assigned to him for the depot, and only GIs would handle the transferring of the Conax containers from the docks to the depot. He said that they would hire more Vietnamese to take the place of Filipinos. As a final statement, he said that he thought it over: he would give us ten days off to clear post. I figured this gave us nine days to do whatever we wanted, to include doing nothing.

The night crew felt damned good about what we had accomplished. I don't think we solved the entire thievery problem, but we sure as hell stopped it for the present time from inside the PX depot. Maybe it was our imagination, but it seemed that the GIs working permanently with the depot gave us more respect.

Mullins and Ritter didn't say a whole lot about the departure of the Filipinos, but both seemed much happier after they were gone. They hung around us much more after the Filipinos were gone. I'll never know for sure, but I believe they were compromised into a situation that they were happy to get out from under before it blew up in their faces. I always had, and still have, a gut feeling that the Lieutenant was in it pretty deep with the Filipinos and saw a chance for instant riches slip through his fingers. For the next four weeks, our life was pretty boring and mundane but no one was complaining. Overall this was good duty, especially for Vietnam.

BEFRIENDING THE LAUNDRESS

When we got back to our barracks, after the Captain talked to us, there was a fairly tall, dark Oriental woman waiting for us. She did not look Vietnamese. She talked with a fair English accent. She asked if we wanted any clothes washed. I told her that I did. Just about everyone in our tent wanted some clothes washed. I gave her the clothes off my back and put on a pair of stateside fatigues. They were heavier than the jungle fatigues and felt constricting against the body. I told her that I needed the clothes back early in the afternoon. She took about six sets of fatigues with her and said she would pick up the rest the next day. By 1400 hours, she had all the fatigues back to us. They were clean and neatly folded. She knew whose clothes belonged to whom. I paid her and gave her a tip. Crandall said I shouldn't tip her, she will expect it the next time and pretty soon she will raise her prices. I didn't give a damn what Crandall thought. He only saw life for what was in it for him.

After lunch, some of us decided to celebrate our success at solving the PX thefts. We went into the Vietnamese section of Cam Ranh and hit a few bars. Most of the bars in Can Ranh carried American beer. I probably had one more beer than I should have. I didn't get any sleep after getting off work that morning. I didn't sleep before going to work that evening. This was going to be a long night. I pulled second watch. During my watch, I sat down to rest on the building supplies in the middle of the compound yard. I dozed off. The night Lieutenant decided to take a walk through the yard at that time. He saw me sitting there and came up to talk to me but instead found me asleep. He woke me and commenced to raise proper hell. My only excuse was that I did not intend to fall asleep, but I hadn't been able to sleep lately and it caught up with me. When I sat down to rest, my eyes took advantage of the situation. He apparently felt he had done his job, so he let me go with the butt-chewing.

The next day a few of us decided to go swimming, but first we had to go to the PX on main post to buy swimsuits. We caught a ride with a truck that took us close to the main PX. This was a very large PX that had departments similar to a Sears or Penney's store. We checked out the store for some time before buying our swimsuits and heading for the beach. I was interested in looking at the stereo equipment. A clerk told us the quickest way to get to the beach.

The beach was yellow sand, and the water of the South China Sea was an aqua blue-green color. It was one of those hot days where the temps hit at least 110 degrees. I ran into the water and dove under. I thought my heart was going to stop. The water against my warm skin was cold; the volume of seawater kept it well below the air temperature. It took about five minutes for my skin to adjust to the water temperature. There were probably at least 200 people swimming, even a few young American women wearing bikinis. After swimming for 15 minutes, someone screamed and he went running out of the water. He had a big red welt on his leg. Before long someone else screamed and he too had a red welt on the leg. After the fifth or sixth person screamed and left the water, the lifeguard called everyone out of the water. He said a mass of jellyfish had moved into the swimming zone and they had to close the beach until they cleared out again.

If you have contact with a jellyfish, it lets off poisonous fluid that penetrates where the contact was made. It can make some people very ill. I managed to get about a half hour in the water before they closed the beach. There were hoses near the bathhouses where you could wash the salt water off before changing back to your clothes.

After the swim, Oblad, Kampa and I walked around the main post area to check out the place. I decided I would have to come back to the main PX to look at stereo equipment again. If I were going to buy anything, I would have to write home for money.

The tall, dark-skinned woman came to our barracks every day to see about doing our laundry. She spoke broken English well enough so I could carry on an acceptable conversation with her. She was not exceptionally pretty, but she was what I would call handsome for a woman. She carried a steel wash pan with her. If she only had one or two sets of fatigues to wash, she would wash them right outside the barracks and hang them on the tie-down ropes to dry. If there were more, she would take them with her. She was very efficient with her work. Every day she came, I would talk with her. She enjoyed talking while she worked. I told her she didn't look Vietnamese. She said she was Laotian. She said she came from Laos to Cam Ranh Bay, liked it, and stayed. She added there was work here with the GIs. She also said that she could not find this kind of work in Laos. I asked her if she was married. She said that she was, but her husband had been killed. She said she did not have any children.

One morning, I handed her my set of fatigues to clean. She said that, if I buy her some underwear from the PX, she would wash my clothes for free. I asked her what kind of underwear she wanted. She was wearing loose black pants with a loose black smock top. She raised her smock on the side and dropped the waist of her pants about five inches so I could see the underwear. They were men's white cotton underwear briefs. I asked her if she wanted the men's shorts. She said yes. I told her I would buy her some underwear. I asked her what size she needed. I believe she needed a 24-inch waist. A couple of days later I went down to the PX. I looked over the reel-to-reel tape decks and decided that I wanted to buy an Akai brand. I had written home for money but had not received it as yet. Before I left, I found the undershorts. They came in three-to-a-pack and six-to-a-pack sets. I bought the six-to-a-pack set. They cost less than two dollars. The next day, when the Laotian came for the laundry, I gave her the underwear. She was so happy she asked if she could give me a hug. She said she would do all my laundry for free. I told her she could do it for free one time, but that I would pay the rest. She insisted she would do my laundry for free.

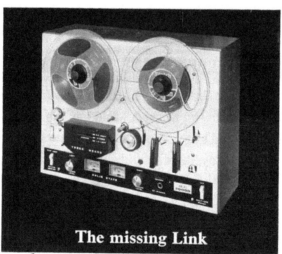

The missing Link
that puts stereo tape into your
Hi-Fi system!

Part of a 1960s ad for an Akai reel-to-reel tape deck.

ENJOYING THE BAY

We worked security at the main PX depot until we had 10 days left in country. Once we were relieved of this duty, we were free to do what we wanted as long as it wasn't getting into trouble. Three times we went to the beach and swam in the ocean. We spent much of our time tromping around the post and visiting the village of Cam Ranh. Compared to Camp Radcliff, this area had a much looser atmosphere. We never heard artillery. There were a few helicopters flying, but nowhere near the volume we became used to in other parts of the country. If you never left Cam Ranh Bay, you would never know there was a war going on in Vietnam.

One evening we got a visit from three American female dancers. They were either very good amateurs or professional entertainers. They seemed to be used to an all-male audience. The basketball court was set up as the dance floor stage. They were dancing to the '50s and early '60s rock music. Crandall was calling them bitches and making other snide remarks about them. He complained that they weren't showing any emotion or feelings. He added that he should go up there and show them how to dance. I told him, "These folks aren't interested in seeing you dance. Besides, they look pretty good to me." After a few dances, they disrobed to bikinis and continued dancing. Crandall couldn't take it any longer. He went up and began dancing with one of the women. As the song went along, with smooth moves and gestures, he worked his way into a kneeling position in front of his dancing opposite. He reached his hand out toward her genital area and then pulled it back and smelled at it. He then waved her away as if rejecting her. She reacted immediately and kicked him in the chest, almost tipping him over backward. The crowd cheered her and jeered Crandall, razzing him back into the crowd. If he had had any thoughts of retaliating, they diminished. He would have had the whole crowd on his back. He came back to our group. I told him, "After that performance, I don't want to be seen with you." He said, "I should have slapped her." I told him, "If you had, the whole crowd would be on your back, and I would be the first one in line." He got the same treatment from the rest of our crew.

Once we got to Cam Ranh Bay, I had written letters to Ray Judy and Ray Kloemken informing them where we were and giving them the lowdown on Cam Ranh Bay. Kloemken had in-country R & R and came to Cam Ranh Bay. He decided to stop in before heading back to Camp Radcliff. He told me that they caught the guy who had been stealing the money from the troops. It was Mears, the supply clerk. He said they also caught the Warrant Supply Officer selling fatigues, beer, and other Army supplies in An Khê. He said that their company had been back at Camp Radcliff for a three-day stand-down and some of the guys went into An Khê. While they were walking around, they saw the Supply Warrant Officer drive up to a business shack. He called out, and two Vietnamese men came out of the shack and the three of them unloaded boxes from the jeep. The two guys went in the front of the shack but no one was around. They heard voices coming from the back. They went back outside and around to the back. They could see into the back room. The Vietnamese were holding up jungle fatigues and looking them over. They watched and saw the Vietnamese hand over money for the fatigues. The GIs reported this and a stakeout was set up. The Warrant Officer eventually got caught in the act of making the sale of Army clothes. Kloemken said both Mears and the Warrant Officer were arrested and were to be court-martialed. I had my suspicions, but now it sure made sense. It was close to suppertime, so Kloemken ate supper with us and then caught a ride back to the airfield where he was staying. He had to catch a flight back to An Khê in the morning.

About four weeks before we were to leave Vietnam, two black guys came to stay in our barracks. One was tall and muscular, the other was smaller and wiry. They each had a pair of boxing gloves and protective boxing headgear. They sparred with each other from time to time. With about a week left in country, the smaller guy tossed me his buddy's boxing gloves and said, "Let's go a round." I put the gloves on and we began to spar. We did the tap-tap thing for about 30 seconds and then I flew into him with a flurry of punches knocking him over a bunk. He said, "Damn, I didn't know you boxed." I told him, "I don't. That's what I learned from street fighting." He told me that I could be a boxer.

When I came back to the tent after eating supper, the muscular guy was waiting for me. He said he heard I could box and he asked if I would box him. With a little encouragement, I told him that I would go three rounds with him, if it lasted that long. I had watched this guy box, and he looked pretty good. We were setting down what the rules would be. His friend would keep the time for three two-minute rounds. We selected a site outside the tent and marked off approximately a ring-sized area in the ground. By the time we got everything settled, word had spread about a boxing match. There were about 30 spectators by now, and more were coming. He put on his headgear and asked if I wanted his buddy's headgear. I replied that I would box without the headgear.

We squared off and his buddy said, "FIGHT!" I respected this guy's ability much more than I did his buddy. He had a much longer reach than I did, so it was tough for me to get in on him. For the first minute, we exchanged and ducked each other's punches. About halfway through the first round, he came at me in a rush firing a couple of hard jabs. One caught me in the cheek and nose. It staggered me. The inside of my mouth was cut up. We didn't have teeth protection. My eyes were blurry. He knew he had me hurt, so he came in again at me. I covered my head and ducked under his punches. He was much taller than I, so I was looking up under his face, covering with my left hand. I saw his face exposed. As soon as I saw an opening for a punch, it seemed as if everything went into slow motion. I drove my right fist up and caught him under the chin. I put everything I had in the punch, pushing off the ground with my right foot. The punch landed squarely, lifting him off the ground and spinning him around as he went down. His face protector twisted on his head so he was looking through the left ear hole. He tried to get up but fell sideways. His buddy was counting. He tried to get up again and, after he got to his feet, he stumbled sideways and fell again. I pushed my gloves toward Oblad and said, "Take them off. I'm done fighting." I had hit people before, but I had never hit anyone like I hit this guy.

After I had the gloves off, I helped him get his headgear off, and then helped him up to sit on the edge of the tent floor. He said he was still a little woozy, but that he would be okay. I told him, "I didn't think I could hit that hard." He said that he had been hit many times, but he had never been knocked down. He also said that he would have been hurt much worse if he hadn't had the headgear on. When things settled down and the people left, he told me I should take up boxing. He said with a little training I would do okay for myself. He said there's good money in boxing. I told him I didn't think I would be interested in the sport. It took at least five days to clear up the inside of my mouth. That was all the reason I needed to stay out of boxing.

Oblad heard from Sgt. Harrin that one of the soldiers from B Company 5th of the 7th Cav was in the hospital in Cam Ranh Bay. He didn't know who it was. I was going down to main post to pick up a tape deck, so I said I would stop at the hospital to see who it was and to visit. The hospital did not have any 5/7 Cav soldiers. Actually, most of the soldiers in the hospital at Cam Ranh Bay were Korean soldiers from the White Horse Division. Since I enjoy meeting people from other countries, I asked a group in a ward right off from the nurses' station if any of them spoke English. There were a few who spoke understandable English. We talked about where they were stationed, how they got wounded, and other small talk. I told them that I was with the Cav and we were in operations with the Tiger Division. They said that the Tiger Division was up north. They said it was bad up north, much worse than where they operated. I had always heard how bad it was in the Mekong Delta, where these guys were stationed.

From the hospital, I went to the main PX and purchased a tape deck. It was packed in a large box and was fairly heavy. I had to carry it back with me. I lugged it to the main road and immediately hooked a ride that took me past the signal company. I spent the night wrapping and labeling the tape deck for transporting back to the world when I flew home.

The next day, I went back to the PX and bought a power amplifier stereo unit to operate the tape deck, speakers, and turntable. Again I hooked a ride that took me past our unit. The following morning, I went back to the PX and purchased a studio-grade turntable. I bought each item separately instead of all at one time, because I had to carry them back to the signal company, which was no easy chore. After buying the turntable, I went to the main road and hooked a ride right away. After we left main post, I told the driver where I was headed. He said that he could get me there, but we'd have to make a few stops first. I asked him where all he had to go. By the time he finished listing all the stops, I figured it would be mid-afternoon before I got back. I told him he could drop me off at the north intersection and I would walk the two miles back to the signal company. He said that it would be a long haul carrying the box. I told him I did a lot of humping this past year, I didn't think the two miles would be too tough.

At about 1100 hours, he dropped me off. The sun was scorching hot and radiating off the sand. Again the temps were close to the 110-degree mark. Since coming to Cam Ranh Bay, it didn't rain more than two or three times. Much of Vietnam had tropical rainforest conditions. However, this region did not receive much rain. I guess that is why the whole area was one big sand dune. I set a fast pace for myself. The sooner I got back, the sooner I could cool down. I made the trip in about a half-hour. I stepped into the tent and set the turntable on my bunk. Petters came up and handed me a bottle of cognac. He said he got his shipping orders for home, have a drink. I put the bottle up and took a hearty slug of the liquor. My throat was parched. The booze choked off my air. I couldn't breathe. I looked around for a canteen but could not find one. I was gasping for air, but nothing was going into my lungs. According to what was said later, my face was beet red. I'm not sure how long this lasted, but it seemed like an eternity. I thought I was going to die right there. I knew that I was moments away from passing out, and then some air got into my lungs. It was not enough, but it kept me from passing out. I gasped some more and a little more air went in. After 10 or more gasps, the breathing began more evenly, but I couldn't talk. When I tried, I only wheezed. Someone had run off and found a canteen. He handed it to me. After a few swallows, my voice came back. Up to this point everyone was serious and, I suppose, worried. But now they started laughing. I told them, "This would really look good in the papers back home. 'Soldier chokes to death on alcohol.'"

There were five or six GIs from our group who got their orders for returning to the States. None of the night crew got orders. This was July 29. I figured that the rest of us should get our orders the following day, which was the case. However, for the rest of this day, there was a lot of nervous anticipation. I was feeling it. Those orders to get out of Vietnam were like a God-sent gift.

Personnel destined to return to the U.S. wait at the Bein Hoa air terminal for a National Airlines flight home. Credit L.T. Gault SPC4, Feb. 15, 1968. U.S. Army photo. NARA 111-CC-64761. Photo courtesy of the National Archives at College Park, Md.

DEROS

When the orders came, we had the rest of the day to pack our things and prepare for the trip back to the States. The following morning, a truck picked us up along with all our gear, and we were transported to some metal barracks buildings close to the airfield. Once there, we were assigned a barracks where we could stack our belongings. We each found an empty cot and put the belongings on or under it. We were told where the mess hall was located and told that we had the balance of the day to hang out. We were told not to wander too far because we could be called at any time to fill a seat on a plane. If nothing came before then, we were due to leave the next morning. We were told that there would be a departure meeting at 1900 hours that evening in a building they nick-named the HRC (Home Rehabilitation Center). We ate lunch and sat around, trying to relax. Everyone was tense. Perhaps their thoughts wandered like mine: I was thinking about what home would be like. What changes would there be? I knew I had changed. How would I act? Before I went into the service, I never used the F-word. It just wasn't in my vocabulary. Since coming to 'Nam, every sentence out of my mouth contained the word. First you heard it, then you used it, and then it became habit. I knew Mom would not approve or want to hear it. Could I just stop using it? I hoped so.

Even though I was anxious to get home, in some ways it scared me. I had adapted to Vietnam. Now I would have to adapt to being home. I still had three months left in the service after a four-week military leave, but I figured I could do the last three months standing on my head if I had to. Nothing they could throw at me would be as bad as this past year. I got to thinking about our trip coming to Vietnam. This right away brought me to all the soldiers who were not going home like I was. I thought about Tom Gray, Dennis Benedetti, Louie Albanese, Del Crockett, Charlie Heaps, Tracy Jones, Patino, Samaripa, Sandoval, and all the others who died. I wondered how many of the wounded would be invalids for the rest of their lives. I felt lucky the way things turned out for me. I had thoughts of the plane crashing before we made it home. I put them out of my mind, but they were there.

At 1900, hours there were more than a hundred soldiers sitting in classroom desks in the HRC building. This building had air conditioning. It felt cold inside. An E-7 took charge of the meeting. The first order of business was to tell us when our plane would leave in the morning. If you were not on the plane at departure time, there were always a few people waiting to take your place. If you missed the plane, there would have to be new orders cut, and it would be three more days before you would be able to leave.

Then he said you are to turn in any military property that is not part of your military issue. If you are caught with any unauthorized military property, you would be detained, and you would miss the flight home. He held up a black pen that has US Government stenciled on it. He said this is military property. If you have one, turn it in. You don't want to miss a flight home over a 20-cent pen. He added that is how picky things can be. So if you have any military property on you now, drop it in the bag on the way out. He said, "If you have any unauthorized military property in your travel gear, get it out and leave it in the barracks. No one will say anything to you. If you get caught with unauthorized property you will be in deep shit."

Then he said, "In the past year you have all come to use language that you probably never used before coming over to 'Nam. You might want to start practicing on not using it from here on." He added, "When you get home and your Mom comes to give you a big hug, she will not appreciate you saying, 'how you f---ing doing, Mom?'" This got a laugh, but he was serious. Unless you really thought about what you were saying, it was natural to use the F-word as an adjective describing anything and everything.

We were given tags to put on our belongings for shipment home. At 0700 hours, all luggage and boxes for shipment home were to be lined up outside our barracks. They would be trucked to the airfield and loaded on the plane. We would not see them again until we got off the plane at the Seattle-Tacoma airport. Once back in the States, all items would be transported to a hangar where we could reclaim them. There would be customs agents from the Drug Enforcement Agency (DEA) checking all baggage for illegal drugs and other illegal items. At this point he told us that, if anything illegal was found in our belongings, we would be arrested and dealt with in accordance with U.S. laws. With final words of warning and caution, he dismissed us.

When we left the building, the heat hit us again. Even though it was nearly dark, the temperature was close to 90 degrees. Tomorrow would be the big day to go back to the world. Everyone in this group had looked forward to this day since August 2, one year ago. They were all upbeat, excited, anxious and, maybe like me, even a little afraid. I had mixed emotions about going back to the world. Yes, I was anxious to get back but, at the same time, it was saddening for me. There's a strong bond between people who put their life and faith on the line for each other. I lost some very close friends to the war. Once we separated ways, I would probably never see the other friends who made it back to the world. I felt I was leaving a part of my heart and soul behind.

More than once, I thought about possibilities that could delay the trip or, even worse, the remote possibility of a plane crash over the sea. I didn't want to think about these things, but I couldn't help it. I said some prayers asking God to watch to see that we made it safely home. Everyone seemed happy but I'm sure they were having the same thoughts as me. As a group, we talked but we all seemed to be reserved and holding back on celebrating. A little before midnight, we decided to go into the barracks and hit the cots. I couldn't sleep. I seldom slept well in Vietnam. But this night I got no sleep. I figured I would get sleep on the plane going stateside.

The night dragged on and morning finally came. We dragged our luggage out and lined it up as instructed, then went to the mess hall for breakfast. About mid-morning, trucks came and took us to the airfield. We stood around waiting outside the terminal. There was a Northwest 727 passenger plane sitting near the terminal. As we were standing there, two GIs came out and rolled a movable staircase up to the loading door on the plane. The door was already open. A short time later, a Sergeant (SFC) and two E-5 Sergeants came out and told us that we would be boarding the 727. The SFC said, "As I call your name, you go to the staircase and show your orders to one of the E-5s. After verification, load onto the plane and move to the rear, filling the seats from back to front." A few people ignored the "from back to front directive," but no one made an issue of it.

My name was called fairly early, so I was sitting well behind the wings. I ended up on the right window. An E-8 older Sergeant sat down beside me. He was with the 1st Cav also,

436

but from another battalion. We made introductions and made small talk, waiting for the rest to load. When the last seat was filled, the door was closed. The flight attendants made their way down the aisle to see to it we were belted in as the plane began to move. The head flight attendant gave us a welcome, made a few comments about going back to the United States, and then recited the general emergency procedure. By now the plane was on the runway. She secured herself in a seat and the plane took off. As soon as it became airborne, there was a cheer, and then a relaxed sigh throughout the cabin.

BACK TO THE WORLD

The pilot came on the intercom with his welcome and flight itinerary, and we settled back for the long ride. We were stopping in Japan for about an hour and 15 minutes to refill the fuel tanks, and then we would fly directly into the Seattle-Tacoma airport.

Once we were settled in, the E-8 beside me told me, "When you get home, people who were in the service during World War II or the Korean War will be telling you how tough they had it." He said, "I served in the infantry in both of those wars, as well as this war. During the previous two wars, even if you were in battle, as soon as the battle was over, we had fairly easy duty maintaining the ground we took." He added, "Vietnam is much different. Every day is another day you can get killed. From the infantry point of view, this war was worse than any war fought in modern times." Then he added, "Don't let those old-timers shit you on how tough they had it. They didn't have it as bad as you had it." He finally said, "One year in Vietnam convinced me to hang it up and retire." He had four months left in the service and he would be a civilian.

The plane landed in Japan for refueling. The pilot told us it might be a good idea to get out and stretch because the balance of the flight would take around 10 hours. Just about everyone got off the plane and milled around and under it. Once we were in the air again, the pilot told us we would be flying over the top of the world. Instead of flying across the ocean, west to east, we were going north over the pole and coming south over the Alaskan interior to Washington.

The flight, from Japan to Washington, began with a lot of chatter bouncing around the cabin of the 727. An hour into the flight, the tone became very subtle and somber. I tried to sleep, but sleep wouldn't come. When we had landed in Japan, I couldn't get my ears to clear as we descended. Now I had a headache. The air-conditioning in the plane seemed to be too cold. I had been too long living in the sultry heat of Vietnam; now the 70-degree climate in the plane was a chill. I tried to think what life at home would be like again. It seemed like years ago when I left for Vietnam. I was only a year older, but it seemed as if I had aged 20 years.

What would it be like to see my girlfriend? She had written me letters over the past year; about two every week. She had not written in the last six weeks. Maybe she found someone else? I met her in October 1965 at a dance at the Kimball Playland Ballroom, after a high school football game. She was a senior and I was four years out of high school. We dated three times before I went into the service, and then when I was home on leave. Other than the letters we wrote back and forth, we didn't know all that much about each other. I really liked her, and I hoped she would still be there when I got back. But I wasn't setting myself up for a big letdown.

Most of the flight, my thoughts were of what I left behind in Vietnam and what life back in the world would be like. I felt tired but tense. For a year I had been wound tight with loss, uncertainty, anxiety, and even fright. I still have uncertainty and anxiety. I didn't know it then, but the losses I was feeling were going to be a part of the rest of my life. Even as I'm writing about this, nearly 50 years later, I have tears in my eyes for some close friends who didn't make it back from

'Nam. When I was on the plane that day, I didn't yet realize how immensely wasteful this war was.

The plane landed in Seattle-Tacoma sometime late at night. I'm sure the pilot gave us the local time. All I can remember is that it was late. We got off the plane and were directed to a huge hangar. About 20 minutes later, carts arrived with our luggage. As soon as we had our luggage, we were to get into one of about six lines and move forward in the line until we were first. Customs agents were checking our luggage for drugs and illegal items. I pushed my luggage to the front, opened my duffel bag, and began removing the items, one at a time, for the agent. When this was completed, he allowed me to repack the items, and then I began to open the boxes I had as part of my luggage. As soon as I began to open the first box, he asked what was in the boxes. I told him a tape player, a turntable, and a power amplifier to run the equipment. He told me to close up the tape deck box. He said, "You're not a drug smuggler." He had watched me as I unpacked my duffel bag, and not so much what I was unpacking. Some people they let off easy, and others they put through the mill.

From the airport, we were bused to Fort Lewis Army Base about 20 miles out. At Fort Lewis, we were separated into groups who were getting out of the service and groups who still had time left in the service. I fit in with the latter group. Our group went to a clothing issue dispensary warehouse. We took only our duffel bags off the bus. We were told to take any personal items from our duffel bags and to stack the duffel bags in a pile on a loading dock inside a warehouse. There was a light rain. We were then directed inside the dispensary and, as we did at induction time, we received all new clothing issue of uniforms. We began with undershorts, T-shirts, socks, boots, khaki uniform shirts, dress green uniform shirts, then dress green uniform pants. We put on the dress green pants. There were three women working with the GIs. They would roll up the pants leg to the right level on the cuff and mark it. We were given a tag and a felt marker. We wrote our name and Army ID number (mine was US-55-847-422) on the tag and tied it to a belt loop. We also had to tag the duffel bag we were issued. Two pairs of khaki pants and one pair dress green pants went in last. Once we had all the military issue we would need in our duffel bags, we slipped back into the clothes we had arrived in. The bags were stacked along a wall on the loading dock.

Before we left the warehouse, an NCO told us not to wear our uniforms in public. He said the Vietnam War was not a popular war, and there were protesters at most large airports protesting the war and harassing traveling GIs. He told us to find some civilian clothes as soon as we could and to wear those instead of the uniforms.

We were then bused to a mess hall. We got in the food line. Bob Kampa and I were together. We picked up a tray with a number tent on it. We had our choice of any food item we wanted. There was a huge glass-enclosed cooler that displayed many different cuts of steak. We could pick out any steak in the stock and it would be cooked to our specification. We had a choice of potato and vegetable. There was a huge salad bar. We took our salads and found a table. There were about six milk dispensers with GIs lined up at them. Everyone had two glasses. I filled my two glasses and went to the end of a line as I drank them. I went through the line again and filled them once more and went back to my table. This was the first real milk I had had in a year. When your steak was done, your number was called and you had to pick it up. We didn't have dim lights or soft music, but we had excellent food.

By the time we were finished eating, our military clothes had been hemmed. The clothes were brought to our assigned barracks. The sky to the east was beginning to show the early morning light. Kampa and I decided to forgo sleep and figure out the flight times for planes going to Los Angeles and to San Diego. Kampa was from San Diego. I was flying to Los Angeles to meet my oldest brother Jim. We had to take the same flight out of Seattle. It stopped in Portland, then Los Angeles, and ended the flight run in San Diego. I had my brother's phone number. He knew I was coming but did not know the exact date or time. It was nearly 6 a.m. I called him and told him the flight times but I didn't have a flight number yet. He said he didn't need it; he would find it out when he reached the airport.

By military standards, you have to travel in Class A uniforms, which were the dress greens. We changed into our dress greens and caught a bus to the Seattle-Tacoma airport. I had a lot of luggage to drag along. By the time we had our tickets and the luggage checked in, it was close to boarding time. The plane was a four-prop milk-run type. We would be landing in Portland for 40 minutes before going to Los Angeles. We stayed on the plane in Portland.

The plane landed in Los Angeles at around 10 a.m. Kampa stayed on the plane. We said our goodbyes and that we would keep in touch. We never did. My brother was waiting for me. As we walked through the terminal toward the baggage claim area, we passed a group of about 25 war protesters. They yelled some protest garbage as I walked by. I didn't look at them or act as if I even heard them. Jim said as soon as we get back to his place, he would fit me into his clothes and we would go out and he would buy new clothes for me. He said the Los Angeles area had protesters all over the place.

Jim lived in Downy, a suburb of Los Angeles. He found clothes that I could squeeze into. He was shorter than I and had a smaller waist. We headed to a mall, and whatever I bought I wore out of the store. He took me back to his place and then he went to work. I told him that I hadn't slept in three days so I stretched out on his couch. I managed to sleep for about four hours before waking. I got up, wandered around the apartment. I looked in the refrigerator and saw some beer. I opened a bottle and drank it. I turned on his TV. I hadn't watched TV at all in the past year. The TV didn't interest me, so I turned it off. I eventually lay down again and fell back to sleep. As soon as Jim came home I woke up. A short while later his girlfriend Janet came home. (Janet is now his wife.) After introductions, she changed into more homey clothes and made supper. We had a quiet evening in the apartment. Jim and Janet asked a lot of questions about Vietnam, and I asked questions about their life.

Jim took off work the next day and we were to see some of the sights in the Los Angeles area. After breakfast, the first thing we did was to get an airline ticket to Minneapolis-St. Paul International Airport. The only ones available for a direct flight were in First Class. Then we went to Sea World, took a tour of Ocean Drive, stopped at a place called Lil Abner's (a topless drinking establishment), and then to a steakhouse for dinner before going back to his apartment. I called Eileen, my girlfriend, and my brother Lee in Minneapolis to pick me up at the airport. He said he would pick up Eileen and bring her along.

My flight took off at around 9 a.m. There were still war protesters at the airport, but there were no comments directed at me as I walked past. I sat in First Class on a Boeing 727. There were four gentlemen who came on together and knew each other. One of them noticed my hair was rather short and asked if I was in the service. A year ago, long hair was becoming prevalent; now, everyone younger than 30 seemed to have long hair. I guess my short hair stood out. I told them I just got back from 'Nam and was headed home. From then on, I was their guest on the flight. In First Class, there was no limit to how much alcohol they let you consume. I had four glasses of scotch and water. The first drink tasted awful, but the fourth tasted great. They asked many questions about Vietnam. I only talked in general terms about the war, and wouldn't answer any question I thought was too involved or personal. They respected my not wanting to talk about some things. They were very interested in the first-hand knowledge I could give them, and it seemed to shorten the flight time.

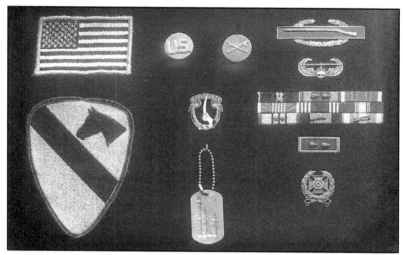

After his time in Vietnam, Bob had earned these ribbons, patches, crests, and badges which he wore on his dress green uniform: First Cavalry Division patch, U.S. Army crest and Cavalry crest, Horseshoe with sword (7th Cavalry crest), dog tag (always worn while in combat), Combat Infantry badge (upper right), AirMobile badge (only the 1st Cav and helicopter pilots and door gunners wear it), Presidential Unit citation (the 1st Cav is the only unit to earn this in Vietnam), and Expert Infantry badge (issued for excellent rifle marksmanship). The ribbons coincide with the medals below, in the same order.

Medals earned by Bob while in Vietnam, from left: Bronze Star with V-Device (issued for valor under fire), Air Medal (issued for 50 or more flights into combat situations), Purple Heart (issued for being wounded during combat), Army Accommodation Medal, Good Conduct Medal, National Defense Medal, Republic of Vietnam Service Medal, and Meritorious Service Medal of Vietnam.

GOING HOME

The plane arrived on time, probably at around 4 p.m. Central Time. When I walked off the tarmac into the terminal concourse, Eileen was there with her sister Bea and my brother Lee. They were excited, and I was cautious and aloof. I didn't realize it then, but I was in a shell, unsure and not trusting. I didn't know how I was supposed to act. I felt out of place. I know I didn't say much. Fifty years later that would seem unreal, but at the time I was a clam.

This was a Thursday. Lee and Eileen had to work on Friday. Bea and Lee had double-dated with Eileen and me; of all things, we had gone to an outdoor movie. We made a fairly short night of it this time, and I slept on the couch in Lee's apartment. Friday afternoon we all went back to the Kimball area and dropped Eileen and her sister off at their farm home. Lee and I headed for our farm home eight miles from Kimball. There was a welcome party of family members waiting for me. My oldest sister Joan was married and her husband, daughter, and son were also there. In our family, it seems everyone talks and no one listens. After the hellos, there were hundreds of questions shot at me. After answering a few, I clammed up. My younger sister asked, "What's it like to kill someone?" I turned around and walked out of the house. The family farm home sat 150 yards from the shore of Pearl Lake. I walked down to the lake and strolled along the shore. I was thinking to myself, this was going to take some getting used to. I didn't know what was going on inside of me but I couldn't take all this attention.

I don't know how long I was gone, but it was beginning to get dark when I came back. Everyone was quieter when I came back. They seemed to understand that I wasn't going to answer their questions at this time.

The night wound down. Those who needed to leave left. Mom saw to it that I had the same bed as when I left home. I crawled into bed and lay there for more than an hour. Once I was sure everyone was asleep, I got up, got dressed, and went outside. I walked behind the house and sat up against a large elm tree on the lawn. I sat there for a long time before I dozed off. I slept two hours. After waking, I took a walk down to the lake again and listened to the lapping of the water in the dark. It was a pleasant sound. I had never noticed it before. I could hear a faint rustling of the tree leaves as a gentle breeze moved them. I had never noticed this before either. In the days that followed, there were many little things like this that I had never noticed before. Being gone and nearly dying brought senses to me that I had always taken for granted. It was like a whole new world opened up for me. Even now, years later, sounds and sights still stir my senses.

In the following days, I slipped the F-word out in my conversations more than I cared to. One morning, Mom was washing clothes, and I was sitting on the basement steps talking with her. I forgot myself and used the F-word in something I was telling her. I got up and left, inwardly chewing myself out. I'm sure she understood, but this was something I had never done and would never do under any circumstances before.

While I was on leave, I had a difficult time adjusting to this home life. Almost every night I waited for the rest of the family to fall asleep, and then I would get up and take a walk in the night. When I felt a need to sleep, I picked the large elm tree and sat up against it. The base of the tree protruded out in two spots and formed a flat area that I could lean against. It was very comfortable for me. Every morning, I would quietly sneak back into the house and go to my bed and be there when the wake-up call came.

Home lifestyle was too laid-back and mundane. I became bored easily. If I could have admitted it, I was actually missing Vietnam. I was missing the friends I had made there, but I was also missing the sounds of artillery, helicopters, and planes. It was too quiet here.

I had 26 days of leave time coming before I had to be back to Fort Carson, Colorado. I dated my girlfriend often. She had met someone else prior to my coming home. After my coming home, he still wanted to see her. Eileen seemed to be torn between the two of us for a short while, but eventually told him it was over. I visited with many other old friends and spent some time in our local tavern where I was weaned on beer. The barkeep was with the Engineers during World War II. As the E-8 on the plane told me, the barkeep filled me in on how tough they had it in World War II. I never brought up Vietnam, but everyone who knew me wanted to talk about it.

BACK TO FORT CARSON

My leave time ended, and I had to go back to Fort Carson for the final 84 days I had left in the service. I was actually looking forward to going. I flew from Minneapolis to Denver and hooked a ride to Fort Carson. Luck had it that I came across a GI in flight who had a car in Denver. He was headed back to Fort Carson and he gave me a ride up to the door of where I had to report. It was late in the day on Friday. I was instructed to find an empty cot in an old wooden barracks and told where the chow hall was located. It was midnight when I crawled onto the cot to sleep. The next morning, a young GI shook me awake and said that I had KP. I was sleepy but came alert very quickly. I asked him since when do Sergeants pull KP duty? He apologized and found someone else to pull KP.

On Monday morning, I was placed with the 3rd Bn 10th Infantry which was located two blocks from the placement unit. I threw my duffel bag over my shoulders and walked to the unit. I had 81 days left in the service. I was placed in a platoon in the weapons squad. I thought, "Oh shit! I'm going to have to carry a machine gun." I made the statement that I wasn't about to carry a machine gun. I made it more to myself than anyone else. An E-5 Sergeant overheard me and said you're going to carry whatever you're told to carry. I told him, "F--- off. It's not necessary to throw your weight around." This set him back a little. By now, he realized I wasn't new to the Army. I never had a chance to get my rank sewed on my uniform so, to him, I was probably just an E-2.

The Platoon Sergeant came in and introduced himself to me. He said the weapons squad leader was going on an extended leave. He said, "You're assigned temporary squad leader." This I could handle. I soon found out this battalion was just put together to fill out the 3rd battalion for a brigade. Fort Carson was comprised of the 5th Division Mechanized. The whole Division was preparing for a move to Vietnam. I would be out of the Army before they deployed overseas, but I was going to have to go through some intensive training with them. As it turned out, they did not train near as much or near as intensely as the 5th Bn 7th Cav did before that battalion went to Vietnam.

John Leither was in this same platoon. He came in the service the same day and rode the same bus from St. Cloud to Minneapolis as I did. He was from Albany, Minnesota. He stayed in Fort Leonard Wood when I went to Fort Carson. He ended up with the 25th Division in Vietnam. He had a 1955 Chevy, so we had a car to get around. We got out of the service together and we came back to Minnesota in it.

The 7th Cav was known as the Garry Owen Brigade. This dates back to the days of the 7th Cav back in Custer's time with the Sioux Indians. As a 7th Cav trooper, when you saluted an officer, you were supposed to say "Garry Owen, sir." The officer would reply, "Garry Owen, soldier." This was supposed to instill pride in you for being a 7th Cav soldier. The 3rd of the 10th Infantry Battalion Commander decided it would be a good idea to instill pride in his men. So, when an enlisted man saluted an officer, he was supposed to say, "3rd of the 10th, with pride, sir." The officer would repeat, "With pride, soldier." This did not go well with the enlisted men. This especially sounded really horse-shit with the soldiers who had come back from Vietnam.

One afternoon, I was walking around the corner of our barracks as our platoon leader came out of the orderly room. I salute him with "Good afternoon, sir." He saluted back and said, "Wait a minute, aren't you supposed to salute with '3rd of the 10th?'" I asked, "Do I have to?" He said, "Yeah, do it right." I saluted again, and said, "3rd of the 10th with pride, sir, and all the other happy horse-shit." He laughed and saluted me again. He said he didn't like it any better than I did but we had to play the game.

Shortly after I arrived, I went back to the 4th of the 12th Cav, about a mile from where the 3rd of the 10th was located. Most of the old guys were there. They said that all they did the past year was train soldiers in Basic Training. As soon as one group left, another group would arrive and they would start all over again. They were more interested in what I had done for the past year. I filled them in on what I wanted them to hear. I didn't talk about everything. Most of the memories I gave them were the good parts. I didn't get into the down times. I guess I built a shield in my mind to protect it. It was good to talk to these guys, and I made the trip to the 12th Cav many times.

Lonnie Edwards had served with the 1st of the 7th Cav at the same time I was with the 5th of the 7th Cav. When we first met, he asked me which Cav unit I was with. When I told him, he said, "You guys were some crazy bastards." I told him I didn't think we were. He said, "The hell you weren't. You ask any other soldier in the Division and they will say the same thing." He added, "You guys liked that war too damned much." I'm not sure how he came to this conclusion, and he didn't specify, but I had heard the same thing before. I suppose if someone does one crazy thing, and the right people hear about it, it might make the whole battalion sound like it's crazy.

The next 80 days slipped by rather quickly. I had the other two wisdom teeth pulled while at Fort Carson. This time the dentist left me with my jawbone. The pain lasted a day or so and I was okay. I played a lot of nickel/dime/quarter poker. I did fairly well at this game, winning most of the time. I never worried about losing, so winning came easy. One particular night while playing poker, I pretty much cleaned just about everyone out of their money. A few wanted to borrow money from me to play against me. I told them I don't play against my own money. One of them told me I wasn't going to make or keep my friends the way I played poker. I told him, "I play to win or I wouldn't play at all." I also told him, "If a friend gets mad because I beat him in poker, then I guess I didn't have a friend in the first place." I also said, "I have two weeks left in the service. Once I'm gone, I'm sure I won't be seeing any of you people any time soon." I also told him, "This Division is headed to Vietnam. Whether you know it or not, some of you are not coming home alive."

A CIVILIAN

The last day came and we were heading home. Back in Basic Training, my first paycheck was screwed up. Like the paymaster said at that time, there wasn't enough time during my military career to straighten it out. My last paycheck was also screwed up. We could have left the base at 0900 hours but, instead, I had to wait until 1300 hours to go to headquarters to get my final military payment. This set our run for home back a little more than four hours.

On the way home, we had three ex-GIs splitting the gas expenses: John Leither who owned the car, Doug Kultzer who was with the 4/12 Cav and was from the Grey Eagle/Swanville area, and me. We drove all the way through, stopping only for gas, an occasional quart of oil, and food. I was dropped off in Minneapolis, on Laurel Avenue at Eileen's apartment, at about 4 p.m. the day following our departure.

Once out of the service, I had no idea where my life would take me. I wasn't sure what I wanted to do. I decided to go to college at St. Cloud State University. I would take General Ed classes until I had a career goal I could focus on. I had the month of December to adjust to civilian life again. I got together with old friends, drank some beer with them, saw a lot of Eileen when we could get together. She worked for General Mills in Golden Valley and lived in Minneapolis during the week. She came home most weekends. Things weren't the same for me. Everything else was like it was when I left, but I had changed so much, I didn't seem to fit in like I did before. I felt like the proverbial square peg in a round hole.

Everyone was planning and getting ready for Christmas. I was hoping to get it behind me. I could not get excited about the Christmas season. The year before, my Christmas was in a hospital in Japan. There was more sadness and bitterness during that Christmas season than I could ever forget. Christmas was a downer for me. To this day, some 50 years later, Christmas is still a down time of year for me. I dislike Christmas music, and despise Elvis Presley's "Blue, Blue Christmas." As the Christmas season gets closer, the more depressed I feel. Usually, by the end of January, I begin to recover from the Holidays. I have become a Christmas Holiday Scrooge.

January 8, 1968, was the first day of classes for me. It was strange being back in school. It was almost eight years since I had graduated from high school. I felt like an old man in with the kids. I dug into my classes. I knew that, if I were to have any success in school, I would have to make a habit of hard study. My classes, in order, were History, Geography, Psychology I, and Art. They were all morning classes. The Art class met two days a week, and each of the other classes met four days a week. I had staggered time off between classes. Usually, when a class didn't meet I would go to Atwood Center, grab a cup of coffee, and study. I soon developed some friends who, like me, were fresh out of the service and trying to find their place in life. As time went on, more vets found our group. Within three weeks, there were eight of us, all veterans meeting in the Atwood Center.

St. Cloud State is a very liberal college. In 1968, protesting the Vietnam War was a campus extra-curricular activity. About three weeks after I began college, four individuals approached me in the hallway just outside my History class. They had all the information I had to give the college to get GI funding for going to school. They said they were organizing a protest of the war and wanted me to join them. They felt that if they could get a few vets in the protest group, it would stand better with them and their cause. I told them I was not interested. I also told them that I still had friends in Vietnam and I was not about to become part of a protest movement that may make life worse for them. This group had a hard time taking no for an answer. As I walked away from them, they began calling me names including a woman- and baby-killer. I doubt they knew it, but how close they were they would never know.

The next day, when I left my History class, two students walked up behind me in the hall and began the name-calling again. I ignored them and walked to my next class, which was Geography. This class was held in an auditorium. I always tried to find a seat on the aisle. I didn't like to be squeezed in. When I sat down, a couple of students sat behind me and began the name-calling in whispers, but so I could hear them. I ignored them for the entire hour, hoping they would give it up. The next time my History class met, I again got the name-calling treatment when I left the classroom. Heading to my Geography class, instead of sitting in an aisle seat, I found one in the middle of a group of other students so my personal fan club could not get close to me. This harassing name-calling went on for most of the school quarter, but the frequency diminished after a couple of weeks.

Immediately after my initial encounter with the protesters, I met with a few of the other vets and told them about it. At this time, none of the others had been approached as yet. This soon changed. Within the next week, eight of us were approached. There was one vet in our group who had retired from the Navy. He retired a Captain, which is the equivalent of a full Colonel in the Army. He was the only person not approached. We discussed it and he suggested we start a vets club as a support group to mentally combat this harassment. He also suggested that we keep it informal, so it doesn't draw too much attention. We worked it out and came up with one day a week in which most of us could get together for a meeting. Meanwhile, we would still get together even more informally throughout the week. Sometime later, this group formally became the St. Cloud State Vets Club.

Even though our group was informal, we still attracted a fan club of protesters. They initially occupied the tables we usually took when we got together. We found other spots to meet. The protesters always searched us out and, as time went on, they gained more numbers and momentum. There was a side room that was used for larger gatherings. Our retired Navy Captain pulled some strings and arranged for us to meet in the side room on our specified meeting day. One day, a group of about 15 tried to block our entry into the room. Because of a fire code, there was a back door to the room; we used that.

Toward the end of the quarter, I had to decide if I wanted to stay in school. I was doing okay with the studying, and I was surprised how well I did in mid-term tests. My heart wasn't in college though. Before I went into the service, I was a drywaller by trade. That is, I hung sheetrock, I taped sheetrock, I sanded sheetrock, I painted and texture-sprayed sheetrock, and I cussed sheetrock. By chance, I met a contractor for whom I had done work in pre-service time. He said he had a couple of houses ready for taping and wanted to know if I was interested. The student GI money didn't reach far enough, so I said why not.

I taped the two houses but found out I could not handle the working over my head very well. At first, I thought I was out of shape so I put extra effort into getting back into shape.

Eventually, I realized the gunshot injury to my upper back and shoulders was giving me the problems. Instead of getting in shape, my shoulders and back ached more, and I eventually tore a muscle in my right shoulder. I finished the two houses, but it took much too long a time to do so. I knew I had to give up this line of work.

I finished the school quarter and did not sign up for the following quarter. I got an A in Psychology, a B in History and Geography, and an incomplete in Art. I apparently missed one project I was supposed to turn in. I missed this class a few times because I was working on the two houses.

Life never was the same for me as it was before I went in the service. I didn't seem to have a purpose. I went to work for Jim Theisen Construction, but physically I could not handle the work. After some extremely strenuous days, I would get so sore that I had a hard time sleeping. I knew I had to find something else, but I didn't know what it would be. I tried going to the St. Cloud Technical College for an electronics trade, but my math was not up to par. I had serious thoughts of going back into the service.

Two years passed by, and I still felt as if I was playing a ball game in a different field than the rest of the team. I didn't fit in. I socialized with my old friends, but I felt out of place. What was important to them seemed extremely trivial to me. When someone talked about a problem, inwardly I would think, they don't know what a problem is. Before the service, I was always happy-go-lucky in attitude. Now, I was reserved and distant. I kept most things inside me. Eileen once told me that I really changed after coming out of the service. There were times when I just wanted to pack some necessities in a bag, grab a rifle, ammunition and fishing gear, and take off to live off nature. I became overwhelmed by this thought. I knew that, if I did it, I would be checking out of normal life forever.

I loved Eileen, and this was the only reason I never took this route in life.

Bob and Eileen Kunkel have been married 49 years as of July 2018. They raised four children, and enjoy four grandchildren as well.

❦ MARRIAGE AND A CAREER MADE FOR ME

Eileen and I were married in July 1969. Three months later Eileen, became pregnant. I still worked for Jim Theisen. Winter was coming on and there was not enough work to keep us busy. I was going to get laid off over the winter months. This scared me and I began looking for other work. The want ads of the *St. Cloud Times* was advertising for a Jailer/Dispatcher. I could pick up an application at the Stearns County Sheriff's Department. I answered the ad and was hired to begin work March 1, 1970.

Working with the Sheriff's Department for about six months, I knew law enforcement would be the career for me. I eventually went to patrol, became a patrol supervising Sergeant, then, in January 1977, a Captain. I remained a Captain for the rest of my career, but the career had many changes in that position. I retired as the Jail Administrator at the end of February 1999, 29 years later, what I consider to be a full career.

Before I retired, I was offered a job as Licensed Officer for security around the four-building campus of the government area. It was part-time and it paid half my insurance. I worked at this for three years. During this time, without the pressures of my former job as the Jail Administrator, I began having problems with what eventually turned out to be PTSD, Post-Traumatic Stress Disorder. After a strong urging from the County's Veterans Service Officer, I went to the St. Cloud Veterans Administration for an interview with a veteran counselor. After the interview and a written test, I was told that I would be set up to talk with a psychiatrist. After the interview with him, I was told that I was a classic example of what constituted PTSD. A short while later, I was set up with a counselor for weekly sessions.

Bob Kunkel worked for the Stearns County Sheriff's Office for 32 years before fully retiring.

Law Enforcement was tailored for me. In Vietnam, I became used to and relished the uncertainty of situations, plans, and priorities. In Vietnam, there was an uncertainty of life itself. While it scared the hell out of me, it also took me to the edge, and I felt good afterward. Law enforcement was not nearly the edge-dwelling that Vietnam was, but there was an uncertainty of the job and a frequent change of priorities from day to day and even from hour to hour. While most people like to plan their day and follow a routine, I am at my best with frequent newly developing situations and problems.

Eileen and I have four wonderful children, three boys Todd, Troy and Travis, and a girl, Tennelle. They are all unique and different. We are very proud of them. When things got a little rough between Eileen and me, the children were the bond that kept us together and focused.

After retirement, writing this book became a new challenge for me. This is something that I could never have envisioned 50 years ago; however, I certainly wish I had made an after-the-fact diary shortly after getting out of the service. It certainly would have helped for recollection of names, events, and details.

This memoir represents one story of one person who went through a personal hell in Vietnam. Even in this hell, there are many fond memories that I keep, especially of the soldiers I served under and with. There are thousands of stories like mine, but each is very different because of perception and what was in the mind at the time of an encounter, whatever that encounter may have been.

If an old vet begins to tell you a story of a part of his life some day, listen to him. He may be getting something off his chest that had been hidden inside too long.

The Kunkel family at daughter Tennelle's wedding: (from left) Eileen, Travis, Tennelle, Troy, Todd, and Bob.

I'm not sure what, if any, benefit will come of this personal history, but it's a done deal now. I hope my children and their children will keep it as a memory of their father and grandfather.

GLOSSARY:

ARVN – Army of the Republic of Viet Nam soldier or unit

Battalion – Infantry tactical maneuvering unit consisting of about 750 men

Battery – Tactical artillery unit with an infantry company

Birds – Helicopters

C-4 – Powerful plastic explosive carried in one-pound blocks; the explosive charge in a Claymore mine

Charlie – Viet Cong or enemy soldier

CIB – Combat Infantry Badge

Claymore – Claymore Antipersonnel Mine; directional pellet explosive used in stationary positions, it uses a one-pound block of C-4 and 600 small steel balls and is detonated by a blasting cap fired from a distance by a hand-held electrical device

CO – Commanding Officer

Como wire – Two-strand coated wire used for land communication

Company – Primary maneuver unit of a battalion, comprised of about 175 men at full force; commanded by a captain with an Executive Officer second in command and a 1st Sergeant as senior NCO

CP – Command Post

Dinky Dau – Mentally retarded Vietnamese

Deuce & a Half – Two-and-one-half-ton truck

Gunship – HU-1B helicopter heavily armed for close-fire support

H & I – Harassing and interdicting fire, a preplanned concentration of random fire against suspected enemy targets, or at random in free-fire zones to harass the enemy and deny him free movement

Hamlet – Small group of Vietnamese families living in one location

Ho Chi Minh sandals – Footwear made from rubber tires and tied to feet

Hooch – A single-family dwelling

HQ – Headquarters

JP-4 – High-test fuel used for all vehicles in Vietnam

Kau-Ke-Dau – Vietnamese term to kill

Klick – Slang for 1000 meters, 1 kilometer

LP – Listening post

LST – Land-to-Sea Transport Vehicle

LZ – Landing Zone for helicopters

Medevac – Evacuation of wounded by helicopter

Montagnard – Local tribe people not considered Vietnamese

MOS – Military Occupational Specialty

Mule – One-seat motorized cart used for light loads for a short distance

NVA – North Vietnam Army, regular army soldier, not Viet Cong or guerrilla

PC – Personnel Carrier

Piaster – Vietnamese money

Platoon – About 47 men at full force, divided into four squads and commanded by a Lieutenant with a Sergeant First Class second in command and senior NCO

Point, Point Man – Lead man or lead unit in an infantry movement

PRC 25 – Radio for military communication

Pogue – Soldier who is a sluff-off

Punji Stake – Bamboo stake sharpened and dipped in feces to cause injury and infection to feet and legs

Rucksack – A canvas pack to carry miscellaneous items

Shrapnel – Metal chunks used as lethal or injurious materials in war

Scrip – Military money used in place of greenbacks (American money)

Squad – Eleven-man tactical unit of a platoon

XO – Executive Officer, second in command of a company, battalion, or brigade

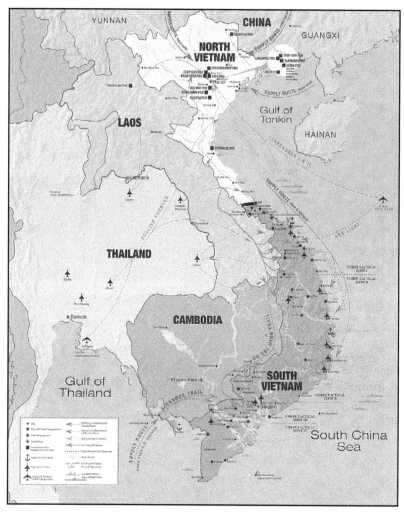

Tactical map of important operations in Southeast Asia during the
Vietnam War era. Map courtesy of Vietnam War Commemoration,
Arlington, Virginia.

Index

A

Agent Orange 91
ambush 31, 103, 104, 109, 117, 119, 135, 153, 168, 172, 190, 366

B

Bangalore torpedoes 355, 356
bayonet 83, 211, 213, 229, 230, 309, 352
beachhead landing 83, 85
boxing 76, 427, 428, 429
Bronze Star with V device 329

C

cave 141, 142, 143, 144, 145, 146, 158, 369, 370
CH-54 flying cranes 289
Chinook helicopter 120, 307, 308, 339, 386
Christmas 261, 268, 269, 270, 271, 456
church 28, 31, 63, 133, 186, 189, 190, 191, 325, 355
Claymore bag 136, 309, 310
Claymore mines 98, 99, 104, 107, 136, 153, 168, 215, 309, 310, 343, 344, 345, 352, 356, 464
cliff 44, 45, 51, 113, 117, 135, 136, 137, 138, 387
communion 180
Como wire 101, 309, 344, 345, 372, 464
concertina wire 98, 102, 107
C-Rations 49, 53, 54, 56, 98, 101, 104, 110, 122, 125, 133, 144, 152, 153, 154, 155, 183, 196, 205, 212, 214, 215, 216, 228, 304, 316, 358, 366, 387
cribbage 79, 393

D

DEET 88, 100
DEROS (Date Eligible Return from Overseas) 176, 415, 417, 433
Derringer 76, 162
Dinky Dau 122, 202, 206, 207, 209, 313, 464

E

elephant grass 107, 187, 188, 191
English soldiers 57
entrenching tool 53, 71, 189

F

flares, artillery 56, 362
flares, mortar 56

G

Garry Owen 69, 452
generator 161, 289, 308
glow-tape 50
Golden Gate Bridge 74
green bamboo viper 92
green-line duty 287, 293, 381, 394, 395, 396
grenade 38, 39, 99, 108, 113, 127, 131, 132, 136, 145, 146, 172, 173, 174, 179, 202, 234, 246, 297, 337, 343

H

hand grenade 108, 132, 145, 337
Harassment and Repel 161
helipad 116, 157, 159, 161, 162, 167, 307, 309, 311, 332, 358, 366, 383, 385
heroin 127, 246
H & I (Harassment and Interdiction) 127, 217, 218

Ho Chi Minh sandals 298, 464
homesick 162
hospital 126, 130, 237, 241, 245,
 248, 251, 252, 253, 254, 255,
 257, 258, 259, 260, 261, 269,
 270, 274, 275, 276, 277, 281,
 282, 296, 297, 305, 313, 356,
 371, 401, 429, 456
H&R 161
humping (walking) 90, 199, 233,
 291, 309, 314, 316, 400, 430

I

interpreter 124, 125, 130, 168, 203,
 210, 211, 316

J

jeep 42, 46, 90, 286, 291, 293, 340,
 341, 376, 380, 381, 395, 396,
 411, 416, 426
jungle boots 149, 179

K

KIA 146, 221, 243, 303, 334
Korean War 49, 439
KP 64, 451

L

LAW (Light Anti-tank Weapon)
 171
leech 121, 189, 190
life jackets 74, 75

Locations:
 7th Field Hospital 254, 257
 8th Engineers' EM Club 115, 294,
  338, 375
 An Khê 18, 85, 87, 90, 92, 94, 97,
  106, 289, 290, 292, 310, 312,
  327, 380, 426, 427
 An Khê River 87, 90, 289
 An Khê, new 92, 292
 An Khê, old 92, 290, 292
 An Lão River 311

An Lão Valley 18, 309, 311, 322,
 329, 337, 339, 368, 377, 386
Australia 375, 376
Binh Dinh Province 18
Bong Son 18, 308, 311, 340, 371
Cambodia 17
Cambodian border 97, 366
Camp Holloway 106
Camp Radcliff 85, 87, 90, 106,
 114, 134, 156, 286, 289, 338,
 341, 355, 368, 373, 380, 394,
 425, 426
Central Highlands 18, 311, 366
Colorado Springs 23, 58, 61, 62,
 63, 70, 73
Dak To 361, 362
Denver 46, 61, 62, 63, 451
EM Club 115, 294, 295, 338, 342,
 375, 376, 381, 383
Fort Carson 23, 25, 26, 46, 47, 63,
 73, 449, 451, 452, 454
Fort Dix 213
Fort Leonard Wood 19, 20, 21,
 452
Fujisawa 254, 255, 277, 283
Hanoi 88, 89, 164
Happy Valley 221
Hawaiian Islands 80
Ho Chi Minh City 17
Japan 247, 248, 254, 273, 274, 276,
 277, 278, 279, 285, 373, 393,
 396, 439, 440, 456
Johnson Air Force Base 254, 272,
 273, 281
Kansas 25
Laos 17, 423
LZ English 307, 308, 309, 327,
 330, 337, 338, 339, 340, 342,
 343, 344, 349, 351, 353, 355,
 363, 369, 370, 371, 373, 377,
 379, 380, 383, 389, 393, 394
LZ Hammond 156, 305
Mang Yang Pass 97, 106
Mekong Delta 259, 429
Minneapolis 19, 22, 37, 444, 451,

452, 455
Missouri 19, 21, 38
North Central Coastline 18
North Central Highlands 18, 311
Oakland 73, 74, 224
Okinawa 80, 81
Pacific Ocean 79, 82, 274
Philippines 252, 254, 412, 413,
    418, 419, 420
Pleiku 18, 97, 106
Pueblo 70
Qui Nho'n 18, 82, 97, 106, 116,
    237, 241, 248, 270, 289
Qui Nho'n Bay 82, 106, 289
Saigon 17, 283, 396
San Francisco Bay 74
South China Sea 17, 18, 80, 81,
    116, 274, 422
St. Cloud 22, 341, 452, 455, 456,
    458, 459, 461, 462
St. Paul 20, 444
Tachikawa 255
Taiwan 77, 126, 222
Taipei, Taiwan 77, 222
Tan Son Nhut 283
Tokyo 255, 272, 279
Watkins 19
Yokota 254, 273

LRRPs (Long Range Recocnnais-
    sance Patrols) 218
LST 83, 85, 464

M

M1 Garand rifle 211, 214
M16 124, 136, 183, 199, 206, 222,
    286, 310, 332, 352
M40 rockets 131
M60 43, 124, 318, 332, 390
M60 machine gun 43
M79 grenade launcher 131, 132,
    173, 297, 330
machete 181, 209, 210, 213, 314
M.A.S.H. 237, 245
Mass 31, 179, 180, 355

medic 108, 157, 166, 171, 203, 207,
    247, 253, 278, 294, 318, 325,
    327, 350
Memorial Day 61, 64
Mexican bar 59, 60
Military Police 37, 41
missile 49, 50
monkey 101, 102, 357, 358, 381
Montagnard 109, 110, 221, 464
morphine 171, 235, 236, 237, 241,
    266, 267
mortar attack 87, 89, 90
mortars 89, 120, 286, 344, 361, 362,
    368, 386, 387, 388, 390, 391,
    392, 393
MOS 41, 292, 301, 400
mosquito 17, 87, 88, 100, 161, 165
mosquito nets 87, 161, 165
mosquito repellent 88
motor pool 41, 42, 43, 45, 52
MPs 31, 37, 46, 73, 295, 374, 402,
    412, 418
mule 159, 163, 164, 165, 332, 358,
    359, 361, 366
muzzle flashes 56

N

NCO Club 80, 272, 273, 274, 276,
    277, 282, 283
New Year 29, 274, 275, 276, 321,
    382
non-issue weapons 77
Novocaine 281, 282
nurse 125, 241, 242, 243, 244, 245,
    247, 248, 252, 254, 257, 258,
    266, 267, 268, 269, 282, 330,
    331, 429
NVA (North Vietnamese Army)
    185, 190, 191, 195, 210, 224,
    225, 246, 311, 365, 464

O

Operation Irving 18, 116, 147, 149, 164
Operation Pershing 18
Operation Thayer 18, 149, 150
orangutan 102
Ordination 379

P

patrol 50, 51, 55, 90, 103, 104, 111, 117, 136, 153, 154, 155, 162, 168, 218, 221, 290, 296, 302, 303, 312, 313, 363, 390, 405, 461
PCs 52, 53, 56, 58
penicillin 244, 245, 248, 254, 257
people
  Blake 61
  Hare 73, 80, 81, 126, 127, 296
  Nowacs 64

People:
  Aby, Rich 150
  Albanese, John 290
  Albanese, Lewis 261, 290
  Aragon, Luis 108, 126, 190, 203, 207, 235, 331, 350
  Ascher, Allen 94, 234, 235, 323, 324, 325, 330
  Baldwin, Sgt. Clarence 296, 304, 316, 317, 339
  Beaupre 310, 333, 334, 335, 337, 344, 345, 346, 393
  Benedetti, Dennis iii, 124, 131, 141, 144, 184, 186, 261, 434
  Bentz, Danny 100, 131, 132
  Bob Mobley 19, 20
  Bronson, Lt. 351, 366, 390
  Brown, Dr. (psych. at VAMC) 14
  Brugstad, Brad 259, 277, 278, 279, 280, 281, 282, 283
  Bullock, Major 338, 339, 344, 345
  Burton, Johnny 334
  Callister 361

Carmichael, Stokley 46, 47
Carter, Sgt. 223, 390
Cartwright, Hoss 29, 30
Carver, Billy 367
Childs, Frank 365, 367
Clark, Roger 41, 44, 49, 50, 51, 53, 54, 55, 56, 58, 61, 62, 63, 64, 65
Clems, Roger 41
Cooper, Sgt. Frank 218, 227, 229, 230, 235, 236, 237, 241
Crockett, Sgt. Delmar 141, 143, 144, 193, 291, 334, 335, 434
Dalton 361
Dobbins 29, 31
Doc 108, 109, 126, 134, 156, 157, 171, 188, 190, 191, 207, 235, 236, 248, 249, 315, 318, 325, 326, 327, 331, 332, 350
Dowling 33
Duggins, Sgt. "Bull" 34, 38
Eileen 267, 268, 444, 447, 449, 455, 459, 460, 461, 462
Elvis Presley 261, 456
Feldkamp 77, 78, 263, 264
Fitzpatrick 61
Franchez 67
Frank, Lt 104, 128, 131, 137, 138, 141, 144, 147, 150, 152, 153, 155, 156, 168, 169, 171, 177, 178, 179, 183, 184, 186, 187, 191, 194, 197, 198, 199, 203, 205, 206, 207, 209, 222, 223, 224, 225, 226, 227, 228, 229, 230, 292
Gaffey, Hugh J. 73, 74, 80
Geyer, J. 367
Gibson, Capt. 351, 352, 353, 365, 366, 367
Glowiak, Frank 221
Gonazles, Joe 262
Gonzales, Joe 262, 361
Gould, William 334
Grady, Capt. 194, 210

Gray, Tom iii, 79, 101, 102, 142, 144, 145, 146, 172, 183, 212, 213, 214, 215, 261, 311, 318, 326, 334, 335, 434

Greek 179, 352, 353

Guist, Leonard 29, 32, 33

Hanahan, Colonel 303, 325, 328, 333

Hanoi Hannah 88, 89

Hare, 1st Sgt. Dayton 73, 80, 81, 126, 127, 296

Harrin, Sgt. 399, 401, 403, 405, 408, 419, 429

Hawkins 76

Heaps, Charles 366, 367, 434

Hennesey, Tom 260, 277, 278, 279, 280, 283

Heronema 77, 132, 184

Higgins 30

Hitti, Capt. John iii, 73, 78, 92, 104, 124, 126, 134, 137, 144, 150, 174, 175, 179, 181, 182, 183, 185, 186, 187, 188, 189, 190, 191, 193, 194, 195, 205, 209, 210, 212, 215, 216, 218, 235, 236, 262, 263, 297, 298, 299, 301, 302, 303, 305, 316, 317, 318, 323, 325, 326, 327, 331, 332, 338, 339, 349, 350, 351, 380, 381, 383

Ho Chi Minh 164, 464

Holcomb 361

Hutnam 290, 301, 302, 303

Inez, Sgt. 74, 77, 78, 98, 102, 103, 137, 141, 150, 155, 203, 207, 209, 223, 264, 311, 335, 359

Jettis, Tom 80, 81

Jones, J.T. 65

Jones, Tracy 325, 326, 434

Judy, Ray iii, 79, 94, 100, 101, 102, 124, 126, 152, 153, 154, 168, 183, 193, 194, 199, 209, 210, 211, 212, 213, 214, 215, 217, 218, 222, 261, 262, 263, 290, 295, 296, 297, 298, 299, 302, 303, 323, 326, 328, 334, 366, 371, 390, 391, 426

Kampa 77, 113, 332, 333, 334, 337, 349, 358, 359, 361, 366, 400, 407, 414, 415, 416, 417, 423, 442, 443

Kloemken, Ray 100, 124, 141, 142, 144, 145, 146, 184, 187, 198, 199, 294, 295, 297, 312, 313, 317, 321, 334, 371, 390, 391, 426, 427

Kuhler (medic) 278

Kultzer 58, 59

Kunkel 25, 27, 158, 223, 379, 395

Kunkel, Fr. Charles 379

Laner 33, 34

Lilly 29

Love, Charles 221

Lunde, Jeff 36

Manning, Tom 97, 98, 102, 104, 105, 106, 107, 113, 116, 131, 132, 176, 177, 178, 183, 184, 185, 198

Maroun, Major General Delton 48

Matera 102, 103

Mathews, Fay 79

Mathies, Tom 19, 26, 28, 29, 30, 31, 32, 35, 36

McCarthy, Sen. Eugene 379, 380

McGee, Terry, Stearns County Veterans Service Officer 14

Mears (supply clerk) 373, 374, 377, 426, 427

Merten, Lt. 244, 245, 307

Milbur, Sgt. 94, 342, 375, 376, 380, 381, 383, 394

Miles, Sgt. 104, 111

Miller, Larry 273, 333, 334, 335, 337, 340, 342, 343, 344, 345, 393

Mitzner 158, 159, 160, 161, 162, 163

Mobley, Bob 19, 20, 21

Moore, Colonel Harold 329, 330

Moore, Sgt. 89, 90

Murgatroyd 77, 131, 173, 174

Nehr, Sgt. Jeffery 117, 119, 135, 136, 137, 138, 141, 142, 143, 144, 145, 146, 149, 156, 167, 168, 179, 184, 186, 188, 189, 191, 193, 194, 206, 210, 211, 214, 218, 311, 352

Nguyen, Sgt. (interpreter) 124, 125, 190, 210, 211, 316, 331

Nuss, Sgt. 309, 329, 332, 333, 334, 341, 349, 353, 361, 373, 374, 377, 380, 383, 389, 393, 394

Oblad 115, 371, 377, 383, 385, 387, 388, 389, 390, 393, 394, 395, 396, 400, 405, 406, 407, 408, 410, 411, 414, 415, 416, 417, 423, 428, 429

Olexy, Terry 81, 329, 342, 343, 352

Olin, Ray 94, 328

Pabone 223

Patino, Sgt. Pablo 103, 104, 334, 434

Patrick, Lt. 333

Petters, Spec-4 John 127, 128, 374, 395, 430

Peyton, Sgt. 26, 27, 32, 329, 330

Phillson, Robert 88, 89

Pollack 221

Powell 155, 358, 359

Rainer 38, 39

Red Dog (medic) 294, 295

Register, Dorsie 367

Reiser 171

Rock, Sgt. 318

Salvi, Rodney 286, 287, 338, 373, 380, 383, 394

Samaripa, Jesse "Sam" 223, 225, 227, 228, 229, 230, 233, 234, 235, 236, 237, 241, 242, 243, 434

Sandoval, Vincente 76, 367, 368, 434

Schmitt, Jerry "Smitty" 313, 334

Schreimf 356

Schuck, Bob 223, 224

Shaffer, Charles 334

Silsby, Sgt. 76, 91

Slick 76, 77, 91, 92

Sommers 199, 361, 363

Stangley, Colonel Marten 48

Stawicky 66, 67

Stearns, Lloyd 367

Sutton, Larry 25

Sweat, Col. Trevor 70, 73, 95

Theisen, Delroy 341

Theisen, Jerry 341, 376

Theisen, Jim 341

Underwood, James 244, 245, 247, 269, 270, 272, 274, 275, 277, 279, 280, 281, 283, 285, 286, 287, 289

Velasques, Juan 196

Walker, Charlie (and his band) 270, 271

Walters 186, 202, 361, 363

Ward, John 201, 202, 230, 272

Westmoreland, Gen. William 95

Wilbur, Sgt. 287

Wren, PFC John 114

Zachery 91, 92, 325

pilot 67, 92, 128, 179, 321, 322, 439, 441

pistol 73, 76, 162, 163

pogues (rear-echelon paper-shufflers) 115, 328, 332, 396

pool 31, 32, 58, 64, 280

prayer 162, 179, 221, 224, 225, 231, 243, 245, 248, 257, 334, 436

priest 179, 355

PTSD (Post-Traumatic Stress Disorder) 14, 461, 462

punji 18, 111, 399

Purple Heart 343

R

radio 64, 88, 104, 131, 137, 144, 146, 171, 177, 205, 209, 215, 218, 222, 235, 290, 297, 302, 325, 328, 332, 333
rattlesnake 51
red ants 111
Red Cross 268
rhinoceros bug 100
rifle 33, 46, 47, 57, 91, 98, 103, 114, 124, 128, 132, 136, 141, 143, 177, 187, 209, 211, 214, 231, 232, 233, 263, 264, 302, 307, 310, 314, 321, 324, 340, 345, 352, 370, 459
rifle range 33, 46
ROKs 120, 130, 135
rosary 162, 224
R & R 77, 126, 222, 373, 374, 375, 376, 377, 394, 426

S

S-1 Intelligence 66
salve 157, 158, 160, 163, 165
sand bags 89, 106, 159, 163, 164, 165, 166
scrip 93, 292, 293, 340, 465
search-and-destroy 170, 172, 182, 201, 316, 326
short-timer 176, 392
Sky Pilot (priest) 355
sleeping bag 51, 52, 55, 56, 57
snake 17, 51, 52, 91, 92
snow 17, 27, 55, 56, 274
sorghum 228, 230
spider 107
spider holes 103, 188, 189, 190
Stars and Stripes 83, 85
Stars and Stripes Forever 83
storm 81, 82

T

tank 46, 52, 57, 58, 90, 171, 289, 343, 366, 367, 439
ten-stepper snake 92
tent 49, 50, 51, 53, 54, 55, 56, 87, 88, 89, 90, 92, 94, 116, 157, 158, 159, 160, 163, 164, 166, 197, 212, 214, 215, 236, 286, 307, 309, 331, 337, 355, 381, 400, 401, 402, 414, 415, 416, 417, 418, 421, 427, 428, 430
Tet New Year 321
Time Magazine 125, 126
troop ship 73, 80
tunnel 121, 143, 144, 145, 146, 283, 314
tunnel rats 121

U

Units:
1st Air Cav 18
1st Battalion, 2nd Cav 283, 285, 286
1st Bn 7th Cav 120, 130, 131, 365, 366, 368
1st Bn 9th Cav 223
1st Bn 12th Cav 370
1st Bn 77th Armor 48
1st Cav Division 90, 115, 283, 285, 286, 365, 366, 380, 381, 436
1st of the 77th Armored Battalion 41, 46
1st platoon 29, 31, 76, 167, 171, 175, 176, 181, 182, 185, 216, 295, 321, 351, 390

2nd Battalion of the 19th Artillery 26

2nd of the 77th Armored Battalion 41

2nd platoon 18, 34, 69, 117, 127, 134, 158, 167, 171, 175, 180, 182, 185, 186, 189, 197, 201, 209, 217, 218, 221, 225, 226, 227, 230, 233, 261, 289, 294, 301, 304, 313, 321, 328, 329, 335, 352, 353, 361, 362, 365, 371, 381, 390

3rd Bn 77th Armor 48

3rd platoon 26, 31, 36, 122, 129, 130, 167, 175, 218, 221, 223, 226, 227, 229, 244, 289, 294, 307, 352, 399

3rd squad 18, 106, 117, 133, 150, 227, 290, 301, 304, 312, 361, 390

4/12 Cav 41, 48, 69, 455

4th Division 246, 270

4th of the 12th Cavalry 41

4th Troop, 12th Cav 48

4th Troop, 12th Squadron iv, 41

5th Bn 7th Cav iv, 67, 69, 75, 76, 77, 80, 83, 87, 88, 97, 120, 158, 283, 286, 287, 293, 294, 295, 303, 329, 343, 358, 365, 367, 368, 371, 400, 429, 452

7th Cav iv, 18, 67, 69, 87, 88, 97, 116, 195, 196, 283, 286, 287, 295, 329, 365, 366, 367, 368, 371, 394, 395, 400, 429, 452, 453

9th Cav 223, 225, 226

25th Armored Cav 66

25th Division 259, 452

A Company 38, 153, 195, 225, 226, 227, 228, 229, 304, 365, 370

B Company v, 18, 73, 77, 83, 97, 104, 119, 122, 164, 167, 170, 195, 221, 225, 226, 261, 262, 286, 287, 289, 294, 296, 305, 332, 333, 337, 338, 339, 349, 351, 352, 355, 356, 359, 361, 363, 365, 367, 368, 373, 374, 389, 393, 399, 407, 429

C Company 80, 160, 163, 164, 194, 330

D Company 120, 195, 369

USS Hugh J. Gaffey iv, 73, 80

V

Veterans Affairs Medical Center 15

W

wallet 260, 261

war games 47, 57, 58, 286

watch 20, 36, 37, 48, 55, 74, 81, 97, 104, 105, 113, 134, 144, 145, 152, 153, 163, 164, 182, 183, 191, 259, 277, 281, 293, 312, 317, 323, 324, 327, 345, 390, 391, 395, 404, 408, 409, 421, 422, 436

waterfall 113

wild cat 107

wisdom teeth 281, 282, 454

World War II 49, 211, 255, 439, 449

wristwatch 55

About the Author

Robert Kunkel grew up on a farm on Pearl Lake in central Minnesota. His family raised dairy cows, beef cattle, and pigs. Bob was right in the middle of 11 siblings, with five older and five younger. He had three sisters and seven brothers, one of whom was a Catholic priest.

In 1965, at age 22, Bob's draft number came up and he would be training for the infantry by the end of that year. Not long before heading to basic training Bob met Eileen Wagner, a high school cheerleader and Prom Queen, at a dance after a football game. An accidental meeting, Bob sort of rescued her from an unkempt country bumpkin who kept trying to dance with her. They dated a few times, but it wasn't something he expected to survive his two years in the Army. He wasn't even sure he'd make it home alive.

Bob credits his survival to superb Army training, and he relied heavily on prayer especially while in Vietnam. He returned home during a tumultuous time in America, and he eventually found his path: law enforcement was the perfect career for him. As he prepared for retirement, haunting memories from Vietnam bothered him more and more. Psychiatric help for his PTSD started him jotting down some of the details that filled his thoughts, and that was the beginning 18 years ago of this memoir. His Vietnam experiences as an infantry soldier still haunt him, but he feels that he can cope with them better now.

Bob and Eileen are retired and live in a home they built together on a lake not far from where they grew up. They raised four children, and are active in the lives of their four grandchildren.

SUPPORT

If you are a Veteran, there are a number of resources available to you if you believe you may have P.T.S.D., depression, or medical issues related to your service. Start with your local Veterans Affairs Medical Center, or check out available resources and VA locations at *maketheconnection.net*.

The National Suicide Prevention Lifeline is available 24 hours a day, 7 days a week: **1-800-273-8255.**

CPSIA information can be obtained
at www.ICGtesting.com
Printed in the USA
LVHW051510170519
618251LV00013B/507/P

9 781513 639222